BADGES of the BRIGADE

VOLUME ONE
THE BOYS' BRIGADE

First published in 2000 by RB Publishing
116, Aldridge Road,
Little Aston
Aldridge
WALSALL
WS9 0PF

ISBN 0 - 9521381 - 1- 5

Design & Layout by **Robin G A Bolton**
Typeset in 10pt Book Antiqua by **RB Publishing, Little Aston, Aldridge, Walsall.**

Printed and bound in Great Britain by
Warwick Printing Company Limited,
Theatre Street, Warwick, CV34 4DR

Also available from RB Publishing:
Boys of the Brigade Volume 1. ISBN: 1 - 870708 - 50 - 4
[Vol. 1. Originally published by SB Publications]
Boys of the Brigade Volume 2. ISBN: 0 - 9521381 - 0 - 7

BADGES of the BRIGADE

VOLUME ONE

THE BOYS' BRIGADE

Rob Bolton   Les Howie   Bob Mandry

The Authors

Robin G. A. Bolton, B.Ed.

Rob, as co-ordinating editor, has gathered together and presented this story of BB Badges. His narrative enriched by his photographic collection and own inimitable chatty style throughout, is an attempt to endow the volume with readability, as well as being entertaining, factually correct and intellectually stimulating. He draws frequently on his long BB experience in the 'ranks' and as an officer in the West Midlands whilst applying his wide knowledge of brigade history and badge collecting. Rob's solid, quiet, humorous and persuasive manner has kept this work on target which was to create a first-class, easy-to-read and useful reference work for both the expert and casual reader, but above all, without his breadth and depth of knowledge this work would have been impossible.

Leslie G. Howie, M.A. (Hons), Dip.Ed.

Les, brings a wealth of high quality, professional, painstaking research to the volume. Revelling in detail substantiated by both historical insight and social context, his contribution can be appreciated all the more when studying the 'References' section of this work. Les leaves no stone unturned as he digs up the historical facts which are then carefully scrutinised and analysed before revealing a glittering wealth of hitherto unknown gems. His own BB experience in Edinburgh is fully exploited as is his familiarity with Scottish academic institutions.
Les has undertaken the proof-reading of the work, no mean task, requiring a first class grasp of the language combined with a deep knowledge of the subject.

Robert Mandry Cert. Ed.

Bob's contribution to the book comes from his twin interests of collecting and photography. Bob has built up a reputation for his vast knowledge of BB badges, in particular the different vasrieties of each badge resulting from years of production.
To Bob there can be beauty in a badge, because of the aesthetic quality of a miniature masterpiece, because of the skill and expertise that went into its manufacture or because of the differences that occur between one variety and another.
Bob's skilled photography brings out the best of these wonderful little creations. He seems equally at home on T.V's 'Collectors Lot' or administering the BB Collectors' Club. Bob has listed every BB Badge and variety ever produced in the UK or Ireland, a work which required great expertise, patience and diligence and for which serious collectors will be grateful for many decades.

Contents

Volume One

BADGES of the BRIGADE

2. Efficiency/Service Badges

BADGES of the BRIGADE

3. Proficiency Badges

SPECIAL PROFICIENCY BADGES

PROFICIENCY BADGES

BADGES
of the
BRIGADE

BADGES
of the
BRIGADE

4. Buttonhole & Special Mufti Badges.

BADGES of the BRIGADE

BADGES of the BRIGADE

BADGES of the BRIGADE

Preface

It is, without doubt, the use of badges and medals which transform a uniform into a 'military' uniform. Badges of rank, function and status all feature in the regimental concept of life. Rewards for proficiency, attendance, and endeavour have a clearly visible place in a military society which delights in a clear-cut, idealised and labelled world, a parody of daily adult reality.

Nineteenth Century Origins

As a result of the increasing militarisation of British society from the 1860s onwards, large numbers of middle-and working-class males became associated with the armed forces, but not as regular, professional soldiers. It was possible for a man's everyday reality of work and family to become suspended, for the weekend or evening, when he could 'cross over' into a parallel military world as a member of the local 'Volunteers'. William A. Smith was one such 'Saturday Soldier' a young, single, Glasgow businessman, not yet thirty years old, member of the 1st Lanarkshire Rifle Volunteers and Secretary of the Free College Church Mission Sunday School in North Woodside Road Glasgow. Experiences in the YMCA as a young man and the Volunteers no doubt affected his whole approach to church work. Smith, used to positive leadership and discipline, found the unruly behaviour and disinterest in his Sunday School boys went very much against the grain. The year was 1883 and the solution he proposed was to form an experimental group. From the outset the experiment was destined to succeed; the model was there in the shape of his

Volunteers and this was linked to a deep Christian commitment. Smith found that he was able to combine the two, and also to see things from the boys' point of view. Suddenly there it was, The Boys' Brigade. He knew that boys like things clear-cut, and to know where they stand. They like order, they need to develop good habits and they need training, as Smith saw it, 'as soldiers of Christ'. The first parade was held on October 4th 1883 without any uniform, but at the end of the first session, on the first Annual Inspection, 25th March 1884, the boys paraded wearing red rosettes in their buttonholes, homemade by William Smith's newly-wed wife, Amelia. These were, in effect, the first BB uniform badges.

Imperial Influence

Throughout the early years of the Brigade Movement the Boys' Brigade, and those modelled on it, such as the Church Lads' Brigade, (Founded by a Capt. of the Berkshire Volunteers), Jewish Lads' Brigade, (founded by a Regular Army Officer) and Catholic Boys' Brigade were considerably influenced by an Imperial military establishment very much at its zenith and, what's more, in vogue at the time in the eyes of the nation's youth. The warlike 'manly' symbolism quite openly adopted by many of the churches lay comfortably alongside the heroic and jingoistic influences of an Empire 'marketed' both liberally and lucratively to young and old alike through magazines and books simply busting at the seams with muscular adventure stories. The anchor, lifebelt, shield, sword, armour, laurel wreath, crown, lion and star were emblems, not only familiar to the empire's armed forces, but also to the readers of

penny magazines and bible scholars alike. It is no coincidence then, that the cross-fertilisation between the military 'means' and the religious 'end' epitomised in the brigades should spawn a wealth of badges and medals steeped in such glamorous symbolism.

Nostalgia

Interest in the history of the brigades has been growing. Since 1983, when The Boys' Brigade reached its centenary, there seems to have been an almost constant outpouring of nostalgia as Boys' Brigade Companies and Battalions, The Church Lads' & Church Girls' Brigade, and the Jewish Lads' & Girls' Brigade all paused to look back over their first hundred years. For many former brigade boys the one tangible record of their service was a handful of badges and medals retained long after uniforms and accoutrements had been returned to the Company Quartermaster. The social historian is, however, able to learn much from these artifacts.

Collecting

There has been a developing interest in the collection of brigade badges, perhaps, because, like the military badges they sought to emulate, the quality and range has been decreasing rapidly during the last twenty years or so. It is the aesthetic character of these small metal objects which gives them a value which anyone who has studied jewellery or 'miniatures' cannot fail to appreciate. A number of books have been produced recently which focus upon the badge as an object of 'art'. There is a fascination for this corporate jewellery which has been with mankind since the dawn of time. Where possible we have used enlarged photographs to show the detail and intrinsic 'beauty' of a badge.

The idea for a 'Brigade Badge Book' grew from:

Collectors

The number of collectors appears to be increasing, especially those interested in badges of the Boys' Brigade and the Church Lads' Brigade. Accurate descriptive detail of all known badges is required so that collectors may further their enjoyment of the hobby.

The Lack of existing reference works

The almost complete lack of any comprehensive reference work other than hundreds of old manuals, minutes and magazine articles, particularly in respect of the CLB, JLB and other smaller brigades. There was also a need for a full revision of the existing, but incomplete, BB badge booklet originally produced in **1980** and revised in **1985**.

Social History

The growing general interest in the social history of the brigades, and other uniformed youth organisations, as described in works such as: 'Sure & Stedfast' by John Springhall, Brian Fraser and Michael Hoare (**1983**), 'The Character Factory, Baden Powell & the Scouts' by Michael Rosenthal (**1986**), 'Baden Powell' a biography by Tim Jeal (**1989**), 'Fall-In, The Church Lads' & Church Girls' Brigade' by Johnny Conn (**1992**), 'Boys of the Brigade' (Vols 1 & 2) by Robin Bolton (**1991 & 1993**). and 'A Good Jew and a Good Englishman' by Sharman Kadish (**1995**). In addition many local publications of

substance have been produced by companies and battalions.

Groups have also been formed with the sole purpose of exploring aspects of brigade history. The BB Badge Collectors' Club (**1994**) and The Church Lads' & Church Girls' Brigade Historical Group. (**1996**) being two recent examples.

The archives of The Boys' Brigade and The Church Lads' and Church Girls' Brigade are being developed and will, no doubt, be available for public research within the next few years.

Brigade Insignia

There is a growing realisation that the development and use of Brigade insignia is one of genuine historical interest. This under-researched aspect of the brigades' histories certainly has its own story to tell. A story often full of political, religious and artistic ideals as well as, perhaps surprisingly, intrigue and conflict. There seems to have been a 'Golden Age' of Brigade badges perhaps from **c 1918 - c 1968**. This legacy of half-a-century remains with us and may never be repeated.

Production Changes

Changing production methods have meant an end, in recent years, to the jobs of many skilled workers and the closure and amalgamation of British factories and workshops complete with their Victorian machinery: a microcosm of what has happened to British industry in the post-war period. There is a need to record not only the badge, but also the often ingenious production methods. A full 'Glossary' of terms is included to aid description and understanding.

A Catalogue

There was also a clear need for an illustrated catalogue of brigade badges and medals for use by dealers in militaria and antiques. At present the market-place is encum-

bered by almost complete ignorance of brigade badges and medals which benefits no-one, especially the new collector.

These Volumes provide pictures and descriptions of all the badges known along with some of their major features. The appendix issued with Volume 1 provides the full detail of all BB badges for the serious collector, giving particulars of all types, stampings, variations, etc..

Stories

Conflicting tales about brigade badges, their origin and use based on heresay, rumour and unsubstantiated evidence are widespread. We have detailed all of our sources under the heading 'References' for each badge where appropriate.

Heritage

Lastly, but perhaps of the greatest importance, is the wish of the compilers of this work that the past and present members of the brigades may have available a thorough accurate and readable account of what is indeed a significant part of their heritage.

Two Volumes

For both ease of reference and economy the book has been divided into two volumes. Volume 1 concentrates on the badges of The Boys' Brigade and Volume 2 the other brigades. The 'Glossary' of terminology and details of Badge description are covered in Volume 1, whilst the locations and processes of badge manufacture are given in Volume 2. Where possible some of the items of common interest between brigades, such as 'Cadets', have been given a common introduction. Reference photographs have been reproduced actual size unless stated otherwise.

The Scope of these Volumes

We decided to focus upon:

- Badges and medals of organisations within the United Kingdom and Eire.
- The uniformed brigades for boys and unisex brigades.
- Brigades of a religious foundation.
- Metal and plastic badges and medals.

These parameters have been set with some difficulty and they mean that a complete listing of every badge, for instance including those in cloth, has in no way been attempted. What we have endeavoured to do is to go back to original sources, where possible, in order to establish the pedigree of each badge. Dates have been particularly carefully researched and are as accurate as we can be certain of at the time of going to press. We make use of actual size photographs where samples were available to us and include line drawings where they were not. There has been the temptation throughout to construct a history of the organisations through the medium of their metal insignia. This is not an impractical idea, but beyond our remit. Naturally, stories surrounding the badges and their protagonists have been included along with a few light-hearted comments. Some badges have been included which perhaps should not have been. Most modern tin 'fun' badges have been deliberately omitted.

A frustrating task

The limitations of time, cost and the availability of primary sources have been paramount in our research. The ravages of two world wars upon brigade archives and records cannot be underestimated. Supply details and lists of awards were often simply thrown out by brigade organisations moving premises and looking to streamline their operations in the **1970s** and

1890s

A PIPER OF THE 100TH GLASGOW COMPANY.
From a Drawing by J. HANNAN WATSON, Captain.

1980s. Some details were retained, however, sometimes unofficially by people who simply couldn't bear to see them disposed of. Changes in the meaning of terminology over the years also makes research difficult. 'Badges' described in some publications actually turn out to be medals or even chevrons! Detailed manuals and pocket books which must have made sense to members eighty years ago can read as 'gobbledegook' today. Often, factories producing large quantities of brigade badges in the past have been closed for years and their records destroyed. Even personal recollections must be subjected to critical scrutiny after many decades.

The mostly non-military nature of the brigades often provides the researcher with evidence of a bewildering casuality as regards the introduction of new awards and the phasing-out of the old.

Ignorance of, and intolerance with, the restrictions placed upon the use of a badge, cost, availability, distance from the nearest company, religious denomination, age of members and interpretation of rules all played their part. Last, but not least, is the sheer bloody-mindedness of many individuals, only able to flourish in a truly voluntary organisation. More often than official documentation would have us believe, companies and battalions of the BB, for instance, decided for themselves which version of the correct uniform they would adopt. They would decide how badges would be worn - and which ones. It must also be said that the 'woolly' nature of some so-called regulations only served to encourage the folk who wished to drive the proverbial coach and horses through them. For instance, just trying to find out dates of introduction of certain BB badges or uniform, or when something was supposed to be 'phased out', etc., can be frustrating and singularly unrewarding. Very little tended to be recorded, or communicated to the members. Badges issued as recently as the **1990s** cannot be tracked down even by the BB's official archivist! A favourite ploy is to make certain uniform or badges 'unavailable' and force members into adopting something else. The latter method always meant that years later, sometimes twenty years later, some officer would be wearing the most disreputable looking accoutrements because he hadn't ever been told that they were no longer official uniform. Some companies and battalions of the CLB mixed and matched up to four variants of the uniform at any one time.

Things to come

It is hoped that at some time in the not too distant future the girls' organisations can be included, as can the wealth of cloth and wire badges. There is too, we feel, scope for the inclusion of belt buckles, swagger canes, buttons and other items of uniform in a future publication. Where the progenitors of metal badges have been those in worsted or wire, they have, for the most part, been included here.

The story of brigade badges provides a fascinating insight into a world of youth which, although all but gone, steadfastly remains after more than a century of continuous development. That long period of growth, change and decline is here monitored, described, analysed and catalogued. Needless to say, perhaps, but it must be stated, that the information contained in this volume is, to the best of our knowledge, correct at the time of going to press. New material is, however,

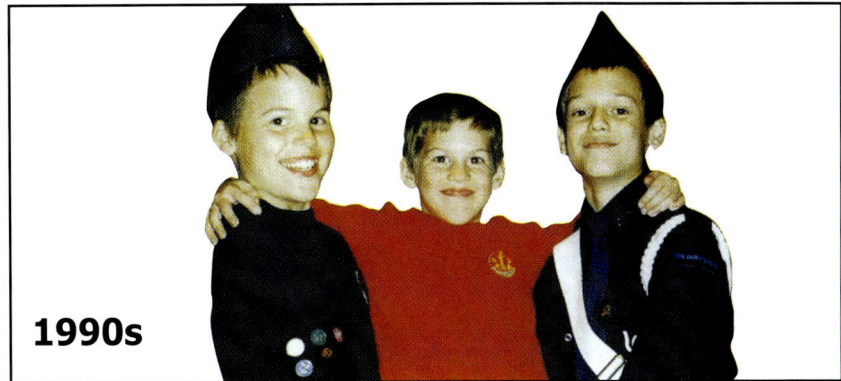

1990s

coming to light every year. Space has been left in the appendix for information to be inserted, e.g. new badges. Many references include question marks and remarks such as 'possibly' or 'said to be'. The authors would be pleased to hear from anyone who can add to the detailed information.

Whatever your particular reason for using this book: collector, dealer, former member, social historian, or an interested member of the public, we trust that you will find something here.

R. Bolton.
Editor.

The Boys speak out ... in December 1958:

'Sir- ... the greatest of joys is giving without expecting any reward. If badges were given for every loyal deed, we would be lowering the standards of the 75 years, and taking away the incentive to duty and proficiency.'
S/Sgt. M.J.Day, 10th Luton Company.

'Stedfast Mag' the Boys' Brigade's own monthly boys magazine ran from **1953 - 1979**. The correspondence columns were often packed full of suggestions from BB boys about how the Brigade should be run. Sometimes serious, usually interesting and often 'whacky', badges were a regular topic of the young correspondents.

His Honour Judge Reg Lockett, BB President, with members of the 5th Croydon Company Pipe Band
Brigade Council 2000, Brighton & Hove

The Boys' Brigade Factfile

The Emblem
The Boys' Brigade emblem is an anchor with the words 'Sure & Steadfast' behind which is a red cross which was the emblem of the Boys' Life Brigade a pacifist Brigade which united with the BB in 1926.

The Founder
Sir William Alexander Smith
[Knighted in 1909, for his Brigade work]

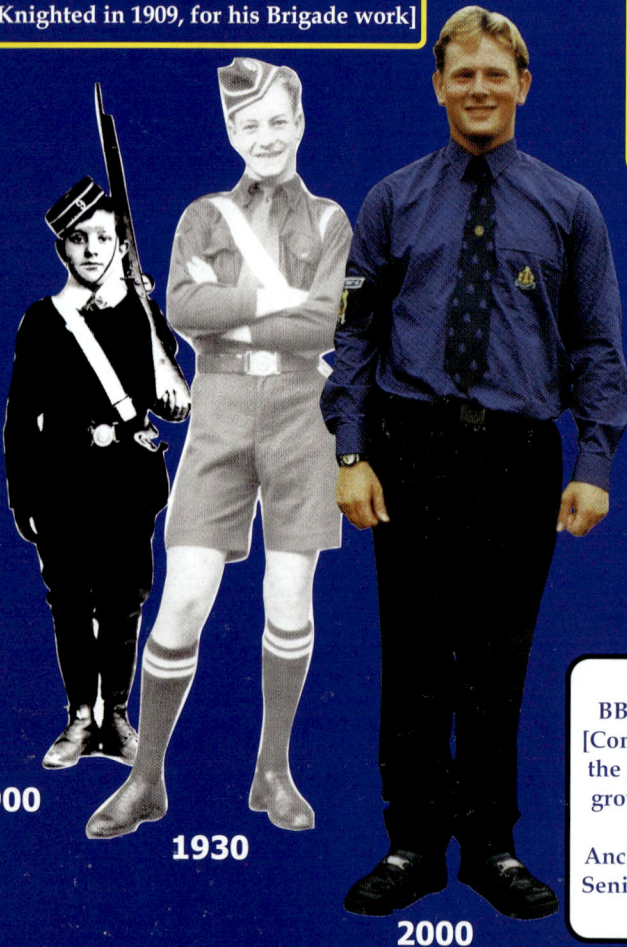

The Brigade's Origins
The Boys' Brigade or 'BB' for short, founded on 4th October 1883, was the first uniformed brigade for boys to develop on a national and eventually international scale. Originally intended as a solution to Sunday School retention and discipline in the North Woodside Church Mission in the West End of Glasgow, it grew rapidly, mainly attracting working boys aged 13 - 18 yrs.

The Brigade Object
'The advancement of Christ's Kingdom among boys and the promotion of habits of Obedience, Reverence, Discipline, Self-respect and all that tends towards a true Christian Manliness.'

The Brigade Movement
The BB played a large part in the development of Scouting in the early years and was copied by many, notably the Church Lads' Brigade, The Girls' Brigade and the Jewish Lads' Brigade. In fact there was an extensive Brigade Movement in the late 19th Century and throughout the 20th Century, all based on the BB method.

National Headquarters
The HQ & Training Centre, Felden Lodge, is located at Hemel Hempstead, Hertfordshire.

1900

1930

2000

BB Structure
BB remains Interdenominational with its individual units [Companies] in virtually all of the Christian Churches. Over the years the lower age limit has reduced, initially with the growth of Junior organisations more recently integrated as Sections within the Brigade. Today, the structure is: Anchor Boys [6-9 yrs], Juniors [8-12yrs], Company [11-16yrs], Seniors[15-18yrs]. There are some 90,000 members in the UK and 500,000 worldwide.

The Patron
H.M. The Queen.

Uniform
BB boys originally wore the accoutrements of cap, belt and white haversack over normal clothing. Over the years, there has been various styles of hat and from the 1920s full uniform options. In 1999, the Brigade adopted a new uniform which for the first time included no hat or haversack.

Introduction

The Badges of the Boys' Brigade, Including The Boy Reserves, The Life Boys, The Anchor Boys, C.O.B.A., & The Stedfast Association.

The people who brought the Boys' Brigade into existence and nurtured it throughout its formative years came equipped with what, on the face of it today, seem to be mutually incompatible ideals: those of christianity and of militarism. Indeed, in the early years, many churches were concerned that the new Brigade was an army 'within' which might erode their christian values. After all the boys of today were, hopefully, the church men of the future.

The early BB leadership was drawn in a large part from the Volunteers, men who found that they often had to justify putting military decorations or ornaments on boys. 'Boys' meant those over thirteen years of age who had normally just left school to find full- time employment. Perhaps the greatest 'sales-gimmick' available to the BB leaders was the ingenious use of equipment or accoutrements, instead of a full uniform like the army. In this way the BB uniform was seen as a sort of compomise, uniform enough to be 'military', but restrained enough to be seen as an extension of 'Sunday best'. All debates concerning badges of the BB need to be viewed within this contextual background. William Smith, who was not born and bred in Glasgow, found difficulty with the puritanical views on uniform and badges with which he was surrounded in the early years. Such views were common in the West of

Sgt. Jones, 13th London Company BB. c1890's
Note the 5-point stars, Drum Badge, 3-Year Anchor, Cravat pin, sergeant's cap with three stripes and drum cover. Sgt Jones is wearing a water bottle and, typical of some drummers, his haversack over the left shoulder.
BB Archive, Felden.

Scotland, whereas in other areas of the country, even within Scotland, there was a liking for the more flamboyant approach. Brigade uniforms, generally, in the Catholic BB, Boys Life Brigade, Church

Lads' Brigade and London Diocesan Church Lads' Brigade exhibited a somewhat divergent nature, mostly stemming from this inbuilt dilemma. The Boys' Brigade was, for many years, firmly anchored in Glasgow, a situation which favoured the minimalist approach. Perhaps the best example was the BB officers' uniform which comprised of a hat with a badge on it: a badge which turned out to be brighter than planned due to the machiavellian manoeuvres of the Founder in dealing with his fellow officers. From **1885** until **1916**, when dull bronze collar badges were introduced, this 'ornament' was the full extent of the deliberately dour uniform, with the one exception being the sheer flamboyance of the small circular buttonhole badges in silver and bronze used between **1897** and **1903**.

Towards the end of the nineteenth century, as the BB method spread throughout the United Kingdom within differing churches, sects, congregations and communities, both rural and urban, a wide disparity began to open up over matters of badges. Uniform was, of course, so simple that it provided very little scope for variation. Proficiency badges, however, suggested to some an area in which experimentation could be tried.

The late **1880s** and the **1890s** were times when the army wore an elaborate dress, khaki not yet being in regular use, and a wide range of badges. Metal badges with brooch or lug type fastenings were common, as were woven wire badges. In keeping with the BB modelling itself on the Volunteers, the various badges which began to appear were inspired by the army. Such badges as Drummer, Bugler, Signaller, Armourer, and Transport were worn on the sleeve, cuff or lapel of the jacket. Badges were not specially made for the Brigade. In fact, only one official, nationally

approved proficiency badge was introduced by the BB in the 19th century. That badge, the Ambulance Badge, was introduced in **1891**. During the early years of the 20th century many quite legal, locally approved badges were being worn. Little need was seen for new national introductions, but those badges which did exist needed to be regularised in terms of their design and award. Critics were starting to voice their opinions. In **1900**, Mr P.D.Adams of London wrote a letter which was read out at the Annual Brigade Meeting and reported in the Gazette:

'I strongly advocate a uniform system. A special sub-Committee should be appointed to draw up the best scheme of marking, and authorize a uniform system of Rewards and Badges, which should be inserted in the Manual, giving the Designs. Ambulance and Band badges are all far too easily obtained, far too frequently worn, and their value is consequently deteriorating.' [1]

Both Efficiency and Sergeants' Proficiency Badges did come into use in the early years, but these were not always truly national in character. Efficiency stars worn on the lower sleeve and sometimes on the lapel were only used by a few battalions between **1886** and **1904**. Diamond-shaped Efficiency Badges, which were recognised nationally and introduced to replace the stars, were optional. [2]

Starting in **1908** with the Bugler's Badge, the Brigade authorities, who had begun to view the increasing diversity of badges with a degree of alarm, finally commenced the regulation of key proficiency awards. National standards were introduced for Signallers', Scouts', Band, Life-Saving, National Service, Gymnastics, Drummers' and Pipers' in the years leading up to union with the BLB in **1926**. The King's Badge was instituted in **1913** combining both

service and proficiency. Approved by the monarch, this badge became the progenitor of a long line of King's and Queen's Badges established as the summit of attainment in the BB badge system.

The Great War affected most aspects of British life, and, by **1918**, changes had started which were to influence the BB in subsequent decades. The BB was not drawn into the government's Cadet Scheme at the outset, but sat on the fence only allowing companies which wished to do so, to affiliate from **1918** onwards. Since some companies would be taking up Cadet affiliation a special khaki uniform, complete with badges, was produced. This was followed by a 'Regulation Grey' uniform. The design of the Cadet Cap and Collar Badges would prove to be very influential because they included a new BB logo and innovative designs used on BB cap badges until **1970** and on collar badges today.

The Boy Reserves, for younger boys, came into being in **1917**. They had metal badges for instructors by **1919** and for boys from **1921**. The widening of the age-range naturally increased the number of badges. The Life Boys replaced the Boy Reserves in **1926** on the union of the BLB and BB. The name Boys' Brigade was retained for the older members, but the BLB Junior Section which had been called 'Lifeboys' transferred it's name. The BB emblem was changed to incorporate the BLB Red Cross behind the BB Anchor.

The badges of the period after union with the BLB are often referred to as those of the 'Golden Era' (or more correctly perhaps a 'Nickel-Silver Era'). From **1927** to **1968** a dozen new proficiency or service badges were introduced. Seven of these badges entered the system within weeks of the union. The BLB's flirtation with Scouting

> Wish I had all those badges !

frosting. Frosting had been a feature of BB badges since that finish had been specifically requested by William Smith in **1885.** Details of the change was given a somewhat 'up-beat' treatment in the BB Gazette of April **1942:**

'As present supplies are exhausted, a change in our Badges will become apparent. Owing to war difficulties some of the plating processes are being dispensed with. The metal used will be precisely as hitherto, but the laquer and the burnishing of parts is being discarded. As at present the badges will need cleaning and polishing, and it will be found that the natural surface responds to such attention more readily than before. From the beginning the new badges should have the well-polished characteristic of those of a senior Boy in an efficient Company.'

It went on to say that the badges should be popular,

'...and here is a shock for you- because of the consequent decrease in price... prices have reverted to the pre-war figures.' [4]

The prices for badges were 6d., except for the King's Badge 2/-, One-Year Service 3d. and Buttonhole 4d..

In the post-war years (from **1946)** a further five badges were introduced, not including special enamelled Duke of Edinburgh's Award Badges. Some badges continued to be worn with coloured felt (red, white or blue) behind to indicate a higher level of attainment. The **1964** Expedition Badge was also very influential, introducing yet another enamelled colour in a badge. The shape, like a TV, was ahead of its time, being the shape chosen for the **1983** awards.

Following the introduction of many of the proposals of the **1964** Haynes Report, leading to an increased number of activities, the rise in badge prices and the grow-

in the years prior to the Great War had given them a large number of proficiency badges both cloth and metal. All badges of the new Brigade had to be metal because, unlike the BLB, the BB had not managed to introduce a successful full uniform. For a time the BB and Life Boys operated with five different boys' uniforms and two officers' uniforms causing a further increase in badges. It was at the time of the BB/BLB Union that the BB Gazette stated that the Brigade Executive meeting in Windermere had decided that as from 1st July **1927** all uniform and equipment,

'...shall be supplied by the Brigade instead of by Contractors as has hitherto been the practice'.

It was stated that this measure should lead to a reduction in price and an increase in quality. [3]

The **1933** BB Jubilee was a time when some special badges were produced, destined to become some of the most famous of all. The Jubilee Buttonhole was so popular the Brigade changed to a similar designed buttonhole badge for general use after the Jubilee. That badge itself became the model for the **1937** and **1953** Coronation Badges. Indeed, the Dechmont Camp Badge was the first fully enamelled badge to be worn on a boy's uniform. There were two officer's Council Badges, also fully enamelled and a bronze Ex-Members' Badge for Glasgow.

Wartime economy restrictions in the Second World War led to a number of changes in BB badges, even though demand was reduced. Enamelling was discontinued in Ambulance and Buttonhole Badges. Some badges, formerly pierced, were produced as solid eg. Long Service, Life Saving, Education and National Service. Thinner metal was introduced as the manufacture of some Buttonhole Badges changed to being shell-stamped. Perhaps the most significant and long-lasting wartime measure was the end of

Badge Poster c.1957

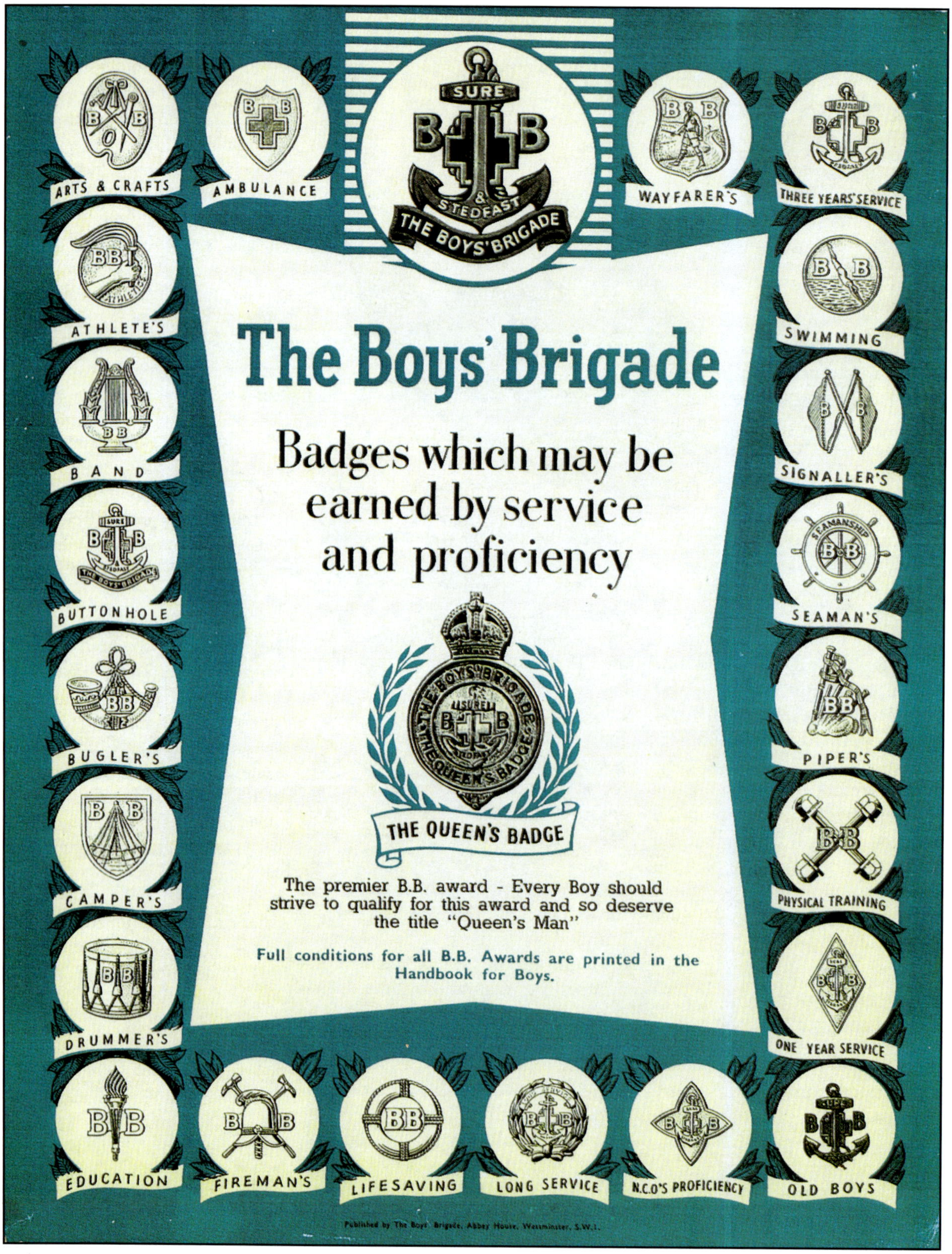

ing number of companies wearing the new full uniform, a new badge system was introduced in **1968.** Companies could now afford new badges and they would not slip down boys' arms when wearing a uniform shirt. The new system included Target Awards in the 'TV' shape, and a whole new range of barrel-shaped proficiency awards made from bronze coloured anodised aluminium. A new President's Badge was introduced to be awarded prior to earning a new Queen's Badge. The President's and Queen's Badges were bland, larger than the proficiency badges and made from enamelled gilding metal. New small-size service badges were also introduced. The proficiency badges achieved the aim of being lighter and of a uniform size and shape, but failed miserably to represent anything other than the fact that the Brigade had sunk to accepting a cheap, nasty, tacky and dull substitute for a badge. To make matters worse the badges sported emblems which were barely decipherable. The unlucky wearers, the boys, hated them, the embarassed officers loathed them whilst the general public just laughed!

In **1978,** the BB authorities were so fed-up with a mounting criticism of the badges, that they decided a change was necessary. New high-impact polystyrene badges, with coloured decal inserts, were produced. Unfortunately, these turned out to be even cheaper and nastier than the aluminium ones. How could it have been possible ? Countries such as Zimbabwe had at this time badges of similar shape and size, far superior in quality to those in Britain. Needless to say the call for reform was very soon in coming.

The Centenary Year, **1983,** saw the introduction of a completely revised badge system. Uniform badges began to appear in the new 'staybrite' finish. Proficiency

badges were reduced to five categories: Adventure, Leadership, Community, Interests and Physical. These badges were made in the same TV shape and size as the Target awards. They were initially enamelled, but soon made from gilding metal with coloured decals under clear epoxy resin. Instead of the earlier cloth surrounds to indicate advanced awards, red and blue plastic surrounds were produced to fit around the badges. Many of the original barrel badges were replaced by foil Credits which boys could stick into a record book in order to qualify for a new badge. These are the badges currently **(2000)** in use by the Brigade.

In **1994,** the President's and Queen's Badges were re-designed. These new principal badges are metal, have coloured epoxy 'enamel' and frosting.

In more than a hundred years many organisations and groups of 'Old Boys' have been formed.

Some like COBA (the Church Old Boys' Association) were uniformed and run like an adult version of a BB company. Others, such as the Old Boys' Union, were simply names on a register. Old Boys Associations and Clubs have, since **1983,** been replaced in many parts of the UK, and the world, by 'Stedfast Associations'.

As the BB enters the new millennium its award badges have much in common with those worn by the early 20th century boy: a few badges in number, difficult to obtain, made from metal and worn as brooches on an armband. They still represent both service and proficiency, and feature the anchor emblem, although the spelling of *'Stedfast'* is now modernised to *'Steadfast'.* Uniform badges have changed very little. The current Officer's Cap Badge simply has the cross of the BLB added behind the anchor on a badge otherwise unchanged since **1885.** The current Warrant Officer's Badge is the one passed by the War Office in **1918** ! The badges of the BB eighty years later, represent a visible link with its history and heritage.

In September **1999** the BB Council meeting in Dundee passed a revolutionary motion introducing a new compulsory 'casual' uniform for boys and officers. Many badges, particularly metal badges, are set to disappear by **2006** along with other formal accoutrements and titles. The BB Council meeting in Brighton, September 2nd 2000, changed the uniform regulations to include hats as an option.

REFERENCES

1 BB Gazette, 1st November 1900. p 39. Mitchell Library, Glasgow.
2 Glasgow Battalion, the largest in the UK, did not use the Efficiency/Proficiency diamond shaped badges at any time.
3 BB Gazette, Vol XXXV, No 10, 1/6/1927 p 150, Mitchell Library, op.cit.
4 ibid. Vol L No. 4 April 1942. p 51.

The Boys' Brigade Emblem: The Anchor

The BB Anchor emblem would seem to be one of the earliest of Christian symbols. An extract from 'The Times' in the early 1950s[1] reads as follows:

'What is believed to be the most ancient Christian inscription yet discovered has been found by a young Italian student of Christian archaeology. The inscription consists of two lines of Latin, scratched on the wall of a building which was almost completely destroyed during the construction of the palace of the Flavians above it. It appears to refer to a celebration of the Eucharist (Communion) in AD78. The design of an anchor appears near the inscription.'

Such anchors are not uncommon in the Catacombs of Rome where they appear on early christian gravestones. The reason given for the use of the symbol is the resemblance of the upper part of the anchor to a Cross.

Hebrews 6: 19:

However, the symbolism of an anchor has not gone unmentioned in the Bible. Apart from the story of Paul's shipwreck in Acts 27: 29 & 30, the Anchor is only mentioned once, in Hebrews 6: 19:

'which hope we have as an Anchor of the soul both sure and stedfast.'

No doubt, the Anchor was known to Christians well before **AD78** as a result of reading the 'Hebrews' letter, although it is not known who wrote it or to whom it was originally sent. [2]

Gordon's Calvary

Tombs in the Holy Land, in particular the Garden Tomb of Jerusalem have 'anchor' inscriptions. The Garden Tomb is sometimes known as 'Gordon's Calvary' because General Charles Gordon of Khartoum became convinced that here he had found the site of Calvary and The Tomb of Jesus. His discovery and announcement came in **1883**! Was this simply a coincidence, or did this influence William Smith?[3]

The whole question of why William Smith chose an anchor is open to much speculation, but it must be emphasised that it is only speculation, as Smith did not record why he had chosen it. It does help, however, to go through the many factors which probably influenced him.

The Anchor was chosen sometime during the summer of **1883** by William A. Smith, James R. Hill and his brother John B. Hill. This was before the first BB meeting in October. The three had been friends for some time and had a lot in common: membership of the YMCA and the 1st Lanarkshire Rifle Volunteers, Sunday School teaching at North Woodside, active interest in the evangelical work of Moody and all three were active businessmen. Peacock states that Smith proposed the crest and motto - and it seems highly likely that he did, but this underplays the role of the Hill brothers, in that joint agreement and a consensus was required. [4]

From 1883

The anchor emblem was not used on any item of Brigade uniform until April **1885,** but it was used with the motto 'Sure & Stedfast' on the first membership card in **1883** and similarly each year thereafter. The choice of what is clearly a naval symbol of an anchor for a quasi - military organisation such as the Boys' Brigade does appear to be a strange one, a point which could not have been lost on either Smith or the Hill brothers who were staunch Volunteers.

Nautical Influences

The sea certainly played a big part in all of Smith's life. His birthplace, Pennyland House, looks out onto one of Britain's most dangerous coastlines. The wrecking of the 'Henry Pochard', whose crew found shelter in Pennyland, *'was one of the lad's earliest recollections.'*[5] When Smith moved to Glasgow and entered his uncle's business the sea and shipping remained important, as the chief market for their 'soft goods' was South America.[6] Even in leisure, Smith was attracted by the sea: next to walking, climbing and skating his favourite pursuit was yachting.[7] Smith's love of both sea and religion must surely have sparked-off allegorical connections.

Family

Peacock states that Smith's family crest included an anchor and Smith:

'... wore a signet ring with that device upon it with the motto: "Sine sanguine victor".' [8]

Smith's family crest was indeed an anchor, described heraldically as an 'anchor in pale'[9] It had a ribbon with the latin motto: 'Sine sanguine victor' and was used on his personal stationery.

The anchor used on Sir William A Smith's Christmas card, 1912.
BB Glasgow Battalion

For Smith this may have added to the attraction of the anchor as a symbolic device, but the allegorical religious connection would have been far more important. It is unlikely that the Hill brothers would have agreed to a symbol simply because it was Smith's family crest.

The Seamen's Chapel/Institute, 9, Brown St, Broomielaw, Glasgow.
Re-built, as above, in 1876, demolished in 1978.
Photo: J. Cooper, collection

Fairbairn's Book of Crests in **1905** detailed various types of anchor used as family crests and of the twelve main types illustrated, the two most similar to the original BB crest had 53.2% use by Scottish families.[10]

One family in Scotland, Stewart-Clark of Dundas Castle, South Queensferry, Edinburgh, used an anchor in conjunction with the motto: 'Sure and Steadfast' which featured on their livery buttons. This emblem and motto was used by the family from c.**1900** (See below).[11]

Anchor Hymn

It has been suggested that the 'Anchor Hymn' (Will your Anchor hold) was the inspiration for Smith's choice, but the earliest publication would seem to be 1st September **1892** when it appears in 'New Hymns and Solos'.[12] A trawl of virtually all of the hymnals produced between **1874** and **1891**, revealed no reference to the Anchor Hymn. In fact, it was not even included in the Church of Scotland Hymn Book until **1973.**

A Hymn entitled 'The Anchored Soul'[13] was introduced from **1876** by Sankey, using the same text from Hebrews below its title. Almost certainly it would have been used during the **1881-1883** Mission. This means that in **1883** it was a fresh and vibrant new hymn, lifting Hebrews 6: 19 to public prominence and, as stated in a contemporary magazine,...

'...they (new hymns/songs) *get into*

the minds and memories - trust also the hearts - of the common people,...'[14]

The Seamen's Friend

It is very likely that Smith and/or the Hill brothers became aware of the 'Anchored Soul' song during **1882-1883**. It is even possible that they may have heard it sung in the Seamen's Chapel on the Broomielaw in Glasgow.[15] The Glasgow Seamen's Friend Society (GSFS), founded c.**1824**, was a strong evangelistic force which supported the Moody and Sankey Missions. It ran the Institute along with another building, the Bethel, in Morrison Street. An interesting possibility is that Smith may have been influenced by the anchor device used on GSFS buildings. Unfortunately, there is hardly any evidence remaining to substantiate the nature of the anchor and none whatsoever to verify Smith's or the Hill brothers' attendance at the venues, or of them even seeing the anchors, but it is not a far-fetched assumption. One publication of the GSFS contains an anchor used as an emblem. It lacks inscription or rope, but does bear an uncanny resemblance to the first anchor used on the **1883** membership card. [16] The bell-tower of the Seaman's Chapel had a stone anchor device (see photo opposite), but there is no conclusive evidence that it was similar to the BB anchor. Mr John Cooper of Glasgow is certain that 'Sure & Stedfast' was inscribed on the anchor and that there was no rope, but the photograph does not show any detail and there are no plans or other pictures remaining. By **1885**, when the BB was blossoming into a national organisation, it would have made sense to differentiate the BB from the GSFS by changing the design of the anchor by adding a rope. The rope would certainly assist a badge - maker when taking into account the fixing of the anchor to an outer ring or more convincingly, a way of securing the 'B's to the shaft and breaking up the space within the emblem.

The Gospel Ship

It is said that there was a 'Gospel Ship' picture which adorned the walls of many Mission Halls in the late 19th Century. Perhaps it graced the inside of the North Woodside Mission. In full sail, the vessel was inscribed with biblical texts. One item marked clearly on the bow was an anchor with the wording 'Sure & Stedfast' with reference to Hebrews 6:19. Unfortunately we have been unable to find an example of this picture.[17]

Symbol of strength

An anchor could, perhaps, act as a proud symbol of Glasgow's industrial and commercial prowess. During the period **1850 - 1914** Glasgow was not only Scotland's commercial capital, but also Workshop and Second City of the British Empire. Between **1870** and **1913**, 18% of the world's output of ships came from the Clyde.[18] Glasgow's dominance in steel, engineering and ship-borne commerce would be suitably represented by a mighty, solid anchor. It was a popular business logo used by firms as diverse as shipping companies and pen makers. [19] Many Glasgow BB Boys would work either in the shipyards or associated industries and services.[20] Smith and the Hill brothers were not, however, founding a secular business; the religious element was obviously uppermost in their minds. Nevertheless, an anchor added the dimension of being a popular and suitable emblem for youngsters from that particular part of Glasgow, bounded by the North Woodside Mission.

Ruling the waves

Of greater importance than any of the above was the popularity of the Royal Navy. During the **1880s** the British Empire was at its most powerful. Crucial to its achievement and defence was the Royal Navy. The often crude and jingoistic popularisation by certain political groups of both Empire and Navy had resulted in a fashion for all things naval from boys' sailor suits to rum. The choice of an anchor emblem simply places it in the spirit of the times; an especially popular symbol among young people.

For Smith and the Hill brothers the most important consideration was an emblem that would distinguish the BB from the Army, express their own muscular form of christian evangelism, clearly state the organisation's aim and be acceptable to robustly masculine teenagers, or those striving to be so. An anchor, which Smith almost certainly proposed, was an attractive and subtle choice.

Foundry Boys

There can be little doubt that a major influence upon Smith and the Hill brothers for both the BB and its emblem, was that of the Glasgow Foundry Boys Religious Society. Since **1861** this organisation had grown and developed in its service to thousands of boys in the Glasgow area and beyond. Well organised and highly visible in the community, the GFBRS had established many branches where boys wore uniform of cap, belt and haversack, drilled, went to summer camp and were taught Christianity. The GFBRS was also at the forefront in the organisation of evangelical religious meetings. Publications and Orders of Service developed by the Society were in common use throughout the City of Glasgow. Before **1870**, the Society's popular Hymn Book,

which had the same format as the eventual BB Hymnal, had on its front cover a drawing of an anchor on a rock along with the verse:

'Which hope we have as an anchor of the soul.' Heb. vi 19.

The title of the book is:
'Hymns selected for the Sabbath Forenoon and Week Evening Evangelistic Meetings'

It was published by Charles Glass & Co. 14, Maxwell Street Glasgow.[21] (See picture on next page)

When the GFBRS Hymn book was reprinted in July **1870** it had a similar format to its predecessor, with the front cover bearing the same inscriptions as the earlier edition except for the additional; wording : *'Enlarged Edition 70th Thousand'* and information that it was now published jointly in Paisley by J & R Parlane and Glasgow by J M^C Callum.[22] The anchor drawing was now considerably modified and transformed. The rock was missing, and the anchor still at a slight angle, was complete with rope. In fact, it was just what became familiar fifteen years later as the BB anchor! It was alike in virtually every respect with the exception of the words 'sure & stedfast' and the 'Bs'. This new edition included more hymns, one in particular, No. 56, called: 'The Golden Shore' is significant. The words reveal much about the renewed symbolism of the anchor:

*'We are out on the ocean sailing,
Homeward bound we sweetly glide,
All the Storms will soon be over,
Then we'll anchor in the harbour;
We are out on the ocean sailing
To a home beyond the tide;
We are out on the ocean sailing,
To a home beyond the tide.'*

This Hymnal, produced in such large numbers, was widely used and had the 'BB' anchor adorning its cover; it is inconcievable that Smith and the Hill brothers would not have used it.

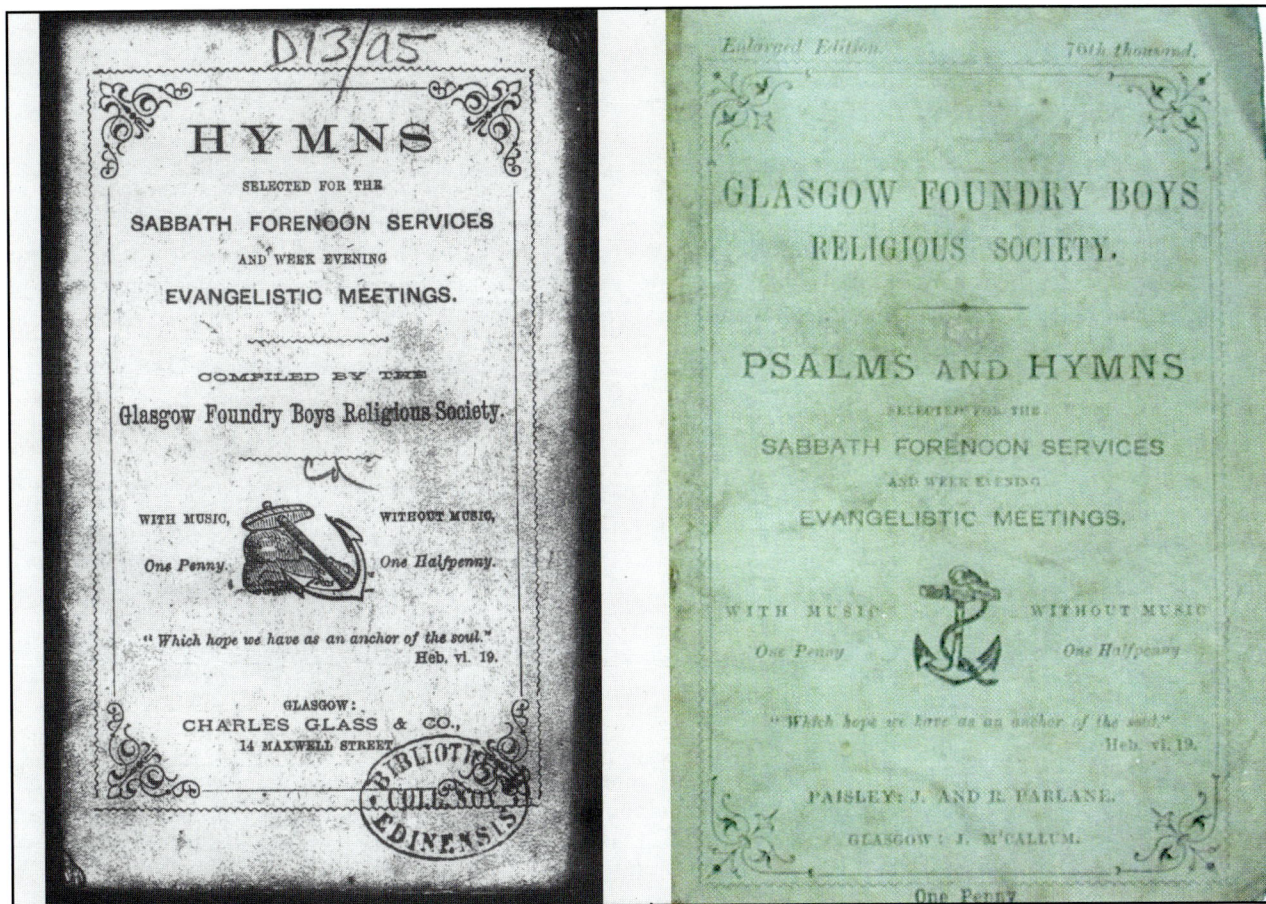

**Left, the cover of the G.F.B.R.S. Hymn book used before 1870
and right the 'enlarged edition' of 1870**
New College Library, Edinburgh

By January **1885**, the 2nd Glasgow BB Company had been formed by J. B. Couper, a close acquaintance of Smith. Like Smith, Couper was a member of the 1st Lanark Rifle Volunteers and a leader of the Glasgow Foundry Boys' Religious Society in the Anderston area. Couper was a member of the first 'Council of The Boys' Brigade' along with Smith, the Hill brothers and four others.[23] Is it then just a coincidence that the Foundry Boys' anchor comes into BB use from **1885**? In the early years of the BB many Companies would be formed under the auspices of the GFBRS so, clearly, the two organisations worked together

Not Foul

A close inspection of the BB anchor reveals that it is not a Royal Navy anchor. Initially, it omitted the rope

which 'fouled' it and, later, even with the rope, it was not fouled as is the Royal Navy version. [24] It could then, be used for its intended purpose. Thus, the allegorical meanings are clear when combined with the motto, signifying a purely Christian aim.

Geneva Cross

When, in **1926**, the Boys' Life Brigade united with the BB their Red Geneva Cross was placed behind the anchor. Fortunately, the cross being so placed renders it officially a cross no longer and so when, in **1935**, the Government instructed the Girls' Life Brigade to remove the Geneva Cross from its emblem there was no need for The Boys' Brigade to follow - suit.

The anchor holds

Today the anchor, as an emblem, has very little meaning to average youngsters who see very much less of ships and the sea. Although still used in a form much as it always was, the anchor is perhaps regarded as a crude 'Victorian' artefact of the industrial and Imperial age, lacking the sophistication of modern technology. Perhaps for this reason the Boys' Brigade today makes use of the initials 'BB' far more than the anchor. The BB **AD2000** Badge, however, is the anchor emblem and the Brigade is raising money to purchase Lifeboats. Perhaps Sir William Smith would approve of the famous symbol he proposed being known to all BB boys across three centuries.

We have an anchor...

the emblem evolves

AD78

A carved anchor from the St. Priscilla Catacombs Rome. This diagram was reproduced in the BB Gazette, (April **1954**) illustrating an article by A. Sandilands.
Sandilands made the tracing of the anchor whilst serving in Italy during the Second World War. He makes it clear that when the stock is placed half-way down the shank and the blades and flukes are shed there is a clear representation of the cross.

1596

In **1902**, the 'Brigadier' Boys' Brigade magazine reproduced this picture of the anchor from a **1596** Spanish Testament held in the Library of the British & Foreign Bible Society.

A hand, let down from heaven, holds up the anchor with the latin inscription 'Anchora Spei' which means 'The Anchor of Hope', an obvious allusion to Hebrews 6: 19:

1870

The anchor emblem used by the Glasgow Foundry Boys' Religious Society on the cover of their **1870** Hymnal. This anchor replaced the original form which included rocks, but had no rope. The new Hymn 'The Golden Shore' had been included which alluded to anchoring in a harbour rather than just on rocks. The similarity with the **1885** BB anchor is obvious, even to the extent of having the rope crossing the anchor near its base, a feature changed in later anchors to allow for clearer reading of the word 'Stedfast'.

1883 - 1885

The original BB Anchor. Note the lack of rope.
This was used on the membership cards for the first three years.
Many other BB publications at this time, such as membership application forms did not use the anchor emblem.
There were no items of uniform which included the emblem until halfway through **1885**.

1885 - 1897

From **1885** the anchor appears with the addition of a rope and sometimes, as here, complete with its own shadow! The 'new' anchor was used on Membership Cards and Proficiency Certificates also appearing in the new 'Officers' Manual'.
It was during the period **1885 - 1897** that the emblem became used on uniform badges and accoutrements often requiring some modifications. In no way was the emblem regarded as 'regulation', many quite 'experimental' anchor forms appeared on all manner of items.

1893 - 1903

During the period **1893 - 1903** this rather 'rugged' anchor was commonly used by the BB. Most often it appeared on the Discharge Certificate or the presentation Book Plate, all produced by Headquarters.
It was however, seemingly not regarded as suitable for letterheads etc with the more refined **1885** version retained in the BB Manual.

1897 - 1926

In **1897** the 'refined' anchor which had been in use since **1885** was re-designed. It replaced the earlier form on Certificates, notepaper, and in the Officers' Manual. It became the form used on Official BB Postcards which were growing in popularity.

With the exception of individually designed items such as membership cards this version of the anchor became the one most widely used right up to **1926**. The fact that the Bs were still free of the main design caused problems for badge and medal designers, a problem which was largely solved when the BLB Cross appeared.

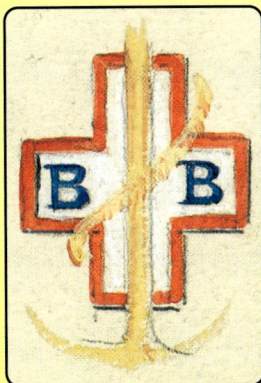

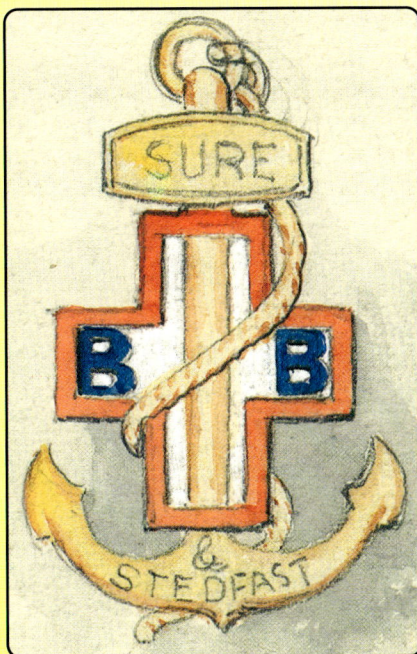

D .L. Finnemore Papers,
11th Birmingham Coy. BB Archive.

1926

The 'Finnemore' Sketches

Discovered in **1996** amongst the personal papers of Sir Donald Finnemore who negotiated the union of the BB & BLB on the BLB side.

These watercolours are thought to have been drawn by Sir Donald himself at the time when discussions about the new combined emblem were taking place. Sir Donald incorporated the B's within the cross (BLB Style) with the red cross, now in out-line, either over or behind the anchor.

Due to his service with the RAMC in the First World War, Sir Donald was aware that the use of the whole Red Cross would be illegal .

These are probably the oldest surviving drawings of the cross behind the anchor.

1927 - 1993

The approved version of the BB Emblem as used for over sixty years in either black and white or coloured form. Initially, it seems, there had been agree-ment that the new emblem of **1927** would have a coloured anchor with a black & white cross but this never seems to have happened. Perhaps the influence of the former BLB Officers was too strong, combined with increasing use of colour in BB publications.

1993 -

The BB Emblem of today with its 'new' spelling of Ste**a**dfast. The logo is still recognised and used thoughout the world.

REFERENCES

1. Quoted by A Sandilands in an article in BB Gazette 'Our Anchor' April 1954. p.65
2. ibid.
3. Article in BB Gazette March 1997 p.51 'The Anchor Cross', Revd John A Pugh.
4. Peacock, R.S. 'Pioneer of Boyhood' (BB 1954) p.32. Gibbon, F.P. 'William Smith of the Boys' Brigade' (Collins, 1934) p.39.
5. Peacock. op.cit., p. 9. Gibbon, op.cit., pp. 9 - 10.
6. Gibbon op.cit., p.15.
7. Ibid., pp. 16 - 17.
8. Peacock, op.cit., p.33.
9. Fairbarn's Book of Crests (4thEd.) Vols I & II, Jack 1905. Plate 161. National Library of Scotland.
10. ibid.
11. Katy Hutchison, Secretary to Sir Jack Stewart-Clark in a letter Letter to L.Howie 20/04/00.
12. New Hymns & Solos: Compiled and sung by Ira D. Sankey. Tonic sol-Fa Edition, Morgan & Scott, London. Inscribed 'Xmas, 1892' Hymn No.128 'Will Your Anchor Hold ?' 'An anchor of the soul, both sure and steadfast' [NB spelling of 'stedfast']
13. Written by Rev. William O. Cushing in 1876 with music composed by Rev. Robert Lowry.
14. 'The Christian' 3.3.1892. p.20.
15. 9, Brown St. Broomielaw, Glasgow. officially called the 'Seamen's Institute' re-built in 1876 & demolished in 1978.
16. 'Another Year's Work Among our Sailors' 1886, GSFS Papers, Mitchell Library, Glasgow.
17. Mr John Cooper. Still on walls of missions in 1950s.
18. Moss, M and Hume J., 'Workshop of the British Empire', Heinemann, 1977, p.3.
19. See advertisements in the Glasgow Herald for any day in 1882-1883 eg. 'Anchor Line' and 'Anchor Pens'.
20. In 1990 this connection was evoked by Bill Bryden's epic play 'The Ship' staged in the former Harland & Wolff Engine Works in Govan. 300 Company Section Boys of Glasgow Battalionb assisted in this powerful and haunting production which con tained many references to the BB. Chillingly poignant was the BB Bugle band at the funeral of a young worker killed in a shipyard accident. Glasgow Battalion 106th Annual Report, pp7-8.
21. In the New College Library, Edinburgh.
22. Ibid
23. Springhall J. et al. Sure & Stedfast 1983, William Collins, p 41.
24. The rope which fouls the RN anchor would make it inoperative but the manner in which the BB rope was later added would not foul it.

BADGES of the BRIGADE

VOLUME ONE
THE BOYS' BRIGADE

1. Uniform Badges

The Officers' Cap Badge

The original metal Brigade Badge

The story of this progenitor of all Brigade Badges is interwoven with the story of the original 1st Glasgow Company BB uniform.

For the first few years of The Boys' Brigade officers were gentlemen who wore what most gentlemen of the day did: a shirt with stiff collar, tie, suit and hat. The hat worn by 1st Glasgow Officers for outside occasions was the bowler. There is not much reliable evidence concerning early uniforms for officers or boys. At the first Annual Inspection held on 25th March **1884** the boys wore no caps or belts only, '... *a small red rosette pinned on the lapel of the coat.*' [1] The official history of The First Glasgow Coy. produced in 1933 gives the Session **1884-85** as the first with distinctive equipment.[2] The stripes are said to have been made by Mrs Smith.

Model Volunteers?

The first photograph of the Company taken outside Garscube House on 9th April **1885** shows the boys in their first uniforms of forage caps (pill-box style), white haversacks and 'S' (snake) belts. The boys uniform was, naturally, modelled on that of the 1st Lanarkshire Rifle Volunteers, William Smith's own unit. These original uniforms show that some of the hats had not yet had the two rings of narrow white (or silver) braid added. The NCO's had rank

displayed by the use of a chevron on the front of the hat as well as on the sleeve, again using white/silver braid. More than twelve months after their first annual inspection much of the uniform detail was hand-made, possibly still by Smith's wife Amelia. The officers in the photograph, Capt. William A. Smith, Lt's James R. Hill and John B. Hill, resplendent in bowler hats, seem to be wearing a home-made lapel badge using the ubiquitous white/silver braid formed into three triangles possibly representing the Holy Trinity or perhaps a Celtic symbol of everlasting life. (See photo page 21). Presumably this was to indicate their rank and membership when 'hatless' indoors. There is no visible anchor here, but a meeting on 26th January **1885** had settled on the crest, title and motto used by 1st Glasgow to be adopted by the entire *'Brigade'* [3] which at that time consisted of 1st and 2nd Glasgow Coys..

Smith fails to get his own way with the cap but succeeds with the badge!

The year **1886** saw the number of companies increase to 44, with a total of 136 officers. The majority of companies were in Scotland, mostly in Glasgow.[4] On the 20th January

1886 the newly formed Glasgow Battalion held its Executive Meeting and discussed the adoption of a suitable uniform cap for officers. A decision was made that a sample cap, '...*suitable for the officers*' be procured and submitted to the next meeting. [5] At that meeting, '...*a sample Glengarry was submitted*'. William Smith was not very keen on this idea as he had already discussed, '...*a stiff cap with a turned down peak...*' with J.B. Hill one of his 1st Glasgow staff. Hill proposed the adoption of such a cap, gladly seconded by Smith. Support for the glengarry was strong, however, with F.P.R. Ferguson of 4th Glasgow proposing, '...*that a Glengarry as exhibited, be adopted with the addition of a* **buckle** *to be approved of by the Executive Committee.'* This was seconded by I. Lammie of the 6th Glasgow. Ten voted for the glengarry and badge and only two for the stiff cap.[6]

BB Buckle

Discussion concerning the design of the 'buckle' is not recorded, but, less than three weeks later at the Glasgow Battalion Council Meeting, a sample of the glengarry made by Messrs. John Blair, who also supplied the boys' caps, was produced. It was stated that they were, '...*preparing a design for a buckle'*. It was none other than William Smith who explained the style of silver buckle which the Committee had agreed upon. Smith had, no doubt, set his heart upon silver as the colour because this was the colour of badge used universally by the Volunteers. In a move which was to be commonplace over the following decades, the whole idea of a bright personal adornment was questioned. Mr Reid, Captain of the 7th Glasgow Coy. *'thought that the Buckle would be better of a bronze colour than silver and made a motion to that effect'*. Thos. Smith Capt. of 11th Glasgow seconded the motion. Peter Whyte, Capt. 18th Glasgow Coy. moved as an amendment that it be silver as ordered which was seconded by Thos. Smith! (The record may be at fault here... it may have been W.A. Smith). Seven voted for the amendment (silver) and eight for the motion (bronze).7 William Smith was defeated once again, but this meeting of **27th Feb**. was not to be the end of the story. Messrs. Blair was proceeding with the silver version, not at all discouraged by Smith:

2nd March '86
Mess. John Blair & Co.
Dear Sirs,
In consideration of your agreeing to do the silver plated ornament for the Officers glengarry Caps at the price of 1/6 each, I beg, on behalf of the Glasgow Battalion Council to guarantee that there will be at least 12 doz. taken off your hands at this price, by the Officers of the Brigade in Glasgow and elsewhere.
Yours faithfully,
Wm. A. Smith. (Signed)
Brig. Secy.
(Postscript)
The ornament to be in dim frosted silver except the letters which may be bright. W.A.S. 8

Just four days after that letter, Smith chaired the Glasgow Battalion Executive meeting and stated that, *'...the Buckle for Officer's Cap would require to be made of silver as originally intended as the work was far too advanced to alter the style.'* No-one seems to have questioned this. 9 Just over a week later, Smith reiterated his point to the Glasgow Battalion Council, again without, it seems, any dissension; who would dare question the founder?.10

William Smith's letter of 2nd March 1886 with his defiant postscript.
BB Archive, Felden.

News spreads

Edinburgh Battalion Council had made the first move to adopt the cap within just over two weeks of the Glasgow decision. The minute book states: *'An Officer's cap, previously adopted by the Glasgow Battalion Council was laid upon the table and after some discussion was approved and adopted.'* 11 When it had, no doubt, had a chance to buy the cap from Messrs. Blair the Edinburgh Battalion approved and adopted the *'Officer's Cap with Ornament'*. 12 (Incidentally, the Edinburgh Battalion, very much less prosaic than their slightly dour Glaswegian colleagues, went on in the late **1890s** to suggest gilt badges and cap buckles for the Battalion President.13) In the first edition of the **1886** BB Manual the first advertisement for the cap and badge appears:

'Glengarry Caps for Officers [as adopted by Glasgow Battalion Council]..... 2s. 6d each.'
'Silver-Plated Ornament representing Crest of Brigade, for Officers' Caps, ...1s. 6d each.'

By the time the second edition was printed in **1886**, the cost of the *'Ornament'* had reduced to 1s. One can only assume that, perhaps, the first gross had been sold out! At the start of **1893** the price of glengarry caps had reduced to 2/3d. and Ornaments to 10d. with Blairs as the only supplier, but by the end of **1893** James Farquharson of London, Garlick & Sons of Bristol and George Binns of Sheffield were also supplying them at the same price referring to the *'Ornaments'* as *'Crests'*. **1895** saw the crest reduced to 9d. with Messrs Leckie Graham & Co. stocking the whole range of uniform accoutrements and not just its traditional leather goods.

In **1899**, a new alternative cap, field-service style, was introduced at a cost of 3/- with a special new badge retailing at 9d. The original badge had become well established, spawning at least two other badges before the turn of the century, the Three Year Anchor (**1888**) and then the Alternative Field-Service Cap Badge.14

Union

In **1927**, upon the amalgamation with the BLB, as well as a new version with the cross behind the anchor at the previous size, it was also considered desirable for an additional smaller version of the Officers' Cap Badge to be introduced. This was for use on the peaked (BLB-style) cap, on a field-service cap (replacing the **1899** badge) and sometimes even on the glengarry. This small Cap Badge, usually frosted as was its larger parent, lasted until about **1960**. It was re-introduced in **1981** after being discussed in detail by the Uniform Study Group. At the Supplies meeting of February **1980** it was agreed that quotations should be obtained, resulting in a badge with a bright chrome finish for use as a Lady Officers' Cap Badge. [15] The same Badge was adopted as an Officers' Epaulette Badge in **1984.**

So which were the earliest types of Officers' Cap Badge?

As this is the oldest of all brigade badges, is it possible to determine the earliest type? It is thought that the first issue of Officers' Cap Badges was shell-stamped. Certainly, such a pre-union type does exist in much smaller numbers than the solid types, and virtually all the post-**1926** types are solid. Both types consist of two components soldered together, viz, the anchor and belt. The shell-stamped type is the only one to include a small ball at the base of the belt runner, (see photo page 16) None of the post-**1926** varieties have this ball even though there are some later types which incorporate shell-stamped anchors. What then is the reasoning behind the theory that the earliest badges were shell stamped and that some had a 'disappearing ball' ?

a. It seems more likely that a small ball on an original die/pattern could be lost rather than simply appear for one edition, although this cannot be ruled-out. The disap-

pearance of a design feature on the badge may be accounted for by a change in manufacturer. Messrs. Blair was either the manufacturer itself, or it dealt direct with the manufacturer, and was the sole supplier until about **1893.** After that date other suppliers may have been able to obtain supplies from different manufacturing sources. The ball could have vanished and the badges could have been produced in solid form. About 2,000 badges had been supplied by **1893** [16]. so it could be that this figure represents the total quantity of shell-stamped 'ball' badges produced, only a few of which remain.

b. Perhaps the manufacturing process was changed at some time in order to cut costs or improve quality. A suggestion has been made that such a change could have been instituted as early as **1887** when Messrs. Blair were asked to quote for the supply of the anchor alone. Smith in his letter wanted it to be, '...*at a very low price*' and gave as his reason that, '...*it could be struck off with the same die as you presently use.*' [17] Evidently this did not happen since there are no known examples of a shell-stamped pre-**1926** Anchor Badge. A month after this letter Smith was again writing to Blair complaining about the quality of the boys' caps. As a footnote he mentions that he wanted to see Mr Robert Blair that morning about the anchors but had not managed to do so. He suggested that Mr Blair call in to see him.[18] We can only assume that Mr Blair, aware that one of his best customers was experiencing problems and requesting to see him about a new order, would have availed himself post-haste. Perhaps the result was a 'better quality' solid anchor badge and eventually a solid re-struck belt section for the Cap Badge? If the latter scenario is correct then the number of shell-stamped cap badges made before the change would have only been in the region of 500. Shell-stamped, pre-**1926** Officers' Cap Badges do

exist with a solid anchor and a re-worked belt surround.

c. There is some anecdotal evidence that the original Cap Badges were indeed shell-stamped. The late Roy Farmer (Ex. Capt 32nd Glasgow Coy.) born c.1900 stated that his father, Capt. Farmer, a founder member of 9th Glasgow Coy., and a friend of W.A.Smith, told him that his original cap badge was of this type.[19]

Without detailed evidence we can only speculate. It is not possible to determine which was the earliest type with any degree of certainty. It is quite likely that two different manufacturers were producing different style Officers Cap Badges at the same time.

Today, the Brigade movement's longest serving 'ornament' is still worn, hardly changed from the original conception except for the addition of a cross behind the anchor. William Smith's silver 'buckle' like his Brigade, continues into the new millennium. In Sept. **1999,** the Brigade Council approved the introduction of a new single uniform for officers which did not include a hat. However, at the Brigade Council meeting of **2000,** the hat was retained as a uniform option, complete with badge.

REFERENCES

1. 1st Glasgow Coy. BB 'Souvenir of Old Members Gathering 14th January 1924'
2. 'For Fifty Years' Jubilee Souvenir of 1st Glasgow Coy. BB 1933. p.7.
3. ibid.
4. Springhall et al.'Sure & Stedfast' History of the BB. 1983. Appendix 1. p.258.
5. The Boys' Brigade Glasgow Battalion Minute Book No.1 [1/1/1] Executive meeting 20/1/1886 Glasgow Battn. HQ.
6. ibid. 1/2/1886
7. ibid. Council 27/2/1886.
8. Letter Book of Brigade Sec. W.A.Smith p.14. Letter 184. BB Archive. BB HQ, Felden Lodge, Herts.
9. Executive 6/3/1886 op.cit.
10. Council 15/3/1886 op.cit.
11. Edinburgh Battalion Council Minute Book 30/10/1886.
12. ibid. 13/10/1886
13. ibid. 7/2/1898
14. The Boys' Brigade Manuals, 1886 [i], 1886 [ii], 1888 [i], 1888 [ii], 1889 [i], 1889 [ii], 1890, 1891/2, 1893, 1893/4, 1895, 1897, 1902. BB Archives. Felden op.cit.
15. Minutes of Supplies Committee. Feb 1980 para 5[d] BB Archive, Felden op.cit.
16. Springhall et al. op. cit. Appendices 1 & 3.
17. Letter Book of Brigade Sec. Letter 496 4th February 1887.
18. ibid. Letter 529, 3rd March 1887.
19. Roy Farmer in conversation with John Cooper, ex-archivist Glasgow Battalion. Information provided by John Cooper, Neilston, Glasgow.

The Officers' Cap Badge

1886 - 1926

BB 001.03

BB 001.10

BB 001 BACKGROUND NOTES

There are two main variations of this badge as a result of the differing methods of production, one is shell stamped with a deep rim, the other is solid. Due to the two- part construction of the badge it is possible to find certain variations with a combination of both construction methods, i.e. a thin shell stamped garter on which is mounted a solid anchor. The anchor emblem can be found with small or large Bs, rope going into the Bs or stopping outside the letters. On the shell stamped anchors the crown can be chined or curved and the deep shell stamped garter has a small ball on the runner motif.

1927 -

BB 002.07

BB 002.23

BB 002.25

BB 002 BACKGROUND NOTES

There are many more varieties of the post-union version for two reasons. Firstly, it had a lifespan almost double that of its predecessor and secondly, after World War II, much smaller batches were produced. There are variations in the garter lettering and the runner motif, the width of the crossbar of the anchor and the lettering of the BB motto. On the reverse, some have a maker's name on either the garter, emblem or both. There are many varying degrees of impressing on the reverse. Originally, the badge was made of nickel but later versions have the 'staybrite' finish.

The Officers' Uniform Buttonhole Badge

A distinction between Captains & Lieutenants

This influential, but most short-lived of BB uniform badges, was never even adopted by some battalions. The reason for this outward disparity stems from the fact that from the outset there was never any real agreement that the badges would be of any lasting worth.

The style of the badge which eventually emerged was, to say the least, somewhat understated. Perhaps this was to please those in the Brigade who were wary of creating a complicated uniform for officers or boys. The Captain of the 2nd Stonehouse (Devon) Coy., Reginald S. Cole, writing in the BB Gazette in **1895** gave his opinion on certain aspects of uniform which was very topical at the time following H.M. Government's legislation to prevent civilians dressing up in military uniform. Cole was opposed to full uniform, but was quite happy to advocate the use of a badge to distinguish between captains and lieutenants:

'If marks of distinction between a Captain and his Lieutenants are required, why not follow the example of a Battalion in the North of England which has adopted the Brigade anchor to be worn in the button hole, that for Captains being gilt and for Lieutenants silver. This badge has the advantage of being visible on occasions when the cap is removed, and marks the wearer as a Brigade Officer.'[1]

Other correspondents to the Gazette at the same time, expounded the more traditional view and questioned the whole concept of making 'captain' a rank in the same sense that 'lieutenant' is a rank. A 'West of Scotland Officer' (Where else!) writing about uniform in **1895**, was concerned that a senior and experienced officer in a large company would be outranked by a young Lieutenant who became a Captain simply by leaving to start a new company of his own. Other reasons were also given:

'...The service of the Officers of The Boys' Brigade is a voluntary service in and of a Christian Organisation, and once connected with a Company, it is not merit or term of service that makes a Lieutenant a Captain, but some unforseen mishap or accident...'

The correspondent reveals his Presbyterian origins in a comment earlier in the letter:

'What could be simpler and more becoming than the Glengarry and Crest worn with a black or blue serge, or other dark cloth jacket suit?... Why should there be a distinctive mark between Captains and Lieutenants?'[2]

Clearly, opinion was divided not just on a uniform distinction, but even as to whether or not there should be any ranks at all. The officer who wrote the above letter actually went on to advocate that they should all be designated as 'officers' with a leading officer given the title 'Senior Officer'.

In spite of clear apprehension from many officers, the first intimation of the badge came in the BB Gazette of March **1897**:

'In order to meet the want felt in some of our Battalions of a means of distinguishing the Captain of a Company from the Lieutenants on parade, the Executive have anuthorised the issue of a Button-hole Badge in two distinct materials (Silver for Captains and Bronze for Lieutenants) as being on the whole, the most convenient and simple form of marking the required distinction. The Executive desire it to be understood that it is left to the discretion of the responsible authority in each case whether these Badges should be adopted or not. It is to be clearly understood that these Badges are only to be used on parade.'[3]

The BB Manual, published in **1897**, had details of the new badges:

'The Executive has authorised the use of Officer's Button-Hole Badges for use on parade, for the purpose of distinction between Captains and Lieutenants (Silver for Captains and Bronze for Lieutenants). The Executive desire it to be understood, however, that it is left to the discretion of the responsible authority, in each case, whether these Badges should be adopted or not.'[4]

Presbyterian equality

It is not clear why the badge was unpopular. Its six-year lifespan and only partial adoption, the result of deliberately permissive regulation, tells its own story. Perhaps the 'ethos' of the BB officer was in question here as pointed out by the 'West of Scotland Officer' in **1895**. The BB 'captain' has been an 'appointment' rather than a rank. On parade, Captains wore, and still wear, the same uniform as any lieutenant. The same uniform rule is applicable to all from the Brigade President to the youngest, newly appointed Lt.. BB officers were, and are, a team of 'equals' led by one of their number appointed by their church. The officers' uniform dress code seems to have stemmed from the simplicity of Presbyterian ministers and congregations, lacking all forms of personal adornment. In the late 19th Century it was very often a matter of keeping a balance between the extravagant military influences of the Volunteers and strict puritanical church pressures. The Volunteer influence permeated the officer ranks and it was thus found necessary to insert warnings about any departure from the simple uniform in the BB Manual. Just before and after the badge regulations it stated:

'No uniform Clothing or belts of any kind are to be worn by Officers of The Boys' Brigade... The Executive would impress upon Battalion Councils and Officers of Companies the importance of avoiding any departure from the simple and inexpensive uniform... it has won for the movement the cordial support of a large section of the Christian public whose sympathy and confidence would speedily be alienated by any unnecessary display of extravagance.' [5]

Inspirational

One battalion where the badge was not adopted was Glasgow. The Annual Report for **1898-1899** quotes the **1897** BB Manual giving it authority not to adopt the badge. It was clearly stated that the badges would not be sold and would not

appear on the *'sanctioned list'.* [6] A similar decision would, in **1904**, be made in Glasgow regarding the One Year Efficiency Badge. For the first time, however, the new badge did appear on one list. In the back of the **1897** BB Manual in the 'Brigade Publications' section, it appeared along with the Ambulance Badge and the Three Years' Service Anchor. The wording from the regulation was repeated in the Manual, including the discretionary proviso:

'Captain's Badge, Silver, 9d each, Lieutenant's Badge, Bronze, 6d each. In Card Boxes, carriage paid.'[7]

Rarely seen on photographs of the time, the buttonhole badge is seen in both forms adorning the lapels of captain and lieutenants of the 94th London Company on a picture in the BB photo-archive. [8]

In October **1903** the BB Gazette carried a curt epitaph for a badge with no future:

'The use of the Button-hole Badge to be discontinued'. [9]

The Editor of the BB Gazette, in March **1921**, under the heading: 'Recorded in March' commented upon the subject of the Officers' Buttonhole Badge introduced in March **1897**:
'In response to insistant requests for some mark to distinguish Captains from Lieutenants on parade, a buttonhole badge was reluctantly authorised, silver for Captains and bronze for Lieutenants. As is not unusual in the

BB, it was found that after all the agitation, only a handful of Officers desired such a badge. Lieutenants did not really wish to be distinguished from their Captains, and so the old order of simplicity continued to rule the Brigade.'[10]

During its short period of use the Officers' Buttonhole Badge must have gained some admirers as it was the inspiration for the Old Boys' Badge, which in turn spawned both the Jubilee and the present Buttonhole Badge. [11] The Boys' Buttonhole Badge, sanctioned in **1911**, was also almost identical in size, shape and design, but with the addition of blue enamel. [12]

It was **1927** before the uniform for officers would again show any distinction between captains and lieutenants with the use of silver cap stars, and silver and black buttons.[13]

REFERENCES

1. BB Gazette 1st April 1895 p 241.
2. ibid.
3. Quoted in the BBBC Newsletter, No 11, July 1985. Muriel D. Gibbs (Brigade Archivist) Editor.
4. The Boys' Brigade Manual. 1897. p 12. BB HQ Felden Lodge, Hemel Hemstead, Herts.
5. ibid. p 12-13
6. Glasgow Battalion Annual Reports. 1896 - 1900, [1/3/3] 1898 - 1899. Glasgow Battalion HQ, Bath St, Glasgow.
7. 1897 Manual op. cit. p33.
8. BB Photo-Archive, Felden. Ref: P/1210.
9. BB Gazette, Vol. XII, 1/10/1903, p 31. BB Scottish HQ, Carronvale, Larbert, Stirlingshire.
10. op.cit. No 3.
11. See section on Old Boys' Badges. p
12. The Badge has both the Anchor and 'B's [See photo] not as depicted in 'Badges of the BB' Archive Press, BB HQ., Ed. M. Gibbs, 1980, Second Edition 1985.
13. BB Manual 1928, p 73. Officers' Optional Full Uniform.

The Officers' Uniform Buttonhole Badges   1897 - 1903

BB 003.01

BB 003.02

BB 003 BACKGROUND NOTES

There seems to be some variation in these lapel buttons. Most types are laminated in two sections, like a button, with a crescent stud, other types being solid. The 'Silver' versions are actually white metal. The obverse detail is raised but the whole obverse is concave on type 003.01 which has the maker's name 'H.W.Miller Ltd B'ham 18', on the stud.

The Officers' Field Service Cap Badge

Officers' Uniform 'B' Droop-peak Cap Badge

Hundreds of Birmingham BB Officers, all wearing Field-Service Caps
At the special Jubilee Garden Party, 11th June **1932**, Bournville.
Hosts Mr & Mrs Barrow Cadbury. [Seated, Front]

From the outset there had been some disagreement concerning the headgear to be worn in uniform by officers. In **1885**, the glengarry was chosen by a majority of one, but there was always a large body of officers who were opposed to it. In **1899,** an optional 'Field Service' cap was adopted along with its own badge. The cap became popular in some areas with the instruction being given that the same caps should be adopted within a battalion:

'Within Battalions there will be uniformity with regard to Officers' Caps...'[1]

The 'remodelling' of the F/S cap was suggested in **1903** and a Sub-Committee formed[2]. However, it was **1912** before a new pattern was announced.[3]

The BB Manual could lay down the law regarding officers' uniformity before **1926**, but it was not able to do so afterwards. In **1926** with BB/BLB union there came upon the scene more uniforms and, of course, this included more caps. The main BLB Officers' Cap was known as the 'Droop-peak' and from **1927** this would feature amongst the options for BB officers' uniform.

From **1927** the Field Service Cap was retained, but the special badge had to be re-designed due to the addition of a cross behind the anchor. In fact, the BB decided upon a small version of the Officers' Glengarry Badge. The Manual allowed for four types of Officers' Cap:

'(1) Uniform A, the Glengarry, and (2) Uniform B, the Droop-peak Cap or the Glengarry. As an alternative to the above, Companies (subject to Battalion Regulations) may adopt a Field Service Cap of black cloth with white (Uniform A), or magenta (Uniform B) piping, and two round silvered buttons at the front.
For all these a special badge with the Brigade Crest is supplied, which is not to be used for any other purpose.' [4]

Clearly, the Brigade considered there to be only one Officers' Cap Crest, now available in two sizes! The BB Supplies Catalogue at the same time, **1928-1929,** does not differentiate between the two. Caps are supplied with *'crests'* (badges). Badges could be bought separately *'plated -9d'* or *'silver-7/6d'*.
In the field, so to speak, the glengarry was worn with the normal full-sized crest, the field-service cap with the new small-sized crest and the Droop-peak Cap with either.[5]

Some battalions were keen to return to the old regulation of having all officers similarly hatted, but for many it was well into the **1930s** before this was achieved. The Droop-peak Cap became unobtainable after the Second World War, so the Field Service Badge was retained adorning the one remaining Field Service Cap, the original **1927** uniform 'B' Cap. The F/S cap was not used much during the **1960s** and dropped out of regulations.[6]

REFERENCES

1. BB Manual 1914, p. 20.
2. BB Gazette 1/10/1903 p 31. D. Aubrey Collection.
3. ibid. 1/09/1912 p3.
4. op. cit., BB Manual, 1928, p 71.
5. Photographic evidence from the period 1927 - 1930s, mainly Birmingham Battalion, shows Officers wearing both cap badge sizes. Presumably this was not done with in a Company, but at a Battalion event such as a Camp the two types can be clearly seen in juxtaposition.
6. R.Bolton has personal recollections of Sir Donald Finnemore, Capt. 1stA B'ham. Coy. wearing the F/S cap well into the late 1960s. Only for official 'National' Brigade duties did he wear the Glengarry eg. as Camp Commandant of the Founder's Camp, Eton, 1954.

The Officers' Field Service Cap Badge   1899 - 1926

BB 004.01

BB 004.03

Field Service Cap Badge - Detail

Pierced gap →

BB 004.03 enlarged

BB 004 BACKGROUND NOTES

Several varieties of this badge, including a hallmarked silver version, are known. Most types have a frosted finish. The most striking variation of the nickel versions is pierced between the top of the anchor crown and the rope passing behind it. (see inset above).

The Officers' Cap - Epaulette Badge (Small)

Field Service Cap Badge   1927 - c.1960
Alternative Uniform 'B' Droop-peak Cap Badge   1927 - c.1945
Lady Officers' Cap Badge   1981 - 2006
Epaulette Badge   1984 - 2006

BB 005.01

BB 005.08

BB 005 BACKGROUND NOTES

The original Officers' badges were produced with a frosted finish. They are solid, made up of two parts as in the larger Officers' Cap Badge, have two lugs and vary little. Although they were officially 'in service' for many years the fact that the F.S. Cap was not widely adopted in 1927 and was infrequently worn after 1945 results in relatively small numbers. The Droop-peak Cap was often adorned with a full-sized Officers' Cap Badge, within the regulations. All the epaulette badges are either chrome plated or 'staybrite' finish and of similar two-part construction to their progenitor. However, there are now two types of fastening on the reverse, lugs or tags. Other differences are to be found in the runner motif, background stipple and lettering style.

The Officers' & W/Os'
Collar, & Epaulette Badges, & Warrant Officers' Cap Badge

groups in the city such as the Foundry Boys' Religious Society. The officers pictured, William Smith and the Hill Brothers (James and John,) are not wearing a uniform bearing any resemblance to the Volunteers. Clearly, they are emphasising the 'civil' nature of the organisation by wearing bowler hats as they had, since the first Inspection. However, a problem which would remain with the BB and its officers for many years had not escaped their attention... what happens to your 'uniform' when you take off your hat?

If scrutinized it will be noticed that the officers are in fact, wearing a collar badge. The badge was a home-made job constructed from white braid formed into a symbol of three triangles.

O n 9th April 1885, the first Glasgow Company of The Boys' Brigade, the elder of the two Companies in existence at the time, lined up to be photographed in the grounds of Garscube House.

The 'Trinity' Badge worn by the first BB Officers.

The 1st Glasgow Company of The Boys' Brigade. The first official photograph, taken in the grounds of Garscube House. 9th April 1885.

The Company had been for a 'March - Out' in uniform. The origins of the uniform for boys is a matter of debate, but certainly it was influenced by the Volunteers as had been other uniformed youth

The first collar badges?

There has been much speculation about the meaning of the badge, perhaps representing the Holy Trinity, or even a Celtic symbol of everlasting life. It can even be read as 'B's' ! Such a badge survives in the Archive of Glasgow Battalion.

The badge was photographed some years ago along with other early Brigade memorabilia and the picture reproduced is an enlargement, now virtually actual size.

Within a few months of the Garscube photograph meetings had been held to discuss the official formation of a Boys' Brigade organisation, there being fifteen companies by October **1885**.[1] Uniform matters would be in the hands of a committee. Typical of most committees, particularly in the early months, there was a great deal of disagreement relating to uniform matters. William Smith and the Hill brothers would now not be able to dictate the uniform for the organisation they had started.

For the next ten years the BB grew and so did the number of officers. If there was an identity problem when not wearing hats not much seems to have been done or said about it. Even in **1897**, when a Buttonhole Badge was introduced, the stated reason for its introduction was to distinguish between captains and lieutenants and its adoption was optional. There was a strong lobby in the Brigade, especially in Glasgow, against 'personal adornment', it being part of the Presbyterian tradition. This was, no doubt, one of the reasons for the Buttonhole Badge's short life.

Badges Added

William Smith would certainly have approved of the wearing of collar badges. His upbringing in the North of Scotland and his

membership of the Volunteers both suggest that the somewhat dour image of Brigade officers was not of his making. Unfortunately, he died two years before the introduction of collar badges, but is frequently shown wearing them on illustrations, even official Brigade publications! The most famous drawing of the founder was that done by eminent Edinburgh artist and BB Captain Tom Curr, - but without collar badges. Someone, obviously not an historian, added them.

By **1915**, it seems certain that there was much discussion about the possible introduction of collar badges. Why this should have suddenly come to the fore is uncertain. There were, of course, more military uniforms around than there had ever been and the habit of smoking had increased due to more advertising. Officers who fancied a smoke, but not in uniform, could simply take off their hat and put it in their pocket, finish the cigarette and then replace the headgear. There was no rule as yet prohibiting officers from smoking in uniform, but the habit was frowned upon.[2]

It was at the Sheffield Council meeting in September **1915** that 70 officers held an evening meeting and passed resolutions regarding possible changes in uniform. One of the three main recommendations was the adoption of a dark-blue serge suit with detachable badges on each lapel.[3] The proposals would be put to the next meeting of the Brigade Executive.

At the first BB Executive meeting in **1916** there was agreement on collar badges:

'...it was decided that specimens of some such Badge in three colours - bronze, gilt and silver, should be before the next Meeting of Executive for decision.'[4]

At the Executive meeting in April the Committee:

'...had before them rough models of the proposed Collar Badge for Officers in gilt, silver and bronze, together with a drawing... ...steps should be taken to proceed with the making of the Badge'

This would only be done if the Northern Committee and the Southern Committees agreed.[5]

Fortunately for the Northern Committee there was agreement and at the next meeting the design for the Officers Collar Badge was approved:

'It was unanimously agreed that the Badge should be produced in Bronze.' To be worn *'...just above the lapel.'*.[6]

A Shade of Bronze

Now it would be a matter of choosing a shade of bronze. It is perhaps as well that there were not many to choose from. The next meeting was faced with the onerous task when two specimen collar badges for officers were exhibited:

'...two shades of bronze being shown.'

The Committee approved the lighter shade.[7]

It was now time to advertize the new badge in the Gazette. The wording of the details perhaps gives a clue to one of the reasons the badges had been called for:

'...the wearing of Collar Badges above the lapel, as is done by Military Officers in service uniform; and an attractive badge has been designed for the purpose.'[8]

The price was 1/6d per pair.

In the same Gazette in which the collar badges were announced was the official notification of the sanctioning of the rank of 2nd lieutenant. They would not wear collar badges, so the tradition of simply wearing a hat would continue after all.

In **1916,** many suppliers were still providing items of uniform and the new collar badge soon became the centre of attention, being produced in two different shades of bronze by the main manufacturers in Glasgow and London. The Northern Committee of the Brigade Executive was called upon to adjudicate in the matter. At its meeting in October **1916** samples of the new collar badges were exhibited from Messrs Farquharson (London) and Messrs Leckie Graham (Glasgow). The Committee complained that:

'...the colour of the Badge was not the same'

The Secretary was directed to communicate with the latter firm regarding this matter, so that they might issue Badges of the same colour as Messrs Farquharson.[9]

We don't know whether Leckie-Graham was making them too light or too dark! If William Smith had still been around, no doubt the silver option would have been chosen, but the dour bronze won the day. There would now be an officers' uniform with three badges, one silver and bright in the cap and two others, singularly dull, decorating the lapels.

It appears from the records that many BB officers treated the new badges with a good deal of contempt. One officer felt inclined to write to the Gazette and his letter was published in April **1921**:

Collar Badges
'Sir, - Has not the time come to consid-er the abolition of these encumber-ances? They are fragile, detrimental to the coat, generally put on at different levels, and serve no useful purpose. I have at home a large quantity of such badges from which the pins have become detached, and as I am one of those persons who think it right to ful-fil the regulations as far as possible, I can see myself becoming the owner of a great many more unless the Brigade Council decides, very properly, to abol-ish them.

Yours faithfully. "Haversack".'

In **1922,** the Gazette included a line drawing to show how the badge should be worn.[10] There was obviously strong feeling that these badges were being worn incorrectly by many officers.

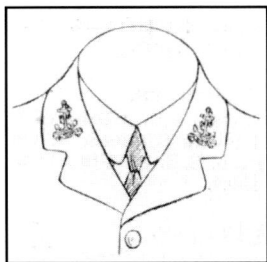

No Adornment

The diagram was later reproduced in the BB Manual. It would be normal to report that these badges, like many others in the BB, became accepted as part of the organisation. The officers' lapel badges are far from normal in this respect and continued to arouse strong feelings nationwide. Mr R. Borthwick, Capt. 17th Leith Company, took his objections to the Brigade Council Meeting at Newcastle in **1923**. His efforts were duly reported in the BB Gazette. Mr Borthwick moved to abolish the badges in...

'...an amusing speech... the gist of which was that BB men did not want any adornment, however simple. Mr L.L. Bilton, Vice-President of the Edinburgh Battalion seconded the motion. He said that these badges were obviously unpopular as Officers would not take the trouble to put them on cor-rectly. Also, they were constantly being lost, so why not abolish them? The motion was opposed on the grounds that the badge was simple, and could not be called an "attrac-tion", and that in Church, or on any occasion when caps were taken off, there was no other means by which we could distinguish a BB man from a stranger... The subject gave plenty scope for chaff, as those who advocated abolition were influenced by the new rule debarring Officers from smoking while in uniform, for if the badge were abolished an Officer had simply to put his cap in his pocket in order to be free to smoke. The resolution was lost by a big majority.'[11]

The Badges Multiply

Not only did the collar badges survive the union of BB and BLB in **1926,** but they actually multiplied in type and style. Like all BB Badges with an emblem, the new **1927** uniform Lapel Badges were given the new crest with a cross behind the anchor. The new united brigade had now an optional uniform for officers - 'Uniform B'. One of the options for uniform under the general heading of 'B' was the wearing of a regulation navy blue tunic with white metal collar badges and a waistbelt. This was the tunic as worn by BLB officers, but with a 'White - Metal' version of the collar badge.

The rank of 2nd lieutenant contin-ued upon union with the BLB, but a new rank of 'Warrant Officer' was introduced; the BLB term for a trainee officer. BLB warrant officers had worn badges of rank, so the BB had to find a further badge. A short, business-like note, part of the minutes of the BB Executive at their meeting in October **1926,** sums up the situation:

'Proposal of Negotiating Committee that a W.O. should wear the same as Officers, but different Collar and Cap Badge. Approved.' [12]

What would the 'different' badge be like?

Cadet Re-incarnation

It transpired that the Collar and Cap Badge selected for warrant officers was a reincarnation of the BB Cadet Officers' Collar Badge which had ceased to be regulation just two years earlier. That badge had been produced in bronze, but the new version identical in both size and design to the old badge, would now be made in white metal. By adopting this badge the BB was saving money on dies, etc. and introducing a badge which was popular. At the same time, the matching 'entwined Bs' cap badge was introduced for use on boys' field-service pattern caps.

It was not long before the bronze collar badges were back in the arena of controversy. Some officers were polishing their bronze badges. A short letter appeared in the Gazette concerning this and stating that the Manual was not unclear on the subject.[13] This opened a veritable Pandora's box, especially when the official reply was printed in the next edition which stated that the badges were *'...bronze'* and *'should not be polished'*, and that a new paragraph to that effect would appear in the Manual.[14] Gazette Correspondence appeared which is here reproduced in full, because it provides a tremendous insight into the badges, and the wearers, of the time.

Emblems of our Cause

'Sir,- In your last issue there is an obvious error in the statement that "the bronze collar badges worn with Officers' uniform 'A' should not be polished." Surely the word "not" is a printer's error, for I cannot believe that such an utterance is issued by Authority. Or perhaps the paragraph was sent in by some indolent Officer who has imposed upon the gullibility of the editor, and seeks to delude the general body into compliance with a habit prompted by his own laziness.

Really, to a BB Officer who insists upon his Boys polishing all the metal fittings of their equipment until they shine like gold, such a question is almost superflous. There is no injunction in the Manual that Officers are expected to wash the back of their necks and wear a fairly clean collar on parade, but such "discreet silence" is surely not to be taken as an indication that such things are not expected of Officers.

For a fraction of the effort we expect from our Boys we can turn our collar badges from dull, dismal, dispiriting brown, hardly discernible at two yards' distance, into glittering ornaments, fit to be worn by one marching at the head of a body of Boys, such as we are privileged to have in our ranks.

Does not this suggestion of leaving unpolished in our own uniform that which can be polished, while asking something more from the Boys, savour of inconsistency? Such a spirit is hard-

ly good enough for the BB.

Visualise, too, the impression upon the minds of the public if, by this little effort, Officers added to their somewhat mediocre appearance that touch of distinction which well polished collar badges impart. What a differernce at Aberdeen, for instance, if all those 800 Anchors had been brightly polished so that they might reflect the rays of the sun into the dazzled eyes of the onlookers, as their wearers marched on Church Parade!

Doubtless, I shall be told that bronze military badges are not usually polished, but that of course is no answer. We wear our badges as emblems of our cause, and in any case the BB is not tied by military regulations. - Yours, etc.
FRANK WESTBROOK,
Captain, 99th London.'

REPLY BY THE BRIGADE SECRETARY,- The statement was correct. When the Collar Badge was instituted some dozen years ago, bronze was chosen deliberately, and universally approved, because it was not "a glittering ornament" to "dazzle the eyes of onlookers." Some distinctive mark was asked for to enable people at any indoor gathering, when caps are not worn, to pick out the men who are BB Officers. That is the sole raison d'etre of the badge. Polish the bronze until it "glitters like gold" and what is the use of choosing bronze? Why not have gilt? How it comes to pass that the Manual omits to state that the badge (though it must, of course, be kept clean) must not be ploished to look like something else, I do not know. Probably, as everyone knew at first, it was taken for granted that everyone would continue to know.

The Cap Badge gives the opportunity to set the Boys an example of polishing.'

A further letter appeared to support the non-polishers, which might not be regarded today as being entirely 'P.C.'

Sir,- How helpless and unpractical the dear men are! I suppose that this is what appeals to us. They need the assurance from HQ that their bronze collar-badges should not be polished. Why don't they ask wife, mother, sister or landlady? We women can tell them that bronze simply mustn't be polished, or it will lose its distinctive tone, and might just as well be plebeian brass. Just keep your bronze free from dust and dirt; and you can get a special oil to put on once or twice a year-just a light touch with a paint-brush. But don't rub,- Yours, etc., H.R.[15]

The reply came in the next edition of the Gazette:

Sir,- The reply of the Brigade Secretary finds me quite unrepentant for having transgressed the spirit of the law by polishing my bronze badges for some years past, and leaves me to conclude that he can never have seen a really well-polished pair. His reply, in effect, is that they are to be worn as articles of uiniform, merely to distinguish us, when uncovered, from the Boys or the Deacons, or the Churchwardens, and not as a means of drawing public attention to the movement with which we are identified.

Is it not possible that the BB is suffering from this policy of modest self-effacement? We believe, don't we, that the Brigade provides the best means at our disposal for the spiritual, mental and physical development of the Boy: then why should we not seek any and every means of advertising it, even to the polishing of our Collar Badges?

"H.R." may be interested to learn that there is at least one Officer's wife who differs from her in this matter, and she was wont to take pride in approving my shining badges when sending me to parade. Now, alas, in deference to the opinion of the Brigade Secretary, these are donned unpolished and in silence, and I hurry through the streets with a shame-faced air to meet the derisive grins and knowing winks of my Boys on parade, when I make my explanation that Officers' Bronze Collar Badges should not be polished.- Yours, etc., FRANK WESTBROOK.

Frank Westwood's dilemma sums up the problems with badge and insignia wearing in the Brigade from the outset. The arguments between Smith and the first Brigade Council were only the start. This debate continues into the 21st Century when the discussion focuses upon the wearing of hats and having any type of formal uniform at all.

Throughout the **1950s, 60s** and **70s** some collar badges were still worn, polished in defiance of the rules. The variety of 'bronze' colours in which they were produced would have horrified the old Northern Committee of the Executive. The abolition of the rank of 2nd Lt. in **1951** didn't affect badges in any way.

Browned Off & Gone to the Dogs

In **1981,** the Brigade introduced the option of wearing a 'full' uniform for officers both men and women. Male officers could wear the former 'Collar Badges' as 'Epaulette Badges' on a sleeve over the shirt epaulette. By **1984,** the options had increased to two types of full uniform for men and three for women. The Epaulette Badges were now described as 'chrome plated' and were not the former collar badges, but the small version of the Officers' Cap Badge originally used as the 'Officers' Field Service Cap Badge' between **1927 - c.1961** [16] and latterly used as the Lady Officers' Cap Badge. The Warrant Officers' Badge was now also chrome-plated providing, in full uniform, a common identity between the W/O's and Lt's..[17]

The dull brown collar 'dogs' which had caused so much heartache were now only one of the alternatives available, remaining regulation only for officers wearing navy-blue jacket suits. If Capt. Westbrook were still on active BB service, he would be very much less shame - faced on parade, resplendent with the 'glittering ornaments' of the new chrome-plated badges fastened into his epaulettes.

At the Brigade Council Meeting in Dundee in **1999** a new set of uniforms for the whole of the BB was agreed. Very early in this millennium the Officers' Collar Badges will disappear, as will probably the very title of 'Officer'!

REFERENCES

1. Springhall et al. Sure & Stedfast. 1983 p. 41.
2. Non-Smoking by Brigade boys was encouraged in many Battalions with the issue of special certificates to those who gave up or never started the habit. Officers were not thanked for openly smoking in uniform.
3. Meeting 11th Sept 1915. The other changes proposed were a walking stick to replace the swaggewr stick and the introduction of a naval peaked cap for officers in non-Scottish companies.
4. Meeting, 28-29 Jan 1916. Northern Committee Minute Book No.1 (1915-1919) Scottish BB HQ Carronvale.
5. ibid. 7th April 1916.
6. ibid. 20-21st May 1916.
7. ibid. 30th June 1916.
8. BB Gazette. Vol XXV No.1. 1/9/1916 p 2. BB Scottish HQ, Carronvale.
9. op.cit. N. Committee. 12th October 1916.
10. BB Gazette, 1/4/1922. Vol XXX, No 8, p 115, Glasgow Battalion Archive.
11. ibid. 1/10/ 1923, Vol XXXII, No. 2. p.24.
12. op.cit. Executive Meeting, 15-16/October, 1926.
13. op.cit. Gazette Vol XXXVII, No 6, 1/2/1929, p 92.
14. ibid. No 7, p 102.
15. ibid. No 8, p 125
16. Uniform option of F/Service cap still in 1960 Manual.
17. BB Gazette June/July 1985 Uniform Regulations pages 100 - 101.

The Officers' Lapel/Collar Badge

1916 - 1926

BB 006.0

BB 006.07

BB 006.04

BB 006.06

BB 006 BACKGROUND NOTES

Colour varaitions occur in this badge due to varying lengths of 'pickling' in the manufacturing process and because some officers cleaned the badges, contrary to regulations. The ribbon lettering varies in size as do the Bs. There is one version (006.04) that has non-pierced Bs. The stick-pin type of fastening is the most common but there are versions having a brooch fitting with an axle-pin.

1927 - 2006

BB 007.01

BB 007.03

BB 007.06

BB 007.15

BB 007.17

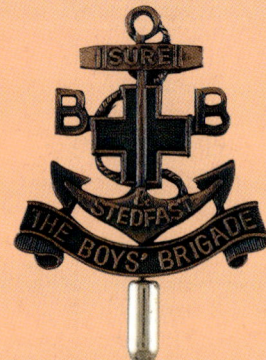

BB 007.27

BB 007.28

BB 007.30

BB 007 BACKGROUND NOTES

NB. THIS BADGE WAS USED AS AN EPAULETTE BADGE FROM 1981 - 1984.

Due to the length of issue, there is a great variety in these badges. The colour range is considerable ranging from a red metal hue through to almost black. Some have a golden brassy appearance. The majority have a stick-pin fastening but tags are found on some versions. The type specifically produced for epaulettes have double clutch pin fastenings. The white metal versions are found with either a frosted or chrome finish and have lugs or tags. There are varying degrees of impressing on the reverse and several makers' names can be identified. Virtually every detail on the obverse varies. A curved brass version exists with two threaded bolts for fixing to Drum-Majors' maces.

The Warrant Officers' Cap, & Collar Badge   1927 -

The Warrant Officers' Epaulette Badge   1981 - 2006

BB 013.15

BB 013.33

BB 013.14

BB 013.01

BB 013.18

BB 013 BACKGROUND NOTES

This badge is found in up to four different formats, due to its variety of uses. Stick pins are used on the collar badge, lugs for the cap badge with tags and clutch-pins for epaulettes. Before the 1980s, the badges were virtually all solid but since then they are fully shell-stamped. The original types had a frosted silver finish, but later they were plain nickel. From 1984, all versions were either chrome-plated or 'staybrite' finish.

The overall size of the badge varies as does the lettering size on the ribbons. The Miller version has noticeably shallow curved scrolls but is invariably the stick-pin variety, perhaps indicating that this maker differentiated between the two main uses for the badge. Early versions have an apostrophe after 'Boys', later ones do not. The earliest lugged versions have the lugs set horizontally, later ones, vertically.

See also BB Cadet Officers' Collar Badge 1918 - 1924

The Boys' Brigade Cadet Badges
& an Introduction to The Brigade Cadet Badges

The Brigade Cadets

The Cadet Movement, a form of preparation for the Volunteer forces which had developed in the Public Schools during the latter half of the 19th Century, had, by the time of the formation of the BB, grown into a more general military training which found its way into many somewhat less 'refined' institutions. Boys clubs, university missions and institutes founded by religious philanthropists were taking military training to the masses of British working boys. The growth of Brigade Cadets, after **1911**, meant that a plethora of special badges and insignia emerged for use within the various organisations. Sometimes these new badges were modifications of existing cadet and regimental insignia, often simply adaptations of brigade badges already in use. When a complete change of dress was required, in order to fulfil the requirements of the War Office, notably a change from cap, belt and haversack 'equipment' to a full tunic uniform, special badges were deemed to be essential appendages.

'a means to an end'

From the outset, the Boys' Brigade like the other religious brigades, had insisted that drill and, by implication, all other military characteristics was only a means to an end and not the end itself. Indeed, the argument that the BB was not a military body had been well developed by **1907** the year that R. B. Haldane, the Secretary of State for War, introduced his 'Territorial Forces Bill'. The Bill provided the legal framework for extending Cadet membership to all existing youth organisations. By **1910**, the BB was being targeted by the War Office. William Smith and, it would seem, a large majority of officers and churches were opposed to the BB being included. The point was made that seventeen was the BB age limit anyway and ex-members could, as they had for years, serve in the Territorials after completing BB service. [1]

The Great War

With the outbreak of the Great War and the rallying to the flag of many thousands of ex-brigade boys, some in special battalions and companies, [2] the attitudes of the brigades and of their sponsoring churches began to change slowly, but surely, in favour of some involvement. The Boys' Brigade Executive, by **1917,** felt an obligation to allow those companies which wished to be recognised as Cadets to have their way. Even by **1919,** however, only 311 BB companies had accepted official recognition with a mere 63 adopting the khaki uniform. [3]

Advantages

Cadet membership for the Brigades held a number of advantages such as grants from the War Office, issue of predominantly khaki uniforms at nominal cost and free loan of camping equipment. On the negative side, the brigades were worried about losing their autonomy and becoming pawns at the disposal of political masters, but independent Cadet units were being set up which would be in direct opposition to the brigades and could, therefore, not be ignored. For the most part, the War Office generally agreed not to allow other Cadet units to exist in the areas which had Boys' Brigade Cadet units. Surprisingly, between **1917** and the early '20s, there was still being fostered in the nation an air of glamour and heroism in the wearing of a full uniform. Even the pacifist Boys' Life Brigade found it necessary to introduce a full uniform whilst the BB introduced an alternative 'Service' pattern cap to maintain interest.

Fighting for the establishment

In **1911**, both the CLB and the London Diocesan CLB (LDCLB) failed to resist the incentives and appeals made to 'sign up' for the military. As Anglican organisations they were both very much part of the 'Establishment' and thus expected to take up the national cause. Walter M. Gee consequently steered his organisation into full Cadet affiliation supported by a senior ruling cabal of septuagenarian military leaders.

Into the fold

Gee's actions of **1911** were mirrored by Everard A. Ford of the LDCLB with the formation of the 5th-14th Middlesex Cadet Battalions and the 1st-14th London Cadet Battalions. In **1918**, the LDCLB Cadet Battalions were re-designated 'CLB Cadets, London Division'. Later the same year the Middlesex Territorial Force Association (TFA) CLB Battalions transferred to the County of London TFA and all 18 LDCLB Cadet Battalions were then designated, 'Church Cadet Brigade of the Diocese of London.' [4] Other brigades were, however, far more ambivalent. The Jewish Lads' Brigade resisted the call until **1915,** finally yielding to the pressures of predicted forthcoming conscription and latent patriotism. [5] The major units of the JLB affiliated to their local regiments, wearing the insignia of the regiment. eg. Birmingham became part of the Warwicks. The Catholic BB, nationally, for the same reasons as the other brigades, was opposed to Cadet affiliation, but it too was eventually absorbed into the scheme by **1917**, long after many CBB companies had already become registered as Cadet units. By **1919**, these Catholic BB Companies were simply being designated 'Catholic Cadets.'

During **1917**, an 'Advisory Council of Brigade Cadets' was formed with the BB President Lord Guthrie as Chairman. The Council comprised: The CLB, CBB, JLB, LDCLB and BB. Other Committees existed in tandem such as the, 'Home Office Juvenile Organisations Committee &

Cadet Sub-Committee' and the 'Staff-Officers Conference of Brigade Cadet Secretaries and Sec.s of certain Territorial Force Associations'. Mr C.E. Ranken [6] represented the BB on the latter two Committees and was responsible for much of the liaison between the BB and the Cadet authorities. A degree of uniformity between the participating brigades was thus established.

Uniformity ?

Brigade Cadet Badges are best understood in the context of the various Cadet uniforms which emerged between **1911** and the **1930s.** Officers in Cadet units wore standard khaki uniform dress usually of the older type with rank stripes displayed on the cuff. Badges and insignia, however, varied considerably. The BB, for instance, had its own specially designed Cadet Officers' Uniform Badges. The LDCLB had its then current blue uniform approved, unchanged, but as a Cadet uniform.

Many companies were directly affiliated to the local regiment with officers wearing the appropriate Cadet officer uniform. Quite often, badges and insignia originally intended to be brass, ended up as woven worsted cloth.

Fig. 1

BB Submissions to The War Office,
November 1917.

Public Record Office. Kew.
Ref.WO 32/4741. 24208

The Boys' Brigade Cadet.

Proposed destinctions to Service Pattern Uniform.

Fig. 2

Above & right

BB Submissions to The War Office,

November 1917.
Public Record Office. Kew.
Ref.WO 32/4741. 24208

9. May be thought Scotch.
10. Suggested Naval Brigade officers.

Fig. 3

THE BOYS' BRIGADE CADET BADGES, 1917 - 1924

The decision by the Boys' Brigade Executive to allow BB companies to take part in the government Cadet Scheme launched the Brigade into a series of lengthy internal discussions and much corrrespondence about uniform and badges with the War Office. However, two badges were to emerge which would stay with the Brigade for many years after the Cadet Scheme had finished: The Boys' Field Service Cap Badge and the Warrant Officers' Collar Badge.

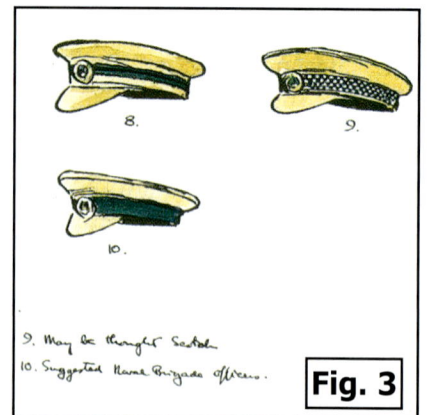

Submissions

The BB application for recognition as Cadets for the whole Brigade (19/11/17) was accompanied by sketches of the possible uniform for Cadets and badge designs.[7] (See Figs 1 - 4) These suggestions were submitted as *'Proposed destinctions*

Lasting Impressions

When the brigades' close association with the Cadet scheme was all but finished in the late **1930s**, little of the specifically Cadet insignia remained. The CLB and JLB, however, retained a high degree of overt militarism although the pre-dominant colour was now blue rather than khaki. In terms of metal badges it was, remarkably, a pair of Boys' Brigade Cadet insignia which outlived all others; one being a cap badge which lasted from **1918** to **1970** and the other a collar badge which was introduced in **1918**, withdrawn in **1923**, and re-issued in **1927**, continuing to the present day.

to Service Pattern uniform' (sic). These splendid drawings were produced by Douglas Pearson Smith, son of the Founder and Acting Brigade Secretary. The designs had already been approved by the Executive.[8] Included in the submission were: a cap badge for service pattern cap and balmoral bonnet, also brass buttons for tunic and shoulder straps. On the shoulder strap brass letters 'BB' would be worn with a 'C' underneath. A BB crest, featuring a foul anchor, would appear on cap badge and buttons. The 'BB' would have the 'C' underneath so as not to confuse it with 'CBB', already used by the Catholic BB. It was stated that the BB had 55,000 boys and if agreed, this should bring '...*the greater part of this force into the Cadets'*.

Anchor Rejected

Towards the end of November **1917** meetings were held between Chas. Ranken and the War Office to discuss the uniform. The outcome was not favourable to the BB. A letter was sent on 10/12/**17** from the WO to the Secretary of the Admiralty regarding the proposed use of the anchor emblem on cap badge and buttons. The reply on 24/12/**17** was not much of a Christmas present from the Lords Commissioners of the Admiralty. Some badge other than the anchor would need to be adopted. The WO reply to the BB on 1/1/**18** could hardly have been worse. The new year was to start with a series of uniform rejections. The Service Dress would be approved except for:

    a. The cap badge
    b. The brass buttons
    c. The cap band
    d. The brass letters BB C.

The cap badge and buttons could not show the anchor. Brass buttons could not be approved due to the expense since they would have to be leather or composition due to the cost of kitting out a potential

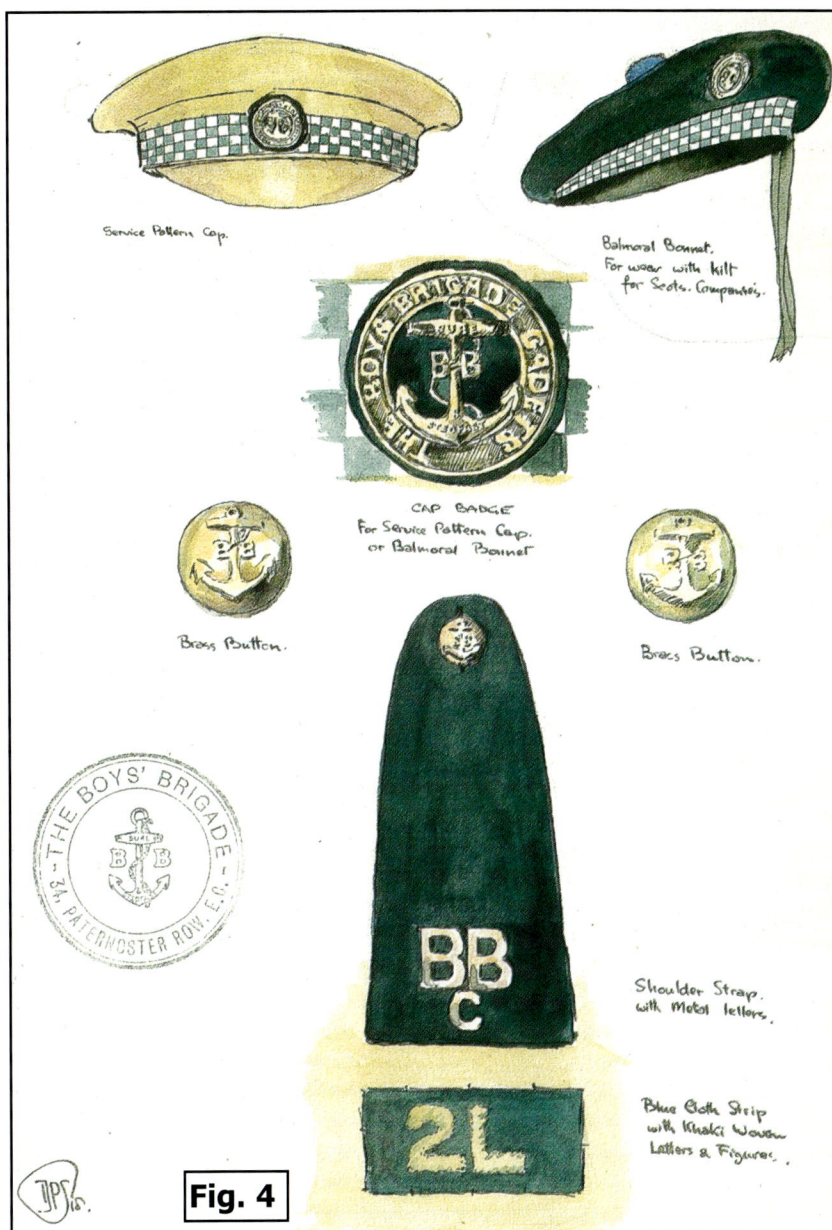

Fig. 4

BB Submissions to The War Office, November 1917.

Public Record Office. Kew.
Ref.WO 32/4741. 24208

55,000 recruits! A suggested blue and white diced cap band could not be used because it was already used by the Lovat Scouts Yeomanry. The shoulder titles must be of worsted embroidery for the same reasons of economy as the buttons. Further letters came from the WO including a rejection of any form of coloured band on the hat. Mr Ranken, however, typical of a BB captain, was not going to give up easily. At the next BB Executive Meeting he submitted alternative designs for approval including the new 'Entwined BB' design.[9] The designs were approved and passed on to the

Fig. 5

**BB
Submissions to the
War Office**
January 1918
Public Record Office. Kew.
Ref.WO 32/4741. 24208

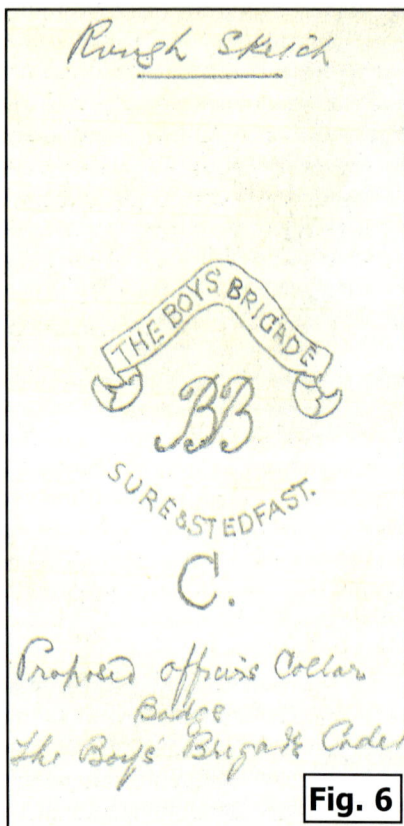

Fig. 6

Army Council on 31/1/**18**. A suggested pattern for an officer's badge was included.

The badges emerge

The modified Boys' Cap Badge was an eight-pointed star with the entwined 'BB' in the centre of a circle with the words, *'The Boys' Brigade Cadets'*. (Fig. 5). The proposed officers badge was illustrated in four parts! (Fig. 6)

1 The entwined 'BB'.
2 The words:'The Boys'
  Brigade' on a scroll fixed above
  the 'Bs'.
3 The words 'Sure & Stedfast' on a
  scroll below the 'Bs'.
4 A letter 'C' fixed below the rest
  of the badge.

On 6/2/**18** the WO approved the new badges, but suggested that the three sections of the collar badge should be joined leaving only the 'C' separate.

The Collar Badge

Undoubtedly the new star badge was popular. The Northern Committee of the BB Executive at its meeting approved of the adoption of the *'Improved'* BB entwined star badge for service uniform cap, *'In brass for Boys and bronze for Officers.'* At the same meeting the Committee also recommended, *'...the adoption of the Collar Badge in Bronze as approved by the Army Council, except that the motto should appear in smaller type above and "The Boys Brigade" below. Badge not to be wider than the present Anchor Badge.'* [10] The new cap badge was also destined to emerge in another form within a matter of a few weeks. Proposals for a Scottish cadet uniform were sent to the WO on 13/3/**18** which included a kilt in 'William A. Smith of Pennyland' tartan and dark blue balmoral cap with red toorey. The cap badge would be as already approved. This uniform was then sanctioned in a letter of 23/3/**18,** but the new one-piece Collar Badge, already commissioned by the BB, still had to be given separate approval. On 11/4/**18** a lead impression was sent to the War Office. A letter of 15/4/**18** at last stated that the new collar badge had been sanctioned.

The 'Alternative' BB Caps & Badges

At the May **1918** Executive Meeting, all the Cadet Badges were approved along with an additional, *'...Alternative Cap Badge'.* [11] The Alternative Cap was, initially, an attempt to meet the needs of those companies which were in the Cadets, but not in khaki. These needs were for greater uniformity on joint parades with units in khaki and the demand from the boys for a hat to replace the 'Pill Box' forage cap which was seen as being dated when worn alongside Cadets wearing 'Service Pattern Peaked Caps'. There were two versions; a peaked service cap of navy blue with white piping around the edge of the crown and, for Scottish companies, a balmoral bonnet with blue toorie. In each case, *'...the star cap badge in white metal'* was to be worn along with the company number which would be worn under the badge.

Finding the Missing 'Link'

Until recently, there existed little evidence as to the exact nature of the 'White metal' badge except that it was considered just possible for it to have initially had the words 'Boys' Brigade Cadets' on it as per the brass version. Recently, however, examples have been found in white metal, shell stamped, non-voided, with two fangs and with the wording 'The Boys' Brigade Cadets'. This 'missing link' had always been considered theoretically possible for the following reasons:

a. The star badge was originally provided for Cadet Companies only and there may have been a white metal issue.

b. The pattern had already been approved by the WO and the badge die already struck, so any badge, brass or white metal, could have been made from it at little extra expense.

c. A motion to the Brigade Council proposed by Rev. J.P. Baker, President, Plymouth Battalion and reported in the BB Gazette of 1st October **1918** states, '...*that inasmuch as it has been found possible, without contravening the Army Council Cadet Regulations, to allow the lads of BB Cadet Companies which do not wear Khaki, to use a* **Cadet Badge** *similar in design to that worn by the lads of BB Cadet Companies which wear khaki, but in another metal...*'.

He goes on to request the use of Cadet Badges for the officers of these Cadet Companies. The motion was seconded and adopted. The question here revolved around the word 'similar'. Did this mean similar design, (i.e. 'star shape',) and/or similar wording?

d. Most Cadet Cap Badges were domed, but there exists a flat version, in brass, similar to the later known varieties of the white metal star cap badge which do not have the word 'Cadets'.

e. In the Archives at BB HQ Felden Lodge, a black and white photocopy of two BB Cadet Badges side by side was found a few years

The Alternative, Regulation 'Grey' uniform
worn by
Pte. Arthur Bullivant
1st South Essex Coy. BB.
Photo. taken January 1921.
BB Archive, Felden.

ago, with one labelled 'W.M' and the other 'Brass'. This, until recently, was the only positive 'evidence' for a white metal badge which included the word 'Cadets'. A photocopy is, unfortunately, inadmissible evidence.

Why have so few of these badges survived?

a. In total, only a small number of white-metal badges are known to exist which probably pre-date the post-**1926** star badge. They are shell-stamped, like the boys Cadet Cap Badge, and not pierced as is the post-**1926** Field-Service Cap Badge. The photographic evidence, of which there is a great deal, suggests that this 'alternative' star badge, not voided like the later Boys Cap Badge, was 'solid'. Detail of the wording on these black and white pictures cannot be seen and whilst the majority look 'white' they could even be polished brass. [12]

b. The Grey Uniform Regulations of **1921** specifically state that the badges for that uniform would bear the words 'The Boys' Brigade' and for Cadet Companies: 'The Boys' Brigade Cadets'. Clearly, there are two types. The only problem here is the official description of **both** types as 'brass'. However, there seem to be no brass star badges surviving without the word 'Cadets', so perhaps that regulation was not followed to the letter!

c. There seem to be far fewer non-voided, white-metal 'alternative' badges than there are brass Cadet Badges. But, this is to be expected because they were only issued from late **1918** and were probably withdrawn during **1924**. Some large battalions, such as Nottingham, reverted to pill box caps in **1922-23** session, and these didn't require cap badges.[13] Of the 487 companies officially registered as Cadets in session **1921-22** only about 90 companies admitted to wearing either the 'alternative cap' or the Grey Uniform.[14]

d. After **1924**, Cadet Badges were no longer appropriate, so another badge should have been used (eg. in Northampton) until the official discontinuation in **1932**. Any new badge adopted after **1927** may not have been the official Alternative Pattern Cap Badge. Most likely it would have been the new, pierced white-metal Boys' Field Service Cap Badge which was available from that date complete with suitable Alternative Cap fastenings - fangs as well as lugs. Some companies continued to use the Alternative Cap well into the late **1930s** (eg. 4th Plymouth), but exactly what cap badge they were wearing remains a mystery.

We can only speculate that there were no brass star boys cap badges that didn't have 'Cadets' on them and there were very few white-metal ones that did!

The 'Grey' Experiment

The massive growth of the 'full uniformed' Cadet Force after **1917** engendered a feeling amongst the membership of the brigades against 'equipment' uniform. This feeling was not totally reflected by the leadership of all the brigades, but, in **1919,** the BB Executive decided to introduce an Alternative full 'Regulation' uniform.[15] The uniform was for use by Cadet or normal companies, and would be Grey, making use of a 'Field Service' pattern cap. (See Photograph) The details of the uniform, when issued, included brass buttons with a BB anchor. (As shown on Pte Bullivant's uniform). A brass 'BB' was to be worn on the shoulder straps for non-cadet companies and the initials 'BBC' by Cadets. It did not state whether the additional 'C' should be under the 'BB' or by the side or if it was produced in brass or worsted. To date no examples of the 'BBC' badge have been found. The Cap Badge would be the eight-pointed star badge in brass. According to the Manual, '...with letters "BB" in centre and bearing the words 'The Boys, Brigade'. For Cadet Companies the wording was to be: 'The Boys'

Brigade Cadets'. [16] The uniform did not catch on, there being only nine companies in 'Regulation Grey' in **1923.**

The Officers' Grey Uniform is even more of a mystery than that of the boys'. The cap badge is described as a '...*bronze badge'.*[17] No mention of 'star' as in the khaki uniform. We can, perhaps, speculate that the cap badge may have been the same bronze badge as worn on the collar of the khaki uniform, but there is no evidence for this. Bronze badges of the type described for the collar are known with both lug fittings and stick - pin, but none with a hat 'tab'. Photographs of officers in Grey uniform either do not exist, or display insufficient clarity to determine detail. (See photo page 36) There are, no known examples (2000) of the Grey Uniform officers' collar badge described as '...*entwined letters "B.B." in bronze.'* [18] which remains just as much of a mystery as the cap badge. It should be noted, however, that the word 'entwined' was used by the BB to describe the two Bs as used in the collar and cap badges. A letter from Chas. E. Ranken acting BB Secretary, addressed to the War Office and sent on March 13th **1918** includes a 'checklist' of agreed uniform and specifies:

'...*Cap Badge as already approved by the Army Council consisting of star with entwined B.B. in the centre...'*[19]

So there may be no mystery at all. It could simply be a way of describing the ordinary Cadet Officers' Collar Badge!

By December **1932,** the Grey Uniform had been discontinued, signifying the end of the entire cadet era for the BB.

REFERENCES

1. Letter from W.A.Smith to London Secretary, 6/6/1910 in response to War Office Memorandum of 21/5/1910. BB HQ. Archive, Felden Lodge, Hemel Hempstead, Herts.
2. 16th Battalion H.L.I. [Glasgow BB], 13th Battalion The Rifle Brigade ['D' Coy.] London BB. 16th Battalion King's Royal Rifle Corps [CLB] etc.
3. Springhall et al. op.cit. p 116.
4. a.The Cadet List 1916. HMSO, Imperial War Museum. Library. Army orders 284/11 [11/5/11] ibid 207/12, 156/13. b. A Register of Territorial Force Cadet Units 1910 - 1922. R.A. Westlake. Army Orders 276/19, 61/20, 116/20, 211/20.   c.The Cadet List 1921 HMSO. Christ Church Harrow & Roxeth Co CL&CGB Archives.
5. Sharman Kadish. A Good Jew and a Good Englishman. 1995 pp 53-54.
6. Charles E Ranken Esq., Capt. 43rd London coy BB. West London Battalion, Belgrave Presbyterian Schools. Acting London [Southern Committee] Secretary.
7. Northern Committee Minute Book No 1. [1915-1919] BB Scottish HQ, Carronvale, Larbert, Stirling. 18/10/17 & 15/11/17.
8. WO32/4741. Public Record Office. 9/Cadets/2723.
9. Minutes of BB Executive. [S.Committee] 25-26/1/1918 BB HQ.
10. Northern Committee Minutes. 21/2/1918. BB Scottish HQ.
11. BB Executive [Southern Committee] 25-26/5/1918, BB HQ.
12. Photographs: Nottingham Battalion Camp 1919/1920. Plymouth Battalion etc. Also William J Lapthorn.'The Boys Brigade in Plymouth 1887-1983' 1983. R. Bolton Collection.
13. 50 Years with the BB, History of Nottingham Battalion & Jubilee Display Souvenir. 1933. p 27. R. Bolton Collection.
14. BB Annual Report 1921-1922 p 11.
15. The BLB introduced a full uniform in 1918 and the CLB attempted to get the whole Brigade in khaki by the end of 1917.
16. BB Officers Manual. 1921 pp 64/65. 'Regulation Grey Uniform.'
17. ibid.
18. ibid.
19. WO32/4741.24208 Public Record Office. Kew.

The Boys' Cadet Cap Badge 1918 - 1924

BB 010.02   **BB 010.03**   **BB 010.06**   **BB 010.7**

BB 010 BACKGROUND NOTES

These badges are either bronze or nickel-silver in colour, shell-stamped and with lugs, tabs, tags or fangs as fastenings. The bronze versions display the usual range of tones in their finish. Some types are domed, whilst others are either flat or convex along the north-south axis. The edges of the badge are either straight or fluted.

The Boys' 'Alternative' pattern badges

The Boys' Alternative Pattern Cap Badge 1918 - c.1927

The Boys' Grey Uniform Shoulder Titles (Non - Cadet Coys.) 1919 - 1932

BB 011.01   **BB 012**

BB 011 & BB 012 BACKGROUND NOTES

BB 011 was introduced at the same time as the Cadet Badge but continued in some areas well into the period of union with the BLB. The badges are fairly flat compared with their cadet contemporaries, shell-stamped with either lug or tag fastenings. The central circular area is smaller than on the Cadet Cap Badge. The edges are straight rather than fluted.

BB 012 was used with the non-cadet version of the Alternative Grey Uniform. It has the same size letters as used in military shoulder titles, linked in the same way with short bars. It has lug fastenings and was generally supplied with a backing-plate. The cadet version of the Alternative Grey Uniform had cloth Bs with a cloth letter 'C' below them.

The Officers' Cadet Badges

Cap Badge   1918 - 1924

BB 008

BB 008 BACKGROUND NOTES

The Officers' Cap Badge is dark brown and solid with the central area fretted/voided. The fastening is two horizontal fangs. There appears to be no variations of this badge.

Collar Badge   1918 - 1924

BB 009.01

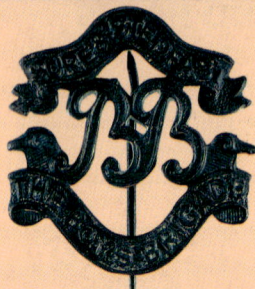

BB 009.02

BB 009 BACKGROUND NOTES

The complete Officers' Cadet Collar Badge was made up of two parts, there being a small brass letter 'C' worn immediately below the main badge. The badge is solid, fretted and has two types: bronze coated brass with two horizontal lugs and a bronze version similar to the standard Officers' Collar Badge with a single stick-pin. There is an apostrophe after the word 'Boys'.

Cadet Letter 'C' worn below Officers' Collar Badge.

A BB Cadet Company
Wearing the Alternative Grey
Uniform. c.1921

The Pipe Band Bandmasters' Cap Badge (Pipe - Majors' Cap Badge)

The BB Bandmaster's Cap, in use in various forms since **1888,** was certainly not in keeping stylistically with a Pipe Band. The boys continued, in some cases, to wear the 'Pill Box' hats until **1970,** but the lobby of opinion (i.e. Scottish officer opinion) for the introduction of the glengarry was strong. Lt.'s and W/O.'s could already wear it, but the problem lay with the Pipe-Major who sometimes was not a Brigade officer. In the eyes of the Brigade he was a 'Bandmaster'. It is usually a necessity for the Pipe-Major to play with the Pipe Band, whereas in the

Bugle or Brass Band the Bandmaster would not. In November **1935,** it was announced in the BB Gazette that:

'In accordance with prevailing opinion in Scotland the use of the Glengarry Cap for Bandmasters of Pipe Bands has been authorised and a special badge for the cap has been designed and is now available at 1s 6d each.' [1]

There can be little doubt about its origin. In the centre was the Three-Year BB Anchor as used on the traditional Service - Pattern Bandmaster's Cap, with the addition of a wreath of thistles. It was similar to that used by Army Pipe-Majors since **1865.** [2]

When the **1976** BB Supplies catalogue was issued there was no Pipe-Majors' Badge listed; it had been discontinued. Stocks had rundown and the costs associated with replacement were, no doubt, con-

Pipe - Major Ian Fleming
5th Croydon Company
Photo: R. Bolton

sidered to be too high for a badge with such a small annual demand.

REFERENCES

1. BB Gazette, Vol XLIV, No 3, Nov. 1935, p 34. BB Scottish HQ, Carronvale, Larbert, Stirlingshire.
2. Edwards & Langley, British Army Proficiency Badges. Wardley Publishing, 1984. p 118.

The Pipe - Majors' Cap Badge   1935 - c.1976

BB 014.01

BB 014.02

BB 014 BACKGROUND NOTES

This is a two-part badge, the BB emblem being soldered to the thistle wreath at four points. One large batch was produced pre-World War II with a frosted finish. Due to less demand in the post-war period only one plain nickel batch was produced. Light-coloured, gilt plated versions may be found, part of a small batch of post-war pieces privately plated by the 5th Croydon Company for use on its sporrans.

Sergeants' & Staff-Sergeants'
Shoulder - Belt Bosses
& Band Music   Pouch Bosses

Col. Sgt. J. Househam, 8th Nottingham Coy.

The shoulder - belt with its badges or 'bosses' is one of the oldest accoutrements in the **Brigade.** At one of its earliest meetings in **1885,** the Executive Committee proposed a cap for sergeants an exact sample of which...

'...should be submitted to the council for approval, as also of the shoulder Belt for Sergeants.'[1]

At that time the pattern of the officers' uniform had not been decided.

At the next meeting both the cap and shoulder belt for sergeants were approved:

'...also belt for boys with new buckle were submitted and approved of with a slight alteration in the pouch of the shoulder belt.'

An early photograph of NCO's and officers of 1st Glasgow, said to be in the session **1885/6,** shows the first sergeants of the BB wearing the leather shoulder belt with bosses. Here they do not wear haversacks as would become the requirement later.[2] (See photo on next page)

For the first twenty nine years of the BB only the sergeants wore shoulder belts, complete with two bosses. Regulation music pouches, mainly for fife-players, were also available from all the main suppliers. Worn in uniform they too came complete with a 'Brigade Boss'.[3] In **1898**, the rank of staff-sergeant was introduced, but at the time this uniform did not include a shoulder belt. There was much debate about the introduction of this with proposals being discusssed during **1903** and **1904,** but the result was that the battalions were: *'Overwhelmingly against'.[4]*

The staff sergeants' shoulder belt was finally introduced in September **1912** and was of exactly the same design as that of the sergeant, having two bosses, one on the pouch and the other on the breast. The width of the S/sergeants' belt was $\frac{1}{2}$" wider than the sergeants'. The bosses were white metal on the S/Sgts' belt, not brass as on the Sgts' belt:

'Staff-Sergeant's Shoulder-Belt.- A Shoulder-Belt has been approved for Staff-Sergeants. Same colour of leather as Sergeant's belt, but superior quality, and $2\frac{1}{2}$ inches wide instead of 2 inches. Mountings in white metal, silver-plated, instead of brass. Price 5s.'[5]

One year was given from 1st Sept. **1912** for companies to effect the transition to the new pattern

Regulations published in the BB Manuals regarding the two different shoulder belts and their bosses have not always been explicit. For instance, in the **1914** Manual, the sergeants' version is termed: *'Shoulder-Belt, with pouch;'* There was no mention of colour of

Officers & Sergeants of 1st Glasgow Coy. c.1886
The first photograph of BB Sergeants with Shoulder - Belts.
Photo: 1st Glasgow Coy. BB. collection

badges, etc.. In the same regulations, on the same page, the staff-sergeants' belt is described thus: '...a Shoulder-Belt, with silver-plated mountings;' The silver-plating, no doubt, needed to be mentioned since this was an embelishment of the common brass which featured in the sergeants' mountings.[6]

As a consequence of union with the BLB, by **1928**, the BB had two sergeants' uniforms, one retaining the shoulder-belt but another without the belt, making use of a red sash. The shoulder - belt was still part of the staff-sergeants' uniform however, for both the new 'A' and 'B' options. The Manual continued to read as it had pre-union in regard to the colour of shoulder belts and bosses, but the bosses would now have the new post-union BB emblem. All BLB belts, boys waist belts and officers shoulder-belts had been black, so the new regulations stated that the 'B' uniforms would have black belts. There is no

specific mention in the regulations of any staff-sergeants' shoulder-belt colour. [7]

In **1927**, the Brigade had made the decision to set up a new 'Equipment Department' so from this time, much of the detail regarding 'official' uniform would be communicated through the lists produced by this Department, a habit which would continue into the next century.[8]

The **1928/1929** price list of the new Equipment Department makes the colours of shoulder - belts and bosses crystal clear, - but not quite. Sergeants would wear a shoulder - belt with brass bosses, 'A' Uniform staff-sergeants a brown leather shoulder - belt with plated bosses and 'B' Uniform staff-sergeants a black leather shoulder-belt. The bosses continued to be supplied in both white metal and 'brass' for the next fifty years virtually unchanged. By the early **1980s** the

BB Equipment Dept., now called 'BB Supplies', started to take measures to reduce costs. Black belts of all kinds were no longer supplied and, by **1984**, the special 'plated' S/sgt's boss was no longer obtainable.[9] Just one year later the BB Gazette announced:

'Only one shoulder belt will be supplied in future. There is a common Style for Sergeants and Staff Sgts.'[10]

Earlier that same year, the Regulations had been updated officially, making it clear that both sergeants and staff-sergeants would wear:

'...a brown shoulder belt with brass boss worn over the left shoulder...'[11]

In the new Uniform Regulations introduced in **1999**, following the recommendations of the Uniform Reform Group, staff-sergeants' and sergeants' shoulder-belts have been discontinued. They are still allowed to be worn during the first few years of the century in companies which have not changed immediately to the new uniform, but will be no longer supplied by Headquarters.

REFERENCES

1. Minutes, Meeting of Executive Committee. 10/12/1885. 22 West Nile St. Glasgow. BB HQ Archive, Felden Lodge
2. Photograph first reproduced in 'For Fifty Years' the 50th Anniversary Book of 1st Glasgow Company. 1933.
3. Adverts in BB Manuals, 1890s, 1902 etc. By James Farquharson, Leckie Graham, George Binns et al.
4. BB Gazette, 1st June 1904, p149. D. Aubrey Collection.
5. ibid. 1st Sept 1912, p 3.
6. BB Manual, 1914, p 19.
7. ibid., 1928, pp 68 - 70.
8. Executive Meeting. 14-15, May 1927. New Dept. to be set up as from 1/July 1927.
9. BB Supplies Catalogue 1983 had plated & brass bosses advertised.
10. BB Gazetrte, Aug/Sept 1985 p 134.
11. ibid. June/July 1985. p 100.

The Sergeants' Shoulder-Belt Boss   c.1886 - 1927

BB 016.02

BB 016.03

BB 016.08 Obverse

BB 016.08 Reverse

The Staff-Sergeants' Shoulder-Belt Boss 1912 - 1927

BB 016.04

BB 016.06

BB 016 BACKGROUND NOTES

These bosses are shell-stamped 'full-shell' and have two horizontally placed lugs for fastening. The most noticeable variation comes in the stamping, some are high-domed, others shallow. The shallow-domed variations have the obverse brass-plated on nickel whereas those with high domes are stamped from brass. The shape of the anchor, ribbon lettering and the small quartered lozenge form the main obverse variations. There is variation too in the centre stipple and ribbon background etching. A notable variety 016.04 has a two-part construction with the central domed circle secured by two small fold over tabs, giving the boss a belt-buckle appearance. When introduced, the Staff-Sergeants' Boss had the frosted finish, otherwise identical production methods to the Sergeants' Boss were employed resulting in similar external variations.

The Sergeants' Shoulder-Belt Boss   1927 - 2006

The Staff Sgts' Shoulder-Belt Boss   1984 - 2006

BB 017.01

BB 017.02

BB 017.05

The Staff-Sgts' Shoulder-Belt Boss   1927 - 1984

BB 017.06

BB 017.09

BB 017.10

BB 017 BACKGROUND NOTES

Designed and produced in a similar manner to the pre-1927 types but generally with a consistent pressing quality. The majority were all high domed and have other differences similar to those described for BB 016. There are two variations which are notable for their lack of consistency. One is an example of a faulty die being used resulting in an imperfection adjacent to the left anchor fluke. The other, the most recent version of the boss, designed for use by both sergeants and staff-sergeants is a very bland affair. It is slightly less domed, has no stippling or etching and a crude anchor design, reflecting the worst of the 1990s cheap production methods.

The Boys' Field Service Cap Badges

Discounting the short period of 'Seniors' cap badges in use between 1967 and 1970 (see the 'Three Year Anchor' section) there have only ever been two main types of The Boys' Field Service Cap Badge: the eight-pointed star with entwined Bs and the chrome anchor with plastic, barrel-shaped surround.

eight-pointed star

The Cadet Cap Badges have been fully covered in another section, but the origin of the first Boys' Field Service Cap Badge, the eight-pointed star, is completely tied in with the Cadet Badges and the alternative to the Cadet Badges introduced in **1918**.

The white metal badge officially started in **1927** after the union of the BB and BLB when there was a need for a boys 'Field-Service' cap as part of the 'B' uniform, most of which had been inherited from the BLB. Pill-box type forage caps had been abandoned by the BLB from about **1918** and they were not happy about going back to wearing them.

A solution to the field-service badge problem was readily available to the Brigade due to the Cadet Badges having ceased only two years before, in **1924**. The 'star' badges had been popular in their various forms for officers and boys. There was also a badge, similar in type which was still being worn by some companies. It was called the 'Alternative Pattern Cap Badge' used on the Alternative 'Service' pattern caps. Alternative pattern caps were popular in some areas

such as Northampton where they had taken over from the khaki cadet caps in **1924**, and were still being used as late as **1931**.[1]

The advantages of the Alternative Pattern Cap Badge were that it was not only readily available, but also made in white metal which would match the numerals on the BB Pill Box. The problem, however, was that it was not fretted in the usual manner of field-service cap badges. The new badge would consequently have to be fretted as had the Officers' Cadet Cap Badges, leaving the 'entwined B's' in the centre. Also in favour of its adoption was the decision that the other 'entwined B's' ex-cadet badge was now officially sanctioned for Warrant Officers.

So the 'new' badge of **1927** was not really new at all. What's more the badge was worn until **1929** on the old BLB Service Pattern Cap with its single row of magenta piping. This was called the 'B' uniform cap and badge. The badges had two 'tags' or 'fangs' on the reverse which pierced the cap material and then folded over for security.

In **1929**, the 'B' uniform cap was changed to that having the familiar two rows of white braid. The new caps were more substantial than the old ex-BLB caps, so the badges were now supplied with two lugs and a spring clip. The old hats continued until **c.1946** in those places where companies which had worn them before **1929** wished to retain the hats along with the rest of the old uniform. This third type was termed uniform 'C'.[2]

Through the decades between the **1930s** and **1960s** the field service

cap with its star badge became very popular, particularly with new companies. Many older established companies wished to retain the 'pill box', but these were regarded as 'old-fashioned' by many boys and officers. The badge was worn on only two caps; the field-service cap for boys and the special sergeants' field-service cap. Smaller $\frac{1}{2}$" numerals, positioned to the side of the star badge, were used instead of the 1" ones found on the pill-box caps.

anchor and plastic

A new blue terylene boys' cap of field service style was introduced in **1970** to replace all previous types. The badge was a small bright silvery non-tarnishable anchor with 'prongs' (The BB name for tags or fangs) and a plastic surround incorporating the company number. The plastic surround was shaped in keeping with the new 'barrel' badge introduced two years before. Surrounds would be of differing colours, one for each tier of the newly re-structured Brigade: yellow for Junior Section, red for Company Section and blue for Seniors.[3]

In September **1999**, the Brigade Council approved a new single uniform without hats, to be introduced immediately and fully adopted by **2006**. A proposal to retain hats as an option, was approved by Council in **2000**.

REFERENCES

1. Albert V Eason, Remember Now Thy Creator, History of the Northampton Battalion , 1982, p 118.
2. The BB Uniform Then & Now, BB Archive Press, 1986. p p 8 - 9
3. BB Manual, 1971, p 66.

The Boys' Field Service Cap Badge

1927 - 1970

BB 015

BB 015

BB 015

BB 015

BB 015

BB 015

BB 015

BB 015

BB 015 BACKGROUND NOTES

Every version of this badge is shell-stamped, 'full-shell'. Some early examples have tags probably designed for use on the thinner material of the former BLB Field-Service cap. Later types have two horizontally situated lugs. There are several variations due to the length of service of the badge but the differences are in the detail. There are different styles of lettering, spacing and in the lozenges at the bottom of the ribbon. The piercing varies considerably and the overall quality of certain strikes is rather poor and lacking in definition. One version of the badge is noticeably smaller in overall size.

1970 - 2006

BB 019

BB 019

BB 019

BB 019 BACKGROUND NOTES

The main variations are in the chrome anchors with fangs on earlier types and a later use of a lug-bar fitting. There are varieties produced with the new spelling of 'steadfast'. Other variations can be found in the insert numbers, the earlier wider types of lettering being self-adhesive with the later being much thinner and glued into position.

Cap Numerals,
Life Boy Pennant numerals, Letters, Chevrons & Stars

When the BB started it was just one company, but as interest grew and futher companies were formed they were given numbers. It was at the meeting of officers which took place in Room No.5 at the Christian Institute Glasgow on Monday 12th October **1885** that the decision was taken to display the number on the front of the cap, if the cap was adopted. At this stage the nature of the uniform had not been fully decided, but there was no doubt about the number:

'... A discussion then took place as to whether or not that company number must be worn on the cap, and it was eventually moved by Mr Kidston & Seconded by Mr Lammie "that if a Company adopted the uniform cap the number of the company must be on the front of the cap." While Mr W.A.Smith moved as an amendment, & Mr Nicholl seconded "that if a Company adopted the uniform cap it is recommended that the number of the Company should be on the front of the cap." On a vote being taken 5 voted for the amendment and 6 for the motion which was accordingly carried by a majority of one.' [1]

The forage 'pill-box' cap was now to be seen with 1" high white metal numerals between the stripes at the front. From **1902**, similar company numbers would also be worn in the Sgts' peaked cap and special bandmasters' caps. Staff sergeants' caps, however, would, as yet, have no numerals.

The Alternative BB Cap of a 'Service' pattern was introduced in **1918** alongside the various cadet uniforms and it had a star shaped

cap badge and company number. The company number used was the $\frac{1}{2}$" size, there not being room for a 1" numeral above the badge.

Union brings more half-inch numerals

Union with the BLB in **1926** brought with it an alternative uniform which included a field service cap and a star badge similar to the Alternative Cap Badge and, like that cap, $\frac{1}{2}$" numerals. These white metal numbers continued to be used until the field service cap with white stripes was replaced by the new blue terylene hat in **1970**.

Staff sergeants were allowed to wear company numbers described as:

'...half-inch white metal figures', in their hats *'At the discretion of Battalion Councils'* from **1924** [2]

The staff sergeants' cap with numbers, or without, was replaced in **1970** with the new cap. The new badge would be used without any plastic surround or numbers. This was virtually a return to the pre-**1924** situation.

Advice on how to clean the numbers was given in the Manual:

'Cap numbers should be carefully cleaned with a soft cloth, but should not be taken out of the cap.' [3]

Plastic Body

Fixing numbers into a pill-box cap was difficult enough when the cap was made from fibre, but, in **1961**, the Brigade introduced hats made from plastic which would easily

split if the lugged numerals were used. To prevent this the screw-fitting became available and advertised in the Gazette as...

'Special Numerals with Screw fitments are now available (6/- doz) as well as small plastic template (1/6 each) to assist in making accurate holes.'

The hats gradually came into use. [4]

Letters

It is not well known that for many years, letters, either instead of, or as well as numerals, were and are worn in the cap. For instance, one of Scotland's most famous companies, the 1st Bearsden, has worn just a letter 'B' in its cap. Since its

The 'Bearsden Bonnets' with the letter 'B'
Photo: 1st Bearsden Coy. The Boys' Brigade.

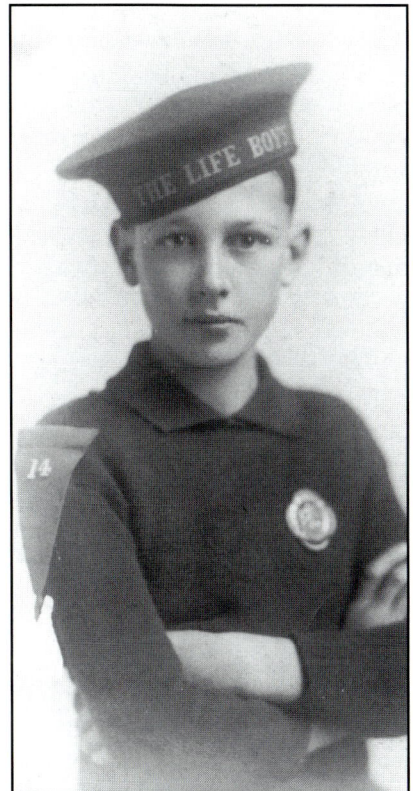

A Life Boy from Stockport wearing the shoulder pennant.
Photo: R.Bolton Collection

formation in **1898**, there has been a single 1" white metal letter 'B' in the pill-box cap and from **1970** a single plastic letter 'B' on the plastic surround of the badge in the new cap. [5] The 1st Bearsden Company History is entitled 'A 'B' in the Bonnet'. Officially, of course, this is breaking regulations, but this has never worried the 1st. Incidentally, one of the most famous BB characters in Scotland, Dr. J. Martin Strang, was Company Captain from **1926 - 45** and again from **1953 -56**. He served on the National BB Executive from **1929** and became a BB Vice - President.

We're 'No 1'

In the early years of the BB it was common for companies to use the initial letter of their village, or town, in the cap by the side of the numeral. For instance, '1S' for 1st Stoke, '1Y' 1st Yeovil, '1H' 1st Hastings, etc., The numeral was almost invariably '1' so on a battalion parade there could be ten companies all wearing the No '1' giving no distinction whatsoever. A similar problem, although not quite so acute, came with the numbers 2 and 3. The use of a letter made common sense. It was in the spirit of the regulation without strictly adhering to it.[6]

We cannot be certain about the use of 1" or $\frac{1}{2}$" letters on caps after **1926** except in cases where a BB battalion was merged with a BLB battalion giving rise to a duplication of numbers from **1927**. One such place where $\frac{1}{2}$" letters were used, on field service caps, was Birmingham. At the time of the union there were ten companies each of BB and BLB, both organisations numbered 1-10, so the former BLB companies used the letter 'A' after the numeral. One of those companies survives today, - the 1st 'A'.[7]

On the shoulder

The same $\frac{1}{2}$" numerals which had been used on the Alternative pattern caps of **1918** were used on the navy blue shoulder pennants of The Boy Reserves, the Junior Reserve of The Boys' Brigade, from **1922** onwards. These numerals and pennants remained after Union with the BLB, on the uniform of the Life Boys, continuing as an option after **1958** until the creation of the Junior Section in **1967**, finally being discontinued in **1971**.

Plastic Power

After **1971** there were no more metal numbers used in the BB. New hat badges now incorporated small plastic numbers. To be pre-

A Life Boy Pennant
(Picture 70% full size).
As here, the company numbers often had to be sewn on to the felt cloth.
This particular specimen adorned Rob Bolton's
L.B. Jumper between **1957 - 1961**.

cise, the new system had a metal badge with a backing plastic surround recessed at the bottom to take squares of plastic engraved with a single digit number filled with blue paint. The recess was large enough for a three digit figure made up of three plastic squares. The numbers have different styles of typeface, but there are basically wide ones and narrow ones.

Stars

Perhaps the most evocative shape ever to appear on a BB uniform over the years has been the 'star'. Much has been written, in this volume, about the Five-Pointed Star, the Sergeants' Star, the star cap badge, or star medals. There are, however, two small stars which appear in the BB firmament at different times, possibly identical in nature, but worn to indicate 'rank' rather than proficiency or attainment. The first was provided for 'Leading Reserves' of the Boy Reserves between **1918 - 1919** to be worn on the right arm midway between shoulder and elbow.[8] The second star came, in **1927,** with the introduction of the optional uniform 'B' for officers, a result of union with the BLB. One option for headgear was the Droop-peak cap and the regulation states:

'If the Droop-peak cap is adopted, a Captain wears one silver star fixed in the middle of the seam of the cap above the badge.'[9]

The uniform which included the Droop-peak cap became unobtainable during the Second World War[10] and was not supplied thereafter.

There is little detailed evidence of the nature of these small stars. If the stars used by the Boy Reserves Leading Boys and the Uniform 'B', Droop-peaked Captains' cap were both of the same design, it would most likely have been the six-pointed, white metal and ridged stars

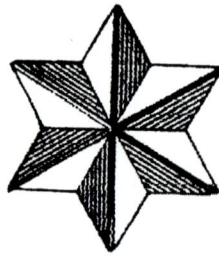

**The BLB
'Good Service' Star**

used by many uniformed organisations and generally available both in **1918** and **1927**. Other evidence would seem to suggest that the captain's star was, indeed, of that type. The BLB used stars to indicate officer ranks, hence the introduction of them after Union. The pattern of BLB stars for 'Good Service' is known and it seems unlikely that the BLB would have supplied two differing six-pointed stars of similar size. [11] It is most likely that they were the same, just different fixings on the reverse.

Photographs of BLB captains wearing what is clearly a six-pointed star are relatively common, although the detail does not show clearly. What does show is the size of the star, worn in the same place as on the **1927** BB Officers' Droop-peak cap.

**A Six-Point Star of the
type thought to be used
on the Droop-peak Cap.**
This example (pictured actual size)
has fixings for sewing.

**A BLB Captain wearing the
Droop-peak cap
with star**
Photo: R. Bolton collection

**A BB Captain c.1928,
wearing the Droop-peak cap
with star.**
Photo: R. Bolton collection

Chevrons

In a radical departure from tradition, in November **1999**, as part of its new uniform, the BB launched a set of metal chevrons for use by NCO's. Since the earliest days of

Continued on page 48

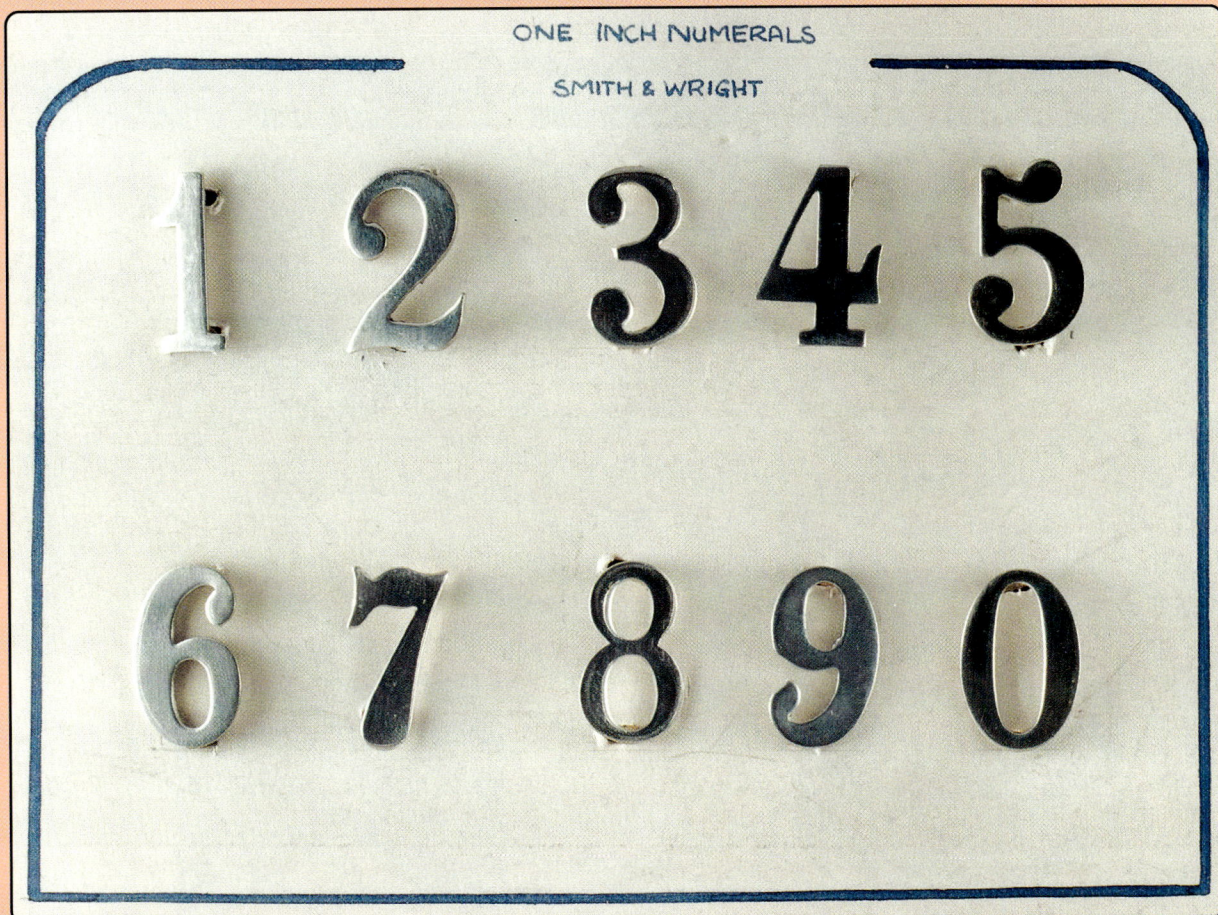

ONE INCH NUMERALS

SMITH & WRIGHT

1 2 3 4 5

6 7 8 9 0

BB 022

BB 021 & 022 BACKGROUND NOTES

The 'Official' pattern numerals are shown here on the cards as they were kept at BB HQ. The variations occur in the fittings with only slight style changes. The 1" having either lugs and bolt fixings, the $\frac{1}{2}$" numbers fangs/tags. Messrs Smith & Wright (Birmingham) was not the only maker and this would account for slight variations.

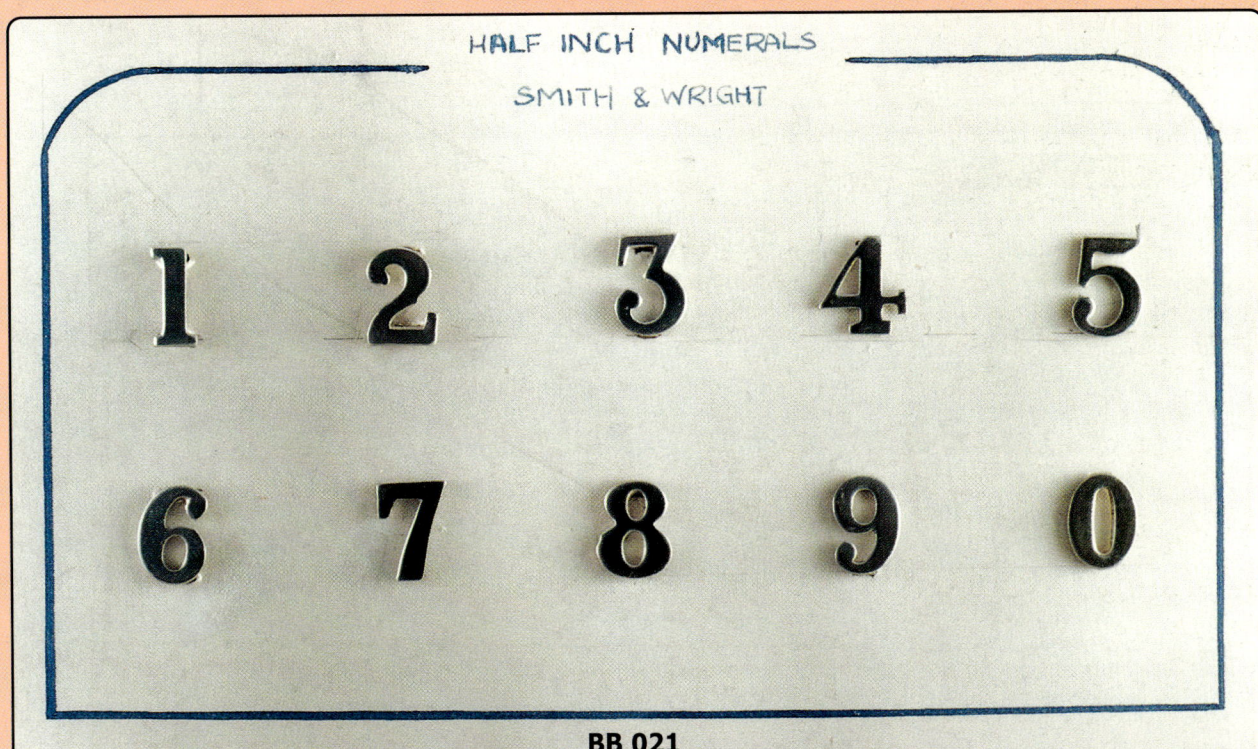

HALF INCH NUMERALS

SMITH & WRIGHT

1 2 3 4 5

6 7 8 9 0

BB 021

NCO's Chevrons 1999 -

BB 020.01

BB 020.02

BB 020.03

BB 020.04

BB 020 BACKGROUND NOTES

These chromed, enamelled chevrons have either a standard tube joint brooch fitting or a bar brooch with safety catch. The first two pieces, BB020.01 & BB 020.02 have standard fastenings and FRCs because they are not deep enough to take bar brooches. There are no variations.

Continued from page 46

1885 BB chevrons have been made from some form of cloth material. Only for colour sergeants' cross flags has there been a woven wire element to a chevron. The chrome-plated, blue-enamelled chevrons are in brooch format so that they can be fixed to an armband, brassard or direct to a shirt. The choice of metal for the new chevrons is more surprising when considered in the context of proposals for the development of BB uniform in the 21st century. There is a move towards less metal badges, possibly smaller than those currently in use. Perhaps the answer lies in the fact that not only are badges under review but the very nature of the 'military' rank structure used in the Brigade. It could be that these metal chevrons are quite short - lived.

REFERENCES

1. Minutes of Glasgow Battalion/Brigade meeting 12th October 1885. BB Archive Felden.
2. BB Manual 1924. Uniform Section.
3. ibid, 1928, p.68.
4. BB Gazette, Vol LXIX, No 6, Aug/Sept 1961 p 119.
5. A 'B' in the Bonnet. The story of the 1st Bearsden Coy. 1898 - 1998. [Private publication]
6. Published example: See 'Youth Empire & Society' J. Springhall, Croom Helm 1977. plate 3 pp 94-97. 1st Hamilton Coy. with '3H' on their hats.
7. Tape-Recorded interview with Mr G. Oakton BEM 18/1/90 Recorded at his home. R. Bolton.
8. BB Gazette, Vol XXVI, No 5, 1st Jan. 1918. p 57.
9. BB Manual 1928, p.73. Officers' Optional Full Uniform.
10. On working Copy of BB Supplies Catalogue used by BB Supplies Officer the uniform is annotated as 'Discontinued' from August 1941. BB Archive, Felden.
11. BLB Boys Manual, Revised Edition 1926, p 34.

BADGES of the BRIGADE

VOLUME ONE
THE BOYS' BRIGADE

Efficiency/Service Badges

Efficiency/Service Badges

Efficiency/Service Badges

Efficiency/Service Badges

Efficiency/Service Badges

Efficiency/Service Badges

2. Efficiency/Service Badges

Efficiency/Service Badges

Efficiency/Service Badges

Efficiency/Service Badges

Efficiency/Service Badges

Efficiency/Service Badges

Efficiency/Service Badges

Efficiency/Service Badges

Efficiency/Service Badges

The 'White' or Five - Pointed Star

The start of the magic

A Star is born

Without a doubt the star was the most glamorous badge never to be issued by BB HQ. In fact, it was probably not even one badge at all, more likely two. The idea of using a star badge probably came from the Volunteers which issued such a badge from **1881,** as a five-year, rifle-drill efficiency award. [1]

The 1st Lanarkshire Rifle Volunteers used the star, worn on the right sleeve, and made from silver (white) wire with a black cloth backing. [2] This was a badge worn by William Smith as part of his LRV (Mounted Detachment) uniform. [3]

Star service

In the third session of the 1st Glasgow Company Boys' Brigade the Company Card included the following passage:

`Boys who have served three sessions in the Company are entitled to wear on the right arm a SILVER STAR, to be presented by the Company, at the close of the third year.' [4]

The details on the card gave the inspection date as 18th March **1886** and reiterated the fact that the star could be worn on and after that date. A well-known photograph exists of the original officers and sergeants of the company (and of the Brigade) said to be **1885/86**. [5] The sergeants are clearly wearing stars which could easily be woven wire stars pinned brooch style. (See page 39) No doubt it would have been too expensive for such awards to be specially produced and a source was readily available, either direct from the 1st Lanarkshire Rifle Volunteers, or from its suppliers. The stars are the same size as Volunteer stars. Pins, probably safety pins, could have been employed to secure them to jackets for each parade. There must be some doubt as to the date attributed to the picture since it must have been on or after March 18th for the stars to be worn. The use of the glengarry cap and badge had only been approved on 15th March **1886**. The latest possible date for this picture in Session **1885/86** would be Thurs. 25th March (Inspection Day) and the last parade of the session. It is unlikely that the hats, belts and cross-belts would have been ready by that time. The date is more likely to be **1886/87**. By the Session **1887/88,** however, the 1st was probably using the new three year service Anchor Badge which came into Brigade Regulations in **1888**. The first BB five-pointed star had come and gone.

A new star appears in the South-East

However, by **1892,** a `white' star had made a come-back to BB uniform, albeit four hundred miles away in West London. [6] The star was now to be awarded as an,

`Efficiency badge for attendance and good conduct.'

It would also be appearing in some quantity since it would be awarded,

`...for each year of efficiency, to be worn on the right forearm.'

**Fives on the forearm...
Sgt. Jones 13th London Coy.
c.1890s**

(Detail of photograph on page 1)

In **1897-98,** this changed to the left forearm. There can be no doubt that this `White Star' was the nickel brooch, smaller than the Volunteer star.

Over the next few years the badge

was taken up enthusiastically by a number of battalions. At a meeting of the Aberdeen Battalion Council on 16th October **1894** the following was reported:

`Samples of efficiency badges were submitted and it was agreed to adopt as the Battalion Efficiency badge a small metal five-pointed star, having impressed upon it the device of an anchor and the letters B.B. to be worn on the right fore-arm.' [7]

So, here is concrete evidence of the nature of the badge. The North London Battalion adopted the badge in the same year as Aberdeen. [8] The star was introduced to the South London Battalion on Jan. 14th **1895** [9] and to Newcastle-Upon- Tyne [10] in the same year. **1896** saw it spread to Bristol [11] and by **1897** it was reported to be in use in Liverpool [12] as well as Brighton. [13] The City and East London Battalion was using the award in **1901**. Glasgow Battalion, notably, rejected the use of this new metal star. For them, the whole idea of extra badges,

requiring armbands and complicated regulations was simply not in keeping with their `purist' principles. William Smith had obviously been in favour, but his views were not typical of the West of Scotland `Covenanting Presbyterians' who wanted to keep the uniform plain and simple. Other battalions took a similar view.

Death of a star

In **1904,** a new diamond- shaped Efficiency Badge, also inspired by the Volunteers, [14] was adopted by the Brigade as a whole, but it remained optional. It was never used in Glasgow. These lozenge shaped badges continued to be called `stars' in London and other Battalions where the White Star had been used. The dainty little star brooches were finally dead, but their `twinkle' lingers like a glamorous unforgettable movie star captured forever on film,[15] or like those miriads of stars in the night sky whose 'magic' light still shines long after their total destruction.

REFERENCES

1 British Army Proficiency Badges, Denis Edwards & David Langley 1984. p.49.
2 Photograph, Exhibit in Glasgow Museum. Volunteer uniforms.
3 Photograph, reproduced in `Sure & Stedfast' Springhall, Fraser & Hoare, 1983 p.35.
4 1st Glasgow Coy. Squad List & Company Card 1885-86. BB Archives, BB HQ, Felden Lodge. Hemel Hempstead Herts.
5 BB Archive Pack. The Boys' Brigade HQ 1983.
6 West London Battalion First Annual Report 1892-1893, p.16. BB Archives, Scottish HQ, Carronvale House, Larbert, Stirlingshire.
7 Minutes of Aberdeen Battalion Council 1894, Aberdeen & District BB HQ, Crimon Place, Aberdeen.
8 North London Battalion, Third Annual Report, 1894-1895.pp.5-7. BB Archives Scottish HQ. op.cit.
9 South London Battalion, Third Annual Report, 1895, BB Archives Scottish HQ.
10 Newcastle On Tyne Battalion, First Annual Report 1895-1896 pp. 11-12 BB Archives. Scottish HQ.
11 Bristol Battalion, Sixth Annual Report, 1896-1897 & Seventh Annual Report, 1897-1898. BB Archives. Scottish HQ.
12 Liverpool Battalion, Sixth Annual Report, 1896-1897 BB Archives. Scottish HQ.
13 Brighton Battalion, Rules & Regulations, 1899-1900. BB Archives. Scottish HQ.
14 Edwards & Langley op. cit., p. 48. Efficiency Badge for Volunteers. Colours included silver on light blue.
15 `The Twinkle of a Star'. Article in BB Gazette, Dec.1985/Jan.1986. p.44

The Five-Pointed or 'White' Star c1890 - 1904

BB 035

BB 035 BACKGROUND NOTES

Only one version of this metal, shell-stamped star exists. It has, the pre-1927 emblem but without the motto on the anchor, and the B's further apart from each other, more into the points of the star. Although it was based on the Volunteer Star which was usually in woven wire format, no attempt has been made to mimic the wire construction as is sometimes found on non-Brigade shell-stamped metal types.

The Three Year Anchor/Three Year Service Badge
The most versatile of badges

The Staff-Sergeants' Cap Badge, The Bandmasters' Cap Badge, The Seniors' Cap & Collar Badge The Lady Officers' Pocket Badge

The emblem fair

This most recognisable of all BB Badges started life as the centre part of the Officers' Cap Badge surrounded by a belt, but began its separate existence, liberated from its constraint, after a decision of the Glasgow Battalion Executive:

31st January **1887**: '...it was decided to recommend to the next meeting of Council that Boys who have served three years be entitled to wear some badge on the right arm such as an Anchor or star.' [1]

Stars had been introduced into the 1st Glasgow Coy. in **1886**. The idea of a badge, however, was followed up by William Smith in a letter to John Blair & Co: [2]

4th Feb '87
Messrs John Blair & Co,
34, Howard St,
Dear Sirs,
Please let me have, early next week, your lowest quotation for the anchor alone, exact as on the Officer's ornament and plated in the same way, but without the ring containing the words 'the Boys Brigade'. The Executive Committee are considering whether they might use the anchor in this way as a badge of so many year's service for the Boys, and if taken up it would be wanted in large quantities, many hundreds at least, and consequently would need to be done at a very low price.
You ought to be able to do it at least as well as any one else, as it could be struck off with the same die as you presently use.
Kindly look into it very carefully & quote your keenest.
There are now 5000 Boys on the roll of the Brigade & new Companies enrolling every week.
Yours Faithfuly,
W.A. Smith,
Brig. Secy.

A month later [3] Smith sought a meeting with Mr Robt. Blair about the anchors. On the 16th of that same month at a meeting of the Glasgow Battalion Executive [4] it was intimated that the Brigade Executive had adopted an anchor as the badge,

'...which Boys who have served three sessions are entitled to wear on the right arm at and after the close of the third session'.

The John Blair advertisement in the new edition of the Manual in **1888** [5] included the adopted badge:

'Three Years Service Anchors, Silver-Plated, with Pin complete for fixing on the right arm, 4d each.'

Presumably not meant literally !

The hut workers in receipt of a lapel decoration

The Three Year Anchor was one of that select group of boys' badges to be introduced in the early years of the movement. The issue of anchors was always in strict accordance with regulations and it took a world war for anyone to consider flexibility in their use, possibly a unique occasion. A Rest Hut for soldiers had been set up in Edinburgh, sponsored and run by the Edinburgh Battalion, which at the start of **1916** brought an unusual request before the Northern Committee of the BB Executive:

'Edinburgh Hut. An application from the Edinburgh Battalion Sec. was submitted for 15 three years service anchors, to be worn by hut workers in Edinburgh. These were granted, and the Sec. was instructed to make it quite clear that they must be issued with the greatest of care to workers only, a receipt being taken for each one, and a promise given that it would be returned when the holder ceased to be a hut worker, so as to obviate the possibility of a Brigade decoration becoming merely a brooch or badge for anyone outside the Brigade.' [6]

Another example of the Brigade's intransigence in relation to anchor badges occured in **1927**, when Lt. Coupar of 147th Glasgow Coy. instituted the uniformed 'Cathcart Old Boys Association' ('COBA') for ex-BB Boys. Initially, the only emblem used as 'uniform' by the Association was the BB Three Year Anchor, a move which did not endear it to the BB authorities who frowned upon the 'irregular' issue of BB uniform. In **1931**, the emblem was changed.[7]

Four, Five & Six Year anchors ?

A report on the Brigade Council Meetings **1919**, reveals what might have been...

'Three Years' service Anchors. Mr Saunders proposed that when a Boy had served for four years with good conduct he should receive a Four Years' Service Anchor (the Three Years' anchor being withdrawn), and similarly after five or six years' service. It would not only encourage the Boys, but would be both interesting and useful to Inspecting officers, who could see at a glance the Boys' periods of service. Mr. F.C. Carey Longmore and Mr. C.J. Youngs supported the motion, which was opposed by Mr. Holmes Scott, Mr. G.C. Garton, Mr. D. Donald, and Mr. G. W. Shannon, who all spoke against unnecessary increase of badges. Mr. T. R. Plowman, approved of the idea, but suggested a Gilt Anchor for the longer period of service. The motion was lost by 37 votes to 29.'[8]

Cap badge Re-incarnation

In **1898,** the anchor badge was used as the new Staff-Sgt.s' Cap Badge in a form different, only in respect of its fastening, from the boys' service award. The Staff Sgt.s' Badge had two pointed tabs or fangs instead of the brooch clip. This was the first official use of the badge for a purpose other than three-year service. The Bandmasters' Cap, which should at this time have had only the company number on the front could, however, sometimes be found bearing the Three Year Anchor. In fact, in **1897**, Messrs. James Farquharson of London had advertised Bandmasters' Caps complete *'with crest'*. No doubt it was concern about such unauthorised use of the badge which led the Brigade to announce in the Gazette that year:

'3Yr Anchors will in future be supplied from Headquarters in the same way as the Discharge Certificates and to simplify the issue no special application form will be issued...'[9]

It wasn't until **1912** that the anchor badge was allowed to adorn the Bandmasters' Cap. Another less well-known use of the pre-**1926** anchor, was by the U.B.B.A., the United Boys' Brigades of America, where it was in use until the late **1980s** when that organisation became unisex and consequently changed its badges.

The post-**1926** anchor, now rather mundanely known as the 'Three Year Service Badge' was also destined to appear in many forms as well as retaining its three year service role. Owing to dissatisfaction with the unsuitable nature of the bandmasters cap for use with pipe bands the Brigade Executive, in **1935**, approved in principle the use of a glengarry with a *'suitable badge'* [10] By **1936**, the new Pipe-Majors' Cap Badge was available, based on the Three Year Anchor, with thistle border. This lasted for forty years before being discontinued.

A bright anchor swings into the sixties

After the Haynes Report of **1964** and the consequent re-structuring of the Brigade in **1966**, the Three Year Anchor on its own showed great versatility when, in a new *'untarnishable'* chrome finish, it provided the cap and collar badges for the new Senior Section of **1967**. The Committee had specifically requested that the collar badges be:

'...in the style of the Three Year Service Badge' [11]

The collar badges had long stick-pins and the cap badges two small pointed tabs. In the same year the use of the original Staff Sergeants' Badge was extended to women Staff-Sgts..

Small(er) is beautiful

1968 saw the final curtain fall on the Three Year Service Badge. The biggest upset of all, however, occurred two years later when a complete newcomer arrived. The new Boys' Cap Badge was designed with a slightly smaller, untarnishable chrome anchor badge. Common to all sections, it was set in coloured plastic surrounds: Yellow-Junior Section, Red-Company Section and Blue-Senior Section. Virtually all the old-size badges had gone for good. Some old badges even surfaced, plated in glorious gilt, re-cycled with fangs, and now clinging to the sides of a BB Weekend Holdall and a Students Bag marketed by the Supplies Department from **1980**. The Staff Sergeants' Cap Badge for men was replaced with the new badge, but without backing. The Bandmasters' and Pipe - Majors' Cap Badge went to the new size as did the Instructors'/Assistants' Cap Badge. The Staff Sergeants' Cap Badge for women came in the new size in **1984**. Finally, the Senior Section Collar and Epaulette Badges became the new size, after an intermediate size was used for a short time. In **1998** the first new size anchors with the 'steadfast' spelling were introduced.

Born again, it lives on yet.

In **1970**, a Lady Officers' Breast-Pocket Badge was introduced, perpetuating the old Three Year

Anchor in a new form as part of a black, cloth-mounted composite badge. This is part of a special jacket and skirt uniform which, since **1984**, has had alternative blouse styles without the use of the Breast-Pocket Badge.

For over a century the Three Year Anchor has been the most recognisable and versatile of all BB badges. Still at the centre of the Officers' Cap Badge, and as part of a lady officers' uniform, it lingers on complete with its traditional spelling of 'Stedfast', a true link with the past.

Hat trick

In September **1999** the decision was taken to change the BB uniform dramatically by **2006.** This should have meant the end of the Officers' Cap along with its badge incorporating the anchor. However, in September **2000**, the hat, complete with badge, was re-introduced as an option.

REFERENCES

1. The Glasgow Battalion Minute Book. No. 1. [1/1/1]. Executive meeting 31/1/1887. Glasgow Battalion HQ. [Stars had been introduced into the 1st Glasgow Coy. by Wm.Smith in 1886.]
2. Letter Book of Brigade Sec. Letter 496, 4th Feb. 1887. BB Archives, BB HQ Felden Lodge, Herts.
3. ibid. Letter 529, 3rd March 1887.
4. The Glasgow Battalion Minute Book No.1 op.cit. Executive meeting 16/3/1887
5. Officer's Manual 1888, BB Archives, Felden op.cit.
6. Minute book of the BB Northern Committee. Meeting 26/1/1916. BB Archives, Carronvale House, Larbert, Stirlingshire.
7. Boys of the Brigade. Vol 2 p110 'Carry On' the COBA Story. R. Bolton. 1993.
8. Gibbs Muriel , Editor: Brigade Archivist, in BBBCC Newsletter, No. 11, July 1985.9. BB Gazette, 1st Nov. 1897. p35.
10. Minutes of The Brigade Executive Meeting 18-19/5/1935, BB Archives, Felden
11. Minutes of Activities & Training Committee. AT/M[66] 2, 10/12/66. Report of Senior Section Activities Sub-Committee. BB Archives, Felden.

The Lady Officers' Pocket Badge   1970 - 2006

BB 018

BB 018 BACKGROUND NOTES

This badge is a three-part construction. The background is a black cloth/card oval bearing two metal motifs with a staybrite finish, the BB emblem and the wreath. Two long tabs are fastened to the wreath which protrude through the backing material to enable the badge to be inserted into the breast pocket. The main variation is in different makers' names on the long tabs, Butler and Firmin. The earlier types being marked 'Butler' and later types 'Firmin' due to the merger of the two companies.

It should be noted that this badge was used as the basis for the experimental seniors' pocket badge which was never adopted. The experimental badge had a blue oval background with clutch-pin fastenings in place of tabs. Samples of these experimental badges do turn up because they were sent to various Brigade staff around the country and should not be interpreted as a version of BB 018.

A white felt surround is supplied with the badge for wear by lady Warrant Officers, (Pictured above) Lieutenants wear the badge without the white surround.

The Three Year Anchor   1888 - 1926

The Staff Sergeants' Cap Badge   1898 - 1926
The Bandmasters' Cap Badge   1912 - 1926

BB 036.05   BB 036.07   BB 036.09   BB 036.14

BB 036 BACKGROUND NOTES

This multi-purpose badge was used in brooch form as the Three Year Anchor having an axle pin with round catch. One version is shell-stamped the rest are solid. Variation occurs on the Bs, the anchor and the rope. The S.Sgts Cap Badge form has tags or fangs and shows similar variations to the Three Year Anchor.

The Three Year Service Badge   1927 - 1968

The Staff Sergeants' Cap Badge   1927 - 1970
The Bandmasters' Cap Badge   1927 - 1970
The Seniors' Cap, Collar & Epaulette Badge 1967 - 1980s

BB 037   BB 037.20   BB 037.03   BB 037.09

> For 'New-Size' Anchor see: 'Boys' Field Service Cap Badge 1970 - '

BB 037 BACKGROUND NOTES

The most common variant of the Badge is the Three Year Service nickel brooch having more than forty types. There are solid and shell - stamped versions, standard tube joints and box joints and most catch types. More than half have some impressing. Variation on the obverse can be divided between wide and narrow crossbar types with additional differences in the lettering. There are types with the Miller maker's name. Variation on the obverse can be divided between wide and narrow crossbar types with additional differences in lettering. The Staff-Sergeants' and Bandmasters' Badges are similar on the obverse to some of the Three Year Service Badges with various tags or fangs on the reverse. The Seniors' Badges are either chrome or staybrite having stick - pin, tags or clutch - pin types.

The Long Service Badge For Boys... and Officers!

Service was the first aspect of the BB boy's life to be recognised with a badge. The Three Year Anchor was first awarded in **1888** and by **1926** was still the main way of recognising Brigade service. The one year Efficiency Badge introduced in **1904** was, however, not used universally. In contrast, the BLB had acknowledged 'Good Service' by the award of a medal after three years with bars thereafter. [1] It is not surprising, therefore, that after **1926** and union with the BLB, the words 'Good Conduct' came into use in the regulations detailing the qualifications for the Three Year Anchor, One Year Service Badge and a new Long Service Badge.

The announcement of the Long Service Badge came in the June **1927** issue of the BB Gazette:

'This is awarded to Boys not earlier than December 31st, in the Session in which they attain the age limit, after serving for not less than four years with good conduct. Design-A laurel wreath surrounding the BB Crest with a scroll bearing the words "Long Service".' [2]

Further details were intimated later in the year,

'Long service badge. Price 6d. it will be worn on the left arm midway between shoulder and elbow, or if the King's Badge is worn, below that badge.' [3]

The laurel wreath idea for the badge may well have come from the National Service Badge introduced in **1915** and, by **1927,** only out of production for a few years. The use of a wreath surround is common amongst British army badges.[4] The Badge was fretted around the BB logo as had been the National Service Badge. The extra cost, and use of energy in passing the badge through the stamping process three or four times, would not meet the utility regulations of the **1940s** which meant the production of some 'solid' badges.

In **1968,** a barrel Service Badge was issued which indicated the number of years' service in Junior or Company Sections. This remained the Service Badge for the **1983** structure of awards.

The Long Service Badge story does, however, have a sequel. The familiar pattern of the Long Service award has been reproduced in a completely new departure from Brigade tradi- tion. In the Gazette of July **1996** the following announcement was made:

'The Brigade Executive has approved a scheme to recognise long service as an officer. There is a new, open certificate which may be awarded for any length of service beyond ten years. Buttonhole badges for men and brooches for women will be awarded as follows: Bronze for 15 years' service, Silver for 20 years' service and Gold for 30 years' service. The awards will be available from 1st September and be administered by Battalions.' [5]

These new Officers' Service Badges are small replicas of the old Long Service Badge. They are for 'mufti' use only and include coloured cold enamelling. Here is a strong link with the past, perhaps the start of a trend.

REFERENCES

1. The Boys Manual, The Boys' Life Brigade, 1926. BLB HQ. p 34. R. Bolton collection.
2. BB Gazette, Vol. XXXV, No 10, 1/6/1927. p 164. Mitchell Library, Glasgow.
3. ibid. Vol.XXXVI, No 4, 1/12/1927. p 54.
4. Edwards & Langley, British Army Proficiency Badges, Wardley Publishing 1984.
5. BB Gazette. Vol. 104, No 5, July 1996. p 104.

STEDFAST MAG CLIPS

The boys speak out... in December 1954:

'Sir-Our Captain has been in the BB for fifty years, and you cannot tell whether he's a new member or an old officer. Cannot a badge be given to an officer for long service?'
Pte. Barry Baker, 2nd Eastbourne Company.

The Long Service Badge   1927 - 1968

BB 038.03

BB 038.06

BB 038.07

BB 038.24

BB 038 BACKGROUND NOTES

This nickel brooch comes in nearly forty versions! Generally it is of solid construction, although there are a few shell-stamped varieties. Early types were frosted and there are some which have been chrome-plated. Joints vary between standard tube and box with a variety of pins and catches. Impressing on the reverse has at least fifteen variations. There are many varieties clearly visible on the obverse, notably the wartime non-fretted version. The fretting varies considerably around the anchor, rope and Bs, note the differences at the base of the anchor. There are types with hatched B's, differing sizes of writing on the ribbon and leaf shapes on the laurel add to the variety.

The Officers' Mufti Long Service Badge   1996 -

BB 491.01

BB 492.01

BB 493.01

BB 493.02

BB 491/2/3 BACKGROUND NOTES

At the time of going to press only BB 493.01 has had a second striking. The badge is in three colours, bronze, silver and gold. The enamel colours, red and blue are identical in all three types. The pins are Bar Brooch safety type on both the mens' badge 491/2/3.01 and womans' long bar brooch 491/2/3 .02.

The Diamond - Shaped Badges

The first of these little diamond-shaped badges entered into Brigade use in 1904 by the 'back door'. By that time a white metal efficiency star had been used by some battalions for more than ten years, but the star had always been optional and was not without its critics.[1] In **1903,** the Brigade Executive discussed,

'...a proposal ...to authorize an efficiency badge for one or two years' service... ...it was unanimously decided that there should be no badge recognising any less service than three years, for which the Anchor is provided.' [2]

However, the matter would not be left to rest there. At a meeting of the Brigade Executive the following summer the matter of the proposed one year efficiency badge was raised again. The Executive considered a resolution passed by the London Council:

'That this meeting of the London Council, over 100 officers being present, while resolving to loyally support the Executive decision regrets their action in declining to sanction the wearing of efficiency badges, and

desires respectfully to point out that such Badges have been issued for many years past in London Battalions under conditions carefully considered and requiring a high standard of attendance; these conditions being published in the Annual Reports presented to headquarters. They affirm that the issue of these Badges proved a strong incentive and a very convenient reward for regular attendance, and that experience has shown that they do not detract from the value of the Three Years' Service Anchor.'

The Executive finally yielded to convincing and overwhelming pressure, from London and elsewhere. The minutes record:

'...Executive felt satisfied that they would be justified in departing from the decision came to in September last with regard to one-year efficiency badges...'

and resolved to approve the adoption of such a badge for the Brigade,

'...but with a view to securing a uniformity throughout the Brigade resolved to take the opinion of the Executives of the various Battalions before laying down regulations for the issue of the badge.' [3.]

The Executive at its meeting in Newport in **1904,** stated that it had considered battalion replies to a questionnaire on the matter and decided that,

*'The form of the Badge to be an upright Diamond.
The Badge to be worn on the right Cuff, two inches from the edge.
The adoption of the Badge to be left to the discretion of Battalions and individual Companies outside Battalions,*

who shall be empowered to raise the standard of efficiency as they may deem right.'

Normally badges would be awarded to boys with two absences or less for drill and bible-class out of a minimum of 24 attendances.[4] Another typical BB compromise, resulting in the Brigade's first discretionary badge and a new set of problems, for instance, how many would be required? An appeal was placed in the Gazette:

'...As the making of these Badges takes some time, the Executive desire to ascertain approximately how many are likely to be required, and with this object in view would be obliged if Secretaries of Battalions and Captains of Companies in which the Badge has been adopted would communicate with the Brigade Secretary, stating as nearly as possible how many are likely to be required during the current session.' [5]

Why choose a diamond?

It is interesting to consider why the diamond/lozenge shape was chosen. Why not a star like the one originally used in the 1st Glasgow company or that used widely in London? The answer seems to come, as it so often does with BB badges, from the Volunteers. Since **1881,** a diamond lozenge was awarded to volunteers:

'Returned as efficient in rifle drill and practice in the last annual return of their Corps.'

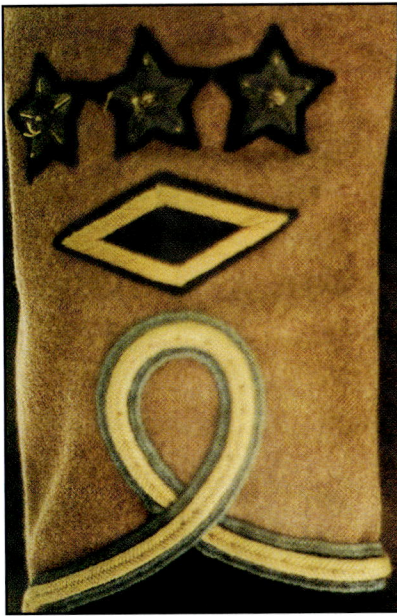

**Detail of right cuff,
1st Lanarkshire Rifle
Volunteers c.1883.**
Photo: Les. Howie Edinburgh.

There was then a progression to a five-pointed star after four or five years. [6] It would, no doubt, have been considered inappropriate for the BB system to start with a star after only one year, particularly with the introduction of the Sergeants' (four-pointed) Star just over twelve months earlier in **1902**. The award of different stars would become rather confusing. William Smith's own experience in the 1st Lanarkshire Rifle Volunteers ('C' Company) would, no doubt, have made him familiar with the efficiency lozenge which was, in his case, black with a grey border.[7] It was probably not Smith, however, who swayed the collective mind of the Executive in **1904**. The London Council Meeting had, in **1903**, already sanctioned an 'Attendance Badge' to replace the star, which was diamond-shaped! The minutes record,

'...[4] Attendance Badges - a diamond shaped badge, which may be worn on a cloth band on right fore arm, to be awarded to Boys putting in 90% of actual attendances, with good conduct, at Parade and Bible Class. The Official

Session must include a minimum of 24 Drills and Bible Class Meetings to be held between 1st September and 31st May...' [8]

Realising that things would be confusing with two stars being awarded for 'efficiency' the London Council had decided to change the rules themselves, only to be squashed by the Executive three months later, hence the strong feelings at the London meeting in June **1904**. So, when the Executive changed its mind and decided to issue a badge, the pattern of a diamond, already in use in London, was the obvious choice, to be worn on the right cuff, just as in the Lanarkshire Rifle Volunteers.

To wear
or not to wear

The splendid compromise so smoothly adopted by the Executive was not universally popular. In fact, the badge seems to have generated considerable acrimony probably for the following reasons:

Firstly, the way it would be worn: on an armband as detailed in the London Council minutes, or perhaps above the cuff, or in the lapel. Where was the consistency longed for by the national Executive? [9] The Manual of **1906** states:

'The Badge shall be worn on the right cuff two inches from the edge, at the discretion of Battalions and individual Companies.'

The **1908** Manual entry suggests that someone must have been wearing the diamond sideways (landscape) like the Volunteers, because as well as changing its

position on the arm, it also states:

'Upright diamond. The Badge shall be worn on the right sleeve, between shoulder and elbow.'

Not that all companies followed the instructions. For instance, the 40th Edinburgh originally wore them on the bottom of the sleeve and changed around **1915** to wearing them high up the arm around the curve of the shoulder, even when the boy had an armband. This tradition continued into the **1960s**. (See photo of Sgt. Maconochie page 99) Companies in London also adopted this method of wearing the badge.

Secondly, the fact that a number of large and influential battalions considered it to be meaningless. Glasgow Battalion never used the badge. By the **1960s,** its absence in Glasgow was defended on the grounds of 'tradition'.[10] Dundee Battalion felt so strongly about it in **1904** that it refused to take any part in any Brigade discussion about its format or use.[11] It was not until **1913** that the issue was raised again in Dundee and the badge, surprisingly, sanctioned. [12]

Thirdly, the qualifications for its award varied considerably when, locally, differing interpretations were put on the 'regulations'. A good example can be found in a reply written by William Smith in **1906** to a Company Captain in the Midlands who had written to him regarding the badge,

'...1st. A Boy is entitled to wear a Badge for every year he wins it, so that by winning it three years, he would be entitled to wear three Badges. 2nd. According to Regulations it is clear that you could not allow more than two absent marks in all, even although you have thirty parades and thirty Bible Classes. 3rd. It is quite within your power to raise the qualifications by deducting marks for lateness or mistakes in drill if you think it right.

All that is laid down is the <u>minimum</u> qualifications. Personally I would consider it rather a risky experiment to take marks off for mistakes in drill, provided a Boy had good conduct otherwise, as it would be very difficult to lay down a satisfactory standard... . ...the more simple and unencumbered...the better.' [13]

Fourthly, an example of potential confusion came in **1918** when the view, of the Northern Committee of the Brigade Executive concerning this badge differed from those of the Southern Committee:

'The Committee note the proposal agreed to by the Southern Committee that a Badge should be issued indicating the number of years service served by each boy with efficiency. It is presumed that this means having a separate Badge for each year. If so, this Committee do not approve of this as it would mean the additional cost involved, the stocking of different badges and the trouble of getting back badges before issuing these for the next session etc..' [14]

Hard to get

There was then plenty of scope for conflict, but generally those awarding the badges kept to the rules, even if they did seem a little harsh at times. The Executive meeting in May **1919** for instance stated that even if boys had been absent due to 'Spanish Flu.' they would not get this badge. [15]

Even after the union with the BLB in **1926** the badge remained optional .[16] The same format, with the addition of the cross behind the anchor, was re-issued as the 'One Year Service Badge' requiring only good conduct and not more than two absences. It continued to be ignored in Glasgow as had the original Efficency Badge. In London, it continued to be called a one year 'star' right up to **1968**. Other areas christened the little diamonds 'pips'. These diamond-shaped badges were generally quite popular during the last twenty years or so of their use, resulting in massive numbers being produced. Each BB boy could earn up to five.

A Diamond is Forever

From **1956** service in the Life Boys could be taken into account and a special diamond-shaped Life Boy Service Badge could be added to the start of a row of five One Year Service Badges for those boys who had served in the Life Boy Team.

The idea of a 'Transfer Badge', which had been discussed as early as **1927**, was inevitable since such a badge had been awarded in the Boys' Life Brigade when Lifeboys transferred into the BLB company. At a meeting of the Executive in January **1927**, it was decided to use a Transfer Certificate indicating Seals won, rather than a transfer badge.[17]

In **1933**, the Executive Committee was approached again by the Liverpool Area to approve a transfer badge. It was not approved.[18] However, by **1955**, times had changed. There were fewer older boys and more Life Boys, but some officers were concerned that senior boys from the Life Boys were leaving before reaching the ranks of the BB. At the Bristol Council Meeting in **1955** a motion from the West of England District proposed a 'Life Boy Transfer Badge'. There was, surprisingly, opposition to this, one critic claiming that it was 'psychologically unsound'. The motion at Bristol was carried by a show of hands.[19] Opposition didn't stop at Council. The Badges Committee of the Brigade Executive received resolutions from Dunfermline, Paisley and Glasgow asking for the award of the badge to be left to the discretion of battalions, as was the situation with the One Year Service Badges. [20] Details of the Life Boy Service Badge appeared in the Gazette:

' Awarded to Boys who have served in the Life Boy Team continuously for not less than two complete years with good conduct, and who have maintained active membership of their Team until the date of transfer to the Company. The badge to be presented by the BB Captain on completion of Recruit Training and worn thereafter on the right arm when in BB uniform. (Note: The Badge will be worn as the first in the line of the One Year Badges.)'[21]

The Life Boy Service Badge was the same size and shape as the One Year Service Badge, but had at its centre the enamelled Life Boy badge which had been popular as a mufti badge since **1930**. When the whole award structure changed in **1968**, remarkably, the diamond-shaped Life Boy Service Badge was retained with a new centre reflecting the name-change of 'The Life Boys' to 'Junior Section'. The enamelled LB emblem was changed to an enamelled BB emblem. The new Junior Section Service Badge was produced in two types: Silver for boys who had served at least two sessions in the Junior Section and Gold for at least two sessions service plus obtaining the Gold Award of the Achievement Scheme. The diamond-shape Junior Section Badge was abandoned in **1971** in favour of the new barrel shape.

For the diamond-shaped service badge, however, **1971** was not actually the end. The new Seniors' Award Badge, although trumpeted with a mute when it was announced in **1991,** has re-introduced the size and shape back to the BB armband. A diamond is, indeed, forever.

REFERENCES

1. See entries on 'The Five-Pointed Star' pp. 50 - 51
2. BB Gazette, Vol. XII, 1/10/1903, p 31. BB Scottish Headquarters, Carronvale, Larbert, Stirlingshire.
3. ibid. 1/6/1904 p 149.
4. ibid. Vol. XIII, 1/10/1904 p.18.
5. BB Gazette, 1st February 1905. p.82. D. Aubrey Collection
6. Edwards & Langley, British Army Proficiency Badges, Wardley Publishing, 1984. p 48.
7. Example of 1st Lanarkshire Rifle Volunteers uniform on display in Glasgow City Museum. August 1995.
8. London Council Minutes. 6/7/1903. BB Archives, BB HQ, Felden Lodge, Hemel Hempstead, Herts.
9. Photographs exist of the Badge being worn on many parts of the uniform. Notably, 13th Cardiff Coy. wearing them on lapels. c1905. R. Bolton Collection.
10. John Cooper, 101st Glasgow Coy. Was told in the 1960's that the lack of one-year badges was 'tradition'.
11. Dundee Battalion, Minute Book, Vol. 2. 7/6/1904.
12. ibid. Vol. 3, 14/2/1913.
13. Letter written by W.A.Smith, Brigade Sec, to Mr Charles A MacGuire, Capt. 1st Aston Manor Company. 22/8/1906. BB Archives, Felden.
14. Northern Committee Minute Book. No 1. 11/7/1918. BB Scottish HQ.
15. Brigade Executive Minutes 16-18/5/1919. Throughout Europe more people died as a result of this influenza pandemic than had died in the First World War.
16. BB Gazette Vol. XXXV No 10. 1/6/1927.
17. Brigade Executive, 17/1/1927. Life Boys Committee.
18. ibid. 8/9/1933. The Liverpool Area was a strong Life Boy area. Supportive letters published in the Gazette: Jan1936 and March 1936 from Jarrow & St. Helens.
19. BB Gazette, Vol LXIV, No 1, October 1955. p 7.
20. Minutes of Badges Committee. 26/5/1956.
21. BB Gazette. No 6 August 1956. p 102.

The Seniors' Award   1991 -

BB 046 BACKGROUND NOTES

The Seniors' Award brooch comes in few varieties due to the lower numbers issued. The Seniors' Award is the only diamond with 'cold enamelling' and a bar brooch fastening.

BB 046

The One Year Efficiency Badge   1904 - 1926

BB 039.01   **BB 039**   **BB 039**   **BB 039**

BB 039 BACKGROUND NOTES

These diamond-shaped brooches were produced in nickel, most having the frosted finish. They are all shell-stamped. Variations occur mainly in the shape of the anchor, one in particular has a flat topped crossbar (BB 039. 01). The anchor flukes and crowns vary considerably and this affects the positioning of the Bs. There is variation in the size of the anchor ring. All examples have axle pin fastenings with round catches.

The One Year Service Badge   1926 - 1968

BB 040.01   **BB 040.14**   **BB 040.33**   **BB 040.82**

BB 040 BACKGROUND NOTES

There are many variations of this diamond service badge. They were produced either shell-stamped or solid, the shell-stamped versions being pre - World War II and early post - war. The solid varieties appeared in the 1950s - 1960s. The main types include wide and narrow, thin and thick borders, bold and fine stipple, long and short ropes and flat or domed shape. Varieties include many different finishes, chrome, gilt, frosted, etc.. There are also many varieties of reverse with differing degrees of impression and depression as the result of stamping. Force marks, joints, fastenings, and makers names all add to the variations. A lugged version exists.

How to identify One Year Service Badge variations

1. Take a group of these badges and divide them into smaller groups representing the **various metals** of which they are made, i.e. nickel, chrome or brass.

2. With one of these 'metal type' groups in front of you divide them again into two further groups, one for **shell-stamped versions** the other **solid**.

3. Consider each of these new groups separately applying the following procedure to both groups: Study the reverse of each badge and place into mini-groups according to the **types of catch and joint combination** that present themselves, eg. copper FRC & standard tube, or nickel hooked etc.

4. Study the obverse of each of these mini-groups sorting out all the **visual differences**.

The Life Boy Service Badge   1956 - 1968

BB 041 BACKGROUND NOTES

Diamond-shaped brooches with blue & white enamelled centre. The main obverse variations occur in the style of centre enamelled badge. Different shades of blue and lettering occur and also the rope loops around the lifebelt vary in height and width. There is also a variation on the reverse with makers-names and fastenings.

BB 041   **BB 041**

The Junior Section Service Badge   1968 - 1971

BB 042 BACKGROUND NOTES

The Junior Section Service brooches have similar variations as their Life Boy progenitors, but having silvered and gilt finishes causes few to be in perfect condition unless unused. Some examples can be found with the pin fittings reversed.

BB 042   **BB 042**

The Post '68 Service Badges & Anchor Boy Achievement Badge

The Brigade Service Badge

In 1968, the diamond-shaped service badges were replaced with a new barrel shape, a shape in common with all the proficiency awards. One of the conditions imposed upon the design of the new badges was that it should be one badge to represent years of service. The idea of a whole row of metal one-year badges worn on an armband was regarded as being impracticable due to weight and the increasing use of shirt - uniforms due in no small measure to the '1963' uniform regulations. Before 1963, there were relatively few companies still using the old full uniform, a leftover from BLB days. Since these one-year badges were optional the main thrust of the argument related to the Three-Year and Long Service Awards at that time being worn on different arms.

The Company Section Activities Sub-Committee met in April 1967 and decided the way ahead for the new scheme:

' Service Awards. General outline agreed, subject to the following:-
(i) Three Year Service and Long Service Badges to be discontinued.
(ii) All Service awards, including

Junior Section Service Badge, to be worn on the left arm.' [1]

At a meeting three weeks later the Activities Sub-Committee laid down the specific design requirements in an interim report:

'one common badge with changeable inserts to show the number of years of service. Three Year Service and Long Service Badges to be discontinued. NB. All Service awards, including Junior Section Service Badges to be worn on the left arm.' [2]

Five months later, the Sub-Committee agreed to recommend the following:

'Service Awards.
(e) a suitable design should be produced, with the numbers 1, 2, 3, 4, 5, 6 and 7 on interchangeable inserts.' [3]

As usual with such proposals, the outline details took a while to translate into badges. It was well into 1969 before the badges were finalised and given approval by the Executive, Activities and Training Committee:

' Service Badge. i)The new service Badge, with the appropriate insert should be made available, this badge to be worn on the left arm, and to replace all the old one year service badges.' [4]

It was late arriving, but the BB now had a new-style Service Badge which was destined to outlive its proficiency cousins.

In 1974, when the Company Section Award Scheme Revision Working Party examined the Service Badges they came to the

conclusion that what had been the 'Company Section' Service Badge should now become the Brigade Service Badge, taking into consideration service in the Junior Section. The Juniors would now feel fully integrated into the 'Brigade' rather than just a 'Training' Section. This would mean that the former limit of '7' would be increased somewhat. The wording of the Working Party minutes concentrated upon the occasion when the new badge would be awarded:

'i)-Agreed that the Badge with insert indicating service should be awarded and worn on promotion to the Company Section.' [5]

The Brigade Service Badge has continued into the new millennium as the only remnant of the once mighty 'barrels'.

The Junior Section Service Badges

The Life Boys finished in 1967 and became the 'Junior Section', so there was, naturally, a need to change the 'Life Boy Service Badge'. Not only had the Life-Boys finished, but also the new Life Boy/Junior Section 'Achievement Scheme', introduced in 1966, meant that some boys would have reached the 'Gold' stage and acknowledgement of this would be required on any new badge.

The Activities and Training Committee meeting in February **1967** was aware that the whole shape of awards was changing and that any new badge would have to fit-in with the new style. However, at this time no decisions had been made regarding the Brigade Service Awards and the lead would have to come from those deliberations. An interim measure was decided upon whereby the old diamond pattern with circular enamelled centre would stay with the new title 'Junior Section' replacing 'The Life Boys'. The 'Gold Award' would be recognised:

'J/S Service Badge'
(b) agreed to recommend that:-
(i) a silver coloured badge be awarded to Boys with at least two years' service on promotion to the Company Section.
(ii) a gold coloured badge be awarded to Boys who gain the Gold Award in the Achievement Scheme.
(iii) Where a Boy has two years' service and has also gained the Gold Award, he should wear only the Gold badge. This recommendation would be for a limited period, until the question of service awards, et., was resolved for the whole Brigade.'[6]

It was **1969** before the Service Badges were complete and the Committees were able to think about changing the format of the Junior Section Badge. The re-design was achieved so that from **1971**, a new barrel-shaped badge became the Junior Section Service Badge. This generally bronze-coloured badge would have inserts 'BB' in silver or gold. In fact, these 'gold & silver' inserts were red letters 'BB' on a gold insert to represent 'gold' and blue letters 'BB' on a silver insert to represent 'silver'.

The new badges had only been in operation for three years when the Company Section Award Scheme Revision Working Party recommended that Junior Section Service be counted into the Brigade Service Badge. There was now no need for

a 'silver' insert, or indeed any insert; a new 'Junior Section Gold Achievement Badge' was required. The Committee:

'ii) requested the Supplies Committee to explore the possibility of introducing an anodised all gold badge with the letters 'BB' in the lower panel.'[7]

In **1976,** the new Gold Achievement Badge was introduced, all -gold as per the recommendation. The idea of an all-gold badge has remained, being changed to a circular shape in **1993**.[8] The circular shape, which matches the Junior Section Achievement Scheme badge, has the spelling 'Ste**a**dfast'. Boys who have gained the Junior Section Gold Achievement Badge wear the badge on the armband as previously, but the same badge is transferred to their Company Section armband on promotion.

The Life Boy and Junior Section Service Badges have come through three changes in shape since **1956**. In addition to the Queen's, President's and D. of E.'s Badges, the left arm awards, in **2000**, consist of a diamond Seniors' Award, a barrel Brigade Service Badge, a circular Junior Section Gold Achievement Badge and a triangular Anchor Boy Achievement Badge. Variety, is, seemingly, the intention here.

The Anchor Boy Achievement Badge

Introduced from 1st May **1997**, to be awarded to Anchor Boys who have completed the Anchor

Achievements in their final year. The Badge was designed by a Committee and it shows. A small triangular enamelled brooch with a letter 'A' it has no 'BB' or other Brigade logo and the brooch bar sticks out at the top and bottom of the badge.

The Gazette stated that the badge was to be:

'worn on armband on right arm for the duration of a boy's service.'[9]

The position for wearing the Anchor Boy Achievement Badge on the Junior Section Armband is in the centre row next to the Service Badge.

Anchor Boys soon grow into Company Section Boys so, in March **1998,** details were published regarding the wearing of the Anchor Boy Achievement Badge on Company Section Armbands:

'The Brigade Activity and Training Committee have (sic) agreed that the Anchor Boy Achievement badge can be worn by Company Section boys. The badge will be worn on the left arm to the left of the Junior Section Gold Achievement Badge...'[10]

It is quite likely that few of these badges will be worn in Company Section Uniform due to the new uniform regulations introduced from **1999**.

REFERENCES

1. Company Section Activities Sub-Committee. 29/4/67,CA/M(67)2. para. m
2. ibid. 16/5/67.
3. ibid. 14/10/67. CA/M/67(4) para 54.
4. Activities and Training Committee. 17/5/69. AT/M(69)2 Para 18.
5. Company Section Award Scheme Revision Working Party. 9/11/74.
6. Activities and Training Committee 18/2/67. AT/M(67)1
7. Company Section Award Scheme Revision Working Party 9/11/74.
8. BB Gazette, Sept. 1993. Vol. 101 No.6 Gold Achievement will be 'phased - in' as current badge is used up.
9. ibid. May 1997. Vol.105, No 4. p.76.
10. ibid., March 1998. Vol 106, No 3. p.50

The 'post 1968' Service Badges

The Company Section Service/ Brigade Service Badge

1969 - 1976   1976 -

BB 043

BB 043

BB 043 BACKGROUND NOTES

The badge was originally issued as a nickel brooch with a standard tube joint. Aluminium versions with bar-brooches followed and then finally it was made in plastic, vacuum coated with silver paint and sporting a clutch pin. From 1976 the inserts bearing the number of years service were extended to take into account service in the Junior Section, bringing the numbers used into double figures. The main difference between the early inserts and the later ones is that originally they were tabbed to fit into holes provided in the badge, but later the holes were removed and the inserts given an adhesive back to fix them in place.

The Junior Section Service Badge

1971 - 1976

BB 044

BB 044

BB 044

BB 044

1976 - 1993

BB 044

BB 044

BB 044

BB 044

BB 044 BACKGROUND NOTES

The 1971 -1976 badges are bronze aluminium brooches with bar-brooch safety fastenings. There is a variety of crest sizes with differing reverse patterns. Sometimes the silver BB Service Badges were adapted by BB captains for use as JS Service as are the two on the right above. In 1976, a Gold - coloured gilding metal brooch was introduced with 'BB' in the square recess. The badge was changed to a plastic gold vacuum coated version with a clutch - pin. The size of the Bs in the square recess vary in size and shape.

The Anchor Boy Achievement Badge   1997 -

BB 047

BB 047 BACKGROUND NOTES

There have been only two batches of this badge produced to date but even so a small variation has occurred in the style of bar-brooch fitting used on the reverse. Inevitably, the colour density of the red enamel has varied between each batch produced. So far all versions have the bar-brooch protruding above and below the basic shape of the badge.

The National Service Badges

Community Service Badges for the First and Second World Wars

During the First World War BB companies were urged to take part in Red Cross work, War Fund collections and to act, for example, as cycle messengers. Much help was given to the civil authorities generally, particularly as the war progressed. Waste paper, bottles, and old metal were collected and orderly buglers regularly helped by blowing the 'All Clear' signal after Zeppelin air raids. Two rest huts were provided for serving soldiers and sailors. One large double-hut was built in Rouen and another in Edinburgh. These recreation huts were staffed by BB officers.[1] A lapel badge was produced after the war and presented to former hut workers to commemorate the Edinburgh Hut **1916-1919**. (See photo, badge BB 311) During the war there had been a controversy over the irregular issue of Three-Year Anchor Badges to the hut workers. (See page 52)

One Hundred Hours

The Brigade was keen to recognise all the Voluntary 'National Service' being done by BB boys, possibly to counteract any criticism which may have stemmed from its lack of enthusiasm to 'sign up' for the Cadets. The BB Gazette of June **1915** had the intimation of a new,

'...National Service Badge... for voluntary and unpaid service performed out of school or business hours in connection with the war... not less than 100 hours to such service.'

It was to be worn on the left arm below the King's Badge. Applications for the award had to be made by Company Captains with the approval of Battalion Presidents.[2] At that time the award had not been produced and no date was fixed due to the makers being busy with war requirements, but a sample was ready for the Northern Committee at its meeting in October:

'A finished example of this badge was shown and the question of price discussed. It was agreed that if possible the price should be 6d., but keeping in view the fact that with the end of the war we might be left with an unusable stock on our hand. This might not be considered possible, in which case the Committee agree to the price being 8d...'[3]

The Badge was ready by December **1915** when it was detailed in the Gazette.[4]

Who's Counting?

Many First World War National Service Badges were sold, perhaps because the war continued for a further three years, or because it was easy to find war service activities. One example is recorded in the minutes of the Northern Committee in **1916** where it states that consideration was made of the application on behalf of four boys in the 7th Dublin Company,

'...whose National Service consisted of

parading in the Dublin University Officer's Training Corps Band...'[5]

After further investigation the Committee approved of the awards.[6] The rather low figure of 2,600 badges awarded is recorded by Muriel Gibbs the BB Archivist in **1985**.[7] There does not seem to be any documentary evidence to support this number; indeed the evidence seems to suggest an oversupply. The Northern Committee had been worried about being left with an *'unusable stock'* and its fears may have indeed been correct, because the badges were still being issued in **1920!** The following statement appeared in the January **1921** Gazette:

'...it is notified that the stock of the above Badge and its accompanying Certificate is now quite exhausted. No further supply of either is being prepared, and no orders to replace lost Badges can be accepted.'[8]

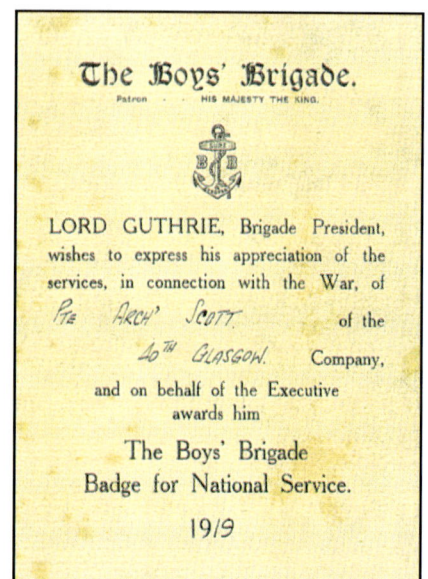

The Certificate which accompanied the award of the
1st World War National Service Badge.

They had, it seems, all been sold, but was this only 2,600 ? The certificate which accompanied the badge is illustrated on the previous page.

A Tendency to 'Decorate' Officers

The BB authorities have always been very strict regarding which badges were allowed to be worn in uniform. However, munition workers badges and other war service badges were allowed. The matter of boys' uniform was covered by the Northern Committee:

'Munitions and War Badges. This matter was dealt with at a meeting of Head-Quarters Committee on 25th March 1915 when it was decided to allow the wearing of such badges. The Northern Committee agree that Boys entitled to wear Munition Workers Badges or other officially recognised War Service Badges should be permitted to continue to wear these when in BB Uniform.' [9]

It is assumed that these badges would be worn in the lapel, and this was certainly the case for officers. The position of officers wearing such badges was also considered by the Committee:

'Wearing of War Badges by Officers in Uniform. The Committee noted whether the wearing of munition or other War Badges by Officers in uniform should be discontinued, owing to them tending towards too much decoration when worn along with the new collar badges. The Committee were of the opinion that the wearing of such Badges was desirable, both from the Officer's and the public point of view and that they should continue to be worn when in Brigade Uniform.' [10]

These war-work badges have not been illustrated in this book, but they do have the same special status as any other non-Brigade badges approved nationally for Brigade uniform wear; a situation much more common in the CLB than in the BB. The only other items allowed by the BB are the medals of the Royal Humane Society.

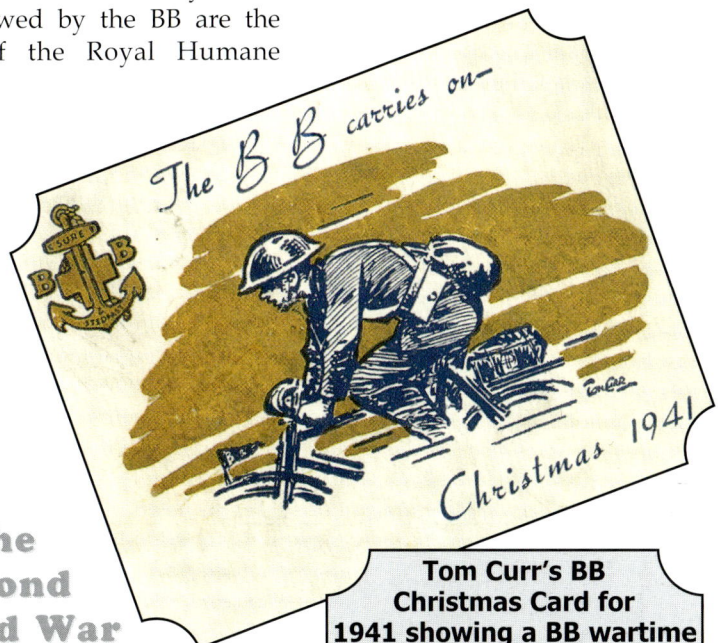

Tom Curr's BB Christmas Card for 1941 showing a BB wartime messenger on 'duty' earning his National Service Badge.

The Second World War

In December **1941,** the Government introduced a requirement that all 16-19 year olds register with their local authority. There was no compulsion involved, but the youths not involved in recognised youth organisations, or pre-service Cadet groups were steered in the general direction of such activities. The government was well aware of the need to involve young people in the war effort, a lesson learnt from The First World War. An official BB National Service Badge was reintroduced soon after the start of the war. Details were intimated in the Gazette of February **1940.** The regulations would apply to work done from 3rd September **1939.** The same regulations would apply as for World War One and the Badge would not be applicable for staff sergeants. The cost would be 8d per badge. [11] There are no details available concerning the numbers produced, but a few different varieties, including a 'utility' unpierced version, probably indicate a large number.

REFERENCES

1. Springhall et.al, Sure & Stedfast. A History of the Boys' Brigade 1883-1983. Collins 1983. pp 107 - 108.
2. BB Gazette, Vol XXIII, No 10, 1/6/1915, p 146. BB Scottish HQ., Carronvale, Larbert, Stirlingshire.
3. Northern Committee Minute Book No. 1. [1915-1919] 28/10/1915. BB Scottish HQ.
4. BB Gazette, 1/12/1915, p. 51.
5. op.cit., N. Committee. 17/4/1916.
6. ibid., 28/4/1916.
7. M. Gibbs. Badges of The Boys' Brigade. BB Archive Press, 1985. p 14.
8. BB Gazette. Vol. XXIX, No 5, 1/1/1921, p 76. Glasgow Battalion BB HQ, Bath St. Glasgow.
9. Northern Committee, op.cit., 26/1/1916.
10. ibid., 12/10/1916.
11. BB Gazette, Vol. XLVIII, No 6, Feb. 1940. BB Scottish HQ.

The National Service Badges

1915 - 1921

BB 054.01

BB 054 BACKGROUND NOTES

There are no real varieties of this badge although some seem to have been frosted and others do not. It is a cut-out badge, solid nickel with fretted centre around the pre - 1927 emblem. The joint is an axle pin typical of the period. The fastening is mounted horizontally, not visible on the photograph above.

1940 - 1945

BB 055.01

BB 055.02

BB 055.

BB 055.05

BB 055 BACKGROUND NOTES

Two distinct variations of this nickel badge exist, fretted and non-fretted. The fretted version is the earliest, produced in 1940, with later types being subject to the utility regulations which means not going through the stamping machine more than once. There are a number of types of the unfretted version, main variations being in the re-design of the emblem and flag and the introduction of stipple in the previously fretted areas. The fastenings are horizontally mounted standard tube joints with round catches typical of the period, making a good benchmark for dating other badges. Frosted versions exist of both main types, but some were no doubt produced without this finish for economic reasons and to accommodate wartime supply restrictions..

VOLUME ONE
THE BOYS' BRIGADE

3. Proficiency Badges

The King's, Queen's, Founder's and President's Badges

The Glasgow Battalion Council proposed the award of a King's Badge in 1913.[1] The Brigade Executive applied to the King for permission and it **was granted.** The conditions for the new badge were agreed at the Executive meeting in Liverpool. The formal announcement of the badge came in October 1913 stating that it would be worn on the left arm between shoulder and elbow. The Scouts' Badge would now be worn on the right arm. [2] It was March 1914 before a picture of the new award appeared for the first time and the Gazette stated that:

'...The Badge is silver-plated and forms a very beautiful decoration...' [3]

The 'Silver plated' reference is the way of describing the 'Frosted Silver' finish used on all of the nickel badges at this time.

The conditions for the award were laid out in the Manual of 1914:

'To be worn when in uniform, on the left arm, between shoulder and elbow, apart from all other Decorations.
The applicant must be recommended by his own Company Captain as suit-

The Founder's Funeral Car, flanked by four 1st Glasgow Coy. Sergeants, outside the College and Kelvingrove United Free Church. 16th May 1914.
Col. Sgt. Arthur Reid can be seen wearing his King's Badge.

able, and must be not less than 16 years of age in the Session in which the application is made.

He must have served for three complete Sessions with good conduct and be of Non-Commissioned rank.

He must have at least 90 per cent. of full attendance marks during the above period at not less than 25 Meetings each for- (a) Drill, and (b) Bible-Class or Sunday School.

He must hold a Non-Commissioned Officers' Certificate of Proficiency obtained after Examination.

He must hold at least two out of the following four:- (a) First and Second

year's Ambulance Certificates. (b) First-Class Swimming Certificate. (c) First-Class B.B. Scout's Certificate. (d) Signaller's, Bugler's, or Band Badge.

Application Forms for this Badge (which is supplied at 1s. post paid) may be had from Head-Quarters or London Office. Service as Staff-Sergeant does not count for the King's Badge.' [4]

Within two months of the introduction of the King's Badge the eyes of the whole Brigade fell upon the First Glasgow Company due to the death of the Founder Sir William A. Smith. William Smith had died in London on Sunday 10th May after attending a meeting of the Brigade

Executive. [5] The first Brigade boy to be officially told of the Founder's death was Col. Sgt. Arthur J. Reid, the 'number one boy in the 1st Glasgow Company'. Arthur was the first boy in the Brigade to gain the King's Badge but his memories of **1914** revolve around the death of Smith. He accompanied the funeral cortege through the packed streets of Glasgow and some sixty years later, he recalled the loss:

'...simply and vividly -
I cried bitterly' [6]

Arthur died at the end of May **1985** after a long and adventurous life. He served in France during the First World War with the 5th Scottish Rifles (the latter title of the 1st Lanarkshire Rifle Volunteers). His work on rubber plantations in Malaya at the start of the Second World War led to over three years in the infamous Changi Jail. Upon returning to Scotland he maintained an interest in the BB, but following the death of his wife in **1977** he went to live with his son in New Zealand.Soon he was actively involved with the local BB there and was appointed Patron of the Companies in the Bay of Plenty area.

Within a few weeks of the Founder's death the world was plunged into the First World War. What should have been a momentous, joyous occasion for the Brigade, the first award of its premier badge, sanctioned by the King, was overshadowed and engulfed by doom and gloom. Even the 1st Glasgow Company when it produced the anniversary book in **1933** looking back over fifty years failed to mention Arthur Reid's King's Badge, or indeed, any others. It was as if they wanted to forget that **1914** had happened.[7]

Minutes which may have recorded the first recipients of the King's Badge were destroyed by bombing in the 2nd World War. The badges

were issued simultaneously by London and Glasgow so it is virtually impossible to be certain who gained the first award.

Mr Arthur Reid, who became the first BB 'Kingsman' in 1914
Pictured with the 2nd Tauranga Coy. New Zealand in 1981. Arthur is wearing a King's Badge.

Various claims have been made to refute Arthur Reid's position as the original 'Kingsman'; notably: Sgt. Frank Edmund Sturch of 1st Warley who received his award on May 18th **1914**. [8] However, Col. Sgt. Reid wore his badge at the Founder's Funeral on <u>16th</u> May **1914**. (see photo. page 70) Arguments revolve around whether the date was when the boy qualified for, or was presented with the badge. Such a dispute broke out in Glasgow between those who thought Reid's badge to be the first and others who favoured Norman Smith of the 19th Coy. [9] Over in Scotland's Capital there were other claimants as specified in the Edinburgh Battalion 28th Annual report:-

'...Early in the Session it (The King's Badge) *was gained by Band-Sergt. Donald Mc Kay Gordon 12th Edinburgh (St John's Episcopal Church) Company and Col -Sergt. Ernest R. Cooper, 15th Edinburgh (Lady Glenorchy's U. F. Church) Company. Others have gained this distinction.'* [10]

It probably all comes down to which company held its annual display and presentation first that year.

To be a holder of the King's Badge was a great honour. Kingsmen were regarded as having reached the peak of proficiency and efficiency within the Brigade. For this reason, in **1935,** when the Brigade decided to commemorate the King's Jubilee, it turned to holders of the badge to provide the main elements of a great 'Jubilee Run' in which thousands of boys participated in a carefully synchronised series of five 'marathon' runs from each part of the UK to finish at the Jubilee Display in the Royal Albert Hall London. King's Badge holders carried copies of a message to the King which were delivered personally to the Duke of York at the display on 16th May **1935**. The

HM King George VI reviews the BB at Windsor Castle, October 1943.
Photo: Central Press Photos

whole run was a triumph of organisation and publicity for the Brigade. [11]

During the decades of the twenties, thirties and forties the King's Badge was unsurpassed as the premier award in the BB on a worldwide basis. The Kings changed (King George V, King Edward VIII and King George VI) but the badge hardly changed at all. The only change in design during this period was the addition of the BLB Geneva Cross behind the anchor in **1927**. The BLB didn't have an equivalent badge, the nearest being the 'First Class Badge.'[12]

Naturally, with the death of King George VI on February 6th **1952** and the accession of Queen Elizabeth II there was a need for a name change. The BB Gazette of August **1952** announced the change:

'... after this Session the Badge will be known as the Queen's Badge.' [13]

The new Queen's Badge was issued complete with name change but, mysteriously, without a change in the crown. A prototype Queen's Badge with a Queen's

Crown does exist but it seems to be a 'one-off' of uncertain date. All the issued Queen's Badges have King's Crowns. Needless to say the 'incorrect' crown was noticed, one indignant S/Sgt wrote to Stedfast Magazine:

'Sir,- when I received my Queen's Badge, I found that the Crown on the top is not her Crown, but the Crown that was used on the King's Badge. Yet the correct Crown was issued on the Coronation Buttonhole Badges. This should be rectified as soon as possible. S/Sgt. David T. Youngson, 18th Hull Coy.' [14]

The Crown remained unchanged. Perhaps this was due to the costs involved at a time when cash was short. During the **1950s** the badge seemed to retain its popularity despite the introduction of The Duke of Edinburgh's Award which seems to have had little effect upon it. One company, the 182nd Glasgow, was able to boast 18 holders of the Queen's Badge in the Company at the same time! [15]

A Queen's Badge presentation was, and is, always a special occasion. Often the badge is presented by the principal guest at a company

Annual Inspection and this was frequently a local newsworthy event. L/Cpl. Tom Carey of 2nd Kilwinning Coy. was unable to attend the annual inspection to receive his Queen's Badge, owing to a football injury. The Inspecting Officer took the badge to Tom's house to present it in person. Due to the usual post-inspection formalities it was 11.15 p.m. before he arrived! [16] Stedfast Magazine during the **1950s** and **1960s** was full of extraordinary Queen's Badge presentations, such as the Mayor or Deputy Mayor of a Town presenting the badge to his or her own son.

The late **1950s** and **1960s** saw much change taking place in the BB Worldwide. The Queen's Badge, like much of the UK awards system, had been used in many countries, but now many wanted to 'do their own thing'. This situation mirrored what was happening politically with the change from British Empire to Commonwealth. Australia introduced a miniature Queen's Badge for wear out of uniform on the lapel, an introduction which would not happen in the UK until halfway through the **1970s.**

In **1962**, for countries not in the Commonwealth, such as The Republic Of Ireland, a new 'Founder's Badge' was instituted to be issued in place of the Queen's Badge under the same regulations. This would become a truly international badge. There is a miniature version which was, for a time, used in Ireland.

The introduction of a new Awards Structure for **1969** was announced in June **1968** and required that there would be a change in the design of the Queen's badge to bring it into line with the new 'barrel-shaped' awards. The new badges would be introduced gradually over two years, with the change-over period ending on 31st August **1970.** Like most primadonna's the Queen's Badge proved to

THE BOYS' BRIGADE

THREE WAYS TO QUALIFY FOR
THE QUEEN'S BADGE

6 BADGES

N.C.O.'s Proficiency Certificate

Badge Badge Badge Badge Badge

THE APPLICANT MUST: A
(1) Be of 16 B.B. age or more and be recommended by his Company Captain as suitable.
(2) He must have at least 90% attendance for each of three Sessions of at least 25 consecutive Drill Parades.
(3) He must have at least 90% attendance for each of the same three Sessions of at least 25 consecutive Bible Class Meetings.
(4) IN ADDITION TO THE N.C.O's PROFICIENCY CERTIFICATE HE MUST HAVE AT LEAST SIX OF THE BADGES LISTED AT THE FOOT OF THIS CHART.

5 BADGES

Advanced Certificate
Advanced Certificate

Badge Badge Badge Badge Badge

N.C.O.'s Proficiency Certificate

THE APPLICANT MUST:
(1)
(2) } AS IN A
(3)
(4) IN ADDITION TO THE N.C.O's PROFICIENCY CERTIFICATE HE MUST HAVE AT LEAST FIVE OF THE BADGES LISTED BELOW PLUS TWO ADVANCED CERTIFICATES IN THE SAME OR DIFFERENT SUBJECTS.

4 BADGES

Advanced Certificate
Advanced Certificate
Advanced Certificate
Advanced Certificate

Badge Badge Badge Badge

N.C.O.'s Proficiency Certificate

THE APPLICANT MUST:
(1)
(2) } AS IN A
(3)
(4) IN ADDITION TO THE N.C.O's PROFICIENCY CERTIFICATE HE MUST HAVE ANY FOUR OF THE BADGES LISTED BELOW PLUS FOUR ADVANCED CERTIFICATES IN THE SAME OR DIFFERENT SUBJECTS.

SUBJECTS FOR WHICH BADGES ARE AWARDED

BOY'S AGES ARE RECKONED AS THAT WHICH THEY ATTAIN BY 31st. MAY

| ARTS & CRAFTS | ATHLETES | BAND, ETC. | CAMPERS | CITIZENSHIP | FIREMAN'S | FIRST AID | LIFE SAVING | PHYSICAL TRAINING | SCRIPTURE KNOWLEDGE | SEAMANSHIP | SIGNALLERS | SWIMMING | WAYFARERS |

Published by the Headquarters of The Boys' Brigade.

Printed in Great Britain.

be awkward and late.[17] For some reason there was a rush on the old awards and this caused supply problems. In **1968**, England, Wales and Ireland sales of the badge had been 888, but, in **1969,** the number more than doubled to 1,740. [18]

Perhaps the idea of a new-style badge was not so attractive to the boys working for the award. The new barrel-shape was rather minimalist in style and finished in mauve enamel. It had, for the first time, no BB emblem or motto. The finish was one of the reasons why the new badge was so late being produced. The Activities and Training Committee was still approving prototypes as late as February **1969**.

'New Queen's Badge.
(a) Approved a new prototype in gold on purple, and suggested that a permanent gold finish should be put on the badge, even if an additional cost was found to be necessary.'[19]

(Note: The original 'silvered' prototype was rejected and the policy of the Queen's Badge being gold, and the President's silver, adopted. This would continue with the new badges introduced in **1994**.)

In addition to the Queen's Badge a new 'President's Badge' was introduced as part of the **1968** scheme. The idea seems to be mentioned first in the minutes of the Coy. Section Activities Sub-Committee in **1967**:

'President's Award. To be gained by a Boy at about age 15 or 16 who qualifies according to regulations similar to the present Queen's Badge requirements.'[20]

Although this new award was intended to be a kind of 'step-up' to the award of the Queen's Badge, the minutes clearly show that it was a way of making the Queen's Badge more difficult since much of its remit was similar to the former Queen's Badge regulations. It was

of a similar shape and design, but slightly smaller than its big sister and also worn on the left arm. The introduction of this extra tier was to act as an incentive for boys to work toward the Queen's Badge.

In **1956,** the BB Badges Sub-Committee was approached by the Gateshead Battalion, who proposed that:

'...a Boy who gains the Queen's Badge should be entitled to wear a buttonhole replica.'

This was not recommended by the Committee. However, the idea was not forgotten. Some eleven years later in **1967** the Coy. Section Activities Sub - Committee agreed to recommend the following:

'(g) a special buttonhole badge should be available for holders of the new Queens Award.' [21]

This was followed by the recommendation being taken up by the Training Committee in February **1968**. [22]

The Meeting of the Brigade Executive in York over 16th/17th May **1970** made a number of decisions regarding uniform including the ratification for introduction of a lapel badge for Queensmen. A design was approved but the Authority of Her Majesty the Queen, as Royal Patron, was required. It was not introduced until **1974**, seven years after it had been first officially recommended. Even then, it was delayed due to manufacturing problems.[23]

The official intimation of the new Miniature Queen's Badge was published in the BB Gazette of April/May **1974**. It would be available *'later this month'* costing just 25p. Unfortunately, this triggered off a mass request from Queen's Badge holders of yesteryear...

'The Miniature of the Queen's Badge, announced in the last issue, is available only to those who have gained the present Queen's Badge and cannot be worn by Boys or Officers who gained previous Queen's of King's Badges. The new miniature is in fact a small replica of the present design, and is linked with the present Regulations which are very different to those applying in earlier years.'[24]

The President's Badge had only been in existence for two years before it too was the subject of a request for a miniature to the Activities and Training Committee.

'29. President's Badge. On consideration of a request from Glasgow Battalion for the production of another buttonhole badge for Boys who gain the President's Badge,
(29) The Committee: Recommended that no further special buttonhole badges should be produced.'[25]

Finally, in **1980,** a lapel version of the President's Badge was produced, a wait, this time, of only ten years.

The new awards of President's and Queen's Badges, in danger of being devalued, were given support, literally, with the introduction, in **1971**, of 'stands' upon which to display them when not being worn. Pictures of these plastic appendages appeared in Stedfast Mag..[26]

Throughout the lifetime of the 'barrel -shaped' Queen's Badges there seems to have been supply problems. The Badge makers were changed: Dowler, London Badge and Button, Toye Kenning, and

Badges Plus. In May **1974**, for instance, the total stock of Queen's Badges in BB Supplies was just 29! Sales in **73/74** had been 304. At the same time there were 810 President's Badges in stock with sales **73/74** having been 838.[27] An apology mentioning safety regulations, enamels and lead content was printed in the Gazette. It stated that it was proving

'...almost impossible to find a substitute of the required quality for this badge...'[28]

The Supplies Sub-Committee at its meeting in February **1980** noted further problems with the Queen's Badge:

'8. AOB. 8(a) The Queen's Badge. The Committee noted that our makers are experiencing problems in obtaining a matching enamel for the Queen's Badge. Health and Safety regulations controlling the lead content of enamels have severely restricted the range of colours available to the industry. The Committee examined samples of alternative choices of colour and finish and agreed that the matter should be referred to the Activities Committee.'[29]

We are told by Mr Bert Hoey, Supplies Officer at the time, that the samples produced here were the very light pink variety. They were accepted, but did not find much favour with the Executive.

In **1983,** the 'Activity Awards' were introduced to replace the proficiency 'barrels'. However, some of the left arm 'barrels' remained, including the Queen's and President's Badges.

The first edition of the Activity Awards was produced with a 'bubble' finish in cold epoxy resin. Decal types appeared in **1984.** The Queen's and President's Badges now looked out of place and the colour had been less than satisfactory. New types of both President's and Queen's Badges were pro-

B. J. Fearnley Photography

H.M. The Queen presents Queen's Badges at Windsor, 30th April 1994.

duced with a similar 'bubble' finish so that they would resemble the new activity badges, eventually using decals under the clear epoxy resin.[30]

Eighty years after the first King's Badge, in **1994**, two completely redesigned models were unveiled, the new Queen's and President's Badges. In many ways the design was retrogressive, but no less acceptable for that, it being the clear intent of the designer Stephen Lane.[31] The new badges were issued with their own miniatures for mufti wear. The BB emblem was back and the badges fully enamelled with a frosted finish on the metal, the Queen's Badge gilt and the President's Badge silver.

The first nineteen of the newly designed Queen's Badges were presented personally by H. M. The Queen, at the Windsor Royal Review on 30th April **1994,** to one Queen's man from each BB District. [32]

REFERENCES

1. BB Gazette, Vol.XXII, No 1, 1.9.1913. p.2. BB Scottish HQ, Carronvale.
2. ibid., No. 2, 1.10.1913. p.18.
3. ibid., No. 7, 1..3.1914. p.98.
4. The Boys' Brigade Manual. 1914. pp 49 - 50.
5. Springhall, J. et al, Sure & Stedfast, 1983. p.105.
6. ibid., and quoted from taped interviews BB HQ. London. Also, Stedfast Mag. No. 40. Jan. 1957.
7. This omission was corrected in the Company book issued for the Centenary in 1983.
8. D. Bailes, 1st Warley Coy, Letter to Stedfast Mag. No. 42. March 1957.
9. Shaw, J. Berend, The Glasgow Battalion of The Boys' Brigade, 1983. p. 42.
10. Edinburgh Battalion, 28th Annual Report, 1913 - 1914, p.27. Edinburgh Batt. Archive.
11. Springhall, J. et al, op.cit. p. 142.
12. The BLB. The Boys' Manual, revised edition 1926. pp 24 - 25. BLB HQ, 56, Old Bailey London. EC4.
13. BB Gazette, Vol'LX, No 6, August 1952. p.98. Mitchell Lib Glasgow.
14. Stedfast Mag. January 1958.
15. ibid. January 1957
16. ibid. June, 1957.
17. BB Gazette, August 1968. p.157.
18. ibid. June 1969 p.105.
19. Activities & Training Committee Minutes AT/M/(69)1 15/2/69
20. Coy. Section Activities Sub Committee Minutes. CA/M/(67)3, 22/7/1967.
21. ibid. CA/M (67)4, 14/10/67 item 54.
22. Activities & Training Committee Minutes. AT/M/(68)1 24/2/68. item 8.
23. BB Gazette, Aug/Sept 1974. p 107.
24. ibid. June/July p 90.
25. op.cit.. AT/M (70) 3. 21/11/70.
26. Stedfast Mag. No 212, April 1971. p.2.
27. BB Supplies Stock Lists May 1974. BB Archive, Felden.
28. BB Gazette, op.cit. 23 above.
29. BB. Supplies Sub-Committee. Minutes. Feb. 1980. p 2. BB Archive.
30. Advertised in BBBC Newsletter. July 1984.
31. Stephen Lane, Lt. 1st New Barnet Coy. Was at the time a London representative on the Brigade Executive and BB Archivist.
32. The Boys' Brigade, Royal Review 1994 Commemorative Brochure.

The King's Badge

1914 - 1926

BB 056

BB 056 BACKGROUND NOTES:

The King's Badge was the largest nickel badge ever to be issued by the BB. There appears to be no variations on the obverse of the badge but it is sometimes very difficult to compare pristine frosted badges with ones which are worn because the eye can perceive the frosted version details as being slightly larger in size. There are various different impressings on the reverse but all the versions have the axle pin fitting with a round catch.

1927 - 1953

BB 057.02

BB 057.05

BB 057.11

BB 057 BACKGROUND NOTES

Naturally, because of the lengthy period of issue there are many varieties of this badge, mainly in the size and style of the ribbon lettering. Some of the varieties are illustrated above. Variations occur in the anchor and letter 'B's. Remarkably, there are few differences in the crown. Some of the badges seem never to have been frosted. Officially, the BB ceased the use of this finish during the life of this edition of the badge. Earliest types have an axle pin but most are found with the standard tube joint and round catch. There is some impressing on the reverse. A chrome, shell-stamped version exists with a standard tube joint and FRC.

The Queen's Badge

1953 - 1968

PROTOTYPE

BB 058   **BB 058**

BB 058 BACKGROUND NOTES

In spite of a relatively short period of issue there are more versions of this badge than either of its predecessors. This is due to the Brigade policy in the post-war years, of purchasing smaller batches of badges in order not to tie up funds in stock sitting on the supply department's shelves. There is variation in the size and style of lettering and emblem, the crown and associated piercing, background stipple and base decoration. On the reverse, there is a large variation in the impressing, joints and catches. One version has a Miller logo and some have completely flat backs making each piece extremely thick and heavy. One badge, possibly a prototype; although it was bought on the open market, has a Queen's crown rather than the King's crown.

1968 - 1984   1984 - 1994

PROTOTYPE

BB 059.01   **BB 059.04**   **BB 059.03**   **BB 059.13**   **BB 059.14**

BB 156.01   **BB 156.09**

The Queen's Badge   Continued

BB 059 & BB 156 BACKGROUND NOTES

The first badges produced were fully enamelled with gilt metal. The example on the left above in silver/chrome finish is a prototype which was not issued. Over the years there was considerable variation in the colour from virtually pink to positively purple. There are variations in the size of the 'B's and the shape of the crown as well as a number of reverse types. The miniature pictured here is enamelled purple as were all before 1984 but there are several variations.

When the Activity awards, introduced in 1983, were changed in 1984 to 'bubble' finish. ie. cold epoxy resin, or clear 'Cold enamel', the Queen's Badge was changed in order to help it fit in with the new awards. No longer were the badges fully enamelled, but printed decals coated with resin. The colour was described as magenta although there was, as can be seen above, much variation. These badges were produced by Badges Plus, Birmingham. The miniature, from 1984, was red enamelled with epoxy coating. All the miniatures have clutch - pin fastenings.

1994 -

PROTOTYPE

BB 060   BB 157.01

BB 060 & BB 157 BACKGROUND NOTES

Messrs. Badges Plus produced these all-new, copper, gilt enamelled badges. The prototypes were not pierced in the crown area and had stippling in the ribbon which was mistakenly enamelled at one stage. The selected version has red and blue enamel in the centre area and a smooth ribbon. The latest version, to be released 2000/2001, will have a bar-brooch fastening on the reverse. The miniature is similarly enamelled but bears the hallmarks of the prototype with a solid crown and stippled ribbon. It has a clutch-pin fastening.

The Founder's Badge

1962 - 1993

BB 063.02   **BB 063.03**   **BB 063.04**   **BB 063.06**

BB 063 & BB 158 BACKGROUND NOTES

As can be seen quite clearly above the major variation in these badges is in the colour, i.e. various shades of bronze and even silver-grey.. On closer inspection of the obverse many other differences become clear notably the variation in the features of Smith's face and particularly the style of his hair.. The lettering around the ribbon varies in style and notably the caption 'Sir William A. Smith' varies in size, being particularly small in the example second from the left above. The second from the left above also shows a variation in Smith's Glengarry, having a narrower band. A Miniature of this badge, produced in 1962, was used for a short time in The Republic of Ireland. In 1993, the latest version was produced with the word 'Steadfast' on the anchor and not 'Stedfast' as on the earlier types. Smith's chin is a little more rounded than on the other types and the rest of the obverse varies in many of the same ways as on the others.

1962 -   **1993 -**

BB 158.01

BB 063.07

The President's Badge

1968 - 1984

1984 - 1994

BB 061.07

BB 061.04

PROTOTYPE

BB 061.03

BB 061.19

BB 154.01

BB 154.04

BB 061 & BB 154 BACKGROUND NOTES

The variations found in this badge lie in three main areas. Firstly, the finish which was originally in chrome with blue and red enamelling; the blue and red colours vary considerably. In 1984, the badge was issued with a 'bubble' finish - an epoxy resin dome. Many of these epoxy domed badges had a paper decal under the resin rather than enamel. One version of the bubble finish is almost green rather than the required blue, a discolouration caused by pouring on the epoxy resin too-hot in the manufacturing stage. Secondly, the emblem and wording varies in size, style and position. Two batches had the word 'steadfast' rather than 'stedfast', the light blue batch being retained by BB Supplies when they became aware of the mistake. Thirdly, the reverse of the badge has a variety of makers' names, pins and catch types. The prototype produced by Miller (see above) is very dark blue bearing little resemblance to the brighter blue of the subsequent issue.

The miniatures display a great deal of variation in finish, colour and makers' names, similar to their larger counterparts. All miniatures have clutch-pin fastenings.

1994 -

BB 062

BB 155.01

PROTOTYPE

BB 062 & BB 155 BACKGROUND NOTES

After only five years or so, several batches of this nickel-plated, enamelled brooch had been produced. The blue colour of the enamel varies from batch to batch but the greatest difference is that after the first batch the motto on the anchor was changed from being raised to being recessed. This change was to assist in the manufacturing process, no longer requiring the lettering to be polished as on the Queen's Badge. The lack of a crown on the badge to hold, made hand-polishing very difficult. The latest version to be issued has a bar-brooch fastening on the reverse. The miniature is almost identical to the large badge except that there is stippling in the ribbon as in the early prototypes. The miniature has a clutch-pin fastening.

The Duke of Edinburgh's Award Badges

The Duke of Edinburgh's Award came into operation in 1956 and was immediately taken up by the Boys' Brigade which became one of the 'Experimenting Authorities'.[1] From 1958, unlike the other Brigades, the BB issued its own metal uniform versions of the Silver and Gold Awards. The application to do so must have been made at the Badges Committee meeting on 23rd February 1957 since the next meeting refers to it under 'matters arising'. [2] At that meeting there was a feeling that even though demand would not be high initially, the buttonhole badge would not be appropriate. The Committee

'...reaffirmed their view that a special badge be cast of a size and design to conform with our present badges, the badge to take the form of the Duke of Edinburgh's Cypher. It was further agreed that for the Gold Standard badge [it] would be worn with a yellow [gold] cloth background shield.' [3]

At the next meeting decisions were made as to the design of the badge.

'Three designs were submitted, and the Committee were unanimous in selecting No 2.' [4]

It was twelve months later, in November 1958 when the official 'mufti' bronze buttonhole badge became available, but the Badge Committee decided not to turn it into a BB uniform badge when it resolved...

'...that the Brigade should not cast a special arm badge.' [5]

Details of the new design for the Silver and Gold Award Badges were given in the April 1958 BB Gazette.

'...in order that a BB Boy gaining the award for the Second and Third Series may wear his Silver or Gold award in uniform, a special design incorporating the Award Badge has been cast [similar to other BB Badges] which will be worn... these Special Badges may be purchased from the Brigade Offices (price 3/-)' [6]

The first two BB members to gain the Gold standard, according to the BB Gazette, were Sgt's Ronald Gray & Lindsay Smith of the 1st Lerwick Coy. [7] It was to be twenty five years before the Bronze Award was eventually converted into a BB uniform badge, when it was included in the new 1983 Regulations. [8]

Unique in its use by institutions and organisations throughout the UK, the question needs to be asked: 'Where did this badge come from ?' or, perhaps more pertinently, from where did The Duke of Edinburgh get the idea ? The answer makes interesting reading and lies in a series of documents to be found in the Public Record Office.[9] The correspondence and literature contained in these boxes relate to the wartime years 1940-1942 and spring mainly from the penetrating influence of Mr Kurt Hahn.

The Experiment

Between 1919 and 1933 Kurt Hahn was Headmaster of the Salem School in Germany, founded by Prince Max of Baden. At the school Hahn based his training on all that seemed to him to be best in the English Public School system. He devised a method of training that would turn a...

'...soft-boned and malnourished post-war generation...'

...into all-round athletes. His school became well known by winning the public schools challenge cup at the White City. With the rise of National Socialism he fled to Britain and set up a boarding school for boys at Gordonstoun in Morayshire. From 1940, for the duration of the war, the school was evacuated to Plas Dinam in Wales. It was, however, at Gordonstoun from 1934 -1939 that Hahn developed his 'experimental scheme' which was to become known as the 'County Badge Scheme', a system aimed at improving the physical training and well-being of boys while at the same time seeking to develop 'character'. An essential part of the scheme was the attainment of set standards. An 'ordinary' badge was awarded for standards within the reach of normal boys and a 'silver' badge for exceptional prowess. The eventual programme was divided into four sections bearing a remarkable similarity to the later D.of E. awards. The sections were: 1. A Physical Test, 2. A Project Test, 3. An Expedition Test and 4. Service Conditions. Initially known as the 'Moray' badge, the scheme, along with the facilities of the school, was thrown open to the rest of the

'County',which was certainly a bold and innovative move.

National Pretensions

Hahn was full of enthusiasm for his 'County' Badge and wanted it to be introduced more widely. To give the badge a 'push' he wrote to 'The Times' in **1938** which published a long letter outlining his 'experiment'. Much interest was generated and he began to push further for the adoption of the badge on a national scale. For Hahn it was becoming something of an obsession; to set right the training of British youth. The badge, he suggested, should be made an essential element of the School Certificate and membership of the voluntary youth organisations might be conditional on taking the badge! Upon the outbreak of war the President of the Board of Education was approached with a view to initiating this scheme for training boys in large numbers as a contribution to the war effort. The whole scheme could, he surmised, be brought under Royal patronage. Naturally, a good deal of cash would be needed to support a scheme involving most of the nation's public schools. However, Hahn didn't get very far with this idea as the Board didn't like his idea of a national pre-military training scheme. Influential supporters, including members of the House of Lords and House of Commons and others, writing in the Times Educational Supplement, ventured to question the attitude of the Voluntary Juvenile Organisations. The autocratic Hahn accused those who failed to support him of 'fiddling with fitness'. In order to implement Hahn's ideas a 'County Badge Experimental Committee' was formed, consisting of University Dons, Public School Heads and other luminaries under the chairmanship of Dr. A.D.Lindsay LLD, Master of Balliol College, Oxford.

**Crossing a River.
A Planned pusuit.**
2nd Gateshead Coy. 1962
Photo: BB Archive.

Sour Pastures, or Sour Grapes ?

The Standing Conference of National Juvenile Organisations including the BB, Scouts and CLB, (which was used to working in conjunction with the Board of Education through the National Youth Committee) was, by **1940,** becoming 'nervous & restive' in response to suggestions relating to the 'County Badge' and its implications. It was, of course, concerned that the Government wished to form a secular National Training Movement which would wipe

them out, perhaps along the lines of the 'Hitler Jugend'. The matter was brought to a head when the Master of Balliol wrote an inflamatory letter to 'The Times' challenging the youth organisations to meet his committee. R.S.Wood, working for the Board of Education brought the parties face to face at a Special Weekend Conference on 11th & 12th January **1941** at Balliol College. Kurt Hahn was present, but his presence only helped to alienate both Wood and the Voluntary Organisations. Hahn's rhetoric was all about, *'purging the poisonous passions'* and *'removing frustration'*. His stated thesis was: *'The pasture of the modern young is sour'* and the *'County Badge'* was a method of healing. Wood was not impressed, as his comments in a later report on Hahn to R.A.Butler the President of the Board of Education seem to indicate:

'...there are some who think that such talk is itself rather poisonous.'

A degree of compromise seems to have been shown, however, by the issue of a joint statement of conclusions regarding the experiment. The answer would be for the County Badge Experimental Committee to produce, as soon as possible, a pamphlet outlining the content of the scheme. In response, on the 14th of January, the Secretary of the Committee rushed through some notes for the National Youth Committee at the Board of Education, but they were not regarded as being sufficient. The requested pamphlet did not appear. Mr Hahn had apparently attempted to write a pamphlet, but, according to R.S.Wood,

'his production was so terrible that it was suppressed at proof stage.'

Seven months later there was still nothing produced by Hahn's Badge Committee.

The Judgement of Archangels...

On January 22nd **1941**, the National Youth Committee, set up by the Board of Education, received details of the badges awarded by members of the Standing Conference of National Juvenile Organisations. [10] A special Badge Sub-Committee with Lord Aberdare as Chairman, collected information throughout **1941** by setting up and distributing a Questionnaire about a possible 'national scheme' similar to Hahn's proposals. Members of this Commitee included Mr. P.B.Nevill Gen. Sec. The Boy Scouts' Association, Mr A.W. Oyler OBE, Church Lads' Brigade, and Mr Stanley Smith OBE, MC, Boys' Brigade Secretary. Submissions made in addition to the questionnaire, were sometimes long and detailed. The Young Farmers Clubs, for instance, sent in details of their use of 'Record Books' and Wales wanted to run its own scheme. The BB thought that a national scheme was unlikely to succeed. The Rev. Harold Peerless, Secretary of the CLB, stated that if 'Character' came into the proposed national scheme:

'it will require Archangels to Judge.'

He went on to say that there should be no element of compulsion as this seemed to imply 'shades of Hitler'. By the end of the year, in its 'Draft Interim Report' the Sub-Committee had come to a decision; there woud be no national scheme. It summarised its reasons for rejecting it:

1 It would not be fair to all youth because facilities were variable.
2 It should be 'Character' training, but there was an undue emphasis on the physical side.
3 It would be difficult to evolve a satisfactory scheme for non-uniformed organisations.
4 Standardisation of training would destroy the distinctive character of the participating organisations.
5 There would be no appeal to over 17 yr olds.
6 There was no clear need beyond existing schemes.

Additionally, there was the possibility of the Government 'recognising' voluntary youth organisations as 'efficient'.

R.A.B.'s rebuttal

Towards the end of **1941** it was becoming clear that Hahn's County Badge Scheme was doomed. In July, R.S.Wood's memorandum to R.A.Butler had emphasised the 'alien' nature of Hahn's ideas and his apparent incompetence. The memorandum mentioned the similarity between Hahn's scheme and the Hitler Youth Movement. The element of 'service', it implied, had only been included in the scheme to placate the voluntary organisations and had been taken from the Board's own circulars! Wood's memorandum introduced the 'few' merits and possibilities of the Scheme using a most sarcastic tone and drawing upon Hahn's own extreme language. In a parody of Hahn, Wood stated:

'I have endeavoured to purge my bosom of the poisonous passions of prejudice'..

...but he obviously hadn't ! A number of additional points were made by Wood which emphasised the unsuitability of Hahn's scheme and concluded with the phrase:

'I believe there are grave doubts about ideas which have to be pressed with the almost brutal persistence which is characteristic of Mr. Kurt Hahn and his supporters.'

It was now only a formality, for the National Youth Committee, endorsed by R.A.B. and the Board of Education to reject the national scheme. The Board stated that since the Youth service was undergoing growth and experiment, the time was 'inopportune.' It could quite easily have added' ...and there's a war on.'

The National Scheme is dead... long live the National Scheme!

In December **1941,** the Government ruled that all 16-19 - year olds must register with their Local Authority so they could be given advice about joining suitable organisations. Any idea of introducing a new National Scheme had been abandoned. On 3rd February **1942,** R.A.Butler wrote to The Rt. Hon. Sir John Anderson at the Privy Council Office effectively closing the County Badge debate. His words sum up the thinking at the time:

'We believe there is a real value in Hahn's ideas and standards, but I do not think the scheme can make any very effective contribution to our Registration plans. It does not stand for any organisation which young people can be encouraged to join, though it does offer a layout for valuable training which existing organisations, or new ones if formed, might adopt.'

Kurt Hahn's scheme had already influenced the start of the 'Outward Bound' movement in **1941**, but immediately post-war there was little scope for 'youth outdoor pursuits' in the context of 'Austerity Britain'. The end of compulsory National Service in **1960,** opened up a 'gap' in youth provision for school leavers which the new Youth Service was designed to fill. That same modern Youth Service would, ironically, be receptive to Hahn's theories, which would work their way through the auspices of one of his first, and most famous pupils. Indeed, a former Gordonstoun student now occupied a position of much influence in British society and so there was an opportunity for Hahn to finally gain respect and credibility for his national scheme.

Phillip's Mentor

In **1933,** an 11 - year old Greek boy called Philip was sent to school in the old Salem nonastery at Baden in southern Germany, mainly to please his German mother. Instead of finding a thriving school, young Philip found himself in the midst of the Hitler Youth. The Headmaster, Hahn, a Jew, had been arrested and membership of the Hitler Youth was compulsory for all pupils except foreigners. Philip returned to Britain only to be followed by Hahn who had been released by the German authorities. In **1934,** Philip was amongst the first intake of 30 boys into Hahn's new school, Gordonstoun, near Elgin. After taking part in most of the physical pursuits and 'character building' programmes at the school, including the 'Moray/County' Badge, he became Head Boy, eventually leaving at the age of 17. Eight years later, just before his marriage to Princess Elizabeth, Philip was created Duke of Edinburgh, a title which remained with him in his role as Queen's Consort from **1952.** [11] Hahn had been one of the major influences in Philip's life, not to be forgotten. His son Charles was sent there although he didn't enjoy it. Phillip's 'Duke of Edinburgh's Award Scheme' was a wholesale copy of the County Badge Scheme complete with its levels and four sections. So-called innovative ideas such as the expedition, keeping a log-book, service to the community and, of course, 'character building', were all cribbed directly from the

Members of 76th Belfast (Cregagh) Coy. approaching Spelga Pass 1968.
Photo: Century Newspapers Ltd. BB Archive collection

County Badge scheme. Thus, the 'national scheme' which had seemed so threatening, so alien in the darkening 'National Socialist' days of the **1930s,** emerged into the real 'Brave New World' of the late **1950s** where it was received with interest and enthusiasm by youth leaders, many of whom had served in HM forces. In **1956,** the same year Bill Hayley's 'Rock around the clock' exploded on to the youth scene, the Duke of Edinburgh's Award Scheme was taken up by thousands of enthusiastic young people. Youth-work would never be the same again.

The first presentation, of eighteen Gold Award Badges and Certificates, by Prince Philip at Buckingham Palace, took place on 4th June **1958**. There were no Brigade recipients. It was decided, however, to hold a further Presentation in the Autumn there being a number of awards 'in the pipeline'. Prince Philip, by this time, had stated that he would like to continue presenting the awards personally. The date of 18th November **1958** was chosen for a further forty-nine presentations.

There were seven BB boys in this second palace presentation. On the 6th September, however, as part of the **1958** Brigade Council Meeting, H.M. The Queen reviewed 1,200 officers and 200 BB boys at Balmoral. On that occasion Her Majesty presented 18 Queen's Badges and Prince Philip 21 Duke of Edinburgh's Gold Awards.[12] Cpl. Kevin Roberts was the first CLB Lad to be presented with the Gold Award at the third presentation on May 22nd **1959**.[13]

REFERENCES

1. Carpenter, P. [Ed] Challenge, The Duke of Edinburgh's Award in action. Ward Lock 1966. p 19
2. Minutes of BB Badges Committee. 25/5/1957 para. 11 [c].
3. ibid.
4. Minutes of BB Badges Committee. 16/11/1957.
5. ibid. 15/11/1958
6. BB Gazette, Vol LXVI, No 4. April/May 1958 p 69.
7. ibid. No 5. June/July 1958 p 88.
8. BB Award Regulations [Company Section] 1983 pp 68-69.
9. Documents filed under ED 124/15 & ED 136/651, [Youth Welfare] Public Record Office, Kew.
10. Submissions included: 'The Use of Badges in the Boys' Brigade', The Boys' Brigade. 'Policy, Organisation and Rules" The Boy Scouts' Association. 'The Training & Efficiency Scheme', The Church Lads' Brigade.
11. Hamilton, Alan. The Royal Handbook, Mitchell Beazley, 1985. p 19.
12. BB Gazette op.cit., Vol LXVIII No 1 Oct/Nov 1958. p 9.
13. Some information in this final paragraph obtained from D of E Award Office, Windsor.

The Duke of Edinburgh's Award Badges

1958 -

BB 064.01

BB 064.04

BB 065.03

BB 065.06

1983 -

BB 066.01

BB 066.03

BB 064 065 & 066 BACKGROUND NOTES

The issued gilding metal part enamelled (BB 064) & (BB 065) and non-enamelled (BB 066) brooches are naturally distinguished by their colour. The Gold Award is gilt with white enamel, the Silver Award chrome with green enamel, and the Bronze Award all bronze finish with no enamel. One or two silver versions exist eg which have not been chrome plated but they were probably never issued. There are two main variations of the obverse; those with a simple border design eg: BB 064.01 and those with a more ornate design eg: BB 064.04. Fastenings on the badges are generally box joints with hooked catches and crook pins or standard tube joints with FRCs. The Bronze Award has only the standard tube joint. Makers' names appear on all three Awards with Miller and Toye Kenning & Spencer on the Gold and Silver and just Toye Kenning & Spencer on the Bronze Award. On the Bronze Award pins are mounted either vertically or horizontally.

c.1957

PROTOTYPE

A number of prototype D of E Badges were considered by the BB c.1957 and one is pictured left, which like the eventually adopted badges, makes use of the oval D of E emblem as produced on the mufti badges.

The Ambulance Badge

The story of the BB's first proficiency Badge.

Like the Boys' Brigade itself, the early history of the BB ambulance shield belongs to Glasgow.

`On a winter night in **1886** at the instigation of 9th (Wellington United Presbyterian Church, Cranstonhill Mission) a class was started for `First Aid to the injured'. The opening lecture, at which detatchments of other companies were present, was given in the hall of Wellington Church by Dr. J. MacGregor Robertson a well known West End General Practitioner who subsequently became an officer in the Company. At the end of the session the Boys were examined on behalf of the St. Andrew's Ambulance Association by Surgeon-Major J. E. Brodie, 3rd Volunteer Battalion, Highland Light Infantry.'*

(J. Berend Shaw)[1]

The earliest evidence of the wearing of an ambulance badge comes from a photograph of the 57th Glasgow Coy. hand - annotated as **1886**. The photograph is clearly from the **1880s** and does show a badge of the style later adopted by the Brigade.[2] (See photo. page 88)

The St. Andrew's Ambulance Association was brought in to examine the 9th Glasgow Company on 8th April **1887**. To those boys who passed, a certificate was issued.[3] The Captain of the Company, Mr. William Kidston (See photo. page 87), who was influential in the Battalion, decided

that the boys should be awarded a badge to wear with their uniform. Just ten days after the Ambulance Examination the matter was placed before the Battalion Executive where the minutes record:

`The Boys of the 9th Glasgow Company who have passed the St. Andrew's Ambulance Association's examination were provisionally permitted to wear the badge submitted, pending the consideration of the whole matter of Ambulance Corps of the Battalion Council'[4]

Kidston's badge was now recognised within the Battalion, but just what was this new badge and where did Capt. Kidston get his inspiration?

Surprisingly, the new badge was not based on that used by the army or volunteers, although it was most likely to have been cloth. Volunteer badges were usually made from silver wire whilst the regular army used gold wire. The cloth army Ambulance Badge (**1874 - 1878**) appeared in Clothing Regulations in **1881**. This badge was a Geneva Red Cross on a circular white background. The Geneva Red cross is made up of five equal sized squares (unlike the BB version) and the copyright is now owned by the Ministry of Defence. However, some other Brigades, such as the CBB and BLB adopted this style years later whilst others, such as the LDCLB, acknowledged from the start that the red cross was for use by the RAMC only.[5]

Almost certainly, Kidston's new badge came from the police. From about **1880** City of Glasgow policemen were permitted to wear a shield-shaped badge almost identical in respect of metal type, shape,

design and size to the one later adopted by the BB. The badge was worn on the right sleeve following the award of a First Aid Certificate. The badge was die-stamped with a cross indented and painted in red, having thinner arms than the Geneva Cross. The badges were of a sew-on type with two small holes made in each of the three corners. The initials `G P' were imprinted on the Glasgow Badges.

Forces such as Govan Burgh Police, Partick Burgh Police and Selkirk also adopted the design, but without initials. Examples are known with the initials `C R'.[6] This design continued to be used by Glasgow Police until about **1906** when a circular design with the wording: `St Andrew's Ambulance Association' was issued. First Aid Badges ceased to be worn by the Scottish Police in the **1930s**.[7]

The new BB badge could have been a brooch type for use with equipment, in which case the blank versions (with no letters) being the most likely. Because of the great cost of making a die it was even more likely, however, to have been a cloth badge which could be made in small numbers for a lower overall initial cost but a higher unit cost.

The scene was set for the gradual introduction into the BB nationally of an official ambulance badge; the first ever BB proficiency badge. In June **1887,** the Glasgow Battalion Council unanimously agreed to form an Ambulance Corps.[8] Further discussions took place on 4th August **1887** when it agreed to leave the issue to the next meeting.[9] That meeting decided to recommend to Council that an Ambulance Committee be formed:

`To control all ambulance work in connection with the Battalion...'. [10]

At the next meeting the Council agreed that the Committee would be elected at the Annual Meeting of the Council.[11] At the first meeting of the Glasgow Battalion Executive in **1888** the following was recorded:

`Ambulance Badge as submitted was approved of, and it was left to the Ambulance Committee to arrange as to price and making up.'[12]

The words *'making up'* would seem to signify that it was, indeed, a cloth badge which was being produced. Presumably, making up meant adding the elastic!

In the early years of the BB it was battalions which took the lead when it came to the award of badges. In Scotland, not surprisingly, it was usually a matter of what Glasgow did today the rest did tomorrow. Edinburgh, however, was not slow in taking up a good idea. In **1888,** the Battalion formed an Ambulance Committee and accepted assistance from the St. Andrew's Ambulance Association. [13] Unfortunately, by **1889,** a dispute arose about the conflicting requirements for the BB Badge and the St. Andrew's Certificate, causing an urgent re-think of strategy.

Naturally, it looked to Glasgow for a solution [14] and was not to be disappointed, although it was kept waiting. At the meeting in April the Ambulance Convener reported:

'...that 13 Boys in one class had just been examined and 12 of these had gained the Ambulance Badge. That a pattern for the Badge was daily expected from Glasgow and would be approved of as soon as possible.'

So, from **1889,** the Glasgow Battalion had their own Ambulance badge, probably supplied by the local firm of Messrs. Geo. Kenning. No doubt, this was the badge adopted by the whole Brigade in **1891**.

The BB Gazette in **1890** carried details of *'Ambulance Work in The Boys' Brigade'* and the article clearly indicates the Brigade approval of the awarding of a badge, when it states:

'On passing the examination, a Boy is entitled to wear a Special Ambulance Badge, when in uniform'[15]

Other battalions around the country were following the lead taken by Glasgow and Edinburgh. In the 1st Annual Report of the Belfast Battalion (**1890-1891**)Ambulance Badges are mentioned, as they are in the 2nd Annual Report of the Sheffield Battalion (**1890-1891**).[16] Edinburgh operated a system based on that of the Volunteers, ie. annual re-examination for the badge which remained Battalion property. A system of illuminated certificates was devised from **1889** onwards and boys could retain those. [17] It was the Glasgow system and badge, however, which was to be favoured by the Brigade.

The 8th BB Annual Report (**1891-1892**) states:

'...if they pass the necessary examination before the recognised Ambulance Association, they receive the certificate and badges which are now granted by the Ambulance Committees of the various Battalions.' [18]

Messrs. Kenning of Glasgow didn't waste any time. It advertised an Ambulance Badge in the Manual of **1891-1892** priced at ninepence-halfpenny. This was probably a woven badge since woven badges were the speciality of Kenning as evidenced by their advertisements for NCO's stripes and colours, etc. in all the early BB Manuals. It is unlikely that Kenning would have had time, or indeed have wished to completely re-design the Glasgow

Officers of the 9th & 32nd Glasgow Coy's at Struchur Camp, 1892.

Top left, Capt. Farmer (32nd Coy).

Mr William Kidston, (9th Coy), seated front right, introduced the BB's first proficiency badge, The Ambulance Badge.

Photo: John Cooper collection

57th Glasgow Coy. c.1887

The photograph above could be as early as 1886, however it is likely to be nearer 1887. The boy second from the right, middle row is clearly wearing an Ambulance Badge of the same size, shape and colour as the badge fist adopted by the Battalion (1889) and the Brigade (1891). Close inspection of the picture reveals the elastic band securing it around the boy's sleeve. (See inset detail)

Photo: Glasgow Battalion Archive.

badge and offer it for sale within a few weeks, so it was most probably the same badge, 'recycled'.

The evidence for an early cloth BB Ambulance Badge is quite compelling if we take into account the stated cost, the cloth-badge manufacturer who advertised it for sale and the use of a cloth-badge by the army. It should also be noted that the later Manual advert made particular pointed reference to the replacement badge being of metal. The fact that in **1889** the Edinburgh Battalion had awaited a pattern from Glasgow demonstrates clearly that it was not the army badge that was being used, but a specific BB design from Glasgow.

One such cloth badge does exist. It was found in Glasgow along with a metal Ambulance Badge. The badge is a machine woven design of the same size and shape as the later metal badge, which is, in turn

similar to the earlier police badge. The background shield is white with a red cross and red letter B's. The white shield is edged in blue. The badge is woven on to a black cloth base which has an elastic fastening enabling it to be worn on the sleeve. Needless to say, the rubber in the elastic has long since perished. It would seem that this could be the oldest official BB proficiency badge in the world![19] For any cloth badge to survive for this length of time is remarkable. The badge was in use in Glasgow from **1887/1888**, by Glasgow Battalion from **1889 - 1891** and by the Brigade as a whole from **1891 - 1893**. It is a sad fact that very few old cloth badges are still around, even 'mass-produced' uniform badges. To find only one remaining, after all these years is not surprising, but we cannot expect many more.

Ambulance work had really taken-

off in the Brigade after **1891** and the demand for badges was no doubt, great. However, many Companies would have found the cost of the cloth badges prohibitve. It was up to the Brigade to do something about this. On the 14th December **1892** the Glasgow Council reported:

'A specimen of the Brigade New Ambulance Badge was exhibited, and was universally admired, its price being Fourpence as against Nine and a half pence for that in present use.' [20]

The Badge was duly advertised in the BB Gazette on 1st January **1893**:

'The BB Ambulance Badge. In Burnished Metal, with Red Cross and letters BB, with pin complete for fastening on the arm. In ordering, give Name, Rank and Age of Boys and state what examination they have passed. This does not apply to Battalions ordering in quantity. Price as follows:- 6d each, carriage paid, for quantities

under one dozen. 5s per doz. carriage paid, for boxes of not less than one dozen. 48s per gross, carriage paid, in lots of not less than half gross.' [21]

The 9th BB Annual Report indicates clearly that official BB Badges were being awarded by **1892/1893**:

'Examinations under the auspices of the recognised Ambulance Associations are held at the close of the Course, and those Boys who are successful become the proud possessors of the new Brigade Badge.' [22]

It is now clear exactly how the unit cost of the new badge was more than halved. The Kenning cloth badge would have been expensive. Metal badges were cheaper to produce once the die had been made. The metal brooch version may also have been easier to produce than that with six holes for sewing and no doubt there was a saving to be made by using a blank already being produced for the police.

By the **1920s** the Ambulance Badge had established itself as one of the pre-eminent Brigade proficiency badges. Its size was larger than the subsequent proficiency awards (Life Saving, Buglers', Drummers', Pipers', Scouts', Signallers' and PT) which meant that it occupied a row on its own when worn on the armband. (See diagram page 155) However, ideas were changing. In **1923** a 8"x 11" Badge Card was advertised in the BB Gazette priced 2/6d. (post-card reproductions of the card were 9d per dozen.)[23] On the card the Ambulance Badge is quite clearly a smaller version and a different shield shape. It is likely that the Brigade Executive realised that with the number of proficiency badges increasing, a smaller badge would be appropriate when re-ordering from suppliers. Obviously, in **1923,** a sample of the new size was available and presumably stocks of the larger size were running low; we simply don't know.

The new badge was basically the five square Geneva Cross and its use was probably illegal, although widely used for Ambulance/First Aid related business. It may be simply coincidence that it appeared at approximately the same time as the BLB became united with the BB (The Red Geneva Cross was the emblem of the BLB).[24]

The **1925** Manual retained the large-sized badge, (see diagram p.155) but, by **1927**, after union with the BLB and an increase in the number of badges, the diagram shows the new small size and different shape (see diagram p. 156).

During its lifetime the Ambulance Badge, like many others, was awarded in conjunction with various certificates. A proposal from Nottingham Battalion, in **1925,** to add bars to the badge was rejected by the Brigade Executive.[25] The **1927** Regulations state that in the 1st Year a certificate would be awarded, followed by a badge in the 2nd Year. The 3rd Year would be followed by a red pocket certificate and the 4th Year by a blue pocket certificate. By **1933,** the addition of red and blue felt cloth shields under the badge became Regulation. Eighteen years later, in **1951,** a 5th Year pocket certificate was awarded and a white cloth shield worn behind the badge. (NB. only one cloth shield is worn) An official notification of a name change to **'First-Aid Badge'** came in **1956**:

'Ambulance Awards: In future the word 'Ambulance' will be superseded by 'First Aid' and all awards will be styled 'First-Aid' awards.' [26]

Within a further decade the use of coloured cloths had been dispensed with.

The ill-fated and much maligned barrel badges arrived in **1968**[27] and replaced all the metal proficiency badges. These were made from bronze-coloured anodised aluminium (see page 146) and brought with them the demise of the Red Cross symbol. The new First Aid Badge depicted a four-handed seat for the transport of injured persons. Perhaps it should have reverted to its former name 'Ambulance' Badge because this means literally 'to transport' someone. Three levels or 'stages' were available using silver and gold inserts to show the 2nd and 3rd stages.

In **1977,** these achromatic lack-lustre awards were changed to make them more 'attractive' by constructing the badge from 'high-density polystyrene' (plastic) and inserting a tawdry red coloured sticker to display the same four-handed motif. Many a BB Captain would be heard exclaiming apologetically at the Annual Company Awards Presentation that he had obtained this year's badges from the inside of breakfast cereal packets!

From 1st September **1983,** (obligatory by Sept. **1984**), a completely new badge scheme was introduced into the Brigade (See page 151). The twenty-four proficiency badges were reduced to five groups, with a single badge awarded for each: Leadership, Adventure, Community, Interests and Physical. First Aid was put into the 'Community' category as a qualification for the award of a new green 'TV'- shaped metal 'Activity' badge. Credits, in the form of foil stickers are now awarded for First Aid at three levels, grades 1, 2 and 3. When two Community Credits are earned the Badge is awarded, a further two Credits qualify for a red 'flash' to be worn behind the

The 4th Cheltenham Company at Camp in Weymouth 1911.
The boys are proudly showing off their Ambulance, Scouting, Signallers', Buglers' and Drummers' Badges. The Buglers' Badge is the old double-bugle cloth pattern obsolete since **1908**. The official BB Signallers' Badge, smaller than the one displayed here, was not sanctioned until the end of the year. It would be another ten years before an official drummer's badge was sanctioned.
The Sgt. is wearing the crossed muskets of a shooting badge, never officially adopted by the whole Brigade.

Badge with an additional Credit earning a blue 'flash'. Redolent of the earlier cloth backings, the red flash is circular plastic and the blue flash is eight-sided plastic. [28]

The introduction of the Ambulance Badge, just a few years after the formation of the BB, was indeed a bold move. A pattern was established for the whole of the next century. It started the BB journey on the long road towards the awarding of armfulls of badges, so diligently worked for and proudly displayed by senior boys. The period from the **1920s** to the **1960s** was truly the 'Golden Age' of Brigade badges. Its termination, in **1968,** signalled the dawn of a new age of cheap and disposable items which was not just confined to the Brigade. A time when the words 'quality' and 'British industry' were in no way synonymous.

To provide badges which were not only poorly produced, but somewhat understated in their size and colour was to fundamentally misunderstand the nature of the folk for whom they were intended, even in the **1960s.** For more than

seventy years many hundreds of uniformed BB boys, often captured for the first time by the photographers of the early part of the century, had peered from countless picture postcards, with arms turned just enough to display their only award, a big shiny Ambulance Badge.[29]
(See photograph, above, of 4th Cheltenham Coy.)

It had been something worth wearing. The barrel badges looked cheap when worn in quantity and diabolical on their own. Could anyone have said that about the doyen of Brigade proficiency badges ?

REFERENCES

1. Shaw, J. Berend , Glasgow Battalion, The Boys' Brigade 1883-1983. St Andrew Press, Edinburgh, 1983. p. 12.
2. Glasgow Battalion The Boys' Brigade, Archives. BB HQ Bath St., Glasgow. Copies in BB Archive Felden.
3. Records of St.Andrew's Ambulance Association. Milton St., Glasgow.
4. Glasgow Battalion Minute Book No.1. [1/1/1] Executive 18.4.1887. Glasgow Battn. HQ.
5. CBB = Catholic Boys' Brigade, BLB = Boys' Life Brigade, LDCLB = London Diocesan Church Lads' Brigade, RAMC= Royal Army Medical Corps.
6. Dinsmor, Alastair, PICA [GB] No 022, Strathclyde, Scotland. Strathclyde Police Museum.
7. ibid.
8. Glasgow Battalion Minute Book op.cit 9.6.1887.
9. ibid. 4.8.1887
10. ibid. 9.9.1887
11. ibid. 24.9.1887
12. ibid. 9.1.1888
13. Barclay, J.P.,'Pill Box & Service Cap' The first hundred years of the Edinburgh Battalion The Boys' Brigade, Edinburgh 1985, p.81.
14. Edinburgh Battalion Council Minutes, 3.4.1889,Edinburgh Battalion Archive.
15. BB Gazette, Vol 1. 1/1/1890. pp 80 - 81.
16. Bound Volumes of Battalion Annual Reports. 1886- Scotttish HQ Archives, Carronvale.
17. ibid., 6.11.1889 & 2.7.1889. Also BB Gazette Vol. V.1.1.1890 p.83.
18. 8th Annual Report p.57 BB Scottish HQ Archives.
19. Found in 'Barras' market, Glasgow 15.11.1998. R. Bolton collection.
20. Glasgow Battalion Minute Book op.cit. Council meeting 14.12.1892.
21. BB Gazette, Vol.II, 1.2.1893, p.203.
22. 9th Annual Report p.14, BB Scottish HQ.
23. BB Gazette, Vol.XXXI, 1.3.1923, p.96, Glasgow Battalion Archive.
24. The Red Cross emblem was used by the Girls' Life Brigade until 1935 when the Government asked them to replace it. The current BB emblem does not incorporate a whole red cross, but a cross bisected by an anchor.
25. Minutes of Brigade Executive 9-10.5.1925. Brigade Archives, BB HQ Felden Lodge. Herts.
26. BB Gazette, Vol. LXIV, No 6 August 1956, p.102.
27. The Boys' Brigade Award Regulations [Company Section] Sept. 1968. pub. March 1968. BB HQ.
28. The Boys' Brigade Award Regulations [Company Section] Sept.1983. BB HQ.
29. R. Bolton, Picture Postcard Collection.

The Ambulance Badge

1891-1893

BB 067

The original (cloth) BB Ambulance Badge

BB 067 BACKGROUND NOTES

This is a machine - made badge in the style typical of early Geo.Kenning badges. The back is sealed with glue. The badge has black elastic sewn to it of sufficient length enabling it to be worn on the sleeve, over a jacket.

1893 - c.1923

Alastair Dinsmor's,
International Police Collection.

Police Ambulance Badge used in Selkirk, in the late 19th Century.

Police Ambulance Badge used in Glasgow from c.1886.

BB 068.01

BB 068.05

BB 068   BACKGROUND NOTES

The gilding metal badge is found only in shell-stamped, brooch form, but there are a number of variations in terms of both overall shape and size as well as the colour of the metal/finish. All obverse features seem to vary: the border, the 'B's, and the cross. There are also variations in the type of joint used. The cross is painted and a common occurence is the re-painting of the red cross, or even filling-in with sealing wax! The nickel-plate is quite thin and sometimes the brassy colour shows through. It is possible that some were produced unplated. The manufacturer is not known.

BB 069

BB 069.07

The Ambulance Badge c.1923 - 1956

The First Aid Badge 1956 - 1968

BB 069 BACKGROUND NOTES

The most common form of this nickel or nickel-plated gilding metal brooch is solid with a red-painted cross. There are many variations, however, the principal ones being the shell-stamped type and those with vitreous enamel in place of paint, or no cross colour at all. [See right]. The latter was issued during and imme-diately after World War Two, with or without a frosted finish. Variation exists in joints, catches, background stipple, cross colour, pin placement and force marks. Some badges have the 'Miller' name on reverse. A particularly important variation is found in respect of the 'B's, some being distinctly outlined. These badges can often be found backed by red, blue or white felt.

The Arts & Crafts Badge

The Badges Committee set up after the union of the BLB and BB in 1926 reported to the BB Executive in May 1927 with suggestions for new badges. The Arts and Crafts Badge was approved, but the design, it was stated, would have to be chosen by the Badges Sub-Committee.[1] The scope of the new badge was intimated in the Gazette less than a month later:

'Arts & Crafts: these include singing, instrumental music, drawing, carpentering, woodworking, metal work, artistic designing.' [2]

Most of these areas had simply not been covered by any BB badge prior to 1926, so it is to the BLB we have to go to discover the extent of the task facing the Committee and the origin of the design that was finally accepted.

Scouting Inspiration

The BLB, from about 1912, had been taking on a wide variety of badges in order to accommodate the demands of Scouting. Towards the end of the Great War when metal was in short supply and the BLB had initiated a change to full uniform, development of cloth badges accelerated. Two of these new cloth badges were 'Handicraft' (1917) [3] and 'Arts' (early 1920s). Much of the detailed syllabus for these awards had been taken from Scouting publications.

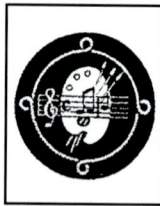

The BLB Arts Badge left and right the BLB Handicraft Badge; the clear parents of the BB Arts and Crafts Badge.

The BLB Arts Badge incorporated an artist's palette as its central motif and the Handicraft Badge likewise had a hammer with its shaft through open dividers. [4] The design idea for the latter probably originated with the Army 'Trade' badge, having hammer & pincers crossed.[5] The two BLB badges had been circular, but with the new badge being produced in nickel the opportunity presented itself for the creation of the unique palette shape with the hammer and dividers superimposed along with a bow to represent the more aesthetic practical arts.

Three for one

In 1968, the new barrel awards were introduced which again separated Arts from Crafts, with a further category of 'Hobbies' being created. There were now three badges replacing one. All the symbols used on the former Arts & Crafts Badge had gone.[6]

Bronze Barrels Banished as Palette is Preserved

The 1983 award system brought a return to one badge covering Arts, Crafts, Hobbies & Music, virtually the same content as the 1927 Arts & Crafts Badge! Now, however, it would be called 'Interests'. [7] With the standardised 'TV' shape the badge artist's problem was similar to that faced by the BLB which also had had two badges. Peter Flewker the designer of the 1983 Awards, came up with a finished design incorporating three of the elements used on the original BLB Badges: musical notes, a hammer and a palette. [8]

REFERENCES

1. Minutes of Brigade Executive meeting. 14-15/5/1927.
2. BB Gazette, Vol XXXV No 10, 1/6/1927. p 165. BB Scottish HQ, Carronvale, Larbert, Stirling.
3. Life Brigade Chronicle, Vol XVI No 5, December 1917. BB HQ, Felden Lodge, Hemel Hempstead, Herts.
4. BLB Boys Manual, 1926. pp 30-31. R. Bolton collection.
5. Edwards & Langley, British Army Proficiency Badges. Wardley Publishing 1984, p 10.
6. BB Award Regulations [Company Section] March 1968.
7. BB Award Regulations [Company Section] September 1983.
8. Brief for Artist. Badge Review Group. May/June 1981. Copy in possession of R.Mandry & R. Bolton.

The Arts & Crafts Badge   1927 - 1968

BB 070.

BB 070.

Arts & Crafts Badge Detail

BB 070.

BB 070

BB 070 BACKGROUND NOTES

There are at least thirty versions of this solid nickel brooch with differences being visible on the obverse and reverse. Obverse types include differing sizes of bow, or Bs, hatched Bs and smooth or stippled palettes. The reverse has standard tube joints with round and FRC catches or coiled pin squeeze or box joints on the hatched B versions. The maker's name Butler or Miller appears on a few types. The pin is usually mounted vertically or sometimes horizontally. There is impressing on some badges along with a variety of force lines and other marks. They can be found with a frosted finish or sometimes chrome-plated.

A Crafts class;
members of the 1st 'A' Birmingham Company outside their church c.1927.

The Athletics Badge

By 1946, the progress of Physical Training in the BB was acknowledged by re-naming the old Gymnastics Badge. Outdoor sporting activities which were taking place would be catered for with the introduction of a new Athletics Badge. The 'arm', the so-called 'severed' arm, which had been a feature of the BLB Physical Training Badge, was incorporated.[1]

The BLB P.T. Badge with the famous severed arm

Actually, it was the hand, wrist and lower arm holding a flaming

'Olympic' torch. The word 'Athletics' was included in the design. Along with the Seamanship Award, introduced at the same time, this was the first proficiency badge to feature a name. All later badges in the pre - '68 series would be 'named', an idea reintroduced for the **1983** Awards.

Very little information appeared in BB publications concerning the issue of this new Athletics Badge. The BB Gazette of June **1946** commented:

'The new Athlete's Badge (sic) and Seamanship Badge, both being preceded by certificates are definitely for seniors.' [2]

Further pointers as to the purpose of the badge appeared in the BB Gazette in February **1947** when the second part of an address by Scottish Secretary H.T.Shirley, to the Brigade Council was published:

'With our new Athlete's Badge (sic), we are setting out on a new adventure- the Athletic adventure. Let us tackle it with enthusiasm, gusto and determi-

nation and, who knows, many a British, European or even World Champion may rise from the ranks of the BB..' [3]

Mr Shirley's prediction turned out to be true for some BB Boys, notably champion sprinter Allan Wells former member of the 9th Edinburgh Coy. who became Britain's fastest man, winning two Gold Medals in the **1978** Commonwealth Games and the 100m Gold & 200m Silver Medals in the **1980** Olympics.

The **1968** barrel badges included Athletics, a badge with an interlocking two-ring design.[4] In the **1983** system Athletics is a named Credit which counts toward the Physical Activities Badge.[5]

REFERENCES

1. The Boys Life Brigade, The Boys Manual, Revised Edition 1926, BLB HQ. p 26. R. Bolton collection.
2. BB Gazette, Vol. LIV, No 5, June 1946. p 73. Mitchell Library, Glasgow.
3. ibid. Vol. LV No 3, Feb. 1947. p 42.
4. BB Award Regulations [Company Section] March 1968.
5. BB Award Regulations [Company Section] September 1983.

The Athletics Badge 1946 - 1968

BB 071 BACKGROUND NOTES

There are few varieties of this nickel brooch. All types have a standard tube joint with a mixture of round, FRC & hooked catches.There is impressing on the reverse of all types. One variety does not seem to have been struck accurately.

BB 071

The Band Badge

The Desire of the Lyre

Distinguishing band personnel, both boys and leaders, was not a problem faced by early BB companies. From 1886 - 1903, band boys could wear forage, pill-box caps, with extra braid. From 1888, Band Sergeants were permitted to wear a peaked cap with extra silver cord and Bandmasters a special army regulation cap with white 'Hercules Braid'.[1] In the **1880s,** it was considered quite proper for the 'Band' to be entirely separate from the rest of the Company. This was the case in Smith's 1st Glasgow.[2] In the **1888** Manual Messrs Leckie, Graham & Co. was advertising:

'Leather music pouches for Bands with shoulder Belt, with Brigade Regulation Boss on front of Pouch.'

These pouches were designed to hold the fife music, fifes being the most popular instrument at the time.[3] The London Council passed a new Regulation adopting a 'Band Badge' in 1903.[4] In a list of 'authorised' Badges & Medals, No. 7 reads:

'Band Badge for Buglers and Drummers or Brass and Flute Bands. By Examination.'

It was after **1903,** when the special boys' caps had been discontinued, that there seems to have been a growth in 'unauthorised' badges, although badges for drummers and buglers had been in use for some years (See photo of Sgt. Jones, 13th London Coy. wearing a Drum Badge and a Band Sergeant's Cap. page 1)

The Band of the 1st Falmouth Coy., 1906.
Note the fife players' proudly displayed lyre band badges worn on armbands on the lower right arm.
NCO's wear the badges above the chevrons. The drummers are wearing the large woven wire drum badge.

R. Bolton collection

For Fifes ?

One of the most popular early 'band' badges appears to have been the Lyre as used in the Royal Artillery to signify a Bandsman from **1856**. [5] The photograph of the 1st Falmouth Coy. **1906** (See previous page) shows the fife players wearing the large 'Lyre' badge. Perhaps smaller versions were being worn in some areas, but there is little visual evidence to substantiate this.

The incentive is there

The introduction of the Bugle Badge in **1909** provided an incentive for a 'Band' badge. Bugle Badges could be awarded to 'Buglers' who were not part of a band. The use of a Buglers' Badge by the Senior NCO of a band, dating back to **1903**, meant an extension of its use which created an anomaly. By introducing a Band Badge the BB could cover all instruments other than bugles; a real 'Band' badge rather than bugle proficiency. Following a meeting of the Brigade Executive, held at York on 7th February **1914,** the introduction of a Band Badge was sanctioned. It would be an alternative to the Buglers' Badge, awarded for any instrument *'other than a Bugle'* the announcement specifically stating that the use of the Bugle Badge by the Senior NCO of the Band would be discontinued.[6] Demand for the new badge was probably quite high, and when it was not immediately available a note was placed in the May edition of the BB Gazette that the new badge would be ready, *'within the next few days'.* [7]

Like the Army & the BLB

The BB Band Badge was based on the most common metal type in widespread use by the army. [8] The

The Band of the 3rd Oldham Coy. Hope Congregational, 22nd May 1913

pattern was simplified by the removal of the supporting wreath, and was virtually identical to the brass BLB badge introduced just two years before.

Tacet bars for the War

Other band related badges may have followed the introduction of the 'Lyre' had it not been for the start of the Great War. Priorities for creating new BB badges changed to those of more national importance such as Life-Saving, Gymnastics and War Service. Not until **1921** were the Drummers' and Pipers' Badges introduced to complete the band awards which would last for most of the next half-century. One interesting decision which probably hastened the introduction of both the Drummers' and Pipers' badges was the widening of the Band Badge regulations to include violinists. In **1919,** the Northern Committee was approached by the 3rd Dundee Coy. to include violinists in the Band Badge regulations. Permission was given for it to award this badge.[9]

Marching Bells

In the **1968** 'barrel badges' the Band Badge, re-named 'Bandsman's

Badge' retained the 'Lyre' symbol. [10] The Lyre was now a much more appropriate design, since, instead of only symbolically adorning music holders, etc., a lyre-shaped, marching glockenspiel band instrument called a 'Bell-Lyra' was becoming popular amongst many BB Bands, pioneered by the 5th Halifax (Elland) Coy., which went on to become the first ever National BB Band Champions in **1976**.

The Lyre is Lost

In the **1983** awards 'Bandsmans' is one of the qualifying components for the Music 'Credit' and currently counts towards the Interests Badge. The 'Lyre' symbol, however, does not appear on the credit, or the badge. [11]

REFERENCES

1. Gibbs, M., 'Banging the Drum'. The story of BB Bands BB HQ Archive Press 1983. pp 15-16.
2. ibid. pp 4-5
3. ibid. p.16. Statistics on the growth of BB Bands.
4. London Council Minutes 6/7/1903. BB archives, Felden Lodge, Hemel Hempstead, Herts.
5. Edwards & Langley, British Army Proficiency Badges, Wardley Publishing. 1984. pp 115-116.
6. BB Gazette, Vol XXII No.7 1/3/1914. p 99 BB Scottish HQ, Carronvale, Larbert, Stirlingshire.
7. ibid. No 9, 1/5/1914. p 134.
8. Edwards & Langley, op.cit., p 116.
9. Minutes of the BB Northern Committee, 13/3/1919 BB Scottish HQ.
10. BB Award Regulations [Company Section] March 1968.
11. BB Award Regulations [Company Section] September 1983.

The Band Badge 1914 - 1968

BB 072.01 **BB 072.03** **BB 072.04** **BB 072.09**

BB 072 BACKGROUND NOTES

Commonly found with a frosted finish (.01) the greatest variation comes in the fastenings for this badge. There are two main patterns of obverse (see below). Obverse variations occur in the B's, stipple size, lyre decoration the pedestal, and strings. Some of the reverse variations are shown above. Earliest types have a horizontal pin with axle joint and round catch. (.01). Other horizontally mounted fastenings have the standard tube joint also with round catches. There is a common fault on one side of the pedestal on a number of varieties (.05). Vertical pinned types come with standard tube joints (.08) and coiled pin, squeeze joints (.09).

The Band Badge - Detail

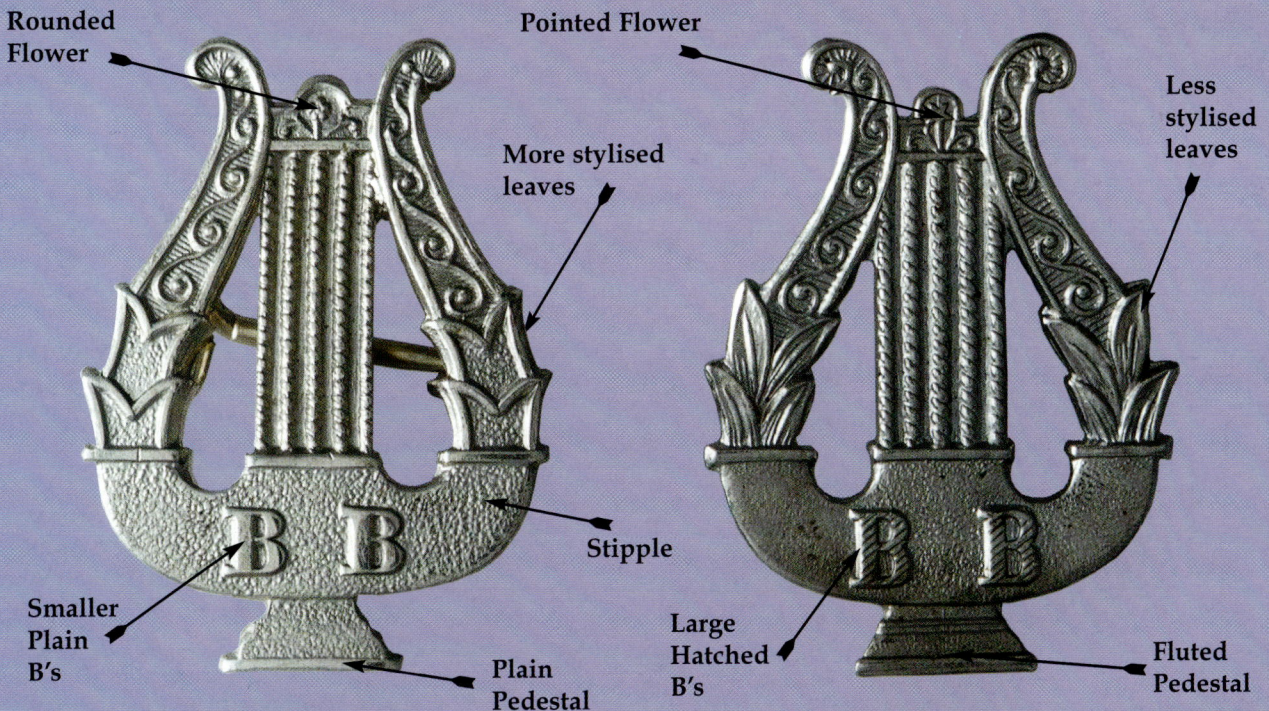

Rounded Flower

Pointed Flower

Less stylised leaves

More stylised leaves

Stipple

Smaller Plain B's

Plain Pedestal

Large Hatched B's

Fluted Pedestal

The Buglers' Badge

Adorned with a horn

T he first official Brigade Bugle Badge was sanctioned in 1908 with the first 'Brigade Issue' being available in 1909.[1] This was, however, by no means the first BB Bugle Badge. Some twenty years earlier, in 1889, Edinburgh Battalion had instituted a badge. [2] In fact, in a sample of 21 battalions awarding badges between 1886 and 1903 which had Annual Reports lodged at the Scottish BB HQ, 76.2% issued a Buglers' Badge. It is not clear whether or not the BB approved of bugle badges being worn by boys in uniform much before 1903. In that year at a Brigade Executive meeting held in Belfast it was decided that:

'The Senior N.C.O. only of a Band (whether a Company or Battalion Band) to wear on his stripes a Bugle Badge.' [3]

Apart from Edinburgh, by 1891 Bristol and Glasgow [4] and, by 1892, West London and Dublin [5] had introduced badges.

'Pre BB Issue' as advertised by the BB

The advertising pages of the BB Manual included buglers' badges in its suppliers lists from 1891/92

when they were advertised as Silver...

'Single Bugle 2/6d, Crossed Bugle 3/6d' [6]

It is likely, but by no means certain, that these badges were silver 'woven wire' (thread) and not solid metal. The supplier was also the maker of NCO's stripes. By 1893 the word 'silver' was not used in the advert and the prices had reduced to 1/9d & 2/6d.[7] The first mention of the material of a bugler's badge appears to be in the Manchester Battalion Report of 1895-1896 where the badge is described as being in 'Worsted'.[8] The design of the single bugle or horn, with cord, and the double version of the same, were both used by the army at the time. The single bugle, dating from 1881, became the one widely used by the Light Infantry and the double crossed bugle, dating from 1877, was used by the King's Royal Rifles from sometime after 1902. [9] (See diagrams page 100). The popularity of the badge must have increased between 1891 and 1903 because the number of suppliers advertising the badge increased to five, the price reduced to 1/8d single and 2/3d double. In 1897, Messrs. J. Farquharson introduced a *'white braid'* version instead of *'silver tinsel'* at prices of 11d & 1/1d, [10] but, by 1902, the only choice for a BB equipment buyer was the *'Silver Tinsel'* version. [11] Without central control as to the procurement of buglers' badges, no doubt many styles of badge were in use. The Annual Report of the Dublin Battalion in 1897-98 for instance, includes a photograph of a Sergeant wearing a large 'coach horn' style buglers' badge. [12]

Detail from a picture reproduced in the Annual Report of the Dublin Battalion, 1897 - 1898. A Sergeant wearing a 'post-horn' style bugle badge.
NB Poor quality original.
BB Archive collection

Becoming Official

The very fact that buglers' badges were obtainable and advertised in the Manual was enough for some Battalions to officially sanction their use, as the experience of the Glasgow Battalion seems to show. In September 1892 it was recorded in the Glasgow Battalion Minutes:

'...A letter was read from Mr Kerr, Capt. 90th Company, asking the sanction of the Committee for some of his Boys wearing the Bugle Badge; and calling attention to the fact that these Badges and the silver Service Anchor while advertised in the Brigade Manual as obtainable for Boys were not placed in the list of articles append-

ed to Rule 11 of the Battalion, articles the wearing of which does not require the consent of the Committee. The required sanction was given to Mr Kerr and the Articles named were ordered to be added to the list.' [13]

Regulation

Until **1914** bugle badges were not always worn by buglers! The **1903** Executive decision had stated:

'...the Senior NCO only of a Band...'.

The bugle represented the whole band. Edwards and Langley seem to suggest that this idea stemmed from the Volunteers, [14] always a strong influence upon early BB decisions. A buglers' badge was regarded as a 'Company Appointment' before **1909.** The Manual of **1908** had the first intimation of the style and a re-positioning of the bugle badge. It stated:

'The Badge to be a single Bugle; worn above the right elbow, in the case of a Non-Commissioned Officer above the stripes.'

In March **1909** the situation was regularised and details of a new badge published in the Gazette:

'In order to bring the issue of the Bugler's Badge into conformity with other Badges for which a qualifying Examination is held, the Executive have arranged that on and after this date (1st March **1909**) the Badge will be issued direct from Head-Quarters and London Office, subject to the conditions laid down in the Manual... The executive have prepared a new and much improved form of Bugle Badge, in the same material as the Three Years' Service Anchor, and will supply it at the rate of 6d each, post paid.' [15]

If there had been any metal bugle badge prior to **1909** the similarity with the Three Year Anchor would not have been alluded to. The new badge was a white metal version of the 'Light Infantry' single bugle with the initials 'BB' added.

Clarification of the rules about wearing the Bugle Badge was required in **1914,** when the new Band Badge came into use. The Bugle Badge was now only to be worn by Buglers:

'The use of the Bugle Badge formerly worn by the Senior NCO of the Band will be discontinued.' [16]

The Buglers' Badge design remained the same for sixty years. In **1927,** the union with the BLB had no effect on the pattern of the badge since by this time, the BLB were using an identical design in brass with lugs and without any initials. [17] In the new Badge Regulations of **1968** the badge, now in its standardised barrel format, bore a rather ignominious mouthpiece and chain design. [18] Neither the bugle, nor any of its parts appear pictorially in the **1983** Award Regulations. The playing of the bugle still counts towards a badge because it is possible as part of the Music Credit regulations of the Interests Badge .[19]

Sgt. E. Maconochie 40th Edinburgh Coy., 1917.
Sgt. Maconochie wears his bugle badge with pride. He ran the Company Band, as well as being Battalion bands' convener for twenty years. Ted served in the Royal Marines and became a State Trumpeter in **1959**. He was a keen BB and military badge collector.[20]
Photo: Jack Gilchrist collection

REFERENCES

1. BB Gazette, Vol XVII, 1/3/1909, p 98. BB Scottish HQ, Carronvale, Larbert, Stirlingshire.
2. Edinburgh Battalion, Third Annual Report, 1889-1890 pp 24 & 27.
3. BB Gazette, Vol XII, 1/10/1903, p 31, Scottish BB HQ.
4. Bristol Battalion, First Annual Report 1891-1892   p 10. Glasgow Battalion, Seventh Annual Report 1891-1892 p 13. BB Scottish HQ.
5. West London Battalion, First Annual Report 1892-1893 p 16. Dublin Battalion, Second Annual Report 1893-1894. p 27. BB Scottish HQ.
6. BB Officers Manual 1891/1892. Advert of Geo. Kenning, Glasgow. BB HQ, Felden, Hemel Hempstead, Herts.
7. ibid. 1893 advert.
8. Manchester Battalion, Second Annual Report, 1895-1896. BB Scottish HQ.
9. Edwards & Langley, British Army Proficiency Badges, Wardley Publishing 1984. p 112.
10. BB Officers Manual; 1897. Advert. of James Farquharson Houndsditch, London. BB HQ.
11. ibid. 1902 advert.
12. Dublin Battalion, Sixth Annual Report 1897-1898, BB Scottish HQ.
13. Glasgow Battalion Minute Book, No 1, [1/1/1] Executive meeting, 22/9/1892. Glasgow Battalion HQ, Bath St.
14. Edwards & Langley, op.cit., p 112.
15. BB Gazette, Vol XVII, 1/3/1909, p 98. BB Scottish HQ op.cit.
16. ibid. Vol XXII No. 7 1/3/1914. p 99.
17. The Boys' Life Brigade, The Boys' Manual. 1926, pub. by BLB HQ. p 30. R.Bolton collection.
18. BB Award Regulations [Company Section] March 1968.
19. BB Award Regulations [Company Section] September 1983.
20. Barclay, J.P. Pill Box & Service Cap. p176.

The Buglers' Badge

Pre 1909

The double bugle was used widely by BB battalions in the years prior to 1909 and could be obtained in metal, woven wire thread (tinsel) or worsted. All of these types may have been worn since there was no national regulation stating the material. Within each battalion, no doubt, the style and material would be constant. The bugles are virtually identical in form to the single one used from 1909.

Crossed Trumpet badges were also in quite common use within the BB prior to 1909. Usually in brass with two or four lugs, they can be found in white metal, wire thread and worsted. They were worn as pictured, or sometimes the other way up. Like all the early 'pre-regulation' badges special arrangements had to be made in order to wear them in 'equipment', armbands, elastic etc.

1909 - 1968

BB 073.01   BB 073.08   BB 073.22   BB 073.24

BB 073 BACKGROUND NOTES

The Buglers' Badge has more than twenty-five variations. Differences occur in the obverse design as well as the usual number of joints, catches etc.. There is a wide variety of impressing. The main features are shown on the enlarged pictures below. A variety exists with the Miller maker's name.

The Buglers' Badge - Detail

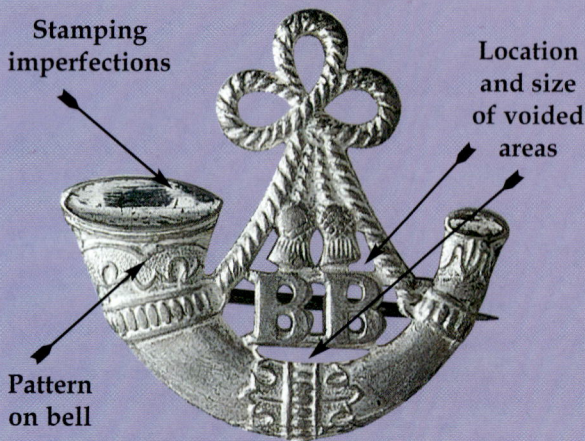

Stamping imperfections

Location and size of voided areas

Pattern on bell

Thickness of cord

Size of tassels

Pattern on horn

Solid or fretted B's

The Campers' Badge

Loitering within tent

I n 1912, the BLB had introduced a Pioneer Badge which was the nearest thing to a Campers' Badge in that Brigade. Aimed at the older company members, it was still regulation issue when union with the BB came about in **1926**. 'Pioneer' was a name given to someone who was part of a camp advance party, those who worked hard before the arrival of the main party by erecting tents, digging pits, etc.. Before the **1920s,** it would have been almost inconceivable for just attendance at camp to imply any degree of camping skill or proficiency. Camping was seen either very much as a 'holiday', an escape from work, the epitome of the easy life, or as a carbon copy of a military experience. Campcraft was not an essential requirement for boys in a large fixed camp where cooking was performed by army or ex-army cooks and teams of staff serviced and maintained everything.

Holiday Camp

In **1926,** the BB, very much in the vanguard of youth camping, had no specific camp awards other than prizes for camp sports and similar activities. For many BB boys camp was simply spending a week away from home in a church hall by the sea. Indeed, in July **1886,** the first BB camp, organised by the 1st Glasgow Coy. under the captaincy

'Spud-bashing' at the N. London Battalion Camp, Romney Marsh, c.1896

Photo: E.T. Menday collection.

of William Smith was held in a public hall in Auchenlochan, Tighnabruaich.[1] The 1st continued to camp there until **1915.** [2] However, by the time the Boy Scouts came onto the scene in **1908** many BB companies were experienced campers under canvas.

A shield from the elements

Just as camping was a much-loved activity within the Brigade, so the little shield badge with the picture of a bell tent became a firm favourite over a period of more than forty years. It was introduced in **1927** after the Pioneer Badge, formerly used in the BLB, had been reviewed as a result of the union. The **1920s** was a time when youth outdoor activities were being encouraged for their own sake, re-evaluated, no longer copying the outmoded and politically sensitive military methods. Many BB boys were camping on small company

sites and their holiday at camp was increasingly becoming an additional week away from home rather than the only week. Camp activities could now focus around the camp itself rather than just being a base for excursions or military manoeuvers. The official announcement of the badge was made in the Gazette where it stated:

'For Boys who have attended three BB Camps [In different years] for at least seven days each year with good conduct throughout and have passed a test in pitching and striking a bell tent...design - A Bell Tent with letters BB' [3]

Room to breathe.
The Rugby BB get away from it all in their camp at Conway, 1912.
R. Bolton Collection

Newcomers pitched in changing field

Both the Campers' and Expedition Badges were continued into the new Awards Structure of **1968**, reborn in the standardised barrel shape. [4] The Camping Badge pictured the end-elevation of a more up-to-date ridge tent. The new Awards Scheme introduced in **1983**, grouped Camping as a Credit under the regulations for the Adventure Badge. [5] The Adventure Badge features a stylised lightweight tent and compass rose. In **1998**, the tent became the second longest-lived symbol, other than an anchor, on BB proficiency badges- 71 years! [6]

Pack up your troubles ...

By the **1960s,** static camping under canvas was seen as only part of the BB camping scene, with greater emphasis being placed on 'lightweight' camping. The Duke of Edinburgh's Award Scheme was getting into full swing with camping becoming associated with adventure and expeditions. The old BB Camp Handbook, for many years the bible of BB camping and the source of all of the Camper's Badge test material, had become inappropriate for such activities. The Expedition Badge was issued in **1964** to cover these new outward bound areas of campcraft.

Left: A 'BoB' printed paper rate postcard sent from camp in 1950

REFERENCES

1. 'For Fifty Years' The Jubilee Souvenir of 1st Glasgow BB. 1933. p 7.
2. ibid. p 14.
3. BB Gazette Vol XXXV No 10, 1 June 1927. p 164.
4. BB Company Section, Award Regulations, September 1968. The Boys' Brigade.
5. BB Company Section, Award Regulations, September 1983. The Boys' Brigade.
6. The Red Cross being the longest [1889-1968], 79 Yrs, and the Band Lyre being the third longest [1914 - 1984], 70 yrs.

The Campers' Badge   1927 - 1968

BB 074   **BB 074**   **BB 074**   **BB 074**

BB 074 BACKGROUND NOTES

More than forty years of this major nickel brooch produced perhaps less variation than would be imagined. There are the usual changes in catch, joint etc., on the reverse with the standard tube joint being the most common. The reverse also features numerous impressions. There are varieties with the Miller name and some with the Miller logo. Remarkably, there are few easily discernible differences in the obverse, but the 'devil is in the detail' here. The main areas of variation come in the B's which are either hatched or plain varying in size, and the design of the tent and the grass upon which it is pitched. There are also differences in the background and the overall finish of the badge. There are foreign versions of this badge in circulation (See BB 077 notes).

Campers' Badge - Detail

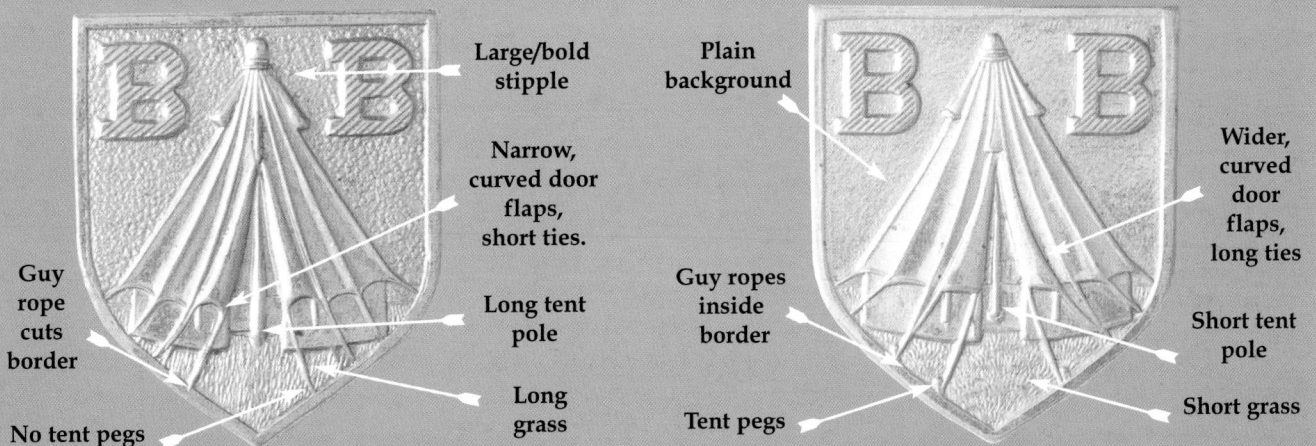

The Drummers' Badge

Like many of the BB proficiency badges, a drummers' badge had been worn officially by many BB Boys for more than a quarter of a century before its official national Brigade recognition in 1921. Battalions were quick to acknowledge the skills of the drummer, no doubt when pressure was applied by their constituent companies. Initially, the Company Drummer was usually an 'appointment' as it was in the army. [1] The pattern of the early BB bugle badges also appears to come from the military. There are a number of photographs showing local Brigade use of the large size worsted/wire badge (See photo. of Sgt. Jones 13th London Coy. page 1) and of 1st Falmouth Coy. Band page 95). This large badge had been in use in the army as early as **1874**. [2]

Brigade beaten by a third of all Battalions

There does not seem to be any evidence of the widespread use of a pre-national metal badge in the BB even though one very similar to that later sanctioned by the Brigade had been in use in the army since **1849**. [3] The earliest extant BB use can be attrtibuted to the North London Battalion in **1894** when it was *'by examination only'*. [4] In the

Manchester Battalion, just one year later, the Drummers' Badge was described as *'worsted'*. [5] A survey of 21 sample battalions from **1886-1903** shows that 33.3% issued a drummers' badge. [6] The awarding of drummers' badges was far from uniform throughout the Brigade. In **1902**, Newcastle- Upon-Tyne introduced it as a *'Sergeant Drummer's Badge'*. [7] At the same time

Edinburgh Battalion introduced a drummers' badge, but didn't get round to a battalion examination for nearly ten years. [8]

Sticking to the Rules

It should not be assumed that all battalions were 'doing their own thing' prior to the official sanctioning of an official brigade badge. The Dundee Battalion, for instance, was careful to abide by the Manual and, in June **1909**, it awarded the new Brigade Bugle Badge.[9] This, not surprisingly, caused a furore among the drummers, so much so that the Band Committee recommended that the Brigade Executive be asked to authorise a drum badge. The suggestion didn't get very far, however, as the minutes state:

' *...after some discussion it was decided to take no further steps as regards this question.*' [10]

However, the issue did not disappear. In the following year the band representative, Mr. Martin, brought up the subject once more when he,

' *...mentioned that the new Drum Badge had been issued by Farquharson & Co., London, and he asked the Executive for permission to adopt this.*' [11]

No action was taken and Dundee stuck by the Manual.

Double 'Whammee' for Paisley

Another Scottish battalion, Paisley, put a proposal to the Brigade Executive at its meeting in January **1921**. [12] Drummers were anxious to get their own BB badge. A Band Badge (Lyre) had been adopted in **1914**, but with a choice of only two 'band' badges to represent a wide variety of instruments. Paisley voiced what many others had, no doubt, intimated to their Executive member. The Executive considered,

' *...a proposal from the Paisley Battalion that a drum badge for drummers and a piper's badge for piper's be authorised in place of the present lyre badge, the lyre being considered an unsuitable emblem in these cases.*'

The issue of the badges was approved on the same conditions as the present Band Badge. Details of the designs were left in the hands of the Southern and Northern Committees. No boy would be allowed to wear more than one 'band' badge. For any battalion to achieve the successful introduction of two badges at one meeting, must count as a memorable achievement.

'Frosted Silver' please

The design of the new official Drummers' Badge was naturally one that matched up with the others in use in **1921**. It was a frosted 'silver' drum in the style of the army metal badge which was in brass. The initials 'BB' were added, in keeping with most of the existing proficiency awards. When the BLB/BB Union came in **1926** the badge remained unchanged as the BLB had used the army pattern brass drum badge since **1912**.[13]

Drumming becomes 'music' ?

In **1968**, the form of the Drummers' Badge was changed to the new 'barrel' shape. [14] The **1983** Awards have drumming as one of the qualifications for gaining the Music credit which retains a picture of a drum. The music credit counts toward the yellow Interests Badge. [15]

REFERENCES

1. Edwards & Langley, British Army Proficiency Badges, Wardley Publishing 1984. p 111.
2. ibid. p 113
3. ibid.
4. North London Battalion, Third Annual Report, 1894-1895, pp 5-7 Scottish BB HQ. Carronvale, Larbert, Stirling.
5. Manchester Battalion, Second Annual Report, 1895-1896. BB Scottish HQ.
6. Battalion Reports, 1886-1903. BB Scottish HQ.
7. Newcastle Upon Tyne Battalion. Eighth Annual Report 1902-1903. Scottish Hq..
8. Edinburgh Battalion, Seventeenth Annual Report 1902-1903 & Twenty-Sixth Annual Report 1911-1912. Scottish HQ
9. Dundee Battalion Minute book, Vol.3. 8/6/1909. Battalion HQ.
10. ibid. 7/9/1909
11. ibid. 7/6/1910
12. Minutes of Brigade Executive, Newcastle-On-Tyne 21-22/1/1921.
13. Report of BLB Badges Sub-Committee, The Life Brigade Chronicle, 1912. pp 36-37. BB HQ Felden Lodge, Hemel Hempstead, Herts.
14. BB Award Regulations [Company Section] March 1968. The Boys' Brigade
15. BB Award Regulations [Company Section] September 1983. The Boys' Brigade

STEDFAST MAG

The boys speak out ... in February 1959:
'Sir - Boys playing the cymbals and bass drum have to have a certain skill. Is there a badge for these players? Some bandsmen have won a drummers' badge for playing the side drum, but also have learned to play the cymbals or bass drum. Surely these players should get an extra badge.'
Cpl. Buckle, 3rd Christchurch Company.

...and in April 1959
'Sir - ... I should like to know what skill there is in belting a couple of pieces of brass together two or three times during each tune... I would refer Cpl. Buckle to the Boys' Handbook which says that badges are not given for self-glorification...'
Cpl. J. A. Murdoch, 51st Manchester Company.

CLIPS

The Drummers' Badge

Pre - 1921

Sew-on wire thread badge used by BB members from the 1890s to 1921. The main problem was that the badge had to be permanently fixed to an armband for use with BB Equipment. See photo of Sgt. Jones page 1 & Drummers of 1st Falmouth Band page 95. Wire thread badges were widely used by various BB Battalions in the 1890s the Drum being perhaps the most common.

1921 - 1968

BB 075.01   **BB 075.24**   **1**   **2**   **3**

4   **5**   **6**   **7**   **8**

BB 075 BACKGROUND NOTES

The drummers' badge varies little on the obverse, most noticeably the hatched Bs type with very precise detail and the plain Bs type with much coarser detail. However, the reverse has a great variety with differing alignment of pins, varying joints and catches. The stamping of the perimeter of the badge including the drumhead falls into eight main variations and these have been illustrated above.

The Education/ Citizenship Badge

In 1927, when the BB and BLB were united and the award schemes amalgamated, there was a clear need for a badge to cover the areas of Citizenship, League of Nations, Scripture Knowledge and Temperance. All of the above had badges awarded under the former BLB regulations. [1] The BB had the Scouts' Badge, introduced in 1911, which could now be discontinued. The Scouts' Badge syllabus had included elements of 'Citizenship' such as the composition of the Union Flag and location of British colonies. The name 'Education' was chosen for a new badge and an appropriate 'Torch of

Knowledge' for the design. The details of the badge were published in June 1927 as:

'...a torch with letters BB' [2]

At first glance a straightforward decision, but it was not quite so simple. From the outset there were discussions about either removing the scripture knowledge component from the award and introducing a separate badge,[3] or making the Education Badge become a Scripture Knowledge Badge. Decisions by the Brigade Executive in 1952 and 1953 allowing three Scripture Knowledge Certificates to qualify for the Badge concerned the Badges Committee greatly. In 1956, it concluded that the purpose of the badge should:

'...encourage a wider outlook on life.' [4]

With the first Scripture Knowledge Badges being awarded in 1959, the Education Badge was finally freed from the thirty years of discussion

and debate about its purpose. It could now be re-named 'Citizenship Badge', a title change which came in officially in 1960. [5]

Life for the badge with a new name was short however, eight years later it was discontinued in favour of the new awards scheme. [6] The new incarnation being the 'International' Badge.

In 1984, the present badge structure was introduced with the green Community Badge, incorporating Citizenship, Civics and International elements.[7]

REFERENCES

1. The Boys' Life Brigade, The Boys' Manual, Revised edition January 1926. Pub. BLB HQ. R.Bolton collection.
2. BB Gazette Vol XXXV p 165, June 1927. BB HQ, Felden Lodge, Hemel Hempstead, Herts.
3. See notes concerning Scripture Knowledge Badge p
4. Minutes of Brigade Badges Sub-Committee, February 1956.
5. BB Gazette Vol LXIII p 47 Feb/Mar 1960. R. Bolton Collection.
6. BB Award Regulations [Company Section], March 1968. The Boys' Brigade.
7. BB Award Regulations [Company Section] September 1983. The Boys' Brigade.

Education Badge 1927 - 1960 / Citizenship Badge 1960 - 1968

BB 076.01   **BB 076.05**   **BB 076.14**   **BB 076.16**

BB 076 BACKGROUND NOTES

There are nearly twenty versions of this badge. Main variations in the obverse include piercing or lack of piercing between B's, and the flame on the torch. There is a version, presumably wartime, with 'solid' B's.There is varying impressing on the reverse with at lest one shell stamped type. Most joints are standard tube with some coiled. Varying catch types are used. Post - war versions have larger Bs and less piercing than the pre - war versions and one post - war version has a larger, straighter edged torch handle.

The Expedition Badge

Leading the way with a compass

The mention of an Expedition Badge in official BB minutes appears to date to a meeting of the Brigade Badges Committee in May 1962. [1] Suggestions concerning the revision of some awards by altering existing regulations were put to the meeting by Mr. R. Peck on behalf of the Sheffield Battalion. He suggested the introduction of an expedition award:

'...which may or may not be an advanced stage of the present Wayfaring award.'

The matter of a separate award was discussed further at the next meeting in December when it was stated in the minutes that:

'...it was agreed to circularise a number of Battalions known to be specially interested in Wayfaring with the proposals submitted by Sheffield Battalion through Mr Peck for the amending of the present Wayfaring awards and the introduction of an Expedition Award.' [2]

There was every reason to suspect that Mr Peck's idea would be implemented. The Duke of Edinburgh's Award had been running for six years carving out an important place in the programme of many companies such as those in the Sheffield Battalion, surrounded by inviting moorland. The

BB had, since the use of the old Scouts' Badge, for example, prided itself on having an award structure for outdoor pursuits that could be managed and run entirely within the normal BB programme. Meetings were held to discuss the new award and its impact on the wayfaring award. Favourable comments must have come in from all concerned since the Badge had been approved by the time the November meeting was held. At this November meeting it was:

'...agreed that publicity for this new award should appear in the Gazette and Stedfast Magazine.' [3]

Designs for the Badge were not finalised in November **1963**, because the same minutes record the following under the heading:

'Expedition Badge Design': *'Two designs were submitted for this new Badge, neither of which the Committee particularly liked, and it was agreed that other designs should be requested.'* [4]

Perhaps this would turn out to be a landmark decision in the light of the influence the eventual design would have upon the entire BB badge system.

The Newcomer

An announcement in the BB Gazette in **1964** signalled the arrival of this influential, albeit short-lived, newcomer to the BB badge family:

'From September Companies will be able to include Expedition as part of the normal BB programme irrespective of the Duke of Edinburgh Awards, though the BB awards are intended to

satisfy the requirements of the Expedition section of the award at the three levels.' [5]

It was very much the herald of things to come. Some twenty years later its 'TV' shape and use of colour would become the norm for all BB awards.

Making the point

Perhaps the most noteworthy feature of the **1964** Expedition Badge was its use of colour, previously used only on the Ambulance/First Aid Badge. Another enduring aspect of the Badge is its compass rose symbol. The compass found its way (appropriately !) on to the **1968** barrel version of the Badge [6] and then on to the **1983** Adventure Badge. Expedition as an award became one of the new Credits. [7] The importance given to the inclusion of the compass was emphasised by the Badge Review Group meeting in May **1981** when it advised the artist Peter Flewker:

'Still some unhapiness regarding the compass. It could be mistaken for a ship's wheel. Star-shaped compass preferred, either with the four cardinal points or possibly a total of eight points.'

Again, at the next meeting in June, the Badge Review Group was not quite satisfied:

'The design needs an amendment to make the Compass points more elongated and so come to a sharper point.' [8]

In other words, it wanted a compass just like the one on the original Expedition Badge.

REFERENCES

1. Minutes of BB Badges Committee, Sat. 26th May 1962. BB HQ Felden Lodge, Hemel Hempstead, Herts.
2. ibid. December 1962.
3. ibid. November 1963.
4. ibid.
5. BB Gazette, Vol. 72, No 6, Aug/Sept. 1964. p 130. BB Scottish HQ., Carronvale, Larbert, Stirlingshire.
6. BB Award Regulations, [Company Section] March 1968. The Boys' Brigade.
7. BB Award Regulations [Company Section]   September 1983. The Boys' Brigade.
8. BB Badge Review Group, Artist's briefing notes c. May 1981 & 6th June 1981. BB HQ..

The Expedition Badge   1964 - 1968

BB 077.01   **BB 077.03**

BB 077 BACKGROUND NOTES

A short-lived nickel part-enamelled badge, the first to have the 'TV' shape, it appears in two main types, light blue enamel and dark blue enamel. There is no other easily discernable variation in the obverse. The Bs are hatched. The joints are all coiled squeeze type with a hooked catch, mounted horizontally. The badges were produced by Miller and have either their name or logo on the reverse. There are many countries that have modelled their badges on the pre - 1968 UK awards and some of these have found their way into the UK over the years. Generally the quality of these imports is not as good as the original UK version and they look extremely bright having a chrome finish. The foreign badges have bar-brooches or other fastenings differing from the UK type.

The boys speak out ... in April 1954

'Sir - We already have badges for athletics and swimming. Why not for cycling? A boy may be a good cyclist, but unable to get a badge for sport, because he is not good enough at swimming or athletics, and thus he may not be able to win his Queen's Badge. The badge could be run on a time trial basis, or a training test basis, where one would have to pass tests in map reading, etc., as well as covering a set number of miles.'
S/Sgt. J. Smith, 29th Birmingham Company.

and ... in January 1957

'Sir - Why not a Cyclist's Badge, with the following qualifications: a ride of 70 - 80 miles in day; a 25 mile run in under one and a half hours; a test on the Highway Code and maintenance of cycle; map reading; holder of first-aid certificate. Even if it is not possible to have a badge, could the BB help cyclists to get together. I do enjoy a lot of cycling and would enjoy the company of a fellow member of the BB.'
L/Cpl. A. England, 1st Banbury Company.

The Firemans' Badge

Saving Life with hatchets and helmet

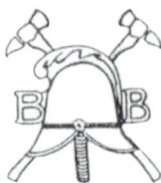

The origins of the Firemans' Badge are quite straightforward and, unlike many others, its introduction in 1927 does not seem to have caused much controversy. It was one of the half dozen new proficiency badges to appear as a direct result of the BB/BLB union in **1926**.

Life Saving

The pre - **1926** history is all from the BLB side, starting with the introduction of a 'Fire Squad's Armlet' in **1904**. [1] Saving life was at the heart of the Life Brigade ethos and after the Ambulance Armlet [1903] the Fire Squad Armlet was only the second proficiency award to be introduced. The feeling in the Brigade seemed to be that an armlet would be

'More prized than a certificate'. [2]

By **1912**, a 'Fire' Badge had been introduced for BLB and GLB. [3] It is by no means certain, but this badge was probably the one illustrated in the **1925** and **1926** BLB Boys Manual; crossed hatchets/axes with a superimposed fireman's helmet.

Pioneering Progeny

The design of the BB Fireman's Badge, was probably inspired by the army 'Pioneer' badge, which consisted of crossed axes, [4] and the badge was probably an 'off the shelf' design since it does not have any distinctive BLB features. Identical badges may be seen with collections of fire-service awards and uniform badges but with a chrome plated finish.[5] Many such badges were used by the BLB in order to save money, in particular the Buglers' and Drummers' Badges. The BLB did use a 'Pioneer' badge, however, with crossed mattock and spade, for awarding to annual summer camp advance parties. [6] The BB had, in some areas, used the army Pioneer Badge as a 'tradesman's' badge before being regulated by the National Headquarters. [7]

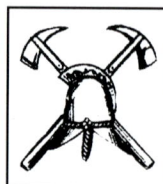

The BLB 'Fire' Badge the clear progenitor of the BB Fireman's Badge

Fire badge is not put out

By **1926,** the BLB had some 27 proficiency badges, not counting the 'class' awards, medals, etc.. It was rare for a BLB boy to retain more than ten of these due to the fact that they were subject to annual re-examination, the system used by the 'Volunteers'. There was also a BLB rule limiting the number of proficiency badges worn on one arm to four. [8] The BB system of boys being awarded a badge which was retained for the rest of their service meant that the number of badges transferring to the new united Brigade had to be considerably reduced. The history and importance of the Fire Badge, however, assured its continuation virtually unchanged.

Evolution not revolution

The official announcement of the new BB Firemans' Badge, described it as:

'...a Fireman's helmet with crossed axes and the letters BB' [9]

This BB Badge was almost identical to its BLB parent except for an enlarged helmet, BB initials, and reversed axes. The regulations contained knowledge of rescue from fire and related First Aid procedures, little changed from the BLB.

The flames are extinguished

This easily recognised badge was discontinued in **1968** and replaced by a barrel-shaped 'Safety' badge bearing a triangular warning emblem containing a picture of stylised flames. [10] Further change was introduced in **1983** when Fire Prevention, First Aid and Safety were all incorporated into the regulations for the new 'Community' Badge. [11]

REFERENCES

1 Life Brigade Chronicle. Vol. III No. 1 Sept. 1904.
2 ibid. Vol. I No.1. January 1903.
3 ibid. 1912
4 Edwards & Langley, British Army Proficiency Badges,Wardley Publishing. 1984. p 14.
5 R. Bolton collection includes a chrome-plated version.
6 BLB Boys Manual 1926. R.Bolton collection.
7 See photograph. R. Bolton Collection. c1890's. NB a 'Trade Badge' was considered by the BB Executive at meetings in 1918 and 1919 but was rejected. [14/9/1918, reply to Chris. K. Butt Letter]. BB HQ. Felden Lodge, Hemel Hempstead, Herts.
8 BLB Boys Manual.op.cit.
9 BB Gazette, Vol XXXV, No 10, 1/6/1927. p 165.
10 BB Award Regulations [Company Section] March 1969.The Boys' Brigade
11 BB Award Regulations [Company Section] September 1983. The Boys' Brigade

The Firemans' Badge   1927 - 1968

BB 078.21

BB 078.14

BB 078.11

BB 078.19

Firemans' Badge Detail

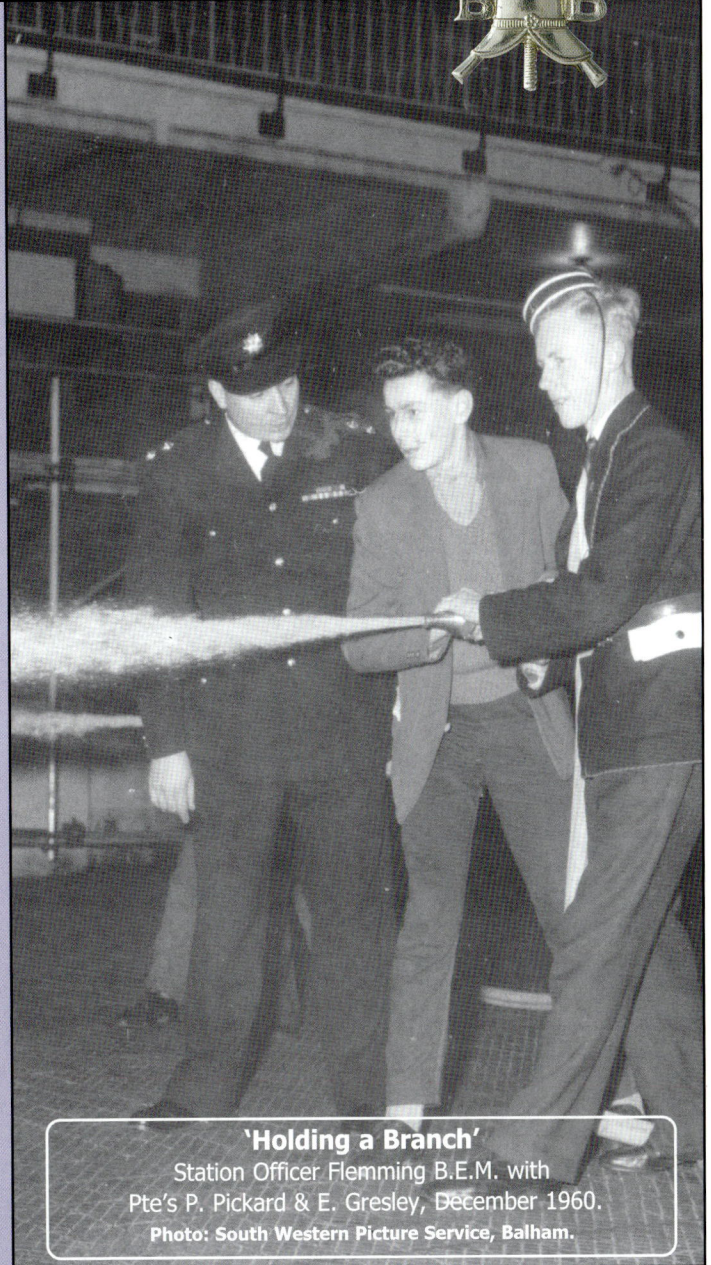

'Holding a Branch'
Station Officer Flemming B.E.M. with
Pte's P. Pickard & E. Gresley, December 1960.
Photo: **South Western Picture Service, Balham.**

BB 078 BACKGROUND NOTES

More than twenty-five versions of this nickel badge exist. Main variations on the obverse include the size and shape of the helmet from small to large and very narrow, wide and narrow chin straps, and varying patterns of plume finial. The decorative rosette which forms the hinge of the chin strap is found in rose (curved) and star (pointed) formats. There is a wartime version with solid Bs. On the reverse the joints are mounted with vertical or diagonal pins, standard tube or coiled joints have varying catches. There is impressing on the majority of types ranging from helmet, plume and chin-strap chain to a very slight depression in the helmet. Like many other badges of this period they can be found with a frosted finish or even chrome-plated.

The Gymnastics/Physical Training Badge

The Spectre of the 'severed arm'

Gymnastics is a long established activity in the BB. As early as the 1890s some companies had their own gymnastic teams. [1] Unlike many badges which appeared after the union of the BB and BLB this badge had been 'up and running' for ten years by **1927**. Dumbell drill, swimming, cricket and football were all regular Brigade activities by the start of the twentieth century. National displays at the Queen's Hall in London and articles in the new Brigadier Magazine[2] encouraged swimming and gymnastic excellence. [3].

Dundee determination

The real impetus for the award of a Gymnastic Badge seems to have come from the Dundee Battalion, particularly after the introduction of The King's Badge in **1914**. A gymnastic class had started in the Battalion around **1899**. [4] By **1911** the activity was being run as a 'Gymnastics Club' administered by its own newly appointed Committee consisting of Messrs. Alexander, Miller, McDonald, Aimer, Arnott and Knowles. [5] Inter-company competitions in dumbell drill plus senior and jun-

ior jumping were introduced. [6] In January **1916**, one of the Committee, Mr Knowles, explained to the Battalion Executive that gymnastics had been omitted from the certificates required for the qualification for the King's Badge. A discussion followed. Mr. Knowles and Mr. Arnott were then requested to:

'...submit a definite scheme which might be submitted to Headquarters with a view to its adoption in connection with this [King's] badge.' [7] One month later Mr. Knowles laid before the Executive, *'...proposed tests for proficiency in Gymnastics which could be adopted for the King's Badge...'.* [8]

Knowles had submitted a full scheme for three years and above.

National Debate

The Dundee Minutes are missing after **1916**, but the story can be picked up in the minute book of The Brigade Executive on 16th September **1916** [9] when a scheme suggested by Dundee Battalion for the award of certificates and badges for gymnastics was considered:

'The matter referred to a Committee consisting of Dr. Morison, Messrs. Shannon and Robertson, Capt. F.W. Stevens and Mr Peacock to consider and report at a later stage of the meeting...[p.2] The Badge shall be issued on or after 31st March 1917... [p.3].'

Yet more debate

The decision concerning the design and nature of the sanctioned badge

was set to have as protracted a passage as its adoption. The Northern Committee looked at some preliminary artwork, making the observation:

'The Committee considered the design of the Gymnastic Badge and were unanimously of the opinion that something more suitable than any of the designs before them could be obtained. The matter was postponed for further consideration.' [10]

Such consideration was given at the next meeting when they had to hand,

'...further designs for the Gymnastic Badge before them, together with another drawing of the design approved by the Southern Committee. They did not think any of the designs submitted suitable and the matter was postponed for further consideration...'. [11]

Again! A week later a new design emerged:

'The Committee had before them a further design approved by the Southern Committee showing the head of Athene as used on the Olympic Games Medal. The Committee approved of this design.' [12]

However, the debate didn't stop there. Another design was to challenge the Greek goddess Athene not with the horse of Poseidon, but a *'severed arm'*. Meanwhile, in the BB Gazette the new Gymnastic Badge was officially intimated:

'To encourage keenness in Gymnastics and Physical Training'

It would be issued on or after 31/3/**1917**. [13] Time was running out for the decision makers. At the next meeting the Committee had the matter of the Gymnastic Badge before it and re-considered the two designs. It was unanimous in its objection to the design showing the arm, for the following reasons:

'a] It suggested a design already used in advertising, b] The over-development of the Biceps is not the ideal of modern Physical Training, c] The severed arm is suggestive of the operating theatre.'

While the Committee unanimously objected to the arm design and thought the other preferable, it considered that something even more appropriate could be obtained, and the Secretary was instructed to ask the Dundee Battalion, which had raised the question of a Gymnastic Badge, if it had any ideas:

'...meantime other members of the Executive might forward any suggestions which they may have for the design.' [14]

At the next meeting,

'The Committee discussed the general lines on which the badge should be designed and the matter was left in the hands of Mr. Orr and the Secretary [D. Smith] to complete before the next meeting of the Northern Committee.' [15]

Finally, the matter was settled two weeks later when it was noted that,

'The finalised drawing of the Gymnastic Badge was before the Committee and was approved.' [16]

But was this the Dumbell design which eventually became the accepted choice ? The answer must be 'probably'. The reasons seem obvious. The initiative for the Badge had come from the Dundee Battalion and this was acknowledged at a later meeting. [17] The best way to solve the dispute over the two competing designs was to accept neither and to seek another design from those previously submitted.

Dumbell simplicity

Crossed dumbells would be an obvious choice for **1917**. BB gymnastic classes, for nearly thirty years, had been run by men associated with the military. They would wear the crossed swords of the Gymnastic Instructor on their shirts. [18] The emblem had been in official use by the army since **1881**. [19] Dumbells were in common use at this time in BB gym classes and their image would have been instantly recognisable, as it is to some extent, even today. The substitution of dumbells for swords may not have happened twenty years before when sword-fighting and its downmarket 'single sticks' were common BB pursuits. In the national climate of **1917**, however, images of war were not considered to be acceptable by many church authorities. There was already a debate about 'Cadets' and the introduction of khaki uniforms. The 'crossed pair' design is, incidentally, a commonly used one in military badges, including flags, rifles, axes, machine guns and bugles.

The badge appears, at last!

The status of the new Gymnastic Badge was ensured, even before its issue, when the Northern Committee agreed that it would be recognised as an alternative to the Signallers', Buglers' and Band Badges for counting towards the King's Badge. [20] Final discussions took place when:

'...Specimens of the finished badge were before the Committee, they agreed that the finished badge was not quite satisfactory and were glad that the matter was being looked into for the further supply of the badge.' [21]

Progress must have been satisfactory because in the BB Gazette of April **1917** the announcement was made:

'Badge now ready at 6d each.' [22]

Perhaps it should have added *'...at last.'*

Time for a change ?

By the early **1930s** 'Physical Training' had become the most popular aspect of what was formerly included in 'Gymnastics'. The BB had just, in **1926**, united with the BLB, an organisation which already had a circular severed arm Physical Training Badge. [23] Ideas were mooted for a name-change and, eventually, South Durham Battalion proposed two badges: PT and Gymnastics. A proposal was put to the Brigade Executive to simply change the name of the badge, where it was moved by Dr. Ridge from Enfield and seconded by Mr. Morgan. They were outvoted 18-4. However, questions concerning the design of a new badge were discussed and it was stated that any suggestions for a new design sent in would be considered. [24] The years leading up to the Second World War were to see PT in the BB reach its zenith. As part of the **1937** Festival of Youth, attended by their Royal Highnesses the King and Queen, more than 800 Boys, all over fourteen years old, performed the largest massed physical training display ever staged in Britain at the Empire Stadium, Wembley. [25]

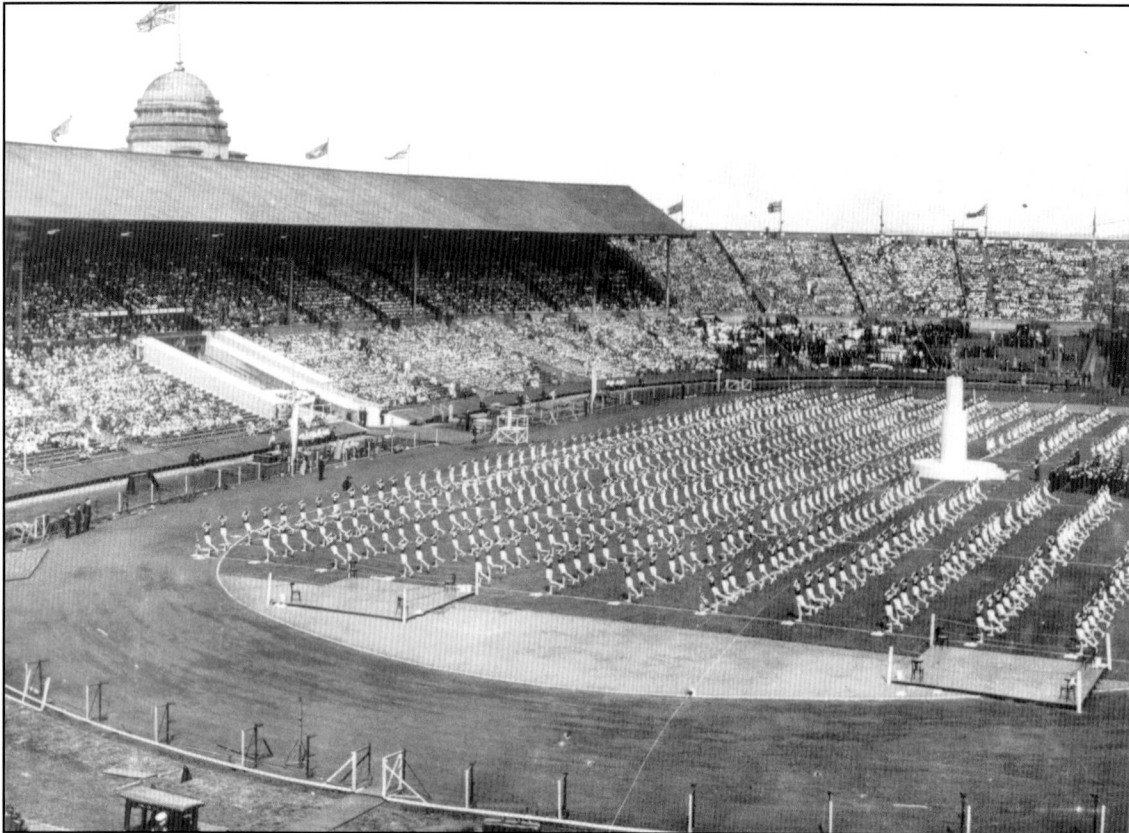

WEMBLEY - JULY 3RD 1937

The Festival of Youth, Empire Stadium, Wembley.
The Boys' Brigade Massed P.T. Display, the largest ever staged in Britain.

Re-named 'P.T. Badge'

The Second World War prevented progress being made towards a new badge, but, in **1946,** a new Athletics Badge, displaying more than just a hint of the 'macabre spectre' of the severed arm, was introduced. Consequently, the Gymnastics Badge was re-named as a Physical Training Badge, a designation it was to retain until **1968.**

One of the simplest badge designs, used in the BB for over fifty years, it had suffered a long and painful birth. However the youthful 'Gym' had emerged vibrantly, tumbling and vaulting into a position of real strength in the BB badge structure, instantly recognisable into its middle age as the 'PT' badge on the

arms of many thousands of BB boys, sadly, to be cut off in its prime.

Under the new badge system the name 'Athletics' was kept along with new badges for 'Physical Recreation' and 'Sportsman's'. [26] In the **1983** Award Regulations a 'Physical Activities Badge' may be obtained, Athletics and Gymnastics being two of the eight 'Credits' available. [27]

REFERENCES

1. '21 Years History'1st Aberdeen Coy.1907, Photograph & Details. R. Bolton Collection. This Company awarded a medal for gymnastics in 1893 to a Col. Sgt. Harry Matthews who later went on to become one of the most prominent Gymnastic Instructors in the Physical Training College in Aberdeen.
2. First edition, January 1901. R. Bolton Collection.
3. The 'Brigadier Badge' for swimming was competed for in the Dundee Battalion. Battalion minute book Vol 2 Sept. 1901-June1905. Dundee Battn. HQ.
4. ibid. Vol 1. 3/10/1899
5. ibid. Vol 3. 3/10/1911
6. ibid. 3/6/1913
7. ibid. 4/1/1916
8. ibid. 1/2/1916
9. Minutes of Brigade Executive Meeting, Glasgow, 16th September 1916.
10. Northern Committee Minute Book No 1 [7th Oct1915-27th Nov 1919] 28/9/1916.
11. ibid. 19/10/1916
12. ibid. 26/10/1916
13. BB Gazette Vol. XXV No. 3. 1/11/1916. p31. BB Scottish HQ. Carronvale, Larbert, Stirling.
14. N. Committee Minute Book No 1. 2/11/1916.op cit.
15. ibid. 9/11/1916
16. ibid. 23/11/1916
17. ibid. 22/2/1917. 'The initiative came from the Dundee Battalion because it had a long-standing certificate scheme for PE ...for each year of a three year course.'
18. 1st Aberdeen Coy. 25 Yrs History. op.cit.
19. Edwards & Langley, British Army Proficiency Badges, 1984. Wardley Publishing, p 18.
20. Northern Committee Minute Book. 1/3/1917 op.cit.
21. ibid. 29/3/1917
22. BB Gazette Vol.XXV 1/4/1917. op.cit.
23. The BLB Boys' Manual. Revised edition. 1926. p 26. R.Bolton collection.
24. Brigade Executive Meeting Minutes, 12-13/5/1934.
25. Springhall, J. et al. Sure & Stedfast, A History of The Boys' Brigade, 1883-1983. 1983. p 143.
26. BB Award Regulations [Company Section] March 1969.The Boys' Brigade.
27. BB Award Regulations [Company Section] September 1983. The Boys' Brigade.

The Gymnastics/Physical Training Badge

1917 - 1968   Title Changed from Gym to P.T. in 1946

BB 079.25

BB 079.09

BB 079.35

BB 079.38

BB 079.28

BB 079.19

BB 079 BACKGROUND NOTES

This solid or shell-stamped nickel brooch comes in nearly forty varieties. The early fasteners are axle pins with round catches, followed by standard tube joints with a variety of catches, later types have coiled pins in squeeze joints. Most shell-stamped types have coiled pins in squeeze joints. There are varying degrees of impressing in the solid types with differing force/production lines. Types with hatched Bs sometimes have either the Butler or Miller maker's name. The pin joint is often mounted at the bottom rather than at the top.

Cork BB Gymnastic Team c.1909
Note the dumbells, bar-bells & clubs
Photo. R. Bolton collection

The Life Saving Badge

In **1913,** the BB became affiliated to the Royal Life Saving Society and steps were taken to introduce a badge. By the end of **1914** an announcement was made in the Gazette:

'This Badge is neatly made in the form of a Lifebuoy, and is very attractive in appearance... it is hoped that this Badge, which will be ready for issue early next year, will greatly increase interest in a most important branch of our work.' [1]

The conditions for the award were given in detail in the same issue of the Gazette, all the tests being taken from the Royal Life Saving Society's Booklet. [2]

The lifebuoy design may have been suggested by the fact that the BLB had, in **1912,** introduced its Life Saving Badge, a metal lifebuoy. A lifebuoy had been used in the BLB for many years as a buttonhole badge and was one of its most important emblems. The BB version had the Brigade emblem in the centre whilst the BLB simply had an 'empty' lifebuoy, because badges were, at that time, shared with the GLB. [3]

In **1927,** it was quite natural for the newly united BB and BLB to retain the Life Saving Award, as this was a badge which they held in common. The centre of the badge was changed to the double 'B' motif to bring it into line with the rest of the proficiency awards. The lifebuoy would become one of the Brigade's most enduring emblems after **1927** as the emblem of the 'Life Boys', the section for younger boys. During the second world war this badge, like many other pierced types, was produced in solid form to comply with the utility restrictions.[4] The lifebuoy was retained for the **1968** issue barrel award for Life Saving. [5] Life Saving forms a Credit component of the **1983** Community Activities Award. [6]

REFERENCES

1. BB Gazette, Vol XXIII, No 4, 1/12/1914 p 50. National Library of Scotland.
2. ibid. p 50 - 51.
3. The Boys' Life Brigade. The Boys' Manual, 1926, BLB HQ. p 36. R.Bolton collection.
4. Massey, Alistair, 3rd Gourock Coy. [joined c1942] supplied evidence of his receipt of a solid version.
5. BB Award Regulations [Company Section] March 1968. The Boys' Brigade.
6. BB Award Regulations [Company Section] September 1983. The Boys' Brigade.

The Life - Saving Badge

1914 - 1926

BB 080

1927 - 1968

BB 080 & BB 081
BACKGROUND NOTES

These nickel brooches are solid and, with the exception of the wartime version, are all fretted. The pre-1927 version has the BB emblem, replaced by two letter B's post-1926. The earlier version has an axle pin with most of the others being the standard tube joint. There is a variety of catches, round, FRC and hooked. Pins are mounted both vertically and horizontally. Only one version has some impressing on the reverse. Variations occur in the fretting around the second 'B'. There are varieties with hatched B's.

BB 081.01

BB 081.07

BB 081.10

BB 081.03

The Pipers' Badge

Ahead of the army !

The Pipers' Badge was authorised at a Brigade Executive Meeting in Newcastle-Upon-Tyne in 1921. [1]

The proposal for a drummers' and a pipers' badge came from Paisley Battalion. The musician's lyre was considered to be an unsuitable emblem for use in the Brigade's some 150 pipe bands. [2] The design of the badge was left to the Southern and Northern Committees. They almost certainly did not get the design from the

Photo:
Aberdeen Journals Ltd.

The pipe band of the 1st Millport Coy. c.1925.

rel format with the Pipers' Badge being retained in the new shape. The design was now limited to the three drones, but no bag. [5] In the **1983** badge structure, Piping is a qualification for the Music Credit which counts toward the Interest Badge. [6] The Music Credit includes a drawing of a set of pipes.

army, which had few such badges at the time and those in use were usually of a wreath design for pipe-majors. The army, unlike the BB, wore full highland dress and had less need for a distinctive badge. [3] The kilt, incidently, was not approved for wear by BB pipe bands until **1949**. In **1939**, a three-drone pipe badge in metal was introduced into the army (The King's Own Scottish Borderers). It was larger, but almost identical in design to the BB Badge. This would seem to indicate that the BB was in advance of the army with this particular badge. [4]

In **1968**, the BB changed the proficiency badges to the common bar-

REFERENCES

1. Minutes of Brigade Executive Meeting. Newcastle-On-Tyne, 21-22/1/1921.
2. Gibbs, Muriel, Banging the Drum, The Story of BB Bands, BB Archive Press, 1983. p 16.
3. Edwards & Langley, British Army Proficiency Badges, Wardley Publishing. 1983. pp 117-118.
4. ibid. p 117.
5. BB Award Regulations [Company Section] March 1968. The Boys' Brigade
6. BB Award Regulations [Company Section] September 1983.The Boys' Brigade

A BB Pipe Band of today

The Pipers' Badge   1921 - 1968

BB 082.09   **BB 082**   **BB 082**

BB 082 BACKGROUND NOTES

Although a scarce badge there are quite a number of variations. The earliest versions were all frosted, double pierced at the top near the longest drone and had either an axle pin or standard tube joint with round catch. Later versions have tube joints with FRCs and single piercing at the top. The reverse displays varying force marks and reveals that the piercing of the centres of the Bs can be either circular or semi-circular. There is an early version with lugs, believed to be part of a set, or sets, of trial badges produced in the wake of BB/BLB union. The BB intention may have been to introduce lugged fittings as an alternative for use on the retained ex-BLB full uniform tunics rather than just brooch fastenings for armbands. There are foreign versions (see BB 077 notes)

The Scouts' Badge
The gilded lily

The fleur-de-lys is perhaps one of the world's most widely recognised symbols. To many people in Britain it means simply the Boy Scout emblem. The original use as a 'Scout' emblem was to represent the North pointer of a compass, indicative of the scout's ability to find his way. Colonel Baden-Powell chose the emblem when he introduced Scouting into the Army when commanding the 5th Dragoon Guards in South Africa around **1897**. First official mention in Army orders dates to **1905**. [1] Army Scouting badges took a number of forms but all were based on the fleur-de-lys.

**Sgt. Herbert 'Nippy' Watts (left)
and Sgt. Herbert Collingbourne (right),**
1st Bournemouth Coy. BB
Photo taken c.1909.
Both attended B.P.'s first Brownsea Island Camp.

Ten BB Boys amongst the first twenty Boy Scout Badge recipients

Major General R.S.S.Baden-Powell, C.B. was a national hero when on Friday 8th May **1903,** he attended the London BB Demonstration at the Royal Albert Hall. As Honorary Vice-President of The Boys' Brigade from **1903** it was inevitable that he would come into contact with many BB Boys. In **1904,** he reviewed the 7,000 strong Glasgow Battalion and suggested in his speech that some form of Scout training would be popular in the Brigade and *'do a great amount of good.'* [2] William Smith, who was admired by Baden-Powell, asked B.P. to adapt his military handbook 'Aids to Scouting' for the training of boys. By **1906,** it was reported in the BB Gazette that Baden-Powell had placed at the disposal of the BB the manuscript of a paper on 'Scouting for Boys'. Various extracts from the paper were reprinted. A year later B.P. organised an 'Experimental Camp' on Brownsea Island in Poole Harbour attended by twenty boys: ten from public schools and ten from The Boys' Brigade. Seven boys from 1st Bournemouth Coy. and three from 1st Poole Coy.. Terry Bonfield, one of the 1st Bournemouth members who attended the camp, recalled that B.P. awarded them a brass Scout badge in two parts:

'At first we were called tenderfeet. we got the bottom part of the scout badge when Baden-Powell made us second class scouts and the top part when we became first class scouts.' [3]

The success of this camp gave B.P. the incentive to let Pearson commence publishing 'Scouting for Boys' in January **1908**. Now the genie was out of the bottle!

Official BP 'Peace Scouts' and BB Scouts

Scouting, originally intended for use within existing organisations such as the BB and CLB, was, during **1908**, being taken up spontaneously by boys all over the country. Baden-Powell, very often assisted by the BB, toured Britain 'selling' his idea. A typical situation was that of Captain Shrapnel of 42nd London (S.Lambeth) Coy. BB who was asked, in **1908**, by the South London Battalion to arrange for a lecture to be given by B.P. on 'Peace Scouts'. The lecture took place in the 42nd's hall after which the 42nd Scout Patrol was formed, said to be the first in London.[4] The growth of Scouting outside the Brigade was of concern to Brigade leaders, but growth within the Brigade very much more so. Some larger battalions issued their own Scouting regulations concerning membership, awards, uniform, etc.. One of the earliest to do so was Glasgow Battalion in January **1909,** when principal advice included keeping activities to non-BB time and not wearing any specific uniform. [5] During **1909,** the Brigade Executive sent a Memorandum to Battalions and Companies as regards Scouting and also asked the following:

'...7. Should a Special BB Scout's Badge be issued? 8. If so, should the Badge be permitted to be worn on BB Parades? 9.Should the Badge be merely a badge of Scout Membership or should it be an award for passing a certain Certificate?' [6]

The Brigade Executive, meeting in London on 7th May, gave careful consideration to the replies from battalions and companies and also considered and approved of the report of the Conference of Representatives of The Boys' Brigade, the London Diocesan Church Lads' Brigade, the Catholic

A Scout Patrol of the 7th Bristol Coy., BB, April 1909
Photo: John Russell collection

Boys' Brigade, and the Jewish Lads' Brigade, held in London on 1st April **1909**, at which it was unanimously resolved:

'That while acknowledging the indebtedness of the Brigades to General Baden-Powell, this Conference is of opinion that the Scouting movement should be carried on by each of the several Brigades as a branch of its own work, independently of the Boy Scouts' organisation, each Brigade adopting its own Badges, Tests, and Certificates if any.'

On the issue of badges it was resolved:

'...3. that a BB Scout's Badge should be issued, subject to Examination, with permission to wear the Badge on BB parades. 4 that a Certificate should be issued for passing a further Examination as a First-Class Scout...'

The Badge was not ready at this stage. A BB Scout uniform was also approved. BB Scouting was, therefore, well and truly launched. [7] The Badge was ready by September **1909** at a cost of 4d carriage paid from HQ.,London Office. One of the more notable BB Badge designs, incorporating the Fleur-

de-Lys and the BB emblem, it was to be worn on the left sleeve between shoulder and elbow. [8] By March **1910** the Certificate for First-Class Scouts was ready and cost 3d carriage paid. [9] The move from Badge to certificate was unusual for the BB, with certificates usually preceding Badges. In June **1910** the Scout Masters' Badge was agreed:

'BB Officers acting as Scout Masters should be distinguished by wearing in their hats the same badge as used in the Officers' Glengarry and Field Service Caps.' [10]

Things were moving quickly because in November **1910** ...

'...the Executive decided to sanction a Special Badge for First-Class BB Scouts...due notice will be given when the Badge is ready for issue.' [11]

This new badge was the 'Gold' version and was destined to last just seven years. The Brigade Executive meeting in July **1917** reduced the Scout Badges to one, but this time, in keeping with other BB Awards, the Second Class would be a certificate and the First Class a badge only. This information was intimated in the October Gazette.[12] The 'new' First Class would be the original nickel badge.

For the sake of change

One thing is clear when investigating the story of the BB Scouts' Badge. It wasn't popular. Scouting didn't really 'take off' within the BB as it did outside. The Edinburgh Battalion in it's 24th Annual Report, **1909-1910** provides some clues about this unpopularity. There is an account of the 'Committee on Boy Scouts' established to investigate the failure to arrange 'Scout Patrols'. It found that BB work was taking up all the available time that officers had and that ...

'...the BB is doing most of the work recommended in the Scouting Handbook...'

The Committee was abolished. Scouting, it seems, was a bit of a 'fad' in the BB which was taken up with enthusiasm in the early days but was unable to sustain any great numbers. Boys wishing to do 'Scouting' as an activity could, after **1908**, simply join a BP Scout Troop. Boys joining the BB were not keen to do 'part-time' scouting in the summer, at camp, or after BB activities were finished.

Just for the Record

There is a unique record of BB Scouting contained in the BB Annual Reports from **1908-1909** to **1915-1916**. Statistics and commentary reveal a somewhat luke-warm enthusiasm.

1908-1909
Scouting was: *'Scarcely sufficiently*

developed'. So far, 414 Officers and 4,361 Boys taken up the activity.
1909-1910
611 Boys passed 2nd Class Exam (Badge);
52 the 1st Class (Cert).
'...Scouting has only been taken up to a limited extent in the Brigade...'
1910-1911
584 passed 2nd Class Scouts Badge; 155 passed 1st Class.
1911-1912
265 passed 2nd Class Scouts Badge;
61 passed 1st Class.
1912-1913
174 passed 2nd Class Scouts Badge;
46 passed 1st Class.
'...it is somewhat remarkable that while every other department of Brigade work has advanced during the past year, Scouting seems to have lost to a considerable extent its interest for the Boys of the Brigade.'
1913-1914
239 passed 2nd Class Scouts Badge;
45 passed 1st Class.
1914-1915
214 passed 2nd Class Scouts Badge; 100 passed 1st Class.
1915-1916
322 passed 2nd Class Scouts Badge; 102 passed 1st Class.

'BB Scouts:...The comparatively small extent to which Scouting is carried on within the Brigade is largely due to the fact that Officers are realising that many of the main features of Scouting such as signalling, swimming etc., have been included in the Boys' Brigade curriculum for over thirty years, and can be carried on as formerly'.

There are no more references in the Annual Reports checked from **1916-1923**. Using the above information it is possible to work out the number of Scout Badges awarded between **1909-1916**.

Silver Scouts = 2409
Gold Scouts = 509.*

*Muriel Gibbs gives the number as 561 but she has included the 52 in Session **1909-1910** who only gained a Certificate. [13]
It is probable that the number of Silver Scout Badges awarded didn't rise above 3000.

La fleur et mort

BB Scouting came to an end in **1927**, six years after Scouts and Scout Badges were abolished in the army. [14] The Brigade Executive met in January and the following appears in the minutes:

'...it was decided to delete from the Manual the present paragraph regarding Scouting, and suggest therefore a paragraph on Open Air work in the summer, which would include a reference to Scouting.' [15]

This failed to materialize. The new Wayfarers' Badge covered most of the former Scouts' Badge syllabus.

REFERENCES

1. Edwards & Langley, British Army Proficency Badges, Wardley Publishing, 1984. p 21.
2. Gibbs, Muriel. The Boys' Brigade & Scouting, BB Archive Press Series, 1983. p 3.
3. Brownsea beginnings for Scouting Adventure. Article in Bournemouth Evening Echo, 4th October 1989
4. 42nd London [S.Lambeth] Coy BB. 21st Anniversary Book, 1912, p 7. J. Russell Collection.
5. BB Glasgow Battalion, Memorandum by the Committee appointed by the Battalion Council to consider Scouting For Boys. Battalion HQ Glasgow, 29th January 1909.
6. BB Gazette, Vol. XVII, No 7, 1/3/1909. p 101. BB Scottish HQ. Carronvale, Larbert, Stirlingshire.
7. ibid. No 9, 1/6/1909, p 154.
8. ibid. Vol. XVIII, No 1, 1/9/1909, pp 2-3.
9. ibid. No. 7 1/3/1910, p 98.
10.ibid. No 10, 1/6/1910, p 146.
11.ibid. Vol. XIX, No. 3 1/11/1910, p 35.
12.ibid. Vol XXIV, No. 2, 1/10/1917, p 24.
13. Gibbs, Muriel, op.cit p 9.
14. Edwards & Langley, op.cit p 21.
15.Minutes of Brigade Executive Meeting. 14-16/1/1927. BB HQ, Felden Lodge, Hemel Hempstead, Herts.

The Scouts' Badge 1909 - 1926

BB 086.01

BB 086.02

Gold
1910 - 1917: First Class

Silver
1909 - 1910: Classless/Second Class
1910 - 1917: Second Class
1917 - 1926: First Class

BB 086 BACKGROUND NOTES

The Scouts' Badges are always full shell and identical except for colour. The 'Silver' being nickel. There are no real variations although some of the 'Silver' badges seem to have been coated with a silver finish. They have a bridge joint which is mounted on a pair of pillars, a coiled pin and a round catch. Pins on these badges seem to be very thin and examples are frequently found with a rusting, broken pin.

Beware of imitations!

WARNING

WARNING

BB Scouts' Badges silver and gold, have been reproduced in silver using dental impression technology. Some years ago, a number of badges were reproduced, perhaps as many as fifty. The quality is surprisingly good although definition on the obverse is poor for a 'shell-stamped' badge. Reverse definition reveals a smooth 'melted' appearance. The best way to reveal these 'fakes' is to check the joint, it should be a version of bridge joint with two pillars supporting the hinge, coiled pin and round clasp. The fakes have a 'box' joint with coiled pin. In the **1980s**, large-sized 'BB Scout Badges' (about 1.5 x correct size) were produced in Poole, Dorset by the Borough Scout Council for the Waterfront Museum. These badges are crudely made and are very 'brassy' in colour sporting two lugs. In the early **1990s**, the large 'fake' badge was replaced in Poole with two smaller replicas sold on a card. The joints of these are single pillar 'squeeze' type with the pin passing over a separate bridge. The replicas are smaller than the real badges, lack quality of definition on the obverse and are brighter than the originals.

Other BB badges 'faked' in the same way as the **Scout Badge** include the **5-pointed Star** and officers' **1897 Silver and Bronze Uniform Buttonhole Badges**. The **Cross for Heroism** and **Old Boys' Union** watch pendant were reproduced in the **1970s** in Wales, using a type of resin.

The Scripture Knowledge Badge

Made in Birmingham

In order to grasp the significance of this badge it is essential to turn back the pages of BB History to the union of the BB and BLB in 1926. The BLB had a Scripture Knowledge Badge which required the recipient to gain:

'...not less than a first class certificate or its equivalent in an examination recognised by the Church or Sunday School'.

It was a circular badge showing an open Bible. [1]

The BLB Scripture Knowledge Badge

Upon unification, much of the badge system of the two organisations was simply amalgamated. Owing to the extreme importance, and sensitivity, of 'Christian Education' within what was now an even more interdenominational and ecumenical Brigade, there was, naturally, a great deal of uncertainty about any prescribed religious teaching which may be considered essential in awarding such a badge. Therefore, regulations for a certificate were introduced which would count towards the newly adopted Education Badge, [2] but the idea of having a separate scripture knowledge badge was rejected.

Birmingham momentum

The main influence to retain some form of scripture knowledge badge had, of course, come from the former BLB leaders, particularly those in strongholds such as Birmingham under the direction of Donald (later 'Sir' Donald) Finnemore. Having not been accepted in the first batch of new awards, clearly it was going to take some considerable time for such a badge to gain favour, but the Birmingham connection would keep up the pressure.

After the Second World War there seems to have been a desire within the Brigade for the badge system to remain virtually unchanged. At a meeting of the Badges Sub-Committee of the BB Executive in 1947, a suggestion for a scripture knowledge certificate and badge was rejected and a general policy statement made. [3] Five years passed before Sir Donald Finnemore brought up the matter again. [4] The proposal this time was to award the Education Badge upon gaining three Scripture Certificates, granted by any appropriate religious authority, over three years. This was considered by the Badges Sub-Committee as being a 'back door' way of introducing a scripture knowledge badge. Its answer was to reject the proposal in the same way that an earlier christian citizenship badge proposal had been rejected. The BB had always been reluctant to introduce any award which attempted to prescribe religious teaching. The Executive, however, decided to go ahead with the idea even though they were not in favour of the principal meeting of the company, the Bible Class, being included in the badge system. [5] So, in effect, the BB had a badge which could be gained by having three Scripture Certificates which did not have to be awarded by the Brigade, and this badge was called the Education Badge! When the Badges Sub-Committee again discussed a motion for a scripture knowledge badge in 1956, a degree of frustration was evident; it made a point of distancing itself from decisions made by the Executive. [6]

Birmingham motion

In 1957, The Birmingham Battalion proposed the following motion at Brigade Council in Nottingham:

'That this council authorises the introduction of a Scripture Knowledge Badge'.

The motion was carried and the matter referred to the Badges Sub-Committee for the drafting of regulations. [7] Decisions about the Badge were made at the meeting in February 1958 when it was even suggested that a more suitable name would be 'Bible Knowledge Badge'. However, six possible designs were submitted for the new badge and one was selected. The chosen circular design had 'Rays' shining out from an open Bible, in very much the style of the old BLB Buttonhole Badges and medals. Finally, the design in a simpler form, ironically almost identical to the former BLB Badge - without the rays - was accepted.

The regulation for the new badge was intimated in the BB Gazette for introduction in the Session **1958/59**. [8] Details of coloured cloth backings for the Badge were also given at the same time. The Badge, awarded for three BB Scripture Knowledge Certificates, could be augmented by the use of a red cloth for gaining the fourth Certificate and a blue cloth for a fifth Certificate.

Birmingham made

To complete the story, the Badge, which had been conceived, framed and sponsored in Birmingham was eventually manufactured there too, by H.W. Miller, Ltd..

Many companies continued the wearing of the badge until **1970**, even though in **1967** a Christian Education Badge was issued as part of the new Awards Scheme and in the new barrel format bearing the Alpha and Omega letters of the Greek alphabet. [9] Currently, the badge which covers Scripture Knowledge is the Leadership Badge having 'Christian Faith' as one of its component Credits. [10]

One of the original drawings for a proposed scripture badge. Note traces of the 'rays'.
R. Mandry collection

REFERENCES

1. The Boys' Life Brigade. The Boys' Manual. BLB HQ 56, Old Bailey, London EC4. January 1926. R.Bolton collection
2. The Boys' Brigade. Handbook for Boys. BB HQ, Abbey House Westminster, 1927. p14.
3. Badges Sub-Committee minutes. November 1947, Abbey House Westminster. Final paragraph reads: .' *'The Committee felt that the present regulations should be continued in operation for some considerable time without any alterations, except in small matters of detail where clarification or interpretation might be required.'*
4. Minutes of Brigade Executive, November 1952.
5. Badges Sub-Committee minutes, January 1953.
6. ibid. February 1956.
7. ibid. November 1957
8. BB Gazette, Vol LXVI, No.6 Aug/Sept 1958 p.107. BB Scottish HQ. Carronvale, Larbert, Stirling.
9. BB Award Regulations [Company Section] March 1969. The Boys' Brigade.
10. ibid. September 1983.

The Scripture Knowledge Badge 1958 - 1968

BB 087

BB 087   BACKGROUND NOTES

Of solid nickel construction the badge has no obverse varieties, all the versions being distinguished on the reverse. The B's are hatched on all types. Coiled pins with squeeze joints and hooked catches are fitted both vertically and horizontally with the maker's name, Miller, in varying sizes and shapes. There is very little impressing on the back.

The Seamanship Badge

Given the BB's jaunty emblem, its founder's known love of sailing and British naval prowess, it is astonishing that no such badge appeared before 1946 by which time the Senior Service was in serious decline. Rather than having any career or recreational intention, the Brigade Executive's proposal to link new seamanship and airmans' awards stongly suggests that the main motivation was national defence. The same with a proposed 'Navigators' Badge' [1] aimed to encourage senior boys either to join the armed forces, or at least be aware of navigation, and other basics should a national emergency arise. All this is wholly explicable given the background of Britain's unpreparedness for WW2 and, in **1946**, the new perceived threat from international communism within a terrifying nuclear age.

The Athletics and Seamanship Badges were introduced in **1946** and both included its name in the design. The helm design for the badge may have been inspired by that used by the RASC (Waterborne Fleet) introduced in the early **1940s** for use by Coxwains, Helmsmen or Navigators, and which came from the training school at Victoria on the Isle of Wight. [2] The army badge being made from worsted was apparently much easier to manufacture than the BB Nickel version which required numerous stampings to pierce all the holes.

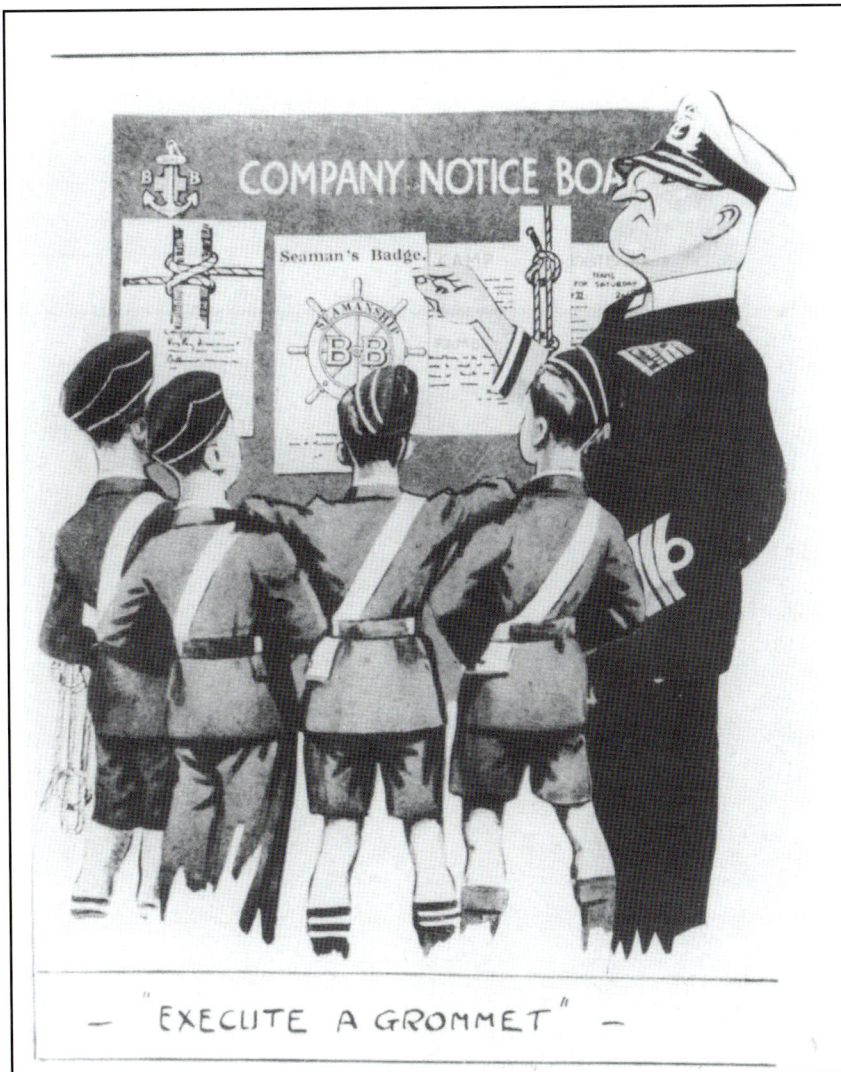

The available records fail to explain why an airmans' badge was rejected. We may, however, surmise that few, if any, companies were involved in such an activity, introduction costs would be prohibitive in those austere times whilst both Scouts and Air Cadets already provided a local option. Seamanship was, on the other hand, already easily encompassed by some BB companies which found it to be a highly successful activity. Nevertheless, given its nature and restriction to senior boys, seamanship would remain a minority pursuit and its badge a much cherished item.

— "EXECUTE A GROMMET" —

**Photo-montage produced by D.Gordon Barnsley MC
former
Birmingham Battalion
Secretary.**
Birmingham Battalion collection.

A Seamanship 'barrel' Badge was included in the **1968** Award Regulations. [3] As part of the **1983** Regulations, Seamanship is a Credit which counts as part of the Adventure Badge. The Credit shows part of a ship's helm. [4]

Some find it surprising that many boys got, and still get, their first 'taste of the sea' in a BB company.

Footnote

You may not recognise the young BB boy in the photograph opposite, a twelve-year-old member of the 2nd Hawick BB Coy.. In **1966,** he became well-known along with his friend John Ridgeway when they rowed the Atlantic Ocean in 92 days from the USA to Eire. Since then Chay Blyth hasn't looked back as regards his nautical achievements.

Photo:
The Boys' Brigade 'Stedfast' Magazine.

was part of the training that would help him in his life both physically and spiritually. In the words of W. Mc G. Eager's book the BB was, and is, involved in 'Making Men'. [6]

Chay has looked back, however, to his youth and the 'good start' he was given.[5] As it happens this included very little in the way of seamanship or sailing instruction. What he probably did get in the BB

REFERENCES

1. Minutes of Brigade Executive, 21/1/1945, BB HQ Felden Lodge, Hemel Hempstead, Herts.
2. Edwards & Langley ,British Army Proficiency Badges, 1984. pp 88 - 89.
3. BB Award Regulations [Company Section] March 1968. The Boys' Brigade
4. BB Award Regulations [Company Section] September 1983. The Boys' Brigade
5. Article: 'Chay Blyth in Edinburgh', Stedfast Magazine No.225, June 1972 p.22.
6. Eager., W. Mc G. 'Making Men' The History of Boys' Clubs and Related Movements. 1953.

The Seamanship Badge   1946 - 1968

BB 083.01

BB 083 BACKGROUND NOTES

This rare badge seems to have only been struck twice during its lifetime, on issue in 1946 and c.1964 towards the end of its life. The early version is the most common; a thinner metal, impressed wheel and copper round catch fastening. The second version is thicker with a non-pierced area to the left of the first letter B. It was an item that badge manufacturers were reluctant to produce for the BB because of the alarming amount of wastage as the whole centre often fell out during the piercing process.

The Sergeants'/NCO's Proficiency Star

The origins of this award, like the Brigade, seem to lie in the Volunteer force in the City of Glasgow.

The Volunteers

The four-pointed badge, originally in silver wire, was given to proficient sergeants in the Volunteer Force from 1878.[1] It was worn in the 'V' of the chevron and was certainly used by the Lanarkshire Rifle Volunteers. By 1914, however, it had fallen out of use in the Volunteers, but had been taken up by the BB as an indication of competence in theoretical and practical drill. The convenor of the Glasgow Battalion Drill Committee made his move in 1894 when he requested permission to grant a proficiency badge

`..in the form of a small star to be worn in the chevron of the stripes, for those who passed the examination for Sergeants recently'[2]

Permission was granted and seventy such awards were made.[3] As part of continuing correspondence in the 'BB' magazine of March 1895 the following information was supplied:

'- A Sergeants' Decoration, in the shape of a star, has been offered by the Glasgow Battalion to sergeants passing a examination (oral and written) in Company and Battalion Drill. The excitement out west, according to our correspondent, is very great, every captain working hard to get his boys through. The examination is to take place about the middle of March.'[4]

By July details of the examination were published:

'Sergeants' Proficiency Star - In the Glasgow Battalion, 79 sergeants entered for the Proficiency Examination in Company Drill, and of these 71 passed ... A record is kept at battalion head-quarters of those who passed, and they each receive a certificate as well as a proficiency star. This star is a neat silver badge with the Brigade crest upon it, and is to be worn above the chevron on the right arm.'[5]

During the session 1896-97 Glasgow Battn. decided to open up the examination to corporals...

`...but to withold the right of wearing the star until a Corporal obtains his promotion.'[6]

Eighty-four passed the examination at the end of that session. The `star' was on the Glasgow Battalion `Approved List' from 1895/96 and available from HQ office, 162, Buchanan St., at a cost of 6d. In the `Report and Arrangements for 1896-1897' it was named as the`Battalion Proficiency star'. Only in 1896 can it be said with certainty that the `star' used by Glasgow is the `Volunteer' pattern four-pointed variety because a `Proficiency Star', of the design later adopted by the Brigade nationally, appears in the corner of a Glasgow Battalion `Certificate of Proficiency

for Non-Commissioned Officers'.[7] A camp photograph of the 32nd Glasgow Coy. taken in the same year shows boys wearing what is clearly a metal star badge.[8]

The idea sweeps the country

It may be assumed from the details above that Glasgow was first with the Sergeants' Star, but North London Battalion also makes reference to the award of a Sergeants' Star `Badge' by examination in 1894 [9] So, who was the first ? Perhaps it will never be known for certain. Bristol [10] and Liverpool [11] Battalions were using them by 1896, Sheffield[12] by 1897, W. London [13] by 1898, City & East London[14] by 1899, and in Perth[15] by 1900 whilst both Nottingham[16] and Hull[17] had introduced the star by 1901. In fact, ten Battalions, 47.6% of all submitting reports to BBHQ, were using the award before it was sanctioned nationally. Needless to say, with such a popular award, acceptance grew each year. The London Council accepted the badge in February 1903 [18] with the Brigade making the following announcement in the October BB Gazette of the same year:

`A Sergeant's Proficiency Star to be issued from HQ at London Office subject to conditions to be laid down.'[19]

In Glasgow this simply meant changing the name from

`Battalion Proficiency Star' to `Brigade Proficiency Star'

in their `Arrangements' for 1904-1905.[20]

THE BOYS' BRIGADE,
Glasgow Battalion.

CERTIFICATE OF PROFICIENCY
FOR
NON-COMMISSIONED OFFICERS.

This is to Certify that Sergeant W. Stewart

of the 19th GLASGOW COMPANY has passed a satisfactory Examination

and has shown himself practically acquainted with the duties of a

SECTION COMMANDER in COMPANY DRILL.

Date, March, 1896.

H. Carr SM. 1.G.W. Examiner.

R. Jeffray Douglas Convener, Drill Committee.

●●●●●●●●●●
The Glasgow Battalion NCO's Proficiency Certificate of 1896, with the first picture of the 'Proficiency Star' and the rather 'rugged' anchor.
●●●●●●●●●●

J. Cooper collection

Star medals

The use of 'Star' Medals rather than brooches must be mentioned, but there is no record of any battalion awarding these in place of a brooch. Examples exist of bronze and silver [21] medals identical in design to the 'Regulation' Sgt.'s Star. During the late **1890s**, these medals were worn on a red, white and blue vertically striped ribbon They were, possibly, advertised

only once in the BB Manual (**1895**) by Messrs James Farquharson of Houndsditch London.

'Bronze Star Medals, with pin hangers 6d each, plated Star Medals with clasp and ribbon 2/- each, Silver Star Medals with clasp and ribbon 10/- each.'

These were more likely, however, to have been the 'Squad' medals which were also then just being supplied by Farquharson. One can only speculate as to the reason why the advertising using the word 'star' was withdrawn. Perhaps simply to avoid confusion.

From star to sticker

The Sergeants' Proficiency Star continued unchanged until the union with the BLB in **1926** when the emblem was updated. During the **1930s** there were moves to get the name of the award changed to 'NCO's Proficiency Star' thus opening up the award to senior NCO's who, in large companies, would never become Sergeants. Mr. F. J. Parkinson, 44th Belfast, one such supporter of a change in the name and regulations, pleaded in the BB Gazette on behalf of those

'...thousands of Corporals in the Brigade [who] year by year qualify in the exam., but are denied the right to wear the badge'.

He was given a robust reply from the editor:

A proficient Sergeant.
Colour Sergeant Maurice Davis 60th
London Coy, Dulwich. c.1914
R. Bolton collection

'...It is "hard lines". If they were members of less efficient and less attractive Companies they would probably be Sergeants, but they have gained more than they have lost through having been trained in first-rate Companies.'[22]

In **1947,** the title of the award was changed to `NCO's Proficiency Star.' In the great awards reformation of **1968** [23] the star fell from the ever present firmament of Brigade awards, losing its special status, to be re-born as a barrel- shaped `Drill Badge' featuring a `King' chess piece design, somewhat ironic since the King has probably the most limited field of movement of any piece. Following the pattern of the certificates which had been awarded for NCO's Proficiency prior to **1968** the new badge was awarded in three stages denoted by the use of silver and gold inserts as per other proficiency awards. The **1977** plastic Drill Badge had a blue sticker. Under the **1983** system [24] Drill is part of the requirement for the `Leadership' Badge, a drill `Credit' sticker is available.

Leadership

The demise of the Sergeants' Star, and of its rather shabby replacement, the Drill Badge, is symptomatic of changes in the ethos of The Boys' Brigade in the latter part of the twentieth century. Any implied association with militarism has been dismissed by some, rather apologetically, as a hangover from the past. The rank of `Private' disappeared in **1981** and drill's importance has continued to decline, becoming a mere 'activity'.

However, the role of `leadership' promoted by the original badge remains firm and deep in the thinking of the BB, so perhaps the 'leadership' badge is a worthy successor.

REFERENCES

1. Edwards D. & Langley D. British Army Proficiency Badges, 1984. p48.
2. The Boys' Brigade, Glasgow Battalion Minute Book No.1 [12.10.1885][1/1/1]. Executive Meeting, 10.12.1894. Glasgow Battalion HQ. Bath St. Glasgow.
3. ibid. Council meeting, 3.4.1895.
4. 'Reid, Herbert, Ed., 'BB' Magazine March 1895. Published by BB Executive.
5. 'BB' Magazine ibid. July 1895
6. Glasgow Battalion Reports, 1896-1900,[1/3/3] Glasgow Battalion HQ.
7. Certificate awarded to Sgt. W. Stewart, 19th Glasgow Coy. March 1896. J. Cooper, Glasgow.
8. 32nd Glasgow NCO's at Strachur 1896, in album 1892-1978. BB Glasgow Battalion Archives, Battalion HQ.
9. North London Battalion, Third Annual Report, 1894-1895, pp 5-7. BB Scottish Archive, Carronvale House, Larbert, Stirling.
10. Bristol Battalion, Sixth Annual Report 1896-1897 & Seventh Annual Report 1897-1898, Carronvale, ibid.
11. Liverpool Battalion, Sixth Annual Report, 1896-1897. p16. Carronvale.
12. Sheffield Battalion, Ninth Annual Report, 1897-1898 p.19. Carronvale.
13. W. London Battalion, Seventh Annual Report, 1898-1899 p.7. Carronvale.
14. City & East London Battalion, First Report, 1899-1900, Carronvale.
15. Perth Battalion, Eighth Annual Report, 1900-1901, Carronvale.
16. Nottingham Battalion, Eleventh Annual Report, 1901-1902, Carronvale.
17. Hull Battalion, Second Annual Report, 1901-1902, Carronvale.
18. Minutes of London Council, February 16th, 1903.
19. BB Gazette Vol XII, 1/10/1903, p.31, Executive Meeting in Belfast.
20. Glasgow Battalion Reports. op.cit.
21. Bronze and Silver, in Private Collections, one Hallmarked B'ham. 1897.
22. BB Gazette Vol XLI March 1933. p.118.
23. The Boys' Brigade Award Regulations, [Company Section] March, 1968.
24. The Boys' Brigade Award Regulations, [Company Section] September, 1983.

STEDFAST MAG

The boys speak out... in February 1957:
'Sir - As drill is part of the discipline of the BB, I think it would be a good idea if there was a drill badge.'
Pte. D. Jones, 10th Wigan Company.

and ...in April 1957:
'Sir - it appears that Pte. D. Jones has not read the Boys' Handbook. He asks for a drill badge - may I inform him that the NCO's Proficiency Certificate and Badge are both based on drill.'
Sgt. F. R. Martin, 90th Belfast Company

The Sergeants' Proficiency Star

c.1895

Star Medals

1902 - 1927

BB 084

STAR MEDALS & BB 084 BACKGROUND NOTES

The Star medal of the same pattern as the Proficiency Star, can be found in bronze and silver. Silver medals hallmarked 1896 are known. The medals are solid with the backs smooth for engraving etc..

The first edition of the official Sergeants' star uses the same die as the medals, solid and with a horizontal brooch fastening. The finish of the badge is usually frosted, whereas the silver medals were not. There is one version that is not frosted and has a vertical pin.

The NCO's Proficiency Star   1927 - 1968

BB 085.01

BB 085.05

BB 085.12

BB 085.17

BB 085 BACKGROUND NOTES

The post-1926 NCO's Stars display a wide variation. The size and shape varies as can be seen from the pictures above. The reverse of the badge displays varying amounts of force marking. Pins are horizontal or vertical with differing joints and catches. The obverse shows variety in the size and style of anchor as well as the lettering. Finishes include frosted and nickel plate. The variations in background stipple size are particularly noticeable.

The Signallers' Badge

Waving the flags for local democracy.

Introduced officially for the whole Brigade in 1911, the Signallers' Badge was one of the early badges to be used by Battalions for many years prior to that date, in response to local demand. Signalling was one of the qualifications for the BB Scouts' Badge, introduced two years earlier, which was not well taken up by the Brigade. Signalling, by the use of semaphore flags was, however, very popular.

Battalions signal the way ahead

The earliest recorded use of a signallers' badge comes in the Third Annual Report of the North London Battalion **1894-1895**, [1] although it is quite possible that other battalions were issuing similar badges at the same time, or perhaps even earlier. The wording of the N. London Report suggests the award of badges at an earlier date when it states:

'These rules do not apply to Boys who were wearing the respective badges on or before January 1st 1895.'

Other battalions also awarded signaller's badges; Liverpool Battalion **1899**, [2] City & East London **1901** [3] and Newcastle-Upon-Tyne Battalion **1902**. [4] Whilst it seemed to be perfectly acceptable to issue and wear signallers'

badges in some battalions, others were keen to 'stick to the book' (The Manual). For instance, Nottingham Battalion in its Annual Report for **1899-1900**, [5] laid down the law:

'No distinctive badges... such as bugles etc. to be worn.'

Volunteer variety

It is clear that anyone travelling the country inspecting BB companies in the period from **1894** until the outbreak of the Great War would have seen a large variety of proficiency badges being worn, both official and otherwise. Battalions were often keen to stick to Brigade regulations, but at the same time needed to satisfy local demands. Even when the Brigade had officially introduced a badge, the basis for its award, and the way it was to be worn. The rules were sometimes very broadly interpreted. In many companies the influence of the Volunteers was strong, leading to further tensions and anomalies.

A rearguard action

The experience of the Dundee Battalion with the signallers' badge is well recorded in its Battalion minutes. The Battalion was awarding a signallers' badge as early as **1908-1909** [6] even though it considered itself to be strict as regards non-Brigade issue of awards. The badge was competed for annually by examination, i.e. the Volunteer system, whereby a boy had to return his badge by May of the fol-

lowing year. [7] The Brigade introduced the Signallers' Badge during **1911-1912,** but a boy only had to compete for this once and, if successful, was then allowed to wear it for the rest of his company service. Dundee Executive do not seem to have fully grasped this point, or else totally disagreed with the concept. Indeed, Dundee was still operating the old annual competition system for the new Brigade Ambulance Badge in **1904**, years after it was introduced. [8] The award of a Signallers' Badge would then, like the Ambulance Badge, be Battalion property and competed for on an annual basis. This situation provoked some considerable comment within the Battalion, especially around the time of the Annual Company Inspections. The Executive decided to contact Headquarters regarding the issue of all badges. [9] The reply from HQ was not the one they had hoped for, so it continued to use its own system and fought a rearguard action. Two years later a compromise was reached; if a boy won the badge for the first time he had to return it the following year as it remained the Battalion property. If he won it a second time, he was to be charged 6d for the Badge, but could then continue to wear it for the length of his service. [10] The divide within the Brigade before the First World War between the old Volunteer group, who dominated Battalions such as Dundee, and a more modernising faction can be clearly seen. Certainly the Dundee 'Black Watch' Territorial Battalion under Col. Walker was supportive of its local BB Battalion. However, the First World War must have dealt a severe blow to the influence of this group. Col. Walker was killed at Loos in **1915**, whilst his 'Dundee's Own' (4th Battalion

Black Watch) was so mauled between March and October **1915** that it had to be amalgamated with another B.W. Battalion. Perhaps this lessening of Volunteer influence helps account for the upsurge of individual proficiency badges and increasing national control from **1916** onwards.

Official flags

In December **1911,** the Brigade Executive announced that they had sanctioned a Signallers' Badge with the same regulations as for the First Class Scouts' Badge. Described as:

'...crossed Signalling Flags, in white metal, silver-plated, with the letters B.B.'.

It was to be worn on the right arm above the elbow. The Badge, when ready, would cost 6d, postage paid. [11]

An interesting point regarding the qualification for this badge was that it was to include the same signalling test as for the First Class Scouts' Badge. A few years later, many in the Brigade would be calling for the Scouts' Badge to be withdrawn because it covered the same syllabus as other BB Badges. At the time, the Brigade was probably making this 'Scouting' activity available to those Companies which did not indulge in Scouting per se. Indirectly, perhaps knowingly, it was loostening its ties with Scouting as an independent activity.

The pattern of the BB Signaller's Badge was probably based on the army badge, first awarded in **1881.** [12] The army badge had crossed flags with disproportionate length sticks. It was made in brass-coloured gilding metal (the type

The 10th Birmingham Coy. Signallers c1913

used by the CLB, BLB and CBB), nickel, or enamel. The BB version in nickel, or nickel plate, reflects the small size of the diagonal bi-colour blue and white semaphore flags commonly used by the Brigade.

Already, by **1968**, with the introduction of the new Proficiency Awards Structure, knowledge of Semaphore and Morse Code was regarded as somewhat marginal. In a matter of months live TV pictures would be transmitted from the moon! Morse Code was retained at the 1st and 2nd stage level, but the use of semaphore flags had gone for good, both from the BB programme and from the symbolism of the badge. [13] In the **1983** Award Regulations, Communications is a Credit gained as part of the qualification for the Adventure Activities Badge. [14]

DASH—
FIRST POSITION.

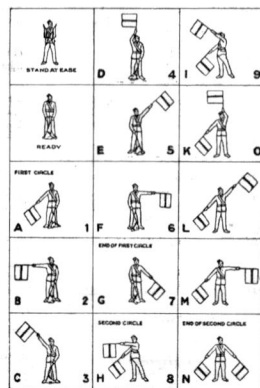

SEMAPHORE ALPHABET, NUMERALS AND SPECIAL SIGNS.

REFERENCES

1. North London Battalion, Third Annual Report 1894-1895 pp 5-7. The award of Drill Badges, Sergeant's Star or Signaller's was stated to be 'by examination'. Scottish HQ Archives, Carronvale, Larbert, Stirling.
2. Liverpool Battalion, Ninth Annual Report, 1899-1900 Scottish HQ.
3. London Committee. First Annual Report, 1901-1902, Scottish HQ.
4. Newcastle Upon Tyne Battalion, Eighth Annual Report, 1902-1903. Scottish HQ.
5. Nottingham Battalion, Ninth Annual Report 1899-1900. Scottish HQ.
6. Dundee Battalion Minute Book, Vol 3, 8/6/1909. Dundee Battalion HQ.
7. ibid. 2/11/1909.
8. ibid. 4/10/1904
9. ibid. 7/5/1912
10. ibid.5/5/1914
11. BB Gazette, Vol. XX, No. 4, 1/12/1911, p 51, BB Scottish HQ.
12. Edwards & Langley, British Army Proficiency Badges, Wardley Publishing 1984 p 16.
13. BB Award Regulations [Company Section] March 1969.
14. BB Award Regulations [Company Section] September 1983.The Boys' Brigade

The Signallers' Badge

1890s - 1911

The brass army - type signaller's flags in use in the BB before 1895 upon which the design of the standardised 'official' BB badge was based.

1911 - 1968

BB 088.01

BB 088.04

BB 088.19

Signallers' Badge - Detail

BB 088 BACKGROUND NOTES

These solid nickel badges have three main versions. The first is pierced between the flags and the sticks and usually has an axle pin or coiled bridge joint witn a round catch. The second version is non-pierced and the surface of the flags is gently curved, it has mainly standard tube joints and FRCs with varying amounts of impressing on the reverse. The third version, made by Miller, is also non-pierced but has an undulating top surface to the flags giving a wavy appearance. The Miller brooch has the characteristic squeeze joint, coiled pin and hooked catch. One variant is engraved with the Miller name.

The Swimming Badge

In at the deep end with a former BLB Badge

In **1927**, there was renewed energy in the BB caused in no small part by the union with the Boys' Life Brigade. Much activity revolved around the amalgamation of the award structures. The BB had introduced ten proficiency badges in 44 years, about one badge on average every four-and-a -half years. The BLB had

meeting in May **1927** [1] and then officially notified in the Gazette:

'The Swimming Badge is awarded to Boys who hold the swimming Certificate in a previous session and pass the following tests... Design - A Diving Figure.' [2]

The design for the new BB Badge came directly from the BLB Swimming Badge introduced sometime between **1912** and **1918**. [3] Selling for a penny- halfpenny the BLB Badge was cloth, circular and with an angled diving figure, virtually identical to the BB Badge. Certainly the ex - BLB representatives on the new Badges Committee would have pressed for

In **1968**, the Swimming Badge continued in 'barrel' form with a diving figure bearing a striking resemblance to the 'caped-crusader' about to leap from one skyscraper to another.[4] A diving figure is illustrated in the **1983** Awards similar to the one pictured on the pre-'68 Badge, but it is on a Credit appropriately called 'Diving'. There is a separate Swimming Credit, which, like the Diving, counts towards the Physical Activities Badge. [5]

The BLB Swimming Badge

Boys of the Brighton Battalion enjoy the swimming pool at their Annual Camp; Glynde, 1934.
Photo: R. Bolton collection

twenty-six, virtually one per year! Six new BB proficiency badges were introduced within the first six months of **1927**. The Swimming Badge was one of these new awards. The Badge had been reported to the BB Executive from the New Badges Committee at its

the retention of the Swimming Badge. Swimming and Life-Saving had been fundamental to the BLB ethos. The BLB held an annual National Competition for the 'Darnell Challenge Cup' probably the most prestigious in the Brigade.

REFERENCES

1. Minutes of Brigade Executive. 14-15/5/1927.
2. BB Gazette. Vol XXXV No. 10, 1/6/1927. p 164. BB Scottish HQ, Carronvale, Larbert, Stirlingshire.
3. Life Brigade Chronicle, Vol XVI No. 6 Jan 1918. 'Prices are increased of the ... Swimming Badge to 1fid'
4. BB Award Regulations [Company Section] March 1968.
5. BB Award Regulations [Company Section] September 1983. The Boys' Brigade

The Swimming Badge   1927 - 1968

BB 089.15   **BB 089.01**   **BB 089.13**   **BB 089.07**

The Swimming Badge - Detail

BB 089 BACKGROUND NOTES

These solid nickel brooches appear in many varieties. Obverse differences occur in virtually all the components, the Bs, the swimmer, the water and the border. The Bs are either hatched or plain. The swimmer has trunks or full costume and is differently shaped as he enters the water. There are frosted and chrome finished versions. The reverse has differences in the arrangement of the fastening, vertical or horizontal. There is variety too in the type of fastening from standard tube joint with round, hooked or FRC catch to coiled or crook pin types with squeeze or box joints. There is some impressing, usually the body of the swimmer on some types and force marks on one type. The Miller maker's name appears in two forms, raised or engraved.

The Wayfarers' Badge
What's in a name?

The 'Great Outdoors' has long held an attraction for boys. At the end of the nineteenth century it was the Brigades, particularly the BB, which pioneered youth outdoor pursuits. The nature of the activities pursued in those days included marching out, skirmishing and semaphore. By the early twentieth century, trek carts were becoming popular as boys and their leaders headed for open country at the weekends - often much nearer to hand than it is today. In **1907,** the BB was the first youth organisation to take on board the new ideas of Scouting at first locally and, by **1909,** with an official Scouts' Badge and uniform. Knot tying, signalling, nature study and mapwork were all included in the Scouts' Badge programme.

Scouts out

In **1927**, with the BLB/BB union, a new award for 'open-air' activities was required. Scouting in the BB had never been popular and in the **1920s** it was particularly unpopular amongst Brigade officers who saw Scouts as a separate, rival organisation. The BLB had abandoned its Scouting Sections in **1922.** [1] Some former Scouting activities were now included in other awards such as the Signallers' Badge. Furthermore, the BLB had been developing its own approach to outdoor activities encouraged by the enthusiasm of the doyen of healthy outdoor pursuits, Mr. Donald Finnemore, as outlined in his illustrated book 'Boys'. The name 'Scout' was to disappear from BB badgework to be replaced with 'Wayfaring'.

A scene on a shield

The Brigade's Badges Committee, in **1927**, reported to the Executive its proposals for the new 'Wayfarers' Badge'. [2] The design was to be chosen by the Badges Sub-Committee. These details were communicated in the BB Gazette:

'Wayfarer's Badge; Note. This Badge is intended to encourage open-air work in the summer. Officers are referred to 'Boys' by D.L.Finnemore... design to be decided by the Badge Sub-Committee' [3]

The Committee came up with a shield-shaped badge picturing elements of outdoor life: countryside, signpost, milestone, footpath, and a walker appropriately attired. Some of the design was, no doubt, taken from the BLB Local Knowledge Badge which included a signpost, path and countryside scene. [4]

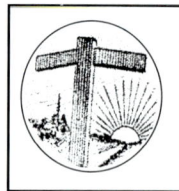

The BLB Local Knowledge Badge

That loathed word

The inclusion in the design of a walker caused a certain amount of comment over the years as fashions changed and a new terminology for outdoor activities emerged. Perhaps the best example comes from the pages of the BB Gazette in **1935**. [5] The Editor reviewed a new book by the popular BB Author Rev. Herbert Reid entitled 'From the Shoulder', being a series of talks to boys. Much praise is poured out about each chapter, until the one entitled 'The Hiker's Opportunity' is reached:

'...possibly one is prejudiced because of the use of that loathed word 'Hiker' in connection with our Wayfarer's Badge. Let us cast out from BB use this detestable American importation of unpleasant associations, and stick to good English terms that have pleasing associations.'

It wasn't only Rev. Reid who could write from the shoulder! Clothing was probably the problem when in an Executive Meeting in November **1945**...

'...it was agreed that a better design for the Wayfarer's Badge should be sought.'

By **1965**, however, change in the design had not happened. The following diatribe appeared in the BB Gazette:

'...Perhaps the Boy who has gained his Wayfarer's Badge values it as a token of his achievement. If he does, that is all to the good, but it ought not to be an excuse for fobbing him off with a token which, in its present design, is a burlesque of the thing it represents...It has one feature and one feature only to commend it, namely, it carries the letters BB....As for the other features of the token, could they possibly have

been more inappropriate to their purposes? Take the costuming of the walker. No lad now in the BB would be seen out walking in such 'gear'. In the days when good Queen Victoria ruled the land such an outfit might have been acceptable to youth, but for the Second Elizabethans. . . never. This model wayfarer is shown in the sketch in The Manual as wearing shorts. As he appears in bas-relief on the badge itself, he appears to be hiking in either riding breeches or long-john underpants! Moreover this fellow is shown on the downhill path. Symbolic of toughness? or of endurance? or of enterprise? No, let us be honest and admit that the affair is a wishy-washy travesty of what it ought to be. It could be argued that, if the letters 'BB' were erased, the thing could serve as a medal for the Turn-again-Whittington Society if there is such a body. ...a BB Course of Instruction is most likely to have trained a would-be wayfarer to rely on

map and compass and not on the signpost and milestone... Yes, indeed, and those features too call for some further consideration. What is the probability of a Boy on a BB organised expedition encountering a milestone of the type shown here? ...Would he also be likely to pass a signpost with its only arms pointing at right-angles to the road he was travelling. Does the Badges Committee of the Executive really know how antiquated and inappropriate this physical token is? If so, does it propose to do anything about it? O.B.P.'[6]

'Plus ça change, plus c'est la meme chose'

In the new Award Regulations of **1968** the name 'Wayfarer's' departed the BB badge system as had 'Scouts' more than forty years ear-

lier. The new Naturalists' and Expedition Badges covered most of the open-air activities. [7] A remarkable comeback occured in **1983**, however, when as part of the Adventure Badge, a Wayfaring Credit was introduced which followed a syllabus almost identical to the one used for the original Wayfarers' qualification. [8]

REFERENCES

1. Rev. M. Foster, The Great World Scout Schism & History of the British Boy Scouts. 1995. Unsupported reference. p 24.
2. Minutes of Brigade Executive Meeting, 14-15/5/1927. BB HQ. Felden Lodge, Hemel Hempstead, Herts.
3. BB Gazette, Vol XXXV No.10, June 1927 p 165, BB HQ
4. The BLB Boys' Manual 1926, p 32. pub. by BLB HQ. R.Bolton collection.
5. BB Gazette, Vol XLIV No. 1, September 1935, p 14. BB HQ
6. BB Gazette, Vol 73, No 3. Feb/Mar 1965, p 201. BB HQ
7. BB Award Regulations [Company Section] March 1969, The Boys' Brigade.
8. BB Award Regulations [Company Section] September 1983, The Boys' Brigade.

The Wayfarers' Badge   1927 - 1968

BB 090.23

BB 090 BACKGROUND NOTES

The many varieties of nickel Wayfarers' Badges are quite distinct when viewed from the obverse. Between 1927 and 1968 at least six major types seem to have emerged with certain key components either altered or completely left out! The walker's dress changes from knickerbockers (knee breeches) to shorts. His stick changes shape, his right arm disappears and his head changes shape. The milestone gets wider, narrower, higher and then vanishes. The finger post gets nearer, further away and is finally gone. The shape of the badge changes from wide to narrow, as does the width of the border. Even the hatched 'B's' have wide and narrow hachuring. The most common joint is the standard tube joint, but crook pins and coiled pins also occur. Clasps vary from round, hooked, and flat-rolled. There are a number of different impressions in the reverse usually the walker's body. The badge was produced by Miller and the name can be found vertically and horizontally. Force marks are quite common.

BB 090 AN ADDITIONAL NOTE ON THE 'FINISH' OF THE BADGE.

This badge is similar to the second one described on the next page which had a 'chrome' finish. When the cost of nickel rose, the makers simply applied a thin nickel coating over gilding metal. This meant that if the badge was polished the coating came off revealing the brassy gilding metal underneath. Chrome-plating was an attempt to stop the need to clean the badge with an abrasive. Just a wipe and it would be bright.

The Wayfarers' Badge - Detail

Willie the Wayfarer

BB 090.01

BB 090.24

BB 090.27

Willie starts his journey in 1927 and is equipped with all the best walking gear of the day. We see him first on .01. Willie wears knee breeches and a smart tweedy hunting jacket. He carries a hooked stick and walks a stony track. The finger-post is indistinct. The milestone is small and the grass short. On .24 Willie is virtually the same as on .01, but is much nearer. The finger-post is now quite distinct and the milestone wider. The fence has more posts and the track surface has changed. The grass is longer and the B's have a different shape. The badge has a chromed finish. Willie appears on .27 now wearing his trendy new shorts, carrying a straight stick and no backpack. His jacket is similar to previous walkers. The grass in the field continues to grow. The finger-post is only just visible, but with no fingers! There is no milestone here. The B's are finely hatched.

BB 090.08

BB 090.21

BB 090.22

On .08 Willie is pictured leaning forward and taking shorter strides. Now he is wearing his smart new jacket. The track is narrower, but no less furrowed. The grass is shorter as is the milestone and the fingers of the post. The walking stick is longer. The Bs are hatched, but are of a different size and shape from previous badges. On .21 Willie strides out manfully. The finger post is still quite distinct and the larger milestone seems to have more information on it. The grass is now so long it masks the fence. The track is still muddy and furrowed but is much wider. The Bs have wide hachuring. Journey's end in sight, there is a final ignominy, it's all change here on .22! Poor Willie seems to now have only one arm, and is his hand in the pocket? He wears shorts and walks a very muddy deeply furrowed track as he passes a small rounded milestone. The fingerpost is much nearer and the grass longer. The fence has been re-erected, the Bs re-positioned and the border of the badge widened. It's 1968 and Willie is destined never to walk that road again.

Plastic or Metal ? The Barrel Badge Story

Key to Background Colours, on page 145

In early 1980, the then Brigade Secretary, Alfred Hudson, probably heartily fed up with the complaints and criticisms about the current badges, put pen to paper and wrote a long explanatory article entitled 'Plastic or Metal ?' which appeared in the April/May BB Gazette.[1] He had inherited a most unpopular set of badges and efforts to improve them had only made matters worse. Typically, Alfred Hudson didn't mince words. It was clear, to the point, yet optimistic. His article tells the story so well that it forms a major part of this section. It is interesting now to be able to support and add to the original article with important evidence from Mr A.E. 'Bert' Hoey, Assistant Secretary, Supplies, in **1967** and Brigade Supplies Officer during the **1970s** and into the **1980s.** Relevant Brigade minutes have also been taken into account. The result is a rare insight into why and how change, for good or ill, is achieved within the Brigade. Particularly poignant is the rôle of Bert Hoey who was given the onerous task of finding a 'more colourful' replacement culminating in the new style awards of **1977**. Alfred Hudson, writing from the perspective of **1980**, starts our story:

You will have noticed in BBSupplies News in the last edition of the Gazette that the Activities Committee is proceeding with its review of the Company Section Award Scheme. Until this is completed we shall carry on using the present plastic badges.

*It may be of interest to trace the development of our present badges. Those of us who are a little longer in the tooth can recall the pride we felt as possessors of a row or more of hard-earned gleaming nickel-silver badges. Maybe we were not so interested in the large and unwieldy certificates that had to be earned before we could qualify for badges but we accepted that this was all part of the system; a system that had remained largely unchanged - except for a few additions and amendments - since **1927** when the badge system was consolidated after union with the BLB.*

*In the **1960s** the Brigade instituted many reforms following the adoption of the Haynes Committee Report. These changes included new activities, new programmes and many exciting new ideas for the Company Section. The certificates for the first-year awards were discontinued and badges were to be introduced at this stage. Clearly a new badge system was needed.'*

After Haynes

Actually, the 'Report of the Haynes Committee on the Work and Future of The Boys' Brigade', which was officially published on Wednesday 19th February **1964**, contained very little direct references to badges at all. Perhaps the most significant observations were that many companies were often not fully using the available badge programme. They were stuck in church halls one night a week, operating a very

basic programme. Outdoor activities and community service needed to be encouraged. The progressive element of the Awards Scheme was praised. Alfred Hudson continues:

'There were problems. As the number of activities increased so did the badges. No less than nine times as many certificates as badges were being issued! Imagine the prospect of boys with badges stretching from the cuff to the shoulder as badges replaced certificates!'

Launched in Birmingham

The proposed new badge structure was approved at the September **1967** Council Meeting in Birmingham [item9] for introduction in September **1968**.

The minutes of The Company Section Activities Sub-Committee from October **1967** are quite revealing:

'Item 54. Design of New Badges.
The Sub-Committee discussed with Mr A.E. Hoey [Asst. Sec. Supplies] various possibilities for the design of the new awards which would be required.
It was noted that the manufacture of these awards would need to be put in hand in the very near future, and that appropriate decisions were therefore required almost immediately.
The Sub-Committee agreed to recommend the following:
Proficiency Badges.
a. badges should be metal, of a silver colour, with a pin fastening.[2]
b. a standard shape should be used.
c. there should be an appropriate design at the top, possibly by means of interchangeable inserts,

to indicate the activity etc. concerned.

d. the appropriate stage should be indicated by a coloured interchangeable insert at the bottom, possibly using the colours, white, green and red for 1st, 2nd & 3rd stages respectively.' [3]

Time was obviously critical here as there were only a few months to go before the badges were required. The existing regulations and awards would be withdrawn on 31st August **1970** and there needed to be an overlap period.

The Sub-Committee reported to The Activities & Training Committee in November, where most of the general principles relating to the new badges were accepted:

'**Item 54. [d]** Agreed that proficiency badge should be metal, with a pin fastening, of standard shape, with an appropriate design at the top to indicate the activity etc., concerned, the approptaite stage to be indicated by a coloured interchangeable insert at the bottom' [4]

The idea of a coloured top, which was interchangeable, had been thrown out.

The Company Section Activities Sub-Committee met again in December **1967**. It now had to re-think its ideas about the badges:

'**Item 71. The Sub-Committee:**
a. Agreed to recommend, if practicable, the idea of a badge in a neutral colour, with bronze, silver and gold inserts to indicate the appropriate stage.
b. Agreed to recommend that the badge should have an appropriate indentation into which the self-adhesive insert would fit.
c. Authorised the Chairman [E.R.Staniford] to approve the final design. [5]

The Activities & Training Committee at its meeting in

February **1968** accepted the designs. The designer, Peter Flewker, had been working on them at Brigade House. Anyway it had little choice as time was short. [6]

Alfred Hudson now details the birth of the barrel badges:

The regulations were tightened up and in order to accommodate more badges in a smaller space the badge designer was instructed to halve the size of the badge. Thus the long, narrow barrel shaped badge was born. The principle of progression from Bronze through Silver to Gold was universally accepted. We therefore adopted bronze badges. The designer, poor fellow, had to leave space on each badge to indicate progression to silver or gold which left just a quarter of the original size badge on which to portray the activity.

Strong pictorial symbols were needed and a great deal of thought was given to their design as so many of the old designs were now no longer appropriate. For instance, Gymnastics was symbolised by dumb-bells which were hardly ever used; a fireman's helmet for Safety [a different emphasis]; a red cross for First Aid [not allowed by International Red Cross]. And yet new designs, good ideas that looked fine even when as large as the old badges [1 inch square] became impossible to identify when reduced to the new format of three-eighths inch.

So most of our old designs had to be replaced and traditionalists lamented their passing, especially as some of the new designs were not readily recognisable.'

Manufacturing Commences

The badges were made by Ludlow of Telford, Shropshire. In a departure from normal practice, only one manufacturer was chosen due to the expense involved.

Problems arise

The Activities & Training Committee at its meeting in February **1969**, just twelve months after the final 'OK' had been given to the awards, noted a further report from the Company Section Activities Sub-Committee:

'**Item 7.** The following points were noted:
[i]   The Sub-Committee was pursuing enquiries concerning the design of the new badges. ' [7]

In May **1969**, Ron Staniford and his Company and Senior Section Activities Sub-Committee in its Report to the Activities and Training Committee made it clear as to just what had been the nature of its enquiries concerning the new badges:

'**Item 18.**
The [Sub] Committee:
[c] Agreed that when it was no longer possible for Headquarters to supply from any source, any of the old type badges..
[ii] the equivalent new award should be made available, any new badges being worn in a separate row above the old type badges.
[e] Design of new badges.
Agreed to recommend that the specialised badges should be improved as soon as practicable with colour being introduced into the top half of the badge, enabling the design to be more distinguishable, and the badge more attractive.
This was not accepted. ' [8]

Discontent had already started and at the next meeting of the Brigade Executive, Activities and Training

Committee, in January **1970**, it would be brought up yet again:

Item 3. Matters Arising.
[iv] Design of new badges [18] [e] Although this recommendation had been turned down by the Brigade Executive in May **1969**, further representations had been received from various parts of the country, and the matter was to be reconsidered by the Brigade Executive.' [9]

Sorry

Supply problems were great in the first twelve months of issue. The BB Gazette of June **1969** reported that, owing to the transfer of the manufacturing from Birmingham to Shropshire, cyanide, used in the anodising process of the bronze badges, was leaking into local rivers and killing the fish. The manufacturing process was stopped and returned by Ludlow to J. R. Gaunt of Birmingham. Presumably all the fish there were already dead ! All this caused delays. Sincere apologies were tendered to the whole Brigade.[10] The badges were still subject to changes in colour due to the imprecise nature of the anodising process. BB Headquarters was supplied with a 'tolerances' card by Gaunt showing specimens ranging from dark to light. Anything received outside the acceptable range was returned to the manufacturer. [11]

Re-think required

At the next meeting, of The Activities and Training Committee in May **1970**, the design of badges was back:

'Item 10. Matters Arising:
[ii] Design of new badges [3] [iv]. The Brigade Executive in January **1970** deferred the matter to their next meeting, requesting additional information, and prototypes were being presented to the Brigade Executive later in the day.' [12]

The Executive decided that samples should be put before the next Brigade Council. These samples, on cards, were sent out to Districts and some Battalions. Two types of card were produced showing specimens of the proposed new badges, manufactured by T.A. Butler & Co [1927] Ltd., of Vittoria St. Birmingham:

The first type of card had Four sample badges on a narrow black armband along with one existing badge. Each card had one design either Drummers or Hobbies. The badges were the same size and shape as the current versions, with similar motifs, but the design was recessed and surrounded by a vitreous enamel coloured panel about two thirds the size of the badge. The colours were yellow, red, green and blue. The wording under the new badges was: 'Possible New Style 2/6d each - 12fi N.P.' and under the other: 'Existing Style 1/5d. each - 7N.P.'
Other information on the card was as follows:
'Brigade Council **1970**, Agenda - Item 10 Badges. If the Council wish to pursue the question of making the current badges more colourful, the samples [above] show colour added to badges:- [a] To make them more attractive to boys.

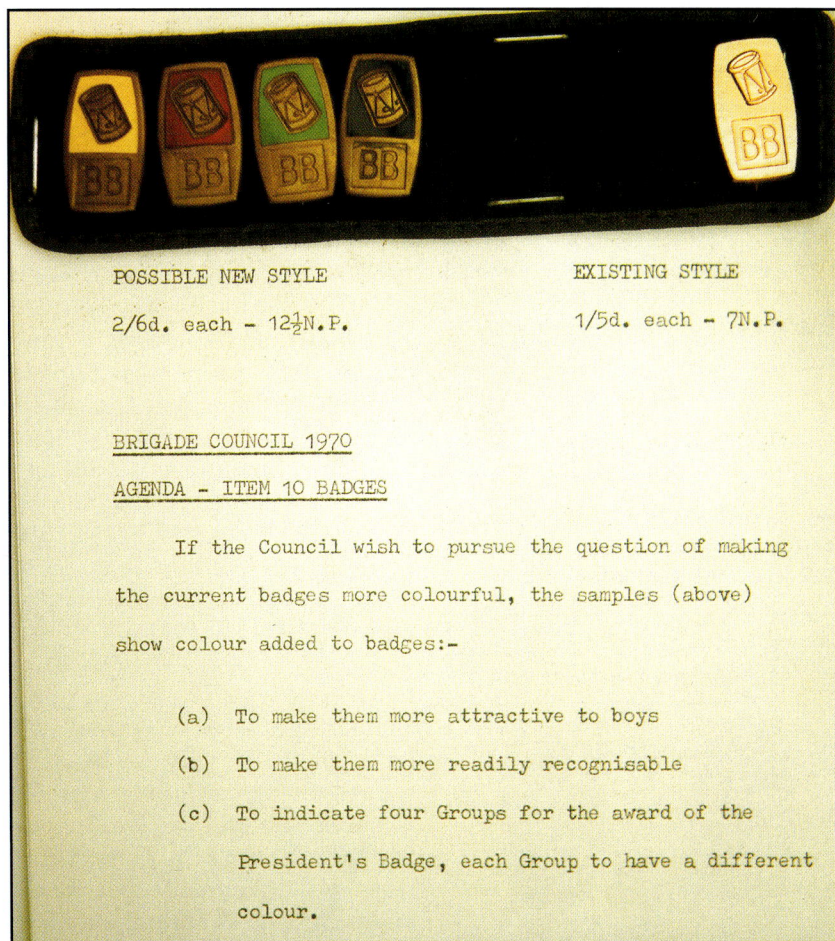

The sample card of proposed new badges
For consideration at Brigade Council 1970

[b] To make them more readily recognisable

[c] To indicate four Groups for the award of the President's Badge, each Group to have a different colour.' [13]

The proposed plastic surround.

The second type of card was about half the size of the first. It had hobbies badges as per the first type. Printed at the top were the words: 'Enamel badges made in the style of the buttonhole Badge would sell at 2/6d.' And by the current type: 'Current style selling at 1/4d'. There was a red plastic surround behind the current sample, cut in the same shape as the badge but larger. The wording describing this was: 'Coloured Surround would sell at 1d.' It is interesting to note that although the surround was rejected on this occasion, the idea was not forgotten. [14]

Small coloured 'BB' inserts in the same four colours as the badges, not distributed with the cards, were made to cover the 'BB' initials at the base of the badge.

Some of the rejected proposals

Here, Brigade Secretary Hudson, unfortunately, got his date wrong, but the rest of his text explains the problem:

*In **1971** [sic] attempts were made to introduce colour to the badges but the idea was not approved by Brigade Council and it was not raised again until **1976**. By now, new factors were having their effect; inflation and currency changes were taking their toll. The raw material for the badges had to be imported from Canada and it was obvious that unless something was done to contain costs Companies would be paying twice the price for their badges in the short space of two years. As some Companies were already spending around £50 on awards this could have had serious repercussions including even the abandonment of the badge scheme by Companies who could no longer meet the new prices.'*

Don't Panic

Alfred Hudson's article skips quickly over the period between **1971** and **1976** because nothing appeared to happen at Brigade Council. The situation was really rather different, perhaps more swan-like in nature, placid and calm on the surface, but with frantic activity going on below. The Brigade was actively seeking to reduce the cost of the badges and to make them more colourful.

In **1974**, activity regarding the re-vamp of the badge system reached fever pitch. A very small start toward saving cash came with the recommendation from the Brigade Supplies Officer in his report S/P [74] 1 of 7th February that plastic inserts, instead of aluminium ones, would reduce the price to 3fip instead of 5fip. At the next meeting of the Supplies Sub-Committee

later in February the following was decided in relation to badges:

1. Prices would be increased from 8p to 9fip, even though there were complaints.
2. Inserts made of plastic would be used when present contracts expired.
3. A working partry was set up to get quotes for cloth badges to replace bronze. [15]

The Company Section Award Scheme Revision Working Party, which required specific details, was scheduled to meet on the 17th May. At that meeting, the Brigade Supplies Officer was invited to introduce all possible alternatives . Information collated over the next two months, leading up to the meeting, included the following selection:

Firstly, a woven cloth badge. Mr A. Shepherd sent details on 5th March complete with sketches of proposed badges. On 11th March the B.S.O. drafted a document for consideration by the Working Party. The document stated that if cloth badges were chosen they would:

a. Need to be bigger than current metal badges.

b. Need to be circular in shape, like the Girl Guides badges.

c. Have a background colour in common, say blue.

d. Have the letters 'BB' in another colour to indicate grade, eg. Bronze, Silver or Gold, possibly in lurex yarn.

e. Cost 8p each, one for each grade = total of 24p. [Present costs, badge plus inserts is only 20fip and likely to reduce.]

The Supplies Committee, it stated, was already aware of the situation regarding cloth badges. It would not like to recommend non-acceptance 'merely on the grounds of finance'. It pointed out that current stocks and forward commitments to purchase, would take at least two or three years to clear. [16]

Secondly, on April 10th **1974,** a

quote was received from Messrs. T.A. Butler of Birmingham for metal badges, similar to those rejected by the Brigade Council in **1970**. The 'Panel Badges would cost 12fip if 25,000 were taken and that excluded VAT. For the same badge without the enamelled panel, but sunken to accept plastic inserts, with the BB supplying and fitting inserts, the cost would be 9p in a simple bronze finish. Twelve days later Messrs. Butler added, 'To supply badges with plastic inserts 11p each plus VAT.' [17]

Thirdly, between 11th April and 10th May, Toye, Kenning & Spencer Ltd. of Birmingham, via their London Office, provided yet more quotes for metal badges. Coloured badges could be supplied at 12p each, but the part cost of 24 different dies would have to be taken into account and an agreement signed to take 120,000, all plus VAT! A cheaper badge described as, '...metal gilt recessed back plates, complete with 24 different design inserts screen printed and gold blocked, fitted brooch attachments' would be 9p each for 120,000 plus VAT and modest die costs, etc.. [18]

Decision time

At the Company Section Awards Scheme Revision Working Party which met on the 17th May, B.S.O. Bert Hoey presented a number of possible suggestions which included the use of different materials and colour for the new badges: cloth, metal and enamel, metal and reverse printed PVC, nickel and plastic. Prices were also included. The Working Party was not keen to change the style or designs of the existing badges, but felt strongly that colour should be introduced. It was agreed that the B.S.O. should

explore the idea of obtaining badges made in plastic, rather in the style of the Junior Section Achievement Badges but...
a. in the style of the present badges.
b. in the colour of the present badges.
c. with the fasteners of the Achievement badges and stabilisers on the back.
d. with a coloured, reverse printed PVC coloured panel in the top part of the badge. This panel to contain the symbol depicting the badge.

The Committee noted that the present style would carry on for several years and new badges would be introduced after existing badges had been substantially reduced. It would not cause objection if the badges were introduced piecemeal. Boys holding the existing style of badge would not be required to change to the improved style. Start of the changeover would ideally be September **1976**. [19]

Following the instructions from the meeting on 17th May the B.S.O. was present at the next Company Section Award Scheme Revision Working Party meeting on 9th November:

'**Item 49. Badge Designs & Titles.** Mr A Hoey-Brigade Supplies Officer, reported on approaches made to various suppliers following the decisions of the May **1974** Meeting of the Working Party. Two types of Plastic badge were presented for consideration:
a. Plastic Low Relief Badge. The design of which conformed to the current style of badge but with a mounted plastic coloured symbol insert and a plastic fixing stud. The production of this badge would involve a specially manufactured moulding tool, the origination cost of which was indicated at approximately 1p per badge. The total estimated selling price to the Brigade would be 12p to 13p per badge [current badges are selling at 9fip each but already there are indications of an increase of at least 1p to

1fip per badge].
b. Reverse Plastic Badge.
-on metal carrier- some limitations were indicated in the size of print reproduction of symbols and again an origination tool would be required at approximately the same cost as the relief badge. The badge could be made available for sale to the Brigade at 12p to 13p each.
The Working Party:
i]expressed a keen interest in the plastic low relief type badge.
ii]requested that approaches be made to the Brigade Supplies Committee through Mr A Hoey, to explore fully the adoption of this general form of award for the Brigade, to be phased in gradually, as and when current stocks of existing awards were exhausted.
iii]invited Mr Hoey, to proceed with the production of a sample engraved relief badge to assertain the degree of clarity in the symbol.
iv]suggested that the plastic symbol inserts be produced in four colours to indicate the spiritual, educational, physical and service elements of the Brigade Award Structure.
v] requested, if possible, that Mr A Hoey be available for the Brigade Activities Committee on Saturday 23 November **1974** to present the Working Party's proposals in respect of Badge designs. [20]

At the end of October and in early November, the B.S.O. had consulted with firms such as Norman Pendred-Cellgrave of Catford Hill London SE6 and Burford & Bunch Ltd of St James's Drive Tooting, London SW17. Both firms had recommended the use of a High Impact Polystyrene, vacuum coated/plated metallic bronze. Burford & Bunch were given the job. Origination costs for moulds, etc., was in the region of £2,500. [21]

Dawn of the Plastic

Although the new badges didn't happen immediately, we can re-join Alfred Hudson's account...

'So plastic badges were introduced involving a high capital cost for the special moulds. Prices were stabilised over a period of three years and this was considered to be an important factor. Colour could be introduced at no extra charge as the symbols were made on separate inserts. Unfortunately, these inserts gave the badges a poor reputation. The first batch were made from a good quality heavy grade plastic; too good in fact! When cut to the small individual units in a press it remained in a dome shape and the adhesive was no match for this. The simple solution was to reduce the gauge of the plastic used and although this was soon carried out it came too late to restore confidence in the badges.'

Perhaps at this point the reasons for the Brigade Secretary's article can be understood. In fact the direct reason can be found in the minutes of the Supplies Committee February **1980**:

'**7. Award Badges.**
The Committee noted that following the decision made by the Brigade Executive, Plastic Award Badges and Coloured inserts had been ordered and were now being supplied [22] for the period ending March **1981**.

The Committee noted that complaints had been received by some members that this decision was not "In the Spirit" of the Brigade Council decision made at Dundee. It would seem that it was thought that some immediate improvement would be made in the quality of badge awards.
The Committee noted that the Supplies News in the BB Gazette for February/March **1980** explained the position.

The Committee decided that request be made that further amplification of this information be given in the Gazette in view of the strong feelings held by many.' [23]

Total Dissatisfaction

The demand to change back to metal grew, culminating in the motion to Brigade Council last year in the name of Yorkshire and Humberside District.

"That at the next quinquenniel review of Brigade Award Regulations, the Brigade awards be improved in quality, in particular, the Company Section Proficiency and Service Awards be changed to metal, bearing a motif in relief, more in keeping with the subject represented. Recognising the possible extra cost which may be involved, this Council accepts the possibility that the range of awards may have to be reduced, as a result of the improvement in quality, but requires that the range and quality of available programmes shall not be adversely affected."

Since Brigade Council, the Activities Committee has met several times. What would have been a minor review and updating of the various regulations etc., has obviously now become a major review. Time will be needed if this review is to be carried out thoroughly and to everyone's satisfaction.

Linked with this review is a comprehensive look at the actual badges, the number we use, the style and design of them and their quality.

All this preliminary thinking will be brought by the Executive to Brigade Council this year in Canterbury.

At York in **1981** Brigade Council will be asked to approve the introduction of the badge award system for implementation by the whole Brigade in September **1982**.

These are the changes envisaged in the longer term. But what about the short term? It was clear that many Companies, anxious for a rapid improvement wanted to abandon the plastic badges immediately and have the metal bronze badges re-introduced without delay.

The Brigade Executive has carefully considered the implications of such a change. They have noted that the visual impact of the metal and plastic badges was the same. Even at close range it was difficult to tell the difference. That the price of the plastic could be guaranteed to remain at 17p for at least another year was an important factor.

The cost to Companies of a quick change to metal would be considerable. More important even than this, however, is the realisation that the demand for change is not confined to a change of material from plastic to metal. The Brigade is looking for more radical changes than this, including new designs. The review of the Award Scheme now in progress and to be implemented in **1982** should provide the answer.

The Barrels No More

Generally, things went as planned. The Brigade Council, at York in **1981,** asked the Review Group to produce a set of definite proposals as mandated at Dundee and

Canterbury. The proposals were outlined in full as a special pull-out section in the June/July **1982** Gazette. The proposed new awards being shown on the cover. The Executive put forward its motion for adoption, part of which read: '...The Executive presents the new scheme and seeks the wholehearted support of Brigade Council **1982** for its full and immediate implementation.' Brigade Council at Keele, Staffordshire, voted in favour and the December/January Gazette carried details of the implementation of the new scheme and, of course, the end of the 'old'.

All old barrel Proficiency Badges and Handbooks would be withdrawn on 31st December **1984**. The new badge structure could be introduced from 1st June **1983** with the new badges being available from 1st September **1983**. What had been born in the W. Midlands was now, ironically, being killed-off there too.

Key to background colours used in this section

Alfred Hudson's Gazette Article. April 1980

Company Section Activities Sub-Committee
[Reports to Activities Committee]

The Activities & Training Committee
[Of the Brigade Executive-decision making]

Company Section Award Scheme Revision Working Party.
[Reports to Activities Committee]

Supplies Committee
Meets to discuss matters relating to Supplies

REFERENCES

1. Hudson, Alfred. [Brigade Secretary] 'Plastic or Metal' BB Gazette April/May 1980. p 77.
2. Sample in R. Mandry collection.
3. CA/M 67 [4] 14/10/67. BB HQ, Archives. Felden Lodge, Hemel Hemstead, Herts.
4. AT/M[67] 3. 17/11/67. BB HQ
5. CA/M67[5]. 16/12/67. BB HQ
6. AT/M [68] 1. 24/2/68. BB HQ
7. AT/M [69]1. 15/2/69. BB HQ
8. AT/M [69] 2. 17/5/69. BB HQ
9. AT/M [70] 1. 10/1/70. BB HQ
10. BB Gazette, June 1969 p 105. R. Bolton. collection.
11. Card dated January 1969. R. Mandry collection.
12. AT/M [70] 2. 26/5/70. BB HQ
13. Sample as submitted. R. Bolton collection.
14. Sample in R. Mandry collection.
15. S/M [74] 1. 22/2/74.BB HQ
16. 5th March 1974. Memorandum from Maker. B.S.O. Notes/Report.
17. Letters from: T.A.Butler. April 10th 1974, & April 22nd 1974. in R. Mandry collection.
18. Letters from Toye, Kenning & Spencer, April 11th 1974, April 30th 1974, May 10th 1974. R. Mandry collection.
19. Hoey, A. [B.S.O.] Report and notes from 17th May 1974 meeting. R. Mandry collection.
20. Coy. Section Award Scheme Revision Working Party 9/11/1974..
21. Letters from Norman Pendred-Cellgrave 29/10/74 & Burford & Bunch 6/11/74. R. Mandry collection.
22. Made by 'Gelaprint' London.
23. Supplies Committee Minutes, Feb. 1980. p 153.BB HQ Archives.

Prototypes   1970

BB 104

BB 104

BB 104

BB 104

BB 101

BB 101

BB 101

BB 101

The Proficiency Badges   1968 - 1976

ARTS

BB 091

ATHLETICS

BB 092

BANDSMANS'

BB 093

BUGLERS'

BB 094

CAMPING

BB 095

CANOEING

BB 098

CHRISTIAN EDUCATION

BB 096

COMMUNICATIONS

BB 099

CRAFTS

BB 097

DRILL

BB 100

DRUMMERS'

BB 101

EXPEDITION

BB 102

FIRST AID

BB 103

HOBBIES

BB 104

INTERNATIONAL

BB 105

LIFE SAVING

BB 106

NATURALISTS'

BB 107

PHYSICAL RECREATION

BB 108

PIPER'S

BB 109

SAFETY

BB 110

SAILING

BB 111

SEAMANSHIP

BB 112

SPORTSMANS'

BB 113

SWIMMING

BB 114

BB 091 - 114 BACKGROUND NOTES

These aluminium, bronze anodised, barrel-shaped badges are all of solid construction having a raised activity motif above recessed initials 'BB' in a recessed square suitable for glueing a square insert with either blue or red lettering 'BB'. The fastenings are bar brooches with safety catches. There is variation in the bronze colouring falling between the maximum and minimum tolerances set by the BB authorities. There seems to be three patterns of finish on the reverse of the issued badges, namely criss-cross, fine stipple and smooth.

The Proficiency Badges   1976 - 1984

ARTS

BB 115

ATHLETICS

BB 116

BANDSMANS'

BB 117

BUGLERS'

BB 118

CAMPING

BB 119

CANOEING

BB 122

CHRISTIAN EDUCATION

BB 120

COMMUNICATIONS

BB 123

CRAFTS

BB 121

DRILL

BB 124

DRUMMERS'

BB 125

EXPEDITION

BB 126

FIRST AID

BB 127

HOBBIES

BB 128

INTERNATIONAL

BB 129

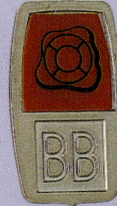
LIFE SAVING

BB 130

NATURALISTS'

BB 131

PHYSICAL RECREATION

BB 132

PIPER'S

BB 133

SAFETY

BB 134

SAILING

BB 135

SEAMANSHIP

BB 136

SPORTSMANS'

BB 137

SWIMMING

BB 137

BB 115 - 138 BACKGROUND NOTES

These are plastic barrel-shaped badges, vacuum coated with a shiny metallic gold paint. They are of solid construction with a central single plastic pin and cone collett on the reverse. The upper part of the obverse is recessed to take a coloured plastic decal with the activity motif printed in black. The lower portion of the obverse is recessed to receive a plastic square with the initials 'BB' in red or blue. Colour and drawings on certain decals vary between print runs but there is very little variation in the overall gold colour of the badge. The reverse colour of the badge reveals that either a rust or a chocolate coloured plastic was used.

The Target Awards

The Junior Section Achievement Scheme introduced in 1966 first gave the Life Boys then The Junior Section something to work for each year. Upon arrival in the Company Section there was a gap when the award of badges seemed distant and possibly the badge programme rather advanced for 11-year olds. In order to bridge that gap between Achievements and BB Proficiency Awards, when the whole badge structure was modernised in **1968**, the idea of introducing two initial awards was suggested.

General Proficiency Awards

The company section Activities Sub-Committee meeting in April **1967** proposed regulations for 'General Proficiency Awards' the regulations initially referred to a 'First Award' and not surprisingly, a 'Second Award'. At the same meeting, titles for the awards were suggested:

'c) Titles- Provisionally recommended that these should be called- Target 1 & Target 2 but agreed to consider further suggestions if any were put forward.'

Clearly there was not much opposition to the name expected because they also:

'f) agreed to recommend that the Supplies Committee be asked to proceed immediately with the production of appropriate awards which would need to be available by December **1967**.'[1]

At the next meeting of the Coy. Section Activities Committee the purpose of the award was reiterated:

'...a different sort of programme, should be introduced for the Boy in his first session, to bridge the gap between the Junior Section and Company Section Work...'

The titles 'Target 1 and Target 2' were now to be recommended by the Committee.[2]

Targets

At the July meeting the Committee again reviewed the name of the award, since another had been suggested, but...

'...agreed that the awards should be known as Target Awards, as previously approved.'[3]

In December **1967** the method of wearing the new awards was decided upon:

'63 Target Awards. The method of wearing awards was discussed, and in view of the fact that, in future, Service awards would be worn on the left arm, (63) The Sub-Committee agreed that Targets should be worn on the right arm, as a separate top row, above proficiency badges.'[4]

Things to come

The two target badges were introduced in **1968**. They were the 'T.V.' shape previously used on the Expedition Badge. Target 1 was 'Bronze' with the red zone of the archery target face coloured in enamel. Target 2 was 'Silver' with the Gold centre coloured in yellow enamel. The badges seemed to be quite popular, which is more than could be said for their barrel - shaped brethren. Sales in **1973/74** were:

Bronze: 17, 105,
Silver: 12, 630.

Sales were so good in fact, that in February **1974**, samples were considered from a new supplier:

'(5) (f) The Sub-Committee approved the samples and directed that these badges should now be obtained from two makers to improve the volume of supplies.'[5]

Parting Shot

Things were going well for the 'Targets', but this was not the case with the rest of the awards scheme. The two badges were about to be sacrificed in the name of change.

The new 'Company Section Award Scheme Revision Working Party' recommended to the Supplies Committee that:

*'(a) Target awards should be discontin-ued from September **1975**.*
(b) New badge to replace this badge be introduced. Name and Design not yet decided but to be in keeping with the rest of the Company Section Awards.'

It seems incredible that the Brigade were going to scrap two successful and popular awards and replace them with just one in the style of the least popular BB badges of all time!

Slings and Arrows

However, sanity prevailed. In the February/March BB Gazette **1976**, the announcement of details of the new award was made. It started off by saying that a: *'multitude of letters and comments...'* had been received. The new badge would be a reten-tion of much of the previous sys-tem and the name 'Target' would stay - back by popular demand. The regulations for the new single 'Target' badge would operate from 1st September **1976**. Unlike the previous system, which ran over the first six months of a boy's entry into the Company Section and was aimed at transfers from the Junior

Section and boys of a similar age, the new badge could be awarded after a three month programme. The other difference spelled-out in the Gazette was that:

'No Boy, no matter his age of joining, will be able to gain other proficiency badges until he has gained his Target Badge.'[6]

The new badge, now virtually 'compulsory', was re-issued as a fully enamelled coloured version of the previous awards, all the colours on the archery target being included.

In **1983**, somewhat ironically, the 'barrel' badges which had so very nearly taken over the 'Targets' in **1976**, were themselves discarded in favour of new 'Activity Awards' - which were now to be produced in the same 'T.V.' shape as the Targets!

Back to Two

The whole 'Target' system in **1983** reverted very much to the pattern of **1968** with a return to two sepa-rate badges. For older boys joining the Company, only the 'Target 1'

programme would be expected to be followed. 'Target 2' being a deeper introduction to the various activities. The two new badges were, in reality one old and one new type. The 'Target 1' being the multi-coloured former 'Target' badge and the all-new 'Target 2' also having a multi-coloured obverse design showing an arrow hitting the Gold.[7]

REFERENCES

1. Coy. Section Activities Sub-Committee, CA/M/(67)2, 29th April 1967. Minutes. No 24.
2. ibid. 16/5/67.
3. ibid. CA/M/(67)3. 22/7/67. Para 40.
4. ibid. CA/M/(67)5. 16/12/67. Para 63.
5. ibid. circa. March 1974. Following the Brigade Supplies Officer's Report of 7/2/74.
6. BB Gazette, Feb/March 1976. pp 71-72
7. The BB Company Section Award Regulations, Sept. 1983. Section 2, p 10. The Boys' Brigade

STEDFAST MAG Clips

The boys speak out... in April 1954:

'Sir - When young BB boys pass their examinations for badges, why are they not allowed to receive them until they are 15 years of age ?'
Pte. Norman Godfrey, 11th Oldham Company.

...and in March 1955:

'Sir - A boy enters the BB at 12 and looks forward eagerly to gaining certain badges. He finds, however, that for the majority of badges, he must be at least fourteen years old. This is one reason why boys tend to "Desert" the Company shortly after joining.'
S/Sgt. W. Williamson, 1st Peebles Company

The Target Awards

Target 1 and Target 2 1968 - 1976

BB 139.01   **BB 139.02**   **BB 139.04**   **BB 140.07**   **BB 140.09**

BB 139 & 140 BACKGROUND NOTES

The obverse of these bronze (139) and nickel (140) coloured, part-enamelled, gilding metal brooches varies very little, although there is a slight difference in some of the Bs and the colours can be either light or dark on each type. The Target 2 badges (140) have either a flat or raised yellow spot in the centre. Generally the differences are found on the reverse but not with the fastenings these being almost all standard tube joints with FRCs, with only a few versions having coiled squeeze joints and hooked catches. The reverse generally has some kind of Butler makers name in small medium or large sizes, or Miller logo. Pieces with a Butler name have either fine, medium or heavy raised stipple Those without name or logo have a criss-cross pattern. There are colour variations mostly noticeable on the reverse of the bronze Target 1 badges (139). On both types there is only one example of impressing on a Target 2 with the target rings just showing.

Target Badge 1976 -1983 and Target 1 1983 -

BB 141.03   **BB 141.17**

BB 141 BACKGROUND NOTES

These gilding metal, gilt brooches come in two main types, decal and part-enamelled.
The decals are coloured and vary, particularly the yellow centre. All the decal badges have the standard tube joint with FRCs. One variety has a clear resin 'bubble' finish over the decal. Variations occur on the reverse of the decal types, mainly stipple size and maker's details. Makers marks include Badges + logo, LB & B (London Badge & Button) and Butler. The Butler name appearing in two sizes. Some reverses are plain or stippled with no other force markings. The part-enamelled types display variation in the blue colour. Some have standard tube joints with FRCs whilst the majority feature bar brooch fittings with safety catches. Generally the reverse is plain although one type does have stipples and the maker; Badges Plus, along with their Tel No., another variety has just the telephone number. Some varieties are recessed to fit the bar brooch.

Target 2 1983 -

BB 142.02   **BB 142.03**   **BB 142.04**

BB 142 BACKGROUND NOTES

The major variation in this badge is the change from a decal on the obverse to a part-enamelled version. The original decal type has two main versions; a light or dark gold finish to the decal. All have the standard tube joints and FRCs. The part-enamelled version varies with respect to fastenings, there being standard tube joints and FRCs on the early batches and bar-brooches with safety catches on the later productions. The first batch of these has white enamelled arrow fletchings.

The 1983 Activity Awards

A metal brooch badge, shaped like a TV screen, with the name of the subject for which it was awarded above a design representing that activity. The badge has coloured enamel and two letter 'B's. This description of the Expedition Badge, introduced in **1964**, could easily have been the design brief for the 'Activity' proficiency awards of **1983**. It is a pity, perhaps, that before the family tradition of BB badge production evolved, like Dr Who, into the next generation there was to come an interregnum of some fifteen years when all that had made BB badges special was sacrificed on the altar of expedient banality. The story of the wretched 'barrel' shaped badges and their demise is covered elsewhere but clearly, a 'back to basics' approach was called for.

A Badge Review Group set up by the Brigade eventually decided upon the reduction of the number of proficiency badges to five with the 'Target' awards being returned to the original two levels. There would be a return to much of what was good about the original pre-'68 badge scheme, but replacing certificates with 'Credits' and the advanced award coloured felts with 'Flashes'. Badges, Credits and Flashes would all need to be designed from scratch. Remarkably, the Brigade approached Mr Peter Flewker, the designer of the 'barrels', to carry out this task. He was the 'poor fellow' referred to by Alfred Hudson, the Brigade Secretary, who had been given just $\frac{3}{8}$" squares on the barrel badges in which to fit his designs.

The design constraints for the new badges and credits would not prove to be quite so demanding as had been the case in the late **1960s**. The new awards would be twice the size of their **1968** counterparts with an area almost four times as big for representative design detail. Between the Canterbury Brigade Council of September **1980** and the York Council of **1981** Peter worked on the designs in consultation with the Badge Review Group.

Surviving minutes, letters and some of the original artwork provide an insight into the development of the new awards. We do not have the complete record. A few snippets of detail, however, give an idea as to the thinking of the BB Executive and the directions explored to produce a set of badges which simply had to be got right. There were two different briefs for the artist and one response from the artist which comes between the two, indicating that the designs were completed under some pressure.[1] The artist states in his response:

'I'm working like the clappers to keep up with this review Groups' sudden urgent requests!'

Here we can concern ourselves with the designs of badges only, although the Briefs and letter also make references to the design of Credits:

'Leadership Badge. The idea of an *'evolving figure' was liked but the title had to read 'Leadership BB' rather than 'BB Leadership'.*

This was duly altered and other changes made, but the 6th June brief ended the badge idea completely:

'The present design submitted by you of three boys is greatly liked but is now judged to be better used as the Leadership Credit. Can you therefore use the design to make this credit.'

So what of the 'Leadership' Badge? The Committee had a new idea all mapped out:

'A new design is suggested and I enclose a rough sketch. The word LEADERSHIP should be at the top but we can now omit the letters BB as we would likw the BB Crest to occupy the design space and this badge to be surrounded by a full Heraldic Wreath complete with cross over tails at the bottom. It may be a good idea to do two versions one with the BB badge and the other with a Buttonhole badge.'

The 'Interests' Badge had the problem of covering a multitude of activities, which provided difficulties for the designer. The Review Groups reaction to an initial design says it all:

'Your problem on choice of subject appreciated but because of crisscrossing of various items that compose the picture it was felt that the recognition of these items was impared. Idea of a bar of music and the choice of the music greatly liked but felt to be impractical. ...Title to stay. Add letters BB. Substitute a single crotchet in place of the bar of music. Show palette and video camera at vertical (or horizontal) position. Reverse video camera

so that eye piece is on right.'

Clearly the Committee were concerned that each item should be recognised, unlike the barrels, and that major BB awards which were being replaced, such as band, must be shown in some way. Eventually a more detailed brief was given with the following reqested to be included in the design:

'a. Any one of the following: a drum, a musical note, a drum major's mace. b. Any one of... a hammer, a saw. c. An artists paintbrush.'

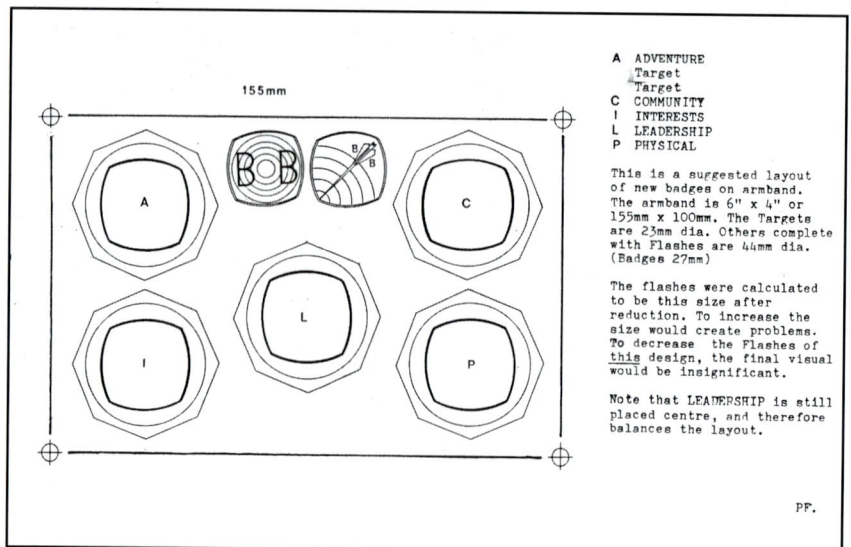

Peter Flewker's layout for the 'Activity Awards' on the armband. The whole assemblage fits into a rectangle 155mm x 100mm

As can be seen from the designs which have survived not all of this brief was followed to the letter.

The initial designs for the <u>Physical badge</u> included a pyramid. Reactions were restrained and *'received with interest'*. Amendments were suggested as follows:

'Add letters BB to design. Strong feeling that the five circles of the Olympiad would be suitable as the basis for a design and perhaps the addition of a Vaulting Horse or Vaulting Box.'

The Review Group were again, giving clear directions to the artist. Further directions followed the next submission:

'A lot of thought and discussion given to this one. It was finally agreed to ask you to substitute a Vaulting Box End-on view instead of the Horse. If it is possible, in the time available to do a further version showing a Vaulting Box side-on View this could prove helpful as the group were not unanimous in their thinking. There is a little worry expressed about the Olympic Rings. It came to me after the meeting that this is probably because your rings are shown by a single line. The

diesinker will make them as solid objects so I think it would be better to give them a dimension by adding a second line to each ring.'

The simplicity of the design for the <u>Adventure Badge</u> was 'especially liked' by the Review Group. They did suggest some modifications however in order to make the detail clear:

'Still some unhappiness regarding the compass. It could be mistaken for a ship's wheel. Star shaped compass preferred either with the four cardinal points or possibly a total of eight points. Add letters BB one each side of tents.' (sic).

The finished compass design bears a remarkable similarity to that of the Expedition Badge of **1964 - 1968.**

The Review Group thought that the <u>Community Badge</u> design was *'excellent'*. They wanted to keep it,

'...even if it means making this in a different manner to preserve the detail.'

There were amendments however:

'Add letters BB. Suggested that omission of part of the wreath on each side would most suitable way to do this.'

(sic) *'Lift up whole design which is thought to be heavy at the base. It needs re-siting in the frame.'*

The artist's reaction was to make the changes and get rid of the Judge. He states in his letter: *'Ammendment:[sic] COMMUNITY Badge Judge removed (...and hung)'*

The hanging didn't seem to worry the Review Group which on 6th June **1981** stated: *'Your revised design approved and generally liked by the group. Thanks.'*

Interestingly, the Target Two badge had not been designed by 6th June **1981** and the artist Brief states: *'Target Two Badge. The Group look forward to having your design at an early date...'*

The badges were ready in time, introduced from 1st September **1983** and generally met with approval.

REFERENCES

1. Two pages of Artist Brief c.May 1981, artist's response letter late May 1981, and further Artist's Brief following meeting of 6th June 1981.
2. BB Gazette. August/September 1986.

Some designs produced during 1981 for the
'Activity Awards'   Proficiency Badges

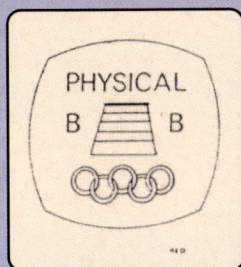

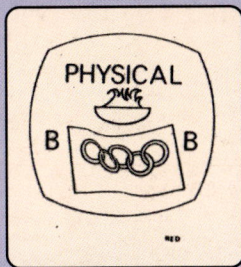

PHYSICAL B B   PHYSICAL B B   PHYSICAL B B

The PHYSICAL badge designs pictured here were amongst the last few to be submitted. The two views of the vaulting box were eventually rejected, presumably because the Review Group could not decide which version to use. The Olympic rings and flame version, right, is virtually identical to the accepted design.

ADVENTURE   ADVENTURE   ADVENTURE B B

The changes to the ADVENTURE badge were mainly in the addition of B's and in the form of the compass. The 'Ship's wheel' version is seen left, with a more complex version and a simple star compass. The Group advised a compass with more elongated sharper points which appear in the approved version.

COMMUNITY   COMMUNITY B B

Designs for the COMMUNITY badge showing the layout before and after the addition of the Bs. The Judge was later removed with just the scales of justice being retained. The wreath design, originally unique, re- occurs on the Leadership Badge.

BB LEADERSHIP   BB LEADERSHIP

Two of the original designs for the LEADERSHIP badge. The Review Group wanted the wording to be reversed with the 'BB' following the word 'Leadership'. Buttonhole badges, haversack buckles, hat angles and head sizes were all criticized on the first design, left, as were double-breasted blazers. The head of one boy was described as 'too skull-like'. Some corrections have been made on the second design, right, but it was rejected for use as a badge and transferred to the 'credit'.

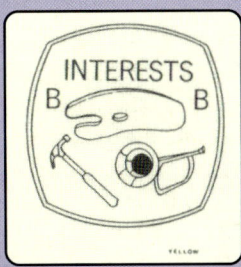

INTERESTS B B   INTERESTS B B   c INTERESTS B B   d INTERESTS B B

Some of the later designs for the INTERESTS badge. The Video camera didn't last long but the artist's palette a favourite from the pre '68 badges develops into an important design element enveloping the other components. Two musical notes represent the band side of the badge with a hammer for crafts. A camera features on the last two designs which, like the palette, was not part of the brief of June 6th 1981. The design labelled 'd' above is virtually identical to the final approved design.

The Activity Awards   1983 -

BB 143

BB 144

BB 145

BB 146

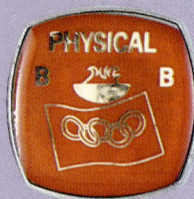
BB 147

BB 147

BB 143 - BB 147 BACKGROUND NOTES

These gilding metal, chrome-plated brooches have been produced in a variety of forms since 1983. Initially colours were tested using the Leadership Badge emblem and the prototypes of these exist (See above). Being the Brigade's first all - coloured proficiency badges the colours had firstly to be set. Leadership: White, Adventure: Turquoise, Community: Malachite Green, Interests: Jasmine Yellow and Physical: Signal Red. There has been some variation however in the way these colours have turned out, due to the differing methods of manufacture. The main two types have been the use of decals under a clear epoxy resin dome and normal use of cold enamel in place of the decal. At least two manufacturers have been used; Messrs Dowler and Badges Plus from Birmingham. Details of the quantities enamelled per day are available from the 1990s viz: BB 143: 600, BB 144: 650, BB 145: 750, BB 146: 700 & BB 147: 750. This shows that although the badges look similar there are differences in production time, usually the result of the design, complicated designs taking longer to enamel. Differences can be readily detected from the obverse in some types (see 147 above) but the reverse details are much more revealing having bar-brooches and a large surface. There are generally seven types as at 2000. The two rivet type with decals on obverse, Dowler name, 1 rivet, 1 rivet with Telephone number, 2, rivet recessed, no rivet, and 2, rivet flat. There are other minor variations in addition. The details of numbers produced were given in the BB Gazette for the session 1985 - 1986[2]. These numbers are a useful 'snapshot' of the proportions of quantities produced. Community: 11,502, Physical: 8,758, Adventure: 8,425, Interests: 7,408, Leadership: 7,293.

PROTOTYPES

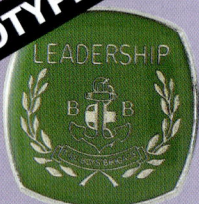

Wearing BB Badges

Service & Proficiency Badges, c.1904 - 1927

Right Arm

Position for Wearing B.B. Badges.

King's Badge (above) Worn on left arm from 1914

NOTE.—The Band Badge is worn in the same position as the Bugler's Badge.

PRE - 1915
1914 MANUAL

Position for Wearing B.B. Badges on the Right Arm.

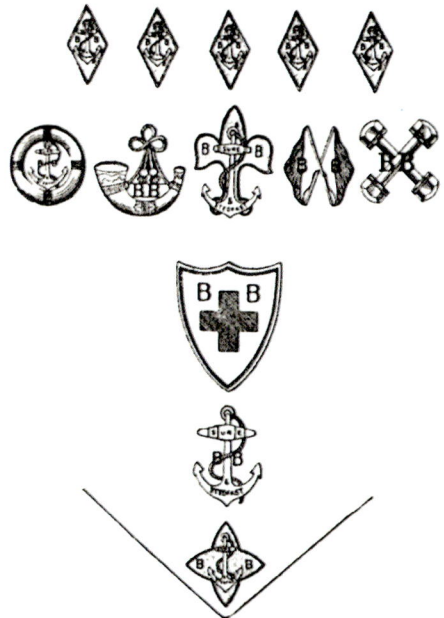

NOTE.—The Band, Drummer's, or Piper's Badge is worn in the same position as the Bugler's Badge.

1917 - 1926
1925 MANUAL

Between 1904 and 1927 as the number of awards increased, so it became essential for the Brigade to detail just how they should be worn. There had been, since the introduction of the three year anchor in **1888**, a wide degree of variation in the way badges had been worn. This variety blossomed with the introduction of proficiency and efficiency awards. Badges adorned coat lapels, cuffs, stripes and caps.

By **1914**, a clear pattern had emerged which was able to be enlarged progressively over the years.

Left:
An armband from the 1890s
5th London Coy. Archive.

Service & Proficiency Badges, 1927 - 1968

Left Arm

Boys attending the **1933** Jubilee camp at Dechmont were allowed to wear the camp badge below the Long Service Badge, during the camp and for the remainder of their service.

In **1953** the Queen's Badge was introduced to replace the King's Badge.

The **1954** Eton Founder's Centenary Camp Badge was worn in the same manner as the 1933 Dechmont badge.

A BB Duke of Edinburgh's Award Badge was added in **1958**.

The **1958** Caribbean Camp Badge was worn in the same manner as the Dechmont & Eton Badges.

The Founder's Badge was introduced in **1962** for use in non-Commonwealth countries such as The Republic of Ireland.

Right Arm

1927 - 1946

2nd World War National Service Badge was worn between Buglers & Ambulance Badges.

1946 - 1952

The positions of the NCO's Star & Three Year Service Badge, switched in **1952**.

1957 - 1968

The Seniors' (cloth) Badge, introduced in **1963**, was worn below the star and anchor which were then placed side by side, anchor first. (See photo p. 157)

Position for Wearing B.B. Badges on the Right Arm.

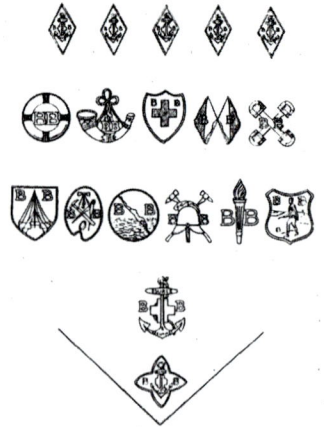

NOTE.—The Band, Drummer's or Piper's Badge is worn in the same position as the Bugler's Badge

Position for Wearing B.B. Badges on the Right Arm.

General Badges to be worn in alphabetical order not more than five badges in a row.

Position for Wearing B.B. Badges on the Right Arm

General Badges will be worn in alphabetical order not more than five badges in a row.

★ The Life Boy Service Badge to be worn here.

Sergeants' Armband with Badges   June 1963

This is the maximum number of awards a boy could wear, complete with all the advanced award coloured cloths. The cloths on these badges had been in the regulations since **1959**. The Seniors' Arm Crest had just come into compulsory use, located in the 'V' of the chevrons with the NCO's Star and Three Year Service Badge alongside. From August 1963 the number of badges with advanced award cloths was increased.

The Advanced Certificate
Felt Cloths 1933 - 1968

In 1933, the Boys' Brigade, in what was an amazingly bold and innovative move, initiated an advanced system of awarding and wearing proficiency badges which was to last for thirty five years and influence BB badge wearing for more than twice that long. The badge in the avant - garde was to be, appropriately, the BB's first proficiency award, the Ambulance Badge. The system involved giving further certificates after the award of badges. These Advanced Certificates were initially indicated by wearing a red or blue coloured cloth behind the badge.

Why Cloth?

It is, unfortunately, not possible to find out exactly what led the BB, in 1933, to extend the award system in this way, but we can make a few observations. The Ambulance Badge was not only the progenitor of all BB proficiency awards, but also it had been the most important award in the newly united BLB. The award system used in the BLB was the one favoured by the Volunteers; the annual re-testing for the award to encourage competence and maintain progress. Upon union with the BB in 1926 the system had been changed to the award of certificates and a single badge, retained by the boy for the whole of his service. No doubt many former BLB Officers would not have approved. After seven years of working the new system, pressure to develop the award of advanced certificates in some recognisable form was probably intense.

The reasons for the choice of representing advanced certificates by wearing a felt beneath the badge

are not recorded. Nevertheless, an explanation can be attempted. It was not possible to wear any form of bar or clasp on a shield-shaped brooch. The solid nature of the award meant that to show up clearly it would have to project from around the edge. Organisations such as The Boy Scout Association had, by 1933, been using different coloured cloths to represent levels of award for some years. The CLB also used different coloured cloths to back the 1st and 2nd class Scouts Badges between 1911 and 1936.

The colours red and blue may have been chosen because they were simply 'BB' colours, as used on the buttonhole badge emblem.

Stages

The introduction of advanced certificates with felt cloths followed six stages:

Stage One was the introduction of the red and blue cloths in 1933. The official announcement in the Gazette read as follows:

'It has been decided that in future Boys passing the Ambulance Examination for the third time will receive with the third year Certificate a red cloth shield to wear under the Ambulance Badge. Similarly with the fourth year Certificate a blue cloth shield will be worn. These cloth shields will in future be supplied with the appropriate Certificates. Officers needing them for Boys at present holding the third and fouth year Certificates may obtain the necessary shields on application at the Brigade Office, giving name and rank of Boy and stating which Certificate he holds. There will be no charge.' [1]

Stage Two was to arrive eighteen years later in 1951 with the award of a white cloth:

'Ambulance- A new 5th year award of a white cloth shield has been approved.' (From 1st September 1951). [2]

No doubt the choice had been between white and gold [yellow] colours for the 5th yr. cloth with the chosen white in keeping with the 'silver/white- metal' nature of the awards.

Stage Three came with the introduction of the Scripture Knowledge Badge in 1958, perhaps not coincidentally, sponsored by the former BLB element within the Brigade Executive who had experienced a progressive award system of tiered badges in the BLB. Just two years previously the Duke of Edinburgh's Award had started within the Brigade using a tiered approach to badges, the first gold awards being made in September 1958 with special D.of.E Brigade Badges also being issued that year. The Scripture Badge Advanced Certificates were designed to fit exactly with the requirements for Bronze and Silver D.of.E awards, there being initially only two advanced awards. The Gazette announced the details of the cloths:

'A Boy gaining a fourth Scripture Knowledge Certificate shall be entitled to wear a red cloth and for a fifth certificate a blue cloth under the Badge.' [3]

Stage Four: In 1959 the Brigade decided to take the larger part of the badge system down the road leading to advanced certificates with cloths. A notification in the Gazette explained its thinking:

'Revised Badge Regulations... The Badges Committee had to consider a badge structure which would not only attract and hold the 12 and 13 year old Boy, but continue to attract him in the

15 and 16 bracket...the Committee felt it wise not to delay the gaining of badges too long and to institute, wherever possible ADVANCED AWARDS, as already exist in First Aid and Scripture Knowledge. Such a practice has been extended to the following in varying degrees- Arts and Crafts, Athletics, Citizenship [formerly Education], Life Saving, Signaller's, Swimming and Wayfarer's- and all are taken into consideration for the Queen's Badge.' [4]

A large coloured chart was produced indicating the number of Advanced Awards for each subject. Reproduced on page 160.

Stage Five: In **1960,** the Gazette carried a notice about a new Advanced Certificate to go with each cloth:

'...by the time the Gazette is published it is hoped that all the new Advanced Certificates will also be ready. As will be seen from the illustrations on this page, the new Certificates are in contemporary design in two colours, the Advanced Certificates being similar in character with the addition of a Seal and Ribbon according to the degree of the Award...the Advanced Certificates [including cloth for wear under the Badges] will be 1s each.' [5]

The full maximum cloths which could be awarded in June **1963** can be seen in the photo on page 157.

Stage Six: By August **1963** additions to the structure of advanced certificates were announced as: 'Revised Badge Regulations' They included Arts and Crafts- 3 Advanced Awards, Citizenship-Age raised by 1 year for Advanced Awards. Life Saving- Advanced Awards raised to R.L.S.S. Award of Merit standard, year raised too. Buglers-2 Advanced Certificates. Physical Training-3 Advanced Certificates, Band, Drummers and Pipers- 2 Advanced Certificates. Expedition-Advanced Certificate, but no direct mention of any felt

The new BB Badges introduced in 1983, with their plastic 'Flashes' the 'true descendants' of the felts.

cloth. [6] The above were proposed in April **1963** before being taken to Brigade Council in St. Andrews. The Badges Committee considered amendments and they were approved by the Executive in November **1963**. The new regulations to start in Session **1964-65.** All proposals were accepted, but with some changes viz: 1. Swimming-Two Advanced Certificates introduced, not just one. [7] The system, refined over more than seventy years, had reached its peak, so, inevitably there was now only one way it could go, and so it did.

The End

The introduction of the new Badges and Awards Regulations in **1968** ended the use of cloths for Advanced Certificates, although plastic surrounds were tried experimentally, (see photo. page 142). The end of subject specific certificates was also announced:

'In view of the new Awards Regulations coming into force with effect from 1st September **1968**, proficiency Certificates with the subject name printed thereon will not be

reprinted. Two "Open" Certificates will be supplied- One for the First and Intermediate Awards and One for all Advanced Awards. The Company Captain will need to arrange to fill in the name of the subject and, in the case of the Advanced Award, whether 1st, 2nd or 3rd Stage.'[8]

Back in a Flash

A sad ending, but the story doesn't finish in **1968**. In **1983,** the new Award Regulations introduced the wearing of Red and Blue 'Flashes' (plastic shapes) behind the badges at Grade 2 and Grade 3 levels. [9] These 'Flashes' are indeed the true descendants of the felt cloths introduced exactly fifty years before.

REFERENCES

1. BB Gazette Vol. XLII, No 3, Nov 1933 p.41.
2. ibid., Vol. LIX, No 4, April 1951 p.70
3. ibid., Vol. LXVI, No 6, Aug/Sept 1958, p.107
4. ibid., Vol. LXVII, No 4, April/May 1959.
5. ibid., Vol. LXVIII, No 4, April/May 1960 p.73.
6. ibid., Vol 71, No 6, Aug/Sept 1963 pp. 130-134.
7. ibid., Vol 72, No 3, Feb/March 1964.
8. ibid., Vol 76, April/May 1968.
9. BB Coy Section Award Regulations, Sept. 1983, Section 3, p.11. para 2. The Boys' Brigade

The Awards Chart for 1959

THE BOYS' BRIGADE AWARDS

CHART SHOWING EARLIEST POSSIBLE SESSIONS IN WHICH AWARDS MAY BE GAINED

AWARD	1st SESSION 11-12 YEARS B.B. AGE 12	2nd SESSION 12-13 YEARS B.B. AGE 13	3rd SESSION 13-14 YEARS B.B. AGE 14	4th SESSION 14-15 YEARS B.B. AGE 15	5th SESSION 15-16 YEARS B.B. AGE 16	6th SESSION 16-17 YEARS B.B. AGE 17
L. B. SERVICE	B					
BUTTONHOLE	B					
ONE YEAR SERVICE	B	B	B	B	B	B
THREE YEAR'S SERVICE			B			
LONG SERVICE					B	
N.C.O's. PROFICIENCY				C	B	
ARTS & CRAFTS	C	C	C B	A 1	A 2	
ATHLETE'S			C	B	A	
BAND, ETC.			B			
CAMPER'S				B		
CITIZENSHIP			C	C	C B	A
FIREMAN'S				C	B	
FIRST AID	C	B	A 1	A 2	A 3	
LIFE SAVING		C	B	A		
PHYSICAL TRAINING		C	B			
SCRIPTURE KNOWLEDGE	C	C	C B	A 1	A 2	A 3
SEAMANSHIP				C	B	
SIGNALLER'S	C C	B	A			
SWIMMING	C	C	B	A		
WAYFARER'S	C	B	A			
QUEEN'S BADGE					B	
THE DUKE OF EDINBURGH'S AWARD				BRONZE	SILVER	GOLD

KEY   C = CERTIFICATE   B = BADGE   A = ADVANCED CERTIFICATES WITH COLOURED CLOTH BEHIND BADGE

Service & Proficiency Badges, 1968 -

Right Arm

Target badges 1 bronze with a red centre, and 2 silver with a yellow centre, are worn above bronze anodised aluminium awards. The award badges are in alphabetical order, no more than seven in a row.

1968 - 1976

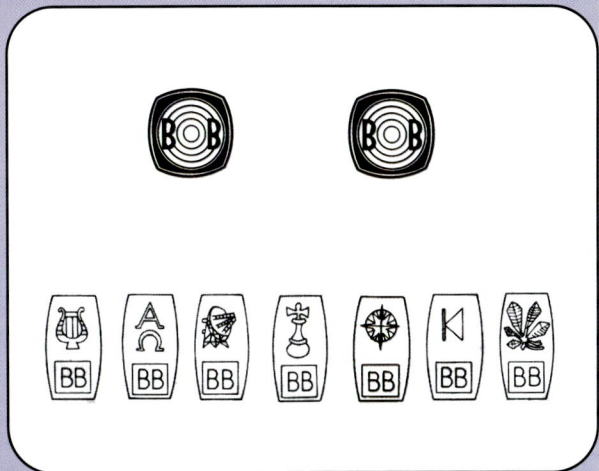

A single multi-coloured target badge is worn above plastic awards with coloured decal tops. The award badges are in alphabetical order, no more than seven in a row.

1976 - 1983

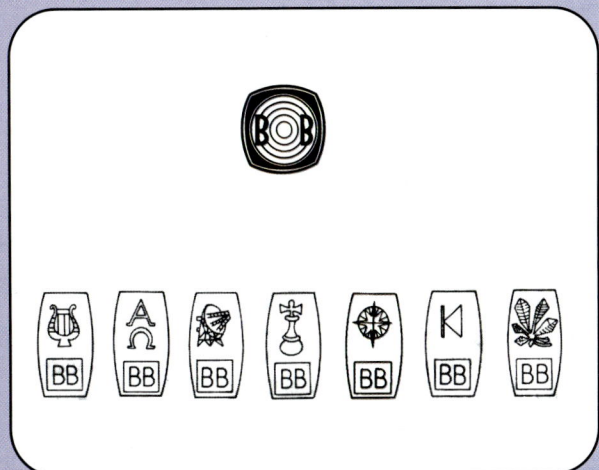

Target badges 1 & 2, both multi-coloured are worn above metal award badges with coloured obverse.

The maximum (illustrated) being five award badges.

Plastic 'flashes' of red or blue may be worn behind award badges to indicate grades 2 or 3.

1983 -

Left Arm

The Queen's & President's badges are worn with the D of E Badge. The Junior Section service diamond, in silver or gold, is worn to the left of the Brigade Service badge.

1968 - 1971

The **Founder's Badge** remains in use in place of the Queen's Badge in non - Commonwealth countries.

The diamond J.S. badge has been replaced with a service badge with the letters 'BB' in silver or gold inserts.

1971 - 1976

A gold J.S. Service badge is now worn to indicate the award of the 'gold' J.S. achievement.

The Service badge now-includes J.S. service. years.

1976 - 1991

The Seniors' Award diamond can now be worn under the Service Badges.

1991 - 1994

1993 New spelling 'St**ea**dfast'

New - style Queen's & President's Badges are worn.

There is a new circular J.S. Gold Achievement Badge.

More than one Seniors' Award may be worn. [Max. 3]

1994 - 1998

1997 'Brassards' authorised for shirt uniform.

The new Anchor - Boy Achievement badge is now allowed to be worn.

1998 -

BADGES
of the
BRIGADE

VOLUME ONE
THE BOYS' BRIGADE

4. Buttonhole & Special Mufti Badges

Special Camp Service Badges

'Special Service' Badges

Camping has been a core BB activity since 1886, so it is surprising that few camp badges exist. Since we are dealing primarily with metal badges, even though they may be used both for uniform and mufti wear, the range is further reduced. Most badges have been produced to celebrate the great international camps, starting with the Jubilee Dechmont Camp of **1933**. At least one Battalion, Manchester, produced its own camp badge. Over the years, major BB camps have been held all over the world, but badges produced for the majority of these are outwith of our remit. The badges detailed here relate only to UK camps, the only exception being one foreign camp attended by UK boys, where the camp badge was allowed to be worn on UK BB uniform.

Only three camps' badges have ever qualified to be officially worn on BB uniform; the **1933** Dechmont, **1954** Eton and **1958** Caribbean. The Dechmont and Caribbean badges were enamelled and multi-purpose, being worn on camp uniform as buttonhole/shirt badges before being consigned to the left arm of the camper for the rest of his service in the ranks. The Eton Badge was produced in a nickel finish primarily for uniform wear. In effect, these badges, worn below the Long Service Badge, are special service badges; they clearly do not demonstrate any particular proficiency or attainment.

The non-uniform badges were produced mainly as souvenirs of the international camps. As such they could sometimes be obtained in both boys and officers versions as well as in tin-plate form. Tin-plate badges were used in **1933** to identify members of different camp companies. The suitability, or otherwise, of wearing a metal badge at camp has been an argument repeated on numerous occasions. In **1963**, the Glenalmond, Scotland, International Camp adopted only cloth badges. Cloth badges were used for the Lilleshall Training Camps of **1958** and **1961** and are now 'de rigeur' for camps worldwide.

1933: The Dechmont, Jubilee Camp

Details of this badge are given in the section concerning the **1933** Jubilee Badges. (see pages 173-177)

1954: The Founder's Centenary Camp, Eton

The playing fields of Eton College played host to two thousand BB boys and hundreds of officers between 12th - 21st August **1954**. The occasion was the Centenary of the Founder's birth being celebrated with a giant international Camp commanded by Sir Donald Finnemore. Hailed as the biggest BB Camp ever, boys attended from as far afield as Singapore, Falkland Islands, USA, Canada, Nigeria and New Zealand. All the numbers associated with the camp seem vast, the large marquee had capacity for three thousand and there were 320 Bell tents. In all 2,200 groundheets and 4,500 blankets were distributed. [1] The BB Gazette

in October **1954** announced that a 'special badge' had been sanctioned for all Boys who had attended this camp and '...*shall be worn in uniform on the left arm immediately beneath the Queen's and Long Service Badges.*' [2] Unlike the Dechmont Camp badge of twenty-one years earlier, the badge was not worn at the camp, but issued after the event. The emblem on the badge was a composite of the **1954** Founder's celebrations logo, a tilted flag, combined with the BB Campers' Badge design.

1958: 75th Anniversary Year, Caribbean Camp

The seventy-fifth year of the BB started with a great International BB Camp at Ardmore in New Zealand held over the last few days of **1957** and the first days of **1958**. It was to be a week in April, however, which many UK BB boys would remember as the peak of their 75th anniversary year celebrations. From April 10th - 18th **1958** the CariBBean International Camp was held at the University College of the West Indies, Kingston, Jamaica. A contingent of 77 officers and boys from the UK were present, the largest overseas contingent, commanded by Mr Tom F Harwood. There were 50 senior boys in the party and all were allowed to wear the special camp badge on their uniform upon their return to the UK and for the rest of their service in the Brigade. The BB Gazette carried the official notification:

'*The Brigade Executive have decided to allow all Boys who attended the*

Caribbean Camp to wear the Caribbean Camp Badge in uniform on the left arm [below the Long Service Badge] for the remainder of their service.'[3]

The official badge, worn as a 'mufti' buttonhole badge at the camp, was gilt with blue enamel incused lettering and the camp logo of a Pelican with stylised sea waves in the background.

There were also tin 'fun' badges and large circular cloth badges produced for the camp. The circular cloth badge was worn as the camp uniform badge.

Between August 16th and 24th another 75th year camp took place, the '750 Training Camp', at Lilleshall in Shropshire for UK boys. This training camp concentrated on sports activities and was led by Sir John Hunt with Rev. David Sheppard as the Camp Chaplain. Only cloth badges were produced for this camp although there was a prototype pin badge produced (See page 166) .The BB's 75th year was something of a disappointment insofar as badges are concerned. Amazingly, the official logo of the anniversary was never produced as a badge.

Manchester Camp Badges

These distinctive nickel badges which have a letter 'C' around a BB emblem were used at the Manchester Battalion Camps from **1936**. The Camps didn't operate from **1940** to **1945,** but the badges, which were awarded to boys who were in the top four tents, came back into use in **1946**. This is an extract from the Manchester Camp Handbook for **1961:**

'Camp Cup & Badges
The Camp Cup will be awarded to the Individual Company (with minimum of Two tents and 16 Boys) having the lowest number of fault marks per boy during the week, for the Tent and Daily

Inspection. In addition fault marks will also be given for defaulting and misconduct, such as late on parade, absent without leave, arriving late in camp at night. Special Camp Badges will be awarded to the top four Tents in Camp.'[4]

This extract certainly gives some idea of the standard required to be in a 'Top Tent'. It seems that about eight boys made up a tent, so approx. thirty-two badges would have been awarded each year which means about 864 over the years. The badges, which were known as 'Tent Pins', could be worn in uniform on the left arm, hence the reason for them being nickel to match the other badges. (although this was technically, quite 'unofficial' since the Brigade controlled the wearing of badges at a national level.) Some boys had three, four, or more by the end of their boy service. Battalion Camps ended in **1967** or **1968** so the 'pins' were no longer issued.[5]

1983: Scone Palace, BB Centenary International Camp

As part of the Centenary celebrations the camp was held between 20th - 30th August **1983** in the grounds of Scone Palace near Perth. The 1,800 senior boys and officers who took part were divided into twelve 'clans'. Camp uniform consisted of a sweatshirt bearing the camp logo.

Two enamelled badges were produced and large tin 'fun badges' with camp logo were sold at the camp shop, but none of these were part of the camp uniform. Camp 'Chieftain' was Col. C. H. K. Corsar. [6]

1986: Ayr, 100 yrs of Camping

At Rozelle Park Ayr 2-12 August

1986, 850 boys, plus girls and leaders attended an outstanding International Camp to celebrate 100 years of BB Camping. Twelve Camp Companies were named after West Coast of Scotland Islands. The highlight was a trip to Tighnabruaich the site of the first camp held by 1st Glasgow Company in **1886**. An plaque commemorating the occasion, situated in front of the Auchenlochan Hall, was unveiled by Viscount Thurso, Brigade President. In a re-enactment of the original camp departure, a parade was held to the paddle steamer 'Waverley' led by the magnificent flute band of 2nd Wishaw Company. On going to the Tighnabruaich Pier the local ladies presented the leading company of campers with a flower and a kiss, capturing a similar incident which had happened a hundred years before. The Waverley departed to the strains of pipe band music from 47th Aberdeen Coy..[7]

1991: Aberdeen International Camp

In August **1991**, 800 officers and boys spent ten days under canvas at the BB International Camp held at Hazelhead Park, Aberdeen. The Aberdeen Battalion was celebrating its centenary. The Camp was divided into twelve companies each taking the name of a Scottish Castle. HRH Prince Edward visited the camp on the first Sunday.[8]

REFERENCES

1. Founder's Camp Souvenir Handbook. p 8.
2. BB Gazette, Vol LXIII, No 1 Oct.1954 p 3.
3. BB Gazette Vol.LXVI No 6 August/September 1958 p 106.
4. Manchester Battalion Camp booklet, Largs, Ayrshire, May 20th -27th 1961. p 9. R. Bolton collection.
5. Dawson, Peter & others supplied Information from, Manchester Battalion, March 2000. Peter actually wore the badges himself.
6. Camp Brochure, BB Scottish HQ. & 'Centennial' Camp newsheet, issue 1 20/8/83.
7. BB Gazette October/November 1986. p 9.
8. BB Gazette, Sept. 1991 pp 118 - 119 and BB Annual Report 1990/1991.

The Camp Service Badges

The Dechmont Jubilee Camp Badge 1933
The Eton 'Founder's Camp' Badge 1954

BB 161

BB 162

BB 161 & BB 162 BACKGROUND NOTES

The 1933 Dechmont Camp Brooch was designed to match the other Jubilee Badges from Glasgow. 2079 badges were issued to boys attending the camp. The enamelled badge with its distinctive 'blue scroll' top, was silvered and consequently is often found rubbed thus exposing the gilding metal. There are no 'varieties' of this badge. The Eton Camp Badge was issued after the Camp to the 2,000 plus boys who had taken part. It has a brooch fitting and there is variation on the reverse. The badge was silvered to match proficiency badges issued at the time, but was not intended to be cleaned.

The Caribbean Camp, Badges 1958
The Centenary Camp, Scone Palace, Perth 1983

BB 163

BB 164

The prototype '750 Camp' Badge 1958

BB 165

BB 163/164 & BB 165 BACKGROUND NOTES

The CariBBean Camp Badge was issued to all boys attending the camp for use in mufti. It has a brooch fastening and is gilt with white and blue enamelling. The wording is incused around the ribbon. The badge was worn as a uniform badge by the UK contingent after their return home. A tin 'fun badge' was also produced. The silver [chromed] and enamelled version of the Scone Palace Brooch was used as a mufti badge for camp members only [1,800]. The gold [gilt] and enamelled version was on general sale. The badge was never worn in uniform.

The Century of BB Camping, Rozelle Park, Ayr 1986
Hazelhead Park, International Camp, Aberdeen 1991

BB 166.01   **BB 166.02**   **BB 167**

BB 166 & BB 167 BACKGROUND NOTES

The Rozelle Camp Brooch was produced in two versions, part-enamelled for officers and fully enamelled for boys. There were 850 boys plus some girls and leaders. The badge was for mufti use only. The Aberdeen International Camp Brooch was produced as a mufti badge for the 800 officers and boys who attended. There is only one version, fully enamelled. Part-enamelled versions do occur, but this is because the enamelling tends to fall out of this badge easily.

The Manchester Batt. Camp Competition Badge   1936 - c.1968

BB 168   **BB 168**   **BB 168**

BB 168 BACKGROUND NOTES

These badges were issued for many years by Manchester Battalion to the top four tents (c.32 boys) at the Annual Battalion Camp. There are a number of variations with different metal finishes and types of pin fastening. One version is smaller in size with consequent variation in obverse detail. Some of the nickel plated badges wear easily to reveal the brassy colour of the gilding metal beneath. it is possible to find unplated versions.

The Bromley Batt. Camp Badge   The 1st Chelmsford Camp Badge

BB 169   **BB 170**

The Buttonhole Badge
Instant Recognition

When the Officers' Buttonhole Badge was discontinued in 1903 there does not seem to have been any strong feeling expressed about its passing. However, the effects of an action are not always immediate and the premature demise of the small circular badge did not devalue its legacy. An affectionate memory of the badge may have lingered long enough to inspire the design of a broadly similar boys' badge.

A good idea

The Gazette of January **1910** included an announcement from the Executive that it thought the idea of a boys' buttonhole badge to be a good one. Council would need to be consulted, and a letter sent to Battalions and companies. Under the heading,

'Proposed Boys Badge for use in Private Life', [1]

Five months later, the results of the letter were published. Naturally, there was a diversity of opinion. The issue would be brought up at the Council Meeting in Brighton in September. [2]

At the Council Meeting:

'The Brigade Secretary laid before the council a synopsis of replies received from Battalions as to the proposed Boys' Badge for use in private life - 21 Battalions, representing 374 Companies, voted in favour of the badge, and 12 Battalions, representing 383 Companies voted against it. Mr E.H. Grigsby (London) advocated the issue of a badge to Boys who have

served one year. Mr. Grigsby said that this would be felt to be a splendid way of letting the general public know more of the BB, and at the same time it would stop the practice of Boys wearing 3 years' service anchors and such badges when not in uniform. Mr J.B.Stubbs (South Essex) said that many of our Boys would not wear the badge, while on the other hand it might fall into the hands of Boys not in the BB who would wear any badge. On the question being put to the vote, the proposal to adopt the badge was carried by 81 votes to 70, the details and conditions of issue to be left in the hands of the Executive.' [3]

It was **1911,** however, before further details were intimated in the Gazette. The Badge would be sold to boys at 3d each, through their captains, and HQ would charge 3d for it. There was a qualification required for the issue of the badge: boys would have to serve...

'...One year with good conduct'. At

this stage the Badge was still *'in preparation'.* [4]

The emergent Badge was the circular, blue-enamelled Buttonhole Badge with the anchor motif which became so familiar over the following two decades.

The **1914** edition of the BB Manual laid down clearly the purpose of the badge:

*'The Executive issue a Boy's Button-Hole Badge, which may be worn in private life only, by Boys serving in the Brigade. **The badge is on no account to be worn when in uniform.**'* [5]

The badge was not particularly popular, being sold at 4d and only to be worn in 'private life'. Some BB captains tried to get the boys to wear one by giving them away free leading to the inevitable abuse summarised in a letter to the Gazette from a Glasgow BB Captain in **1921**:

'For a considerable time I have noticed Boys wearing this badge, who, when asked about their Company, admit that they are not in the BB, and that the badge has been given to them by a brother or chum. Surely a Brigade Boy should value his badge too highly to give it away. What makes it so cheap to him must be because he can have one for the mere asking. Perhaps if Captains laid down that the Badge must be worn, it would be held in higher respect. It lies with Captains to be more discreet in giving out badges...'[6]

In the same Gazette, of January **1921**, it was felt necessary to isssue a recommendation regarding the distribution of the badge:

'It is recommended that the Badge should not be given away free, but should be sold to the Boys at cost price, when they will appreciate it more and will take pride in wearing it.'[7]

The Manual of **1921** issued the rule which sought to redress the problem of status for the badge by allowing it to be worn in uniform and reducing the period of service with good conduct to three months. Now, the wearing of the badge was to be encouraged. The Manual statement of **1914** leaving the adoption of the badge to the discretion of captains, was replaced with the sentence:

'Captains are strongly urged to encourage all the Boys in their Companies to wear the Badge.'[8]

The bonus was that BB boys could simply leave the buttonhole badge on their coats in 'private life' and not have to worry about taking them off for uniform parades. This meant a greater wearing of the badges in mufti than ever before. After only ten years, the BB Buttonhole Badge had come of age.

The design remained unchanged until union with the BLB in **1926/7**.

The Red Cross

In **1927**, the Brigade Executive examined the Report of the Badge Committee set up to produce badges for the new united Brigade. The Buttonhole Badge was considered and the minutes read as follows:

'A discussion took place on the proposal that the cross in the Buttonhole Badge should be in red, strong views being expressed on both sides of the question. Ultimately it was decided, on the motion of Lord Polwarth seconded by Mr Bennet Mitchell that the proposal of the Committee that the cross on the Buttonhole Badge should be in red should be adopted on the understanding that this was the only case in which the cross in the crest would appear in red, and that the cross should in all other instances, whether on publications or equipment, be the same colour as the anchor. The suggestion was made that a cut-out design for this badge might be considered, but in view of the difficulties involved, and the additional expense in a cut-out design it was agreed to proceed with the Badge as described above.'[9]

It should be noted that the use of a cross in red behind the anchor must have obtained widespread approval because just a few months after the Executive ruling against, it was being used on the Membership Card.[10]

The official intimation of the Buttonhole Badge with the new crest appeared in the June **1927** edition of the Gazette:

'Design-circular Badge with the BB Crest in a blue enamel ground with the Cross in Red.'[11]

In the Price List of **1928/29** the 'Standard' Buttonhole Badge was advertised at 4d. A silver Badge was struck for officers at 1/3d. Although the Badge was to be worn for mufti purposes only by

officers, it was in fact, almost a return to the **1897** Buttonhole.

A victim of 'Jubilee Fever'

Jubilee Year, **1933**, was in many ways a turning point for the Brigade. It was the end of an era. Within three generations the BB had increased its numbers to an all-time high. Jubilee fever, which had introduced the successful special Buttonhole Badge, was to be encouraged into the mid- **1930s**. When the official Jubilee Buttonhole Badge, which had replaced the circular one, finished its stint on October 4th **1933** it was decided not to look back to the pre-Jubilee circular design when considering a future replacement. An announcement was made in the Gazette:

'...it has been decided not to revert to the pre-Jubilee Badge, but to issue a new design in gilt with the words "The Boys'Brigade" on a scroll beneath the crest. The price of the Badge has been reduced to 3d. and it should be supplied to Recruits on the completion of their first three months service.'[12]

Those wanting a 'cut-out' design just seven years before had been vindicated. It would be cheaper and not more expensive.

'Mighty Band of Brothers'

Much emphasis was placed by the Brigade upon the wearing of the new Badge. No doubt costs had been reduced by ordering large numbers.

'The Boys should be told something of the significance of the Badge, worn by

men and Boys all over the world, the sign of a great brotherhood banded together to seek the advancement of Christ's Kingdom, and a constant reminder to each of us of our duty and responsibility at all times.' [13]

Whilst the image of the Buttonhole Badge certainly remained untarnished, the badges themselves were decidedly lack-lustre. Keeping the costs down resulted in the use of an inferior finish which caused much concern in the ranks. The initial response from the Brigade was to produce a gold version, the decision being made at the January **1935** Executive Meeting. At the same meeting, the Finance Committee reported that the new Buttonhole Badge had increased receipts by £200. [14] The gold version costing 6s.0d was suitable for presentation purposes and,

'...has longer wearing qualities than the ordinary one...'. [15]

The problem remained for those without the new gold badge. In December **1935**, a letter appeared in the Gazette from *'Shiney'*, a correspondent. He advocated the cleaning of the Buttonhole Badge, a practice formerly reserved for badges of uniform and proficiency:

'The wonderful gilt with which the new badge is so resplendent does not, alas, maintain its pristine freshness for many weeks, and many of us have been sorely tried by the dingy appearance of these badges...The badges clean well and are very easy to keep clean.' [16]

The Badge survives a war and the 1968 Awards Structure

Wartime restrictions caused some modifications to the Buttonhole Badge with non-enamelled versions and thinner shell-stamped metal types being sold. The Badge continued to remain popular and

there were a number of attempts made to make the badge compulsory for wear in uniform. One such

proposal was made to the Badges Committee in **1956**, but this was not recommended.[17] The badge remained primarily for use out of uniform, by all ranks.

Problems with defining the role of the Buttonhole Badge came with the introduction of the new awards in **1968**. No longer could the Buttonhole Badge be regarded as a *'recruits'* award as there were new 'Target Badges' for this purpose. The Executive had not however, forgotten the Buttonhole Badge. At the Company Section Activities Sub-Committee meeting in April **1967** the status of the badge had been discussed and *'Suggestions agreed'* [18] When the Sub-Committee Interim Report was produced in May it was clear just what agreement had been reached:

'Buttonhole Badge. To be presented to

all Boys when they are accepted as members. NB. This badge now becomes a "membership" and not a "service" badge.'[19]

The decision to withdraw the existing regulations on 31st August **1970** completed the official change in status of the Buttonhole Badge. [20] Official recognition, however, was not enough on its own. Members needed to know details of its new status. The **1968** edition of the BB Handbook for Boys virtually ignored the Badge.[21] At last, the Boys Handbook of **1976** finally included the Buttonhole Badge as part of the Company Section uniform. This was the first uniform/mufti badge in the Brigade.[22] The Badge continued to be produced in large numbers with various fastenings being introduced.[23]

The Demise of the Dull

The famous tarnishing tendency of the Buttonhole Badge remained with it for many years. Letters to and from the manufacturer are quite revealing. In January **1971**, the Supplies Department wrote to Messrs. William Dowler of Mott St., Birmingham, regarding the tarnishing of the Badge. Dowler replied:

'...we can confirm that these badges will tarnish being made of gilding metal... which oxidises quite rapidly.'

It offered a solution, at extra cost, and stated that samples would be sent. [24] On 29th January samples and prices were submitted, three samples of each finish on a card. Type '0' was the unlaquered Badge currently supplied. Type '1' was laquered gilding metal which would add 1d to the price. Type '2' was ordinary gilt, but laquered for an additional 2fid. Type '3' was polished, well-gilt and laquered adding 5d to the price. [25] Decimalisation came to confuse matters concerning prices during **1971**, but, even with the best quality badge, the price after conversion should have been less than 15p. By **1975**, the price was 24p. [26] The demise of the dull Buttonhole Badge was a high priority of the Brigade Secretary, Ian Neilson, in **1972**:

'Do you wear a lapel badge which is unintentionally dull? ...I am always saddened when I meet a BB member, Boy or Officer, with a dull and dreary looking lapel badge...Those pieces of blue polishing cloth work wonders and I commend them to you.' [27]

Improvements in the quality of the Buttonhole Badge were still high on the agenda of BB Supplies even in the **1980s**. An announcement of a 'Presentation Quality' badge came in the BB Gazette in **1985**. This new badge was said to be '...made to higher standards of plating and enamelling' it had a safety catch and brooch fitting. This improved badge would cost £1.50p. The standard quality remained in stock at 85p. [28]

'Authorised' no longer!

By far the greatest change to the Buttonhole Badge since **1934** came in **1993** when the Brigade Executive agreed to change the 'Authorised Version' Biblical spelling of 'Stedfast' to 'Ste**a**dfast' and the new spelling appeared on the Buttonhole Badge before any other, due to the large numbers being produced and used. The Buttonhole Badge is known throughout the world as **the** membership badge of the BB.

At the **1999** Brigade Council in Dundee a new uniform for the Brigade was approved. This will mean that jackets are no longer worn and the buttonhole badge returns to 'mufti' status only. The new regulation states that:

'The BB buttonhole badge may be worn by any member when not in uniform.'

REFERENCES

1. BB Gazette, Vol XVII, No 5, 1/1/1910, p 66. BB Scottish HQ. Carronvale, Larbert, Stirlingshire.
2. ibid. No. 10. 1/6/1910. p 146.
3. ibid. Vol XIX, No 3, 1/11/1910. p 35.
4. ibid. No. 6, 1/2/1911, p 82.
5. The Boys' Brigade Manual. 1914. p.51.
6. Knox, John, Capt.154th Glasgow Coy., in a letter to the BB Gazette Vol. XXIX, No 5. 1/1/1921, p 76, Glasgow Battalion BB Archive, H.Q. Bath St.
7. ibid. p 66.
8. The Boys' Brigade Manual 1921, p 67.
9. Minutes of Executive Meeting. 14-16/1/1927. BB HQ Felden Lodge, Hemel Hempstead, Herts.
10. Membership Card, 1928-29. designed by a member of 4th Motherwell Coy.
11. BB Gazette Vol.XXXV, No 10, 1/6/1927, p 163. Mitchell Library, Glasgow.
12. ibid. Vol.XLII, No 1, 1/9/1933. p 2. National Library of Scotland.
13. ibid. Vol. XLIV, No 4, December 1935. p 52. R. Bolton Collection.
14. Minutes of Executive Meeting, 19/1/1935.
15. BB Gazette, Vol XLIII, No 8, April 1935. p 126. R. Bolton Collection.
16. op.cit., BB Gazette December 1935, p 63.
17. Minutes of Badges Committee Meeting, 26/5/1956. BB HQ
18. Minutes of Company Section Activities Sub-Committee 29/4/1967. CA/M[67]2 para. 27 [n] p 6. BB HQ.
19. Interim Report of the Company Section Activities Sub-Committee Concerning A Revised Programme and Awards Structure for Company Sections.Section 1. [Agreed awards] p 9. 16/5/1967. BB HQ.
20. Minutes of Company Section Activities Sub-Committee, CA/M/67/4 14/10/1967 para. 53, [a] 5. p 4. BB HQ
21. BB Handbook for Boys. [Company Section] New Edition, August 1968. BB HQ.
22. ibid. New Edition, December 1976. p 13.
23. The Clutch-Pin fastening was introduced in 1974, available from a new supplier. Supplies Officer's Report 7/2/74.
24. Letter from William Dowler, Mott St., Birmingham. 27/1/1971 to BB Supplies Dept.
25. ibid. 29/1/1971.
26. BB Supplies Price List No 1. August 1975.
27. BB Gazette, Vol. 81, No. 1 Oct/Nov 1972. p 11.
28. ibid. Feb/Mar. 1985.

The Standard Buttonhole Badge

1911 - 1926

BB 173   **BB 173**   **BB 173**   **BB 173**

1927 - 1933

BB 174   **BB 174**   **BB 174**   **BB 174**

The Standard Buttonhole Badge - Continued

1934 - c.1940   **c.1947 - 1993**

BB 175

BB 175

BB 175

c.1940 - c.1947

BB 175

BB 175

BB 175

1993 -

BB 175

BB 173 - BB 175 BACKGROUND NOTES

There are really only two 'generations' of the standard Buttonhole Badge, circular and cut-out. However, due to the union with the BLB, the Second World War and a new spelling of Steadfast combined with the usual changes over many years and a high volume of production there are many variations. There are seventy versions of BB 175 alone!

BB 173 has variety in the material, seemingly made from gilding metal and nickel as well as a silver type. There is also variation in the emblem and in the fastening stud being either crescent or circular. The post - union version BB 174 has similar variation but includes only crescent and foot studs. Remarkably, some versions have an anchor with a rope and more commonly without. The red cross is enamelled and there is an early diamond shaped Miller maker's logo. The cut-out BB 175 was produced in stud and brooch form. Studs are crescent and foot types. Brooch types cover virtually all the main fastening types from standard tube to clutch pin. There is much obverse difference in the size and type of lettering and the anchor lettering raised or depressed. There are types with no rope, differences in the size of Bs and in the colour of the enamelling. The wartime economy buttonholes are nearly all stud type and lack any enamelling. Some types are the normal striking without enamel having been added. There are a few economy types which are fully shell stamped, usually having Foot Studs. The 1993 version has the word 'Steadfast' replacing the traditional spelling.

The Jubilee Badges 1933

Buttonhole, lapel badge for the Brigade to wear in Jubilee Year.
Lapel badge for all Visiting Officers attending the Council Meeting.
Lapel badge for all Glasgow Officers attending the Council Meeting.
Special uniform badge for all Boys attending the Dechmont Jubilee Camp.
Buttonhole, lapel badge for all Glasgow Battalion Ex-Members.

Fifty years after the founding of the BB, the City of Glasgow, birthplace of the Brigade, buzzed with the euphonious clamour of The Boys' Brigade. The celebrations revolved around the fiftieth annual meeting of the Brigade Council on 9th September **1933**. So important was the Jubilee that no less than five different badges were issued. There has, as would be expected with badges of such importance, been much discussion about their classification. The fact is that some of the badges could be classified under more than one heading as will become clear to the reader. Certainly, these influential badges in respect of their high quality of design and production, just as the Jubilee itself, should be seen as a high peak in the terrain of BB history. The Jubilee was both a Glasgow and a Brigade event. There is little scope for separating the events of 9th-11th September **1933**, however, for this was no 'local' celebration. The eyes of the whole BB World were focused on Glasgow.

The Jubilee Buttonhole Badge

Nineteen months before the Great Jubilee Celebration in Glasgow, meetings were being held to discuss arrangements which included the issue of a special badge. The minutes of the Jubilee Celebrations Sub-Committee for England & Wales record that it was agreed that Glasgow should be the main place for celebrations between 9th-11th September **1933**. It was also approved...

'...that a special Jubilee Buttonhole Badge be produced for sale to Officers and Boys on the strength in the Jubilee Session.' [1]

The Badge was agreed at the Executive meeting.[2] By May of **1932** there was a sample of a buttonhole badge in gilt available and the meeting agreed that this would take the place of the current buttonhole for the duration of **1933**.[3] The details of the new badge appeared in the September Gazette:

'Officers should note that during the present session the issue of the ordinary Buttonhole Badge will be suspended. In its place the special Jubilee badge, which consists of the Boys' Brigade crest in gilt with the words "Jubilee 1883-1933" will be worn by all Officers and Boys, and it should be noted that Boys may wear it for the remainder of their service in the Brigade to denote that they were Jubilee members.' [4]

The new buttonhole badge was made up of the new small BB emblem which had been introduced in **1932** for use by Old Boys. The Old Boys Badge was in bronze finish and the Jubilee badge would be the same size, but gilt with blue enamelled scrolls underneath. It was a successful badge; in the first month of its issue, the BB Gazette stated:

'The Jubilee Badge has certainly caught on, and within the first few weeks since its issue, seems to be more generally worn than any badge of the kind we have ever had.' [5]

" A Ticket to Glasgow, Please "

Further comment on sales appeared in the November Gazette:

'Over fifty thousand Buttonhole Badges have already been issued. Their prevalence is noticeable in all the great cities. It is hoped that the rest of the Boys will receive their badges soon... Past Officers and Old Boys are not entitled to wear this badge. The special Badge for Old Boys sanctioned last year is the only Boys' Brigade Badge Old Boys may wear.' [6]

Demand for the badge was maintained into December:

'The demand for the Jubilee Buttonhole Badge is as brisk as ever. The badge is reproduced at the head of this column-Blocks for printing this badge are obtainable at the Brigade Offices at 3s 6d each.' [7]

As **1933** started the badge was still being advertised:

'Captains should see that every officer and Boy entitled to it is now in possession of this Badge, which is such an excellent means of making the fact of our Jubilee widely known. Everybody should get the Buttonhole Badge habit.' [8]

It was the unquestioned success of the Jubilee Buttonhole Badge which was to change the shape of the regular Buttonhole Badge. Gone forever was the circular enamelled badge and in its place a badge based on the fantastically successful Jubilee Button. The decision to kill-off the old badge in favour of the new design was made at the January **1933** Executive meeting when Mr Harvey proposed and Canon Vining seconded that the present Jubilee Buttonhole badge...

'...with a fresh scroll underneath'

...should be the permanent Buttonhole Badge. This was approved. [9] The pressure to extend the wearing of the badge forced the BB Executive to change its mind and by March the following notice appeared in the Gazette:

'By decision of the Executive, authority to wear the Jubilee Buttonhole badge has been extended to past Officers and Old Boys, who are entitled to wear the badge during Jubilee Year.' [10]

The notice of the termination of the Jubilee Badge was linked to the introduction of the newly designed regular Buttonhole Badge:

'The sale of the Jubilee Buttonhole Badge will terminate on October 4th...the form of this badge has proved so popular that it has been decided not to revert to the pre-Jubilee Badge, but to issue a new design in gilt with the words "The Boys' Brigade" on a scroll beneath the crest. The price of the Badge has been reduced to 3d and it should be supplied to Recruits on the completion of their first three months service.' [11]

When the final accounts were done, the Jubilee Badge had been a financial success in addition to its popularity, as reported to the Brigade Executive in **1934**:

'£1, 349 worth of Jubilee Buttonhole Badges sold. Great success.' [12]

Perhaps the greatest achievement of the badge, along with its close relative the Old Boys Badge which was introduced in the same year, was that of 'breaking the mould' of BB buttonhole badges for officers or boys which, until then, had always been solid and circular.

The Jubilee Celebrations Badges

Three badges emerged from the Jubilee Celebrations as perhaps the most recognisable mementos of the occasion, but they started out as one badge.

The Council Meetings Badges

Reporting to the Brigade Executive in May **1932** the Jubilee Committee stated:

'Special Jubilee Badge for wear by Officers attending the meetings would be available and the Committee proposed that the two Boys per Company attending the Camp would be entitled to this badge, to be worn on the arm during the rest of their service as Boys.' [13]

The Badge was to be the emblem for the Jubilee Celebrations organised by the Glasgow Battalion between 8th and 11th September, quite distinct from the national Jubilee Year badges and celebrations. The Council meeting was organised by the Battalion, as was the Dechmont Camp.

The design of the badge incorporated the BB emblem surrounded by a wreath. On top of the badge was the figure of St. Mungo with the wording *'1933, Glasgow, Sept 8-11.'* The word *'Jubilee'* crowned the wreath with *'1883-1933'*. Virtually all the Battalion publications were emblazoned with full coloured 'seals' the same size and design as the badges. The seals were available to affix to locally produced Battalion literature. The common design was modified to produce three distinct badges.

When the Brigade Executive met in September **1932,** it discussed the Glasgow Celebration 'Badge'. Designs in gilt for officers attending the Glasgow Jubilee Celebrations and in silver for the two boys per Company attending the Jubilee Camp were before the meeting and approved. The meeting also considered a special Jubilee One Year Service Badge, but this was not approved. [14] Glasgow had never used the One Year Service Badge, so that was a certain non-starter!

"A Milestone in Youth Work"

Badges for the officers attending the Council meeting were gilt with White, Blue and Red enamel. It was decided to make a distinction between Glasgow Officers and Visiting Officers by changing the enamel colour at the top of the badge from the standard white to red for the Glasgow contingent. There were 1871 Visiting Officers, 389 Visiting Ladies and 1539 Glasgow Officers. [15]

The Dechmont Camp Badge

The Camp of Representative Boys was held at Dechmont, Kirkhill, Glasgow from 8th-11th September, 1933. Boys attending were each presented with a badge. The special camp badges were 'silver' with the colour at the top changed from white to blue. The silvering was done over the gilding metal and was easily rubbed off revealing the bronze colour underneath. It seems strange that the boys' badges, destined to be worn for perhaps four years, should be less durable than the Officers' Council Badge probably only worn for the same number of days.

The first intimation of the badge came in the BB Gazette of December **1932**:

'The Brigade Executive have approved of the issue of a special Jubilee Badge to the two Boys per Company attending the Jubilee Camp. The Badge will be a silver one and will be worn on the arm during the remainder of the Boy's service in the ranks.' [16]

JUBILEE CELEBRATIONS BADGE

Every Representative Boy in Camp will receive, on arrival, a Badge which he will wear during the week-end in the left lapel. After Camp, for the remainder of his B.B. service, he will wear this Badge as a decoration on the left arm, under the King's Badge and the Long Service Badge.

Visiting Officers to the Brigade Council will also wear a Special Badge, and Glasgow Officers a similar one, but with a red scroll at top.

There were 2079 boys at the Dechmont Camp. [17]

'Each Boy was allocated to a Battalion, Company and Tent, and it was so arranged that there was a Glasgow Boy in every tent to do the honours. The camper was then issued with the Official Jubilee Badge, which adorned his lapel during the week-end and later became a decoration worn on the left arm to indicate throughout his BB service that he had been one of the representative Boys at the Jubilee Camp.' [18]

The badge was in fact worn on the left lapel during the Camp and afterwards transferred to be worn on the left arm under the King's Badge and the Long Service Badge. [19]

The Dechmont Tin-Badge

Another badge was worn by boys and officers at the Dechmont Camp. A half-white, half single-coloured Tin Button Badge, mentioned in the November Gazette:

'Each Camp Company is distinguished by a coloured badge, so that Boys may know their Company Officers at sight.' [20]

The Ex-Members 'Hundred Thousand Badge'

In April **1933**, the Glasgow Battalion issued details of a special Jubilee Badge for Ex-Members of the Battalion. It was reckoned that 100,000 Glasgow men had passed through the ranks of The Boys' Brigade between **1883** and **1933**. Badges were to be issued in bulk to companies at the special reduced rate of 1/6d per dozen (postage extra). Single badges were 3d each. (see advert) [21] It is not clear why a bronze finish was chosen, perhaps to conform to the existing bronze 'Old Boys' badge which had been issued by the Brigade. The design and size of the badge is similar to the Celebrations Badges, but the word 'Jubilee' is replaced by 'Ex-Member'. The top is made so that the badge overall takes on a thistle pattern with the wording: 'Jubilee, Glasgow 1933'.

The badges were produced by William Miller of Branston St., Birmingham. On 10th March **1933,** Miller submitted samples from the die and its accompanying letter stated:

'The Silver plated pattern will not wear white indefinitely as it is plated on Red metal. If you require White metal throughout the price would be the same as in bronze ie 15/- per gross.' [22] ('Red metal' is copper.)

It is clear that a number of varieties were considered, but the 'bronze' version was accepted. The reply to William Miller stated:

'We have now definitely fixed on the Ex-Members Badge in bronze finish and I have pleasure in ordering herewith 10,000 Badges, in bronze finish, at 15/- per gross, as quoted. These are now required very urgently and if possible for you to let us have them in hand here by the 1st of April, it will be

of service to us.' Presumably, it was estimated that only one in ten ex-members would buy the badge.

One 'silvered' Ex-Members Badge is known to exist, but this may well be one of the samples submitted by Miller. This badge was given to a former Glasgow Battalion Archivist by an officer who had been a BB Captain and member of the Jubilee Committee. It was stated that this type was given to former Captains of the Glasgow Battalion. This claim is entirely unsubstantiated. [23]

REFERENCES

1. 'Jubilee Celebrations: Report of Sub-Committee for England and Wales 8/1/1932 for consideration of Full Committee at Liverpool.' Printed 12/1/1932, Abbey House. Glasgow Battalion Archive Box J1. Glasgow Battn. HQ Bath St. Glasgow.
2. Minutes of Brigade Executive 23-24/1/1932. BB HQ, Felden Lodge, Felden, Hemel Hempstead, Herts.
3. ibid. 28-29/5/1932.
4. BB Gazette, Vol. XLI No. 1, September 1932, p 2. National Library of Scotland.
5. ibid. No 2. October. p 20
6. ibid. No 3. November p 37
7. ibid. No 4. December p 55
8. ibid. No 5. January p 73
9. Minutes of Brigade Executive. 21-22/1/1933. BB HQ op.cit.
10. BB Gazette, No. 7 p 108, op.cit..
11. ibid. Vol XLII, No 1. September 1933, p 2.
12. Minutes of Brigade Executive. 14/9/1934. BB HQ
13. ibid. 28-29/5/1932.
14. ibid. 23/9/1932.
15. List of Visiting Officers. 50th Meeting of Brigade Council. Archive Box J1. Glasgow HQ.
16. BB Gazette. Vol XLI No. 4. December 1932, p 55. Nat. Lib Scotland.
17. ibid. Vol XLII No. 2, October 1933. p 22.
18. The Boys' Brigade Jubilee Book, McLagan and Cumming, 1933, p 28.
19. The Jubilee Camp of Representative Boys, Dechmont, Kirkhill, Glasgow, 8-11/9/1933, Glasgow HQ Archive Box J1. See also Jubilee Camp Handbook page 11.
20. BB Gazette. Vol XLII, No 3. November 1933, p 48.
21. Advertisement, Glasgow Battalion Archive Box J1. Battalion HQ.
22. ibid. Letter from William Miller, Rec'd. 13th March 1933.
23. Cooper, John, states that he was given the badge by Roy Farmer. [Member of 1933 Jubilee Committee]

The Brigade Jubilee Buttonhole Badge   1932 - 1933

BB 176

BB 176

BB 176

BB 176

BB 176 BACKGROUND NOTES

This small cut-out lapel badge has a crescent stud. The obverse is found in both gilt and bronze versions. The enamel is blue. Examples can be found with both painted and enamelled red crosses, but their origin is unclear.

The Glasgow Jubilee Celebrations Badges   1933

BB 215.01

Brigade
Council,
Glasgow
Officers'
Lapel Brooch

BB 215.02

Brigade
Council,
Visiting
Officers'
Lapel Brooch

BB 161

Boys'
Dechmont
Camp Brooch

BB 215, & BB 161 BACKGROUND NOTES

These brooches are all produced using the same die, but with variation in both the enamelling and metal finish. The Council badges are gilt over gilding metal. The red 'scrolls' indicating the Glasgow Officers' Badge and the white 'scrolls' the Visiting Officers' Badge. The Boys' Dechmont Camp Badge is made from copper with a silvered finish. The example shown here has, typically, lost most of its silvering, since the Boys' Badge was worn for some years as compared with the Officers' badges only being worn for days. The Dechmont Badge has blue enamelled 'scrolls' at the top.

The Glasgow Battalion Ex-Members' Brooch   1933

The 'Hundred Thousand' Brooch

BB 177

BB 177 BACKGROUND NOTES

Although similar in pattern to the Officers' & Boys' Badges there are many differences. The badge is full shell and includes the maker's name Miller, Birmingham, on the reverse. The badge is made from copper or 'red-metal' with a bronzed finish. Exactly 10,000 were produced to supply the expected market of 10% of the possible number of Ex-Members of the Battalion. When the prototype for this badge was discovered c. 1996 it was found packaged with two 'BB 215' badges, one of which was fully enamelled except for the scrolls and the other was completely without enamel. This probably indicates the thinking process behind the development of the badge, for the prototype is a 215 but with the new type scroll and 'Ex-member' ribbon cut into it.

The Royal Badges

The 1937 Coronation Badge

There was little doubt in the minds of the members of the BB Executive in 1936 that a badge to celebrate the forthcoming Coronation would be a good idea. The 1933 BB Jubilee celebrations' badges had been very popular and the new Buttonhole Badge was selling well. But who would be King? When the copy had been written for the December Gazette there had been no official notice regarding Edward VIII's marriage to a divorced U.S. citizen. That announcement came during the production of the Gazette on November 16th 1936, with the abdication coming on 11th December. The next day the Duke of York was proclaimed King George VI. This change of Kings was an added bonus for the BB since, as Duke of York, the King had been present at the Jubilee celebrations in Glasgow. The Gazette announced the badge:

'A BB Coronation Badge will be issued for the use of Officers and Boys during the year, in place of the ordinary Buttonhole Badge. It will have a special significance as the purchase of one will enable each member of the Brigade to contribute to a Coronation Gift to his Majesty's honour.'

The Badge would be ready in the New Year. [1]

Some of the original designs for the Badge have survived (see above) and some include the date of the Coronation, 12th May 1937. The centre of the badge was, of course, the cut-out anchor design which had proved so popular in the 1933 and 1934 buttonhole designs. Eventually, one design was chosen, based on the 1934 Buttonhole with a scroll and crown added to the top. [2] By February 1937 the Badge was ready at a cost of 4/- per dozen or 4d each. [3] The Badge turned out

to be a great success demonstrated by comments in the March Gazette. The demand was stated as being so heavy it was hoped that the manufacturers would *'cope with the supply'*. [4] Evidently, more than one maker was used to produce the badge, since there are at least two distinct crowns and lettering styles indicating different dies. There is no written evidence to suggest that the crowns were designed as par-

Design proposals for the 1937 Coronation Badge.
BB Archive collection.

ticularly 'English' or 'Scottish', as has sometimes been assumed. In fact the crowns represent the St Edward's Crown which is English (the narrower of the two) and the

CORONATION
BUTTON - HOLE BADGE

4D each.   From Brigade Offices

**The completed 1937 badge
is advertised.**

Imperial State Crown. All the badges have the crescent stud fitting to wear in the buttonhole.

The 1953 Coronation Badge

It would have been unthinkable for the Coronation of Queen Elizabeth not to be celebrated within the Brigade. Decisions regarding a badge seem to have been taken with the success of **1937** very much in mind. The new badge followed the same design, but the date was changed and the finish altered from gilt to chrome. The choice of chromium may have been just to produce a clearly different badge from the **1937** model, but it was very much in keeping with the times. Many people were looking for something 'bright' to take their minds off the somewhat austere immediate post-war atmosphere. The design would have saved money - another post-war requisite. The Girls' Brigade adopted the same idea, simply changing the date and Royal cypher on its coronation badges. [5] There had been quite a change in prices over fifteen years, however, with the badge going on sale for 1s 3d. According to the BB Gazette, which announced the new badge, a very heavy demand was expected. The badge, it stated: '...*may be worn thereafter.*' [6] Both brooch and pin versions were available, recognising the move away from lapel buttonholes. The two different crown-designs, similar to those used in **1937,** probably indicates the Brigade's return to the same two badge manufacturers.[7] During the **1960's** & **1970's** there were very many people who wore the badge, claiming it to be one of the best ever produced. Like the glittering Coronation itself, and the conquest

of Mt. Everest at the same time, this badge can be singled out as one of the 'highs' in BB badge production.

The Prince of Wales Investiture Badge 1969

The investiture of Prince Charles as Prince of Wales took place at Caernarvon Castle on July 1st **1969.** The Boys' Brigade in Wales decided to produce a commemorative buttonhole badge to mark the occasion. The badge was a simple design incorporating the emblem of the prince with that of the BB. It seems that the badge was sanctioned for general wear as a buttonhole badge in place of the standard type in both uniform and mufti. However, finding details about it has been difficult. The editor wore his throughout the year, in place of the normal buttonhole badge, but it was optional within the company. The badge clearly has the wording, '*The Boys' Brigade In Wales*' rather than simply '*The Boys' Brigade*', so it was probably supplied from Wales whilst being sanctioned throughout the UK.

The Queen's Silver Jubilee 1977

For all of **1977** Britain was engulfed by Jubilee fever. In many parts of the country BB boys formed guards of honour for Her Majesty as she toured the country. BB Bands,

joined with many other youth bands and participated in a massive 'Salute to the Queen' Jubilee Parade along the Mall. An official Jubilee logo was available appearing on various publications including a Souvenir BB booklet, cloth badge and inevitably, a special buttonhole badge. The new badge was announced in the Gazette:

'...*for Officers and Boys-and suitable for Boys to wear in uniform, a LAPEL BADGE. Metal with coloured design, rectangular shaped...*' [8]

An important additional announcement was made in the Feb/Mar Gazette:

'*The Brigade Executive have agreed that Junior Section Boys may wear the Silver Jubilee Buttonhole Badge when in uniform and it should be worn above the jersey badge.*' [9]

When the new badge emerged, 'it' turned out to be twins. English and Scottish versions were produced, both for the official cloth and buttonhole badges. The main difference was in the crown which appeared as part of the official Jubilee logo. The Brigade recognised for the first time that two different crowns would be used, thus reflecting the rise of Scottish national sentiment during the **1970s**. Unfortunately, the move away from an enamelled badge to one which was a decal stuck into a 'blank' lessened its popularity somewhat. The blanks from all the unsold badges provided the Brigade with a source of cheap, badges for a number of years afterwards: notably the Cleveland Hike, and the Scottish and UK Band Championships. The Jubilee Badge was perhaps typical of the Brigade's, and to some extent the country's, fixation with bland, functional almost 'brutalist' design which emerged, like the proficiency badges and membership cards, as 'cheap and nasty' rather than a bold modern statement.

The 1994 Windsor Royal Review

On 30th April **1994**, in the castle quadrangle at Windsor, H. M. The Queen reviewed around 1,100 senior BB boys and Officers from the UK and Eire. The occasion was originally designed as an opportunity for a ceremonial, public handover of the Brigade Presidency from Lord Thurso to his successor Lord Strathmore. The event turned into a Royal event when H. M. The Queen graciously consented to allow Windsor to be used and to attend personally to review the Brigade. Lord Thurso in his speech

thanked Her Majesty for her patronage and that enjoyed from successive Monarchs since **1896.**

Two Badges were produced for the occasion, one in silver plate for anyone in the Brigade to wear as a souvenir of the occasion, (2,000 produced) and the other in gilt for wear only by the senior boys and officers on parade, (1,200 produced.) The tablet design of the badge, represents the plan of the Castle Quadrangle at Windsor. Like the BB Seniors on the day, lined up on the grass, the Brigade emblem on the badge is set in bright green enamel. Incused in black around the silver or gold 'paths' on the perimeter ribbon of the badge is the wording 'Royal Review Windsor **1994.**' The badge was designed by Stephen Lane, Lt., 1st New Barnet Coy. who at the time was a member of the Brigade Executive, Brigade Archivist and Officer I/C Ceremonial for the Review.

Considering Royal patronage extended over more than a century, there have been relatively few royal badges produced by the BB. None were issued in the first forty years, with occasions such as Queen Victoria's Diamond Jubilee of **1897** and King George V's Silver Jubilee of **1935** being recognised by the BB in other ways than the production of metal badges.

REFERENCES

1   BB Gazette, Vol. XLV, No. 4, Dec. 1936. p 56, Mitchell Library, Glasgow.
2   BB HQ. Archives, Felden Lodge, Hemel Hempstead, Herts.
3   op. cit. BB Gazette, No. 6, Feb. 1937, p. 92. BB Scottish HQ, Carronvale, Larbert, Stirlingshire.
4   ibid. No. 7, p. 110.
5   The Girls' Brigade Archive Collection, GB HQ, Didcot Oxfordshire.
6   op.cit. BB Gazette, Vol. LXI, No. 2, Dec. 1952, p 20, Mitchell Library, Glasgow.
7   Hoey, A.E. Former Brigade Supplies Officer testifies to the fact that the crowns were indeed produced as 'Scottish' & 'English' but were never advertised as such but supplied by the Brigade's two main HQ Depots in London & Glasgow, St Edward's Crown being the English version.
8   BB Gazette, December 1976/January 1977, Vol 85 No. 2. p 34. R. Bolton Collection.
9   BB Gazette, February/March 1977, Vol 85 No 3. p 57.

The 1937 Coronation Badge

S

BB 179

E

BB 178

PROTOTYPE

S

BB 178 & 179 BACKGROUND NOTES

This appears to have only been produced as a crescent stud (points up) lapel badge, no brooch versions having been discovered. It is gilt with red and blue enamel. There are two varieties; one with the Imperial State Crown and one with the St. Edward's Crown. The former has the word 'stedfast' in a straight line and was issued in Scotland. The latter has the word 'stedfast' curved and was sold in England. A chromed, non-enamelled version exists, of the Imperial State Crown type and this was probably produced as a prototype for the 1953 Coronation badge.

The 1953 Coronation Badge

 S    S    E    E

BB 181   **BB 181**   **BB 180**   **BB 180**

BB 180 & 181 BACKGROUND NOTES

This chrome on gilding metal, enamelled lapel badge was produced with both lapel stud and brooch fittings. The red enamel varies in shade between batches and there are the same two varieties of obverse design as in the 1937 badge. The crescent stud has 'points down' on the Imperial State Crown type and 'points up' on the St. Edward's Crown type. Interestingly, the Imperial State Crown versions do not carry the 'Made in England' imprint on the reverse.

The Investiture of The Prince of Wales Badge 1969

BB 182 BACKGROUND NOTES

This silvered, gilding metal, enamelled brooch was produced with red, white and blue enamel. The silvered finish tends to wear very easily thus exposing the metal beneath. There is variation in the fastenings and coatings on the reverse between different production batches. A notable feature is the wording 'Sure & Stedfast' incused in white within the anchor.

BB 182

The Queen's Silver Jubilee Badge 1977

 E    E    S

BB 183.01   **BB 183.02**   **BB 184.01**

BB 183 & 184 BACKGROUND NOTES

The construction is a printed plastic decal set into a gilt on gilding metal brooch. There are two main versions, one with the St. edward's crown (English) and one with a Scottish crown. Two decals were produced with the English crown. The first type BB 183.01 has small lettering on the white ribbon and larger lettering for 'The Boys' Brigade'. Type BB183.02 has the reverse of the first i.e. large lettering on the white ribbon and small lettering for 'The Boys' Brigade'. The latter type has two differently stippled decal holders. The Scottish version, has no gold on the wreath and only gilt on the ribbon scroll.

The Windsor Royal Review Badge 1994

 G    S

BB 185.01   **BB 185.02**

BB 185 BACKGROUND NOTES

This tablet style, enamelled brooch was produced in either gilt or chrome on gilding metal. It was the first 'special' button-hole badge to bear the 'Steadfast' spelling. A 'bronze' version was produced but not officially used or issued.

The BB Centenary Badges

The biggest event in the BB since the 1933 Jubilee... that's how the Brigade heralded the Centenary Celebrations of 1983. Like the Jubilee 50 years earlier, the Centenary was a 'Three in One' event; The 1st Glasgow Company celebrated its foundation on 4th October 1883, Glasgow Battalion hosted the Centenary Council as the Birthplace of the BB, and the BB in Britain and around the world celebrated the fact that the BB had reached its first hundred years.

Centenary year was a big milestone in the history of the Brigade. Started with a bonfire at the New Zealand 'Camp BB 100' at Mystery Creek, and followed by a chain of similar massive bonfires all over the UK, (The editor was privileged to organise the **B**irmingham **B**onfire on **B**arr **B**eacon where, on the stroke of midnight, BB boys in uniform cast flaming torches to ignite the fire). The year included much TV coverage including a special film 'Smith's Boys' and a 'Songs of Praise'. A Royal Review by H.M. The Queen at Holyrood, postage stamps (including UK and Eire issues), the naming of a BR Train, a Centenary History, and a special England v Scotland football match of ex-BB professional players staged at Aberdeen FC under the auspices of (now 'Sir') Alex Ferguson, an ex member of 129th Glasgow Coy.. A new Floribunda Rose called 'The Boys' Brigade' was introduced, the West Kent Battalion broke the record in assembling the World's Largest Band, and 'Centenary Salute' at Ibrox Stadium featured more than 5,000 boys. Every BB boy was presented with a special New Testament and, as they say on show bills, 'much much, more.'[1]

By far the greatest celebrations were focused upon the city of Glasgow and the Council meeting at the end of August 1983. Like the 1933 events, there were a number of badges produced although they were, sadly, lacking in variety. The main badge was the Centenary Buttonhole Badge produced in large and small sizes. This Badge was a reproduction of the Centenary emblem, adopted all over the world, from Singapore and Hong Kong, to Africa and the Caribbean. [2]

The BB Centenary Emblem appeared for the first time on the front of the August/September 1981 BB Gazette. It was designed by Mr David Cherry and chosen from more than seventy entries. David joined the 2nd Thames Valley Company in 1941 following a family tradition. His father had been a member of the 1st London Coy. during the First World War. Better known for his Bugle Band work in which he has acted as an Instructor at Felden Lodge since 1951, David is a professional art designer.[3] An extract from a letter of thanks to David from Brigade Secretary Alfred Hudson, written in August 1981, gives some idea of the undertaking:

'... I am reminded of the incredible amount of work you have done every time I look at the repro sheet bearing 43 different versions of the logo. in preparation for the final selection you produced 33 roughs in colour, twelve further roughs, two special copies of the logo for the Centenary Committee to look at and then, finally, the art work

Centenary Year is launched in the West Midlands
with a massive bonfire on Barr Beacon. Jan. 1st 1983.
Photo: R. Bolton

for the Gazette...All of this you have undertaken with great enthusiasm and high professionalism...'[4]

David Cherry did the calligraphy for the Loyal Address presented to H.M. The Queen on the occasion of her Silver Jubilee and for a similar address presented to Her at the Centenary Royal Review in Edinburgh.

The 'Glasgow 100' Logo

In **1933**, the Brigade's Jubilee Emblem had been the one used by Glasgow for the celebrations in the city. It was used for the Brigade Council and even the national Dechmont Camp. The Official Brigade Jubilee Buttonhole Badge was somewhat dull and uninspiring in comparison. In **1983**, it was perhaps, the other way around. Glasgow had its own 'Glasgow 100' emblem plastered upon everything organised and produced by the Battalion and the BB Centenary logo featured on all 'national' events and literature. Sometimes both emblems could be found together; for instance, a double-decker bus had a version of the 'Glasgow 100' emblem painted on one side and the Brigade Centenary logo on the other. Only two brooch badges featured the 'Glasgow 100' emblem. One, a pewter Ladies' Brooch was sold as a souvenir gift. On this pewter badge the Glasgow emblem design was altered to make the dates **1883 - 1983** and the word 'Glasgow' much larger. The other, produced for the Brigade Council meetings in Glasgow from 26th - 28th August, was a special moulded plastic name badge. (see page 190).

Other badges were produced bearing the Brigade's Centenary emblem, some companies and battalions making use of the design to produce enamelled metal, as well as tin fun badges. The Centenary International Camp at Scone Palace from August 20th - 30th **1983** generated two badges featuring the Centenary logo and is dealt with elsewhere in this book [see page 166]. Unlike the Dechmont, Eton, or Caribbean Camps the Scone badges were not worn in uniform.

The official announcement of the Centenary Buttonhole Badge was rather confusing; in the same Gazette there were two announcements. The first read:

'The Brigade Executive has approved the wearing of the Centenary Buttonhole Badge by all members of the Brigade from 1st September 1982 - the beginning of the Centenary session...'

Then the second:

'...you will see that the Brigade Executive has approved the wearing of the Centenary buttonhole badge from the beginning of the Session 1982/83. Although the Centenary Session does not begin until 1st september 1983, the calendar year of 1983 is to be our Year of Centenary Celebration. So to avoid the need for two badge issues, the Centenary buttonhole badge is being authorised for wear from the beginning of session 1982/83.'

Actually, the 'second' was printed on page 9 and the 'first' on page 12 just to add to the confusion![5]

There is no doubt that the **1983**

Celebrations were on a grand scale, but the BB unfortunately was not. Fewer badge types were produced because numbers in the UK were well below the **1933** figures. There was no parade of 32,000 boys, and no Conventicle with 100,000 unable to get in. However, the raw numbers of badges produced was high. The Centenary lapel badge sold well as can be seen from the minutes of the Supplies Committee in November **1982**:

'Centenary Lapel Badges.
The Committee noted that 65, 000 badges had been sold. A further 20,000 would be delivered during November and December completing our commitment.
(e) The Committee agreed to authorise the purchase of a further 10,000 badges to be delivered in January.'[6]

Ninety-five thousand badges in a period of a few months is quite impressive. The final total was 117,000.[7] No doubt they will keep the collectors' market supplied for many years to come. It is remarkable that the badges in both sizes, were traditionally enamelled in style. In the ten years leading up to **1982** many mufti badges produced for the Brigade had been of the 'Decal' type, notably the **1977** Queen's Silver Jubilee. Perhaps it was here, in **1982**, that the Brigade like Saul, 'saw the light', and became converted, re-discovering that attractive, well-designed and produced badges are popular.

REFERENCES

1. Centenary Year in Pictures. The Boys' Brigade 1984.
2. Centenary Celebrations Book, Glasgow Battalion, May 1983.
3. BB Gazette, October/November 1981, p 9.
4. Hudson, Alfred, Letter to D. Cherry from 25/8/81. R.Bolton Collection.
5. BB Gazette op.cit. pp. 9 & 12.
6. Supplies Committee November 1982. Minute 47.
7. From BB Supplies reported in B.B.B.C. Newsletter July 1984.

The BB Centenary Buttonhole Badge   1982 - 1983

BB 191.01

BB 191.04

BB 191.06

PROTOTYPE

BB 191.09

The Miniature

BB 192

BB 191 & BB 192 BACKGROUND NOTES

Produced in large numbers, the Brigade used different manufacturers to maintain supplies. Each supplier has a distinctive pattern on the obverse, particularly clear in the motto wording on the anchor. The anchor itself varies clearly seen in the ring at the top. Most badges were produced by Dowler (BB 191.01 & BB 191 .02) and so variations occur within this manufactuers badges. Noticeable Dowler variations pictured here include, no 'sure' on anchor, small amount of black enamel and non-enamelled. All of these three 'variations' are probably factory rejects, but some have been sold and worn, presumably by someone assuming that all were the same. Others were produced by The London Badge & Button Co. (BB 191.06) whilst some are plain. The 'Buttonhole' size is cut out but the miniature, only produced by London Badge & Button (BB 192), is circular. The obverse detail on the miniature matches that of the larger London Badge & Button brooch. All the badges have brooch fastenings with some variation in type and placement. There is variety in the position of the Wm Dowler name. A full-shell version also exists as does an example of a badge smaller than the normal buttonhole but larger than the miniature; probably another prototype.

The 'Glasgow 100' Brooch   1982 - 1983

BB 193

BB 193 BACKGROUND NOTES

Strictly speaking this fretted brooch was a Glasgow Battalion badge, but it was advertised nationally by BB Supplies. Produced in pewter by Harkison Jewellery, Scotland. It came complete with brown, jeweller's presentation box. It has an axle pin with safety catch.

Locally issued BB Centenary Badges

BB 194

7th Wishaw

BB 195

Cumbernauld

BB 196

14th Belfast

BB 197

13th Edinburgh

BB 198

Chelmsford Sharing Day

BB 199

1st Banff

BB 200

1st Newport

BB 201

Motherwell

Brigade Council Badges

The Council of The Boys' Brigade was formed at a meeting in Glasgow on 26th January 1885 with representatives of all existing Companies present. It would have been more accurate to say that there were representatives present from both companies since the 'Brigade' consisted only of 1st and 2nd Glasgow Companies. It was decided at that meeting that the 1st annual Council meeting would take place on 12th October 1885.[1] By 12th October there were some fifteen Companies on the roll, twelve from Glasgow and three from Edingurgh.[2]

The Brigade Council was to become the 'Governing Body' of the Brigade, making its rules and monitoring progress. There has been an annual meeting held every year since 1885 and it grew as the Brigade grew. Perhaps the greatest meeting was the one held at the time of the Jubilee in 1933, billed as the 'Fiftieth Annual Council Meeting'. Actually, it should have been the 49th unless we count two meetings in 1885! This great gathering took place in Glasgow, the birthplace of the Brigade after being held, sometimes more than once, in Edinburgh, London, Sheffield, Bristol, Dublin, Liverpool, Manchester, Carlisle, Newcastle, Belfast, Newport, Aberdeen Nottingham, Brighton, Plymouth, Birmingham, Dundee, Cardiff and Swanwick.

Needless to say, as the Brigade grew in size, the event attracted officers from every part of the Kingdom requiring at least one overnight stay, usually longer. Jordanhill College was the main

Drawing by Tom Curr, Edinburgh, for the Brigade Council 1933.

It was reproduced on the back of the menu card for the Official Dinner on Saturday September 9th. 6.45 p.m.

accommodation for 1933. Apart from the actual meeting there would usually be some kind of civic reception, a church parade sundry entertainments and supporting meetings, for instance 'denominational' gatherings. The arrival of Brigade Council was a big event.

The meetings were 'hosted' by a Battalion who would receive often

hundreds of officers as guests. The Battalion would sometimes be celebrating its own anniversary or perhaps there would be a national milestone to celebrate. In 1926, Brighton hosted the '41st' Council and attracted 377 registrations. In 1938, at Dunoon the figure was 588 visiting Officers. Initially, only Company Captains, Executive members and Chaplains were allowed to attend, but, by 1921, long - serving Lieutenants were allowed and all officers from **1952**.[3]

In the first half-century and beyond, officers would wear uniform for all of the official meetings which was liable to cause a few problems with identification given the officers uniform of sober similarity. It was thus the custom to wear identification badges which included the name of the officer along with his or her company or battalion designation.

Special badges produced for Brigade Council tend to vary because they were not all produced with the same purpose in mind. Some, such as those of **1905** and **1909,** were simply 'mufti' badges produced to celebrate the event, no doubt worn unofficially on some uniforms and regarded as souvenirs. In **1933**, the Council badges were produced to fit into the Glasgow Battalion's year - long Jubilee Celebrations with special editions for Glasgow Battalion Officers and Visiting Officers. These badges were just part of a series of badges produced for the Jubilee Celebrations and were worn in uniform by officers for the duration of the main Jubilee weekend. There were badges designed to act both as souvenir mufti badges and conference labels by using cunning little fixing devices to enable a label to dangle below the badge. Printed card badges, tin and plastic, have all been used.

The first metal brooch badge was produced for the **1905** council at Aberdeen. This badge set the standard for the best Council badges which would follow during the next ninety - five years. Enamelled and cut-out in the shape of a thistle it incorporated the BB emblem and the Scottish flag. The name 'Aberdeen' was included, but not the word Council or the date. The next few badges produced followed the same trend, not giving all the details, but cut out to repre-

sent the location. The **1909** badge for the Dublin Council was cut in the shape of a shamrock leaf with the location and date as well as smaller shamrock leaves. It was to be **1925** and the next Dublin Council before a further badge was issued. This too was in the form of a shamrock leaf, but in a politically correct blue rather than green! Not to be outdone the Brighton Battalion for the Council of **1926** produced a fine English Rose, complete with its own fixing for a label. The Jubilee Council of **1933** had two badges in the format of the official Glasgow Battalion Jubilee Badge, described in the Jubilee Section. (See page 174) The visiting officers had a gilt badge with a white enamelled scroll at the top with the Glasgow Battalion officers version having a red scroll. A similar badge, silvered with a blue scroll, was given to boys attending the Dechmont Camp which was also part of the Jubilee celebrations during the same weekend as the Council meeting. The **1938** Council at Dunoon revived the thistle shape complete with BB crest and saltire. Card badges could not, it seems, easily take a form which would be recognisable. They were usually round or rectangular and during the **1930s** developed the idea of incorporating a local crest or coat of arms to signify the area. We can see this pattern clearly on a card badge for the **1929** council. The red hand, BB Crest, name of place and date.

This one belonged to a famous BB personality Mr W. H. Mc Vicker. The card badge for the Oxford Council in **1934** followed an almost

identical pattern. Tin badges imposed similar restrictions to those made of card and the **1948** tin button badge for the Belfast Council took the design straight from the centre of the **1929** badge. The Birmingham tin button badge of **1949** followed similar rules with the emblems of Birmingham and the BB superimposed.

The **1950** badges for the Brighton and Hove Council were a radical departure from all previous designs with a thin metal badge and an etched design which incorporated at the bottom a sea area in which the name of the delegate could be engraved. It seems that originally only the officials for the Council had names engraved such as 'Gilroy O/C Excursions', but many badges with names such as 'Macklin W. Middlesex' and 'Baldwin London' suggest that this was not the case. The Battalion used the badges to identify officers on other Battalion events during the year, since they had '**1950**' but not the word 'Council' engraved on them. For the next Council in St. Andrews, **1951**, the badge took a more traditional form being cut - out and enamelled, but the emblems of St. Andrew and Scotland actually replaced the B's each side of the anchor. Typical of the the period, the badges for **1951** were produced with brooch and stud fittings as would be the Coronation Buttonhole badges of **1953**. In **1954**, Glasgow introduced the first plastic Council badge, an idea it would take up with a vengeance some twenty nine years later. The fourth Council badge of the '50s decade, Aberdeen, **1958**, returned to the tin button style to celebrate the 75th Anniversary of the BB. The only **1960s** badge is a single-colour large tin button from Belfast in **1968**. In the design it almost managed to emulate the 'barrel' shape of the new awards, so perhaps we are lucky not to have any more badges from this decade.

The four badges of the **1970s** reflect the changes and experiments which were taking place in badge making at the time. The Sheffield **1974** badge makes use of a stick - on decal, most famously used for the Queen's Jubilee Badges a few years later. Innovative as usual, the third offering from this Battalion, the Brighton '75 badge is made from aluminium and has crisp, clean colours and splendid detail. Perhaps it was trying to tell the Brigade something? Aberdeen's third Council badge is another trendsetter, departing from any overt BB reference: no emblem, no words 'Boys' Brigade', not even any 'BB' initials. It does make the '76' look like a big letter 'A' in the trendy script popular at the time. [4] Not to be outdone, Manchester produced a decal badge with a '77' forming part of a letter 'M'. If Cardiff had produced a badge in **1978** it would have been difficult to make '78' look like a 'C'!

There was no shortage of badges for the BB Centenary in **1983**, the Brigade Centenary badge, in two sizes, being widely worn. There was even a special women's scarf badge made from pewter, complete with the 'Glasgow 100' logo. The Council Badge, following the precedent of **1954**, was a large moulded plastic name badge with space for paper stick - on labels.

1985 saw another departure from the ordinary with a special 'Brigade Council Choir' badge. Brigade Council was at Birmingham that year.

The nineties was a much better

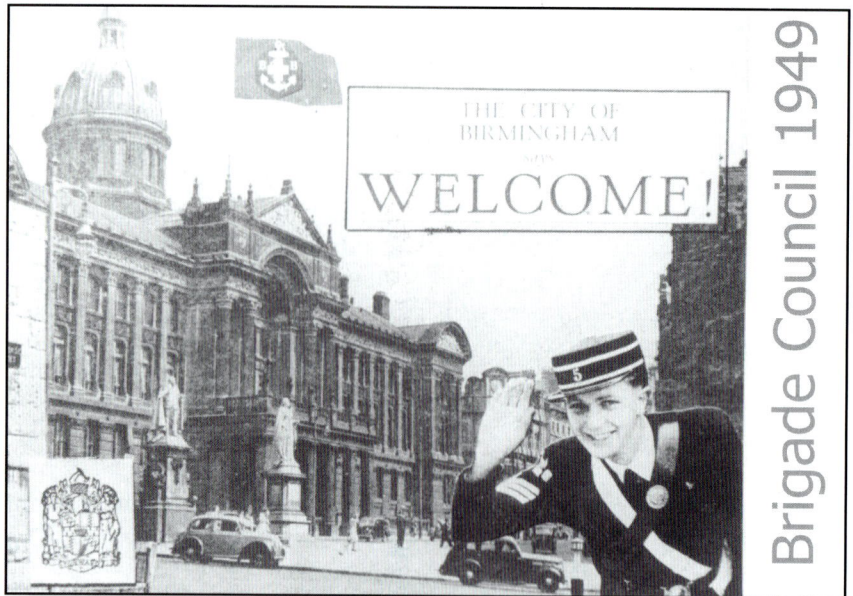

Photo - montage produced by D.Gordon Barnsley MC, Battn. Secy., for the Brigade Council in Birmingham.
Meetings were held at the university. The BB flag is a little larger than the one which actually flew there
Photo: Birmingham Battalion collection

decade for Council badges although it started with a mini- disaster. The Durham Council badges of **1991** were never finished, the centres of the decal badges arrived but no blanks, so no badges were made-up. Unfortunately some seem to have been made up since, appearing in **2000** as 'samples'.[5] In **1993**, the Southampton badge was a landscape ellipse, featuring the early Christian symbol of the fish. For the Inverness Council the badge design reverted to the thistle, but it was less successful, not being cut - out. The **1997** Newcastle badge introduced the colour green for the first time on a Council badge entirely appropriate due to the fact that it was Newcastle, County Down. Originally the **1998** Council badge was to be a pentagon inside a circle, but it was

issued cut - out in pentagonal form. The West Kent Centenary was celebrated by the Council and on the badge. Dundee departed from tradition with its badge in **1999** by including a 'non - BB' anchor in the design.

The first Council badge of the new millennium, Brighton and Hove **2000**, features a BB emblem and the wonderfully exotic skyline of the Royal Pavilion.

REFERENCES

1. Springhall, J, et. al. Sure & Stedfast, A History of The Boys' Brigade 1883 - 1983. p.41
2. ibid
3. ibid. p.43
4. This script is found on a number of badges produced around this period, for instance the GFS [Girls' Friendly Society], junior Members' badge.
5. Appearing in the BB International Auction of Memorabilia 7/10/00, Northampton. Lots 37 & 38.

The boys speak out ... in February 1959:

'Sir - If we adopt Pte. Lewis's suggestion of doing homework on parade, some bright spark will come up with the idea of a "homework" badge.'
Pte. Malcolm J. Clark, 4th Barking Company. (Barking indeed!)

STEDFAST MAG

CLIPS

The Brigade Council Badges

BB 211
1905 Aberdeen

BB 212
1909 Dublin

BB 213
1925 Dublin

BB 214
1926 Brighton

BB 215.1   **BB 215.2**
1933 Glasgow

BB 216
1938 Dunoon

BB 217
1948 Belfast

BB 218
1949 Birmingham

BB 219.02   **BB 219.03**
1950 Brighton & Hove

BB 220
1951 St. Andrews

BB 221
1954 Glasgow

BB 222
1958 Aberdeen

BB 223
1968 Belfast

BB 224

1974 Sheffield

BB 225

1975 Brighton.

BB 226

1976 Aberdeen

BB 227.01

BB 227.02

1977 Manchester

BB 228

1983 Glasgow

BB 229

1985 Birmingham

BB 230

1993 Southampton

BB 231

1995 Inverness

BB 232

1997 Newcastle

BB 233

1998 West Kent

BB 234

1999 Dundee

BB 235

2000 Brighton & Hove

BB National Hike Mufti Badges

BB 241.01

BB 241.02

BB 241.04

Cleveland Hike

BB 242

BB 243

BB 244

West Lowland Hike

BB 245

West Lowland Hike Jubilee

BB Band Mufti Badges

BB 251

BB 252

BB 253

National Band Contest

BB 254

BB 254

Scottish Band Contest

BB 255

Dundee Band Contest
1986

BB 256

Glasgow Central Band

BB 257

Stedfast Silver
Band

BB 258

World's Largest
Band 1983

BB 259

BB 259

BB 259

London Band I.D. 1983

BB 260
Troon 2000

Cross - Country Run Badges

BB 281

Scottish

BB 282

Scottish 1989

BB 283

Scottish 1990

National Centenary Badges

BB 301

Wales

BB 302

Northern Ireland

BB 303

Eire

Junior Section 75th Anniversary Badges

BB 265

BB 266
Clydebank

The Felden 'Brickie' Badge

BB 267

BB 267

They got what they asked for - eventually.

The Boys speak out ... in June 1954

'Sir- ...Why has not the BB a scripture badge ? The object of the BB would be advanced if Boys studied God's Book to obtain this badge. Not only would it be another opportunity for a Boy to win a badge, but it might also be the means of winning Boys to Christ.'
Staff Sgt. David Chivers, 3rd Eastbourne Company.

... in April 1957

'Sir- Why not institute a Sportsman's Badge. Boys who hold the Athlete's Certificate could enter - they should be outstanding in two sports and recommended by the Battalion.'
L/Cpl. K Anspach, 49th Manchester Company

... in June 1954

'Sir - Often Boys miss their one-year service badges through illness of some kind, and thus cannot show the correct number of sessions they have been in the BB. Could not a number, showing the years of service be added to the badges.'
L/Cpl. Ray Faulkner, 30th Brighton Company.

Non-Anniversary Mufti Badges

BB 451

1st Thames Valley

BB 452

16th Nottingham

BB 453

1st Aberdeen

BB 454

BB 454

1st Whitehaven

BB 455

Redbridge

BB 456

85th Birmingham

BB 457

12th Coy

BB 458

16th London
'Billy Bear'

BB 459.01   **BB 459.02**

London I.D.

BB 460

Chelmsford

BB 461

Chester Rd
Brigades

BB 462

Northfield

BB 463

Hartlepool &
W. Hartlepool

BB 464

BB-GB Flags

BB 465

8th Grimsby

BB 466

13th Company

BB 467

12th Glasgow

BB 468

BB 469

Hamilton & Dist.

The Anniversary Mufti Badges

BB 311

Edinburgh Rest Hut. 1919

BB 312

1st St. Andrews 1944

BB 313

Bradford 1954

BB 314

Airdrie, Coatbridge & Dist. 1972

BB 315

1st Cambusnethan 1973

BB 316

1st Bletchley 1976

BB 317

85th Birmingham 1979

BB 318

40th Edinburgh 1980

BB 319

Hartlepool 1980

BB 320

10th Leith 1981

BB 321

1st Fraserburgh 1981

BB 322

1st Newport 1981

BB 323

1st Cupar 1981

BB 324

89th Birmingham 1981

BB 325

89th Birmingham 1981

BB 326

1st Old Kilpatrick 1982

BB 327

8th Airdrie 1983

BB 328

Clydebank 1984

BB 329

5th Wishaw 1984

BB 330   **BB 330**

Glasgow 1985

BB 331

4th Carluke 1985

BB 332   **BB 332**

Edinburgh 1986

BB 333

Ayr 1986

BB 334

49th Glasgow 1986

BB 335

14th West Bromwich
1986

BB 336

Ist Wellingborough
1986/87

BB 337

1st Aberdeen 1987

BB 338

2nd Dumbarton 1987

BB 339

76th Glasgow 1987

BB 340

Sheffield 1988

BB 341

2nd Paisley 1988

BB 342

25th Edinburgh 1988

BB 343
Enfield 1988

BB 344
73rd Birmingham 1989

BB 345
41st Edinburgh 1989

BB 346
1st Alloway 1989

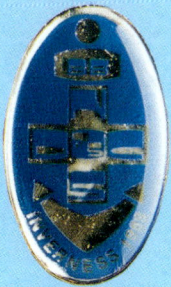

BB 347
N. Scottish 1989

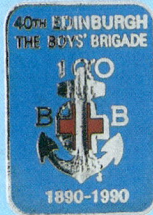

BB 348
40th Edinburgh 1990

BB 349   **BB 349**
Aberdeen 1991

BB 350
Dundee 1991

BB 351

Liverpool 1991

BB 352   **BB 352**

1st Barnet 1991

BB 353

1st Helensburgh 1991

BB 354

1st Auchinleck 1991

BB 355
2nd Cambusnethan
1991

BB 356
2nd Prestwick 1991

BB 357
6th/8th Dundee 1991

BB 358
Nottingham 1992

BB 359.01   **BB 359.02**   **BB 360**   **BB 361**   **BB 362**

5th Aberdeen 1992   1st Harpole 1992   4th Fraserburgh 1992   Glasgow 1993

BB 363   **BB 364**   **BB 365.01**   **BB 366**

Perth & District 1993   Hawick 1993   Somerset 1993   3rd Edinburgh 1993

BB 367   **BB 368**   **BB 369**   **BB 370**

6th Perth 1993   7th Perth 1993   Paisley 1994   1st St.Andrews 1994

BB 371   **BB 372**   **BB 373**

182nd Glasgow 1994   1st Troon 1994   Northampton 1994

BB 374

Cardiff & Vale of
Glamorgan 1995

BB 375

3rd Aberdeen 1995

BB 376

1st Girvan 1995

BB 377

268th Glasgow 1995

BB 378

1st Colne 1995

BB 379

60th Glasgow 1995

BB 380

Oldham 1996

BB 381

3rd Cardiff 1996

BB 382

10th Leith 1996

BB 383

1st Fraserburgh 1996

BB 384

2nd Bearsden 1996

BB 385

1st Morningside 1996

BB 386

3rd Greenock 1997

BB 387

2nd Witham 1997

BB 388

1st Castle Bromwich
1997

BB 389

14th Croydon 1997

BB 390

7th Coatbridge 1997

BB 391

Greenock 1998

BB 392

2nd Sutton Coldfield 1998

BB 393

1st Annaghmore 1998

BB 394

Edinburgh, Leith & Dist. 1998-1999

BB 395

1st Loughborough 1998

BB 396

1st Ellon 1998

BB 397

2nd Gourock 1998

BB 398

25th Glasgow 1998

BB 399

10th Brighton 1999

BB 400

85th Birmingham 1999

BB 401

85th Birmingham 1999

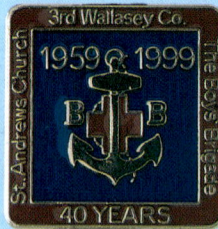

BB 402

3rd Wallasey 1999

BB 403

1st Southend-on-Sea 1999

BB 404

1st Troon 1999

BB 405

1st Margate 1999

BB 406.02

BB 406.01

BB 406.03

6th Mansfield 2000

BB 407

18th West Kent 2000

BB 408

4th Kirkaldy 1993

The AD2000 Badge

As a Christian organisation the BB has been keen to recognise the significance of the Year 2000. The prefix 'AD' Anno Domini, means in The Year of Our Lord. The year **2000** provided an opportunity to celebrate the coming of Jesus to the world, 'the word made flesh', God in human form.

The BB Gazette of May **1998** carried the first details of the new logos for the BB Millennium. One was the rectangular version, as at the top of this page, to go with the BBs square logo. The other, was an heraldic emblem to be used in place of, alongside and to 'complement' the familiar BB Anchor. Both emblems carried the 'AD2000' symbol and would be used from January **1999** until December **2000**.

As part of the Millennium Celebrations the BB worked with the Royal National Lifeboat Institution to raise cash to buy new Atlantic Class Lifeboats to be stationed around the UK.

Special buttonhole badges, as well as other memorabilia, were produced, all based on the heraldic AD2000 emblem. Like other special buttonhole badges this one was sanctioned for wear in uniform during the two years **1999 and 2000**.

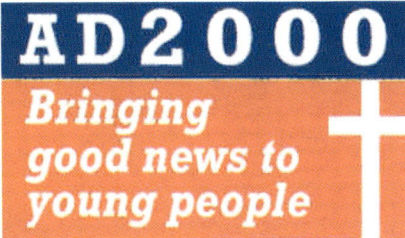

The special buttonhole badges, for the first time, could be ordered as national or 'localised' to give details of a particular company, battalion, district or group. The extra local information could be added on a wider ribbon at the base of the badge as per the Collectors' Club pictured below. Sometimes the top ribbon is also changed as per the 32nd Dublin also illustrated.

Many different 'limited edition' badges have been produced including; Headquarters, London Stedfast Association, companies, battalions and districts. As we go to press the full list has just been finalised and is included on the next page .

Some of the design sketches for the badge are shown below. Naturally the starting point was the normal 'standard' buttonhole.

Designs for the AD2000 Badge

Some companies and groups have produced their own millennium badges. One Company, 101st Glasgow, produced a badge celebrating the fact that the Company, formed in **1912**, was still going 88 years later!

The AD2000 Millennium Badges

BB 500.01
BB Millennium Buttonhole

BB 501
BB Limited Edition Millennium Buttonhole

BB 502.01
101st Glasgow

BB 504.01 see page 247

BB 503.01   1st St. Combs

BB 505.01
Bath 2000

BB 506.01
1st Campsie

The AD2000 Millennium 'Limited Edition' Badges

NORTHERN IRELAND

1st Bangor	1st Glendermott
4th Bangor	1st Lisburn
5th Bangor	Londonderry Batt.
13th Bangor	L'derry B.B.O.B.
1st Ballyclare	4th Londonderry
1st Ballymena	6th LondonderryCo
1st Ballywatt	7th Londonderry
25th Belfast	1st Magheragall
33rd Belfast	1st Muckamore
34th Belfast	4th Newtownards
63rd Belfast	3rd Portadown
93rd Belfast Co	1st Portrush
2nd Benburb	1st Richhill
8th Carrickfergus Co	1st Stewartstown
2nd Coleraine	

SCOTLAND

1st Burghead	11th Hamilton Co
1st Dalry	2nd Inverness
53rd Dyce	6th/7th Inverness
3rd Elgin	1st Mauchline
4th Elgin Co	1st Milngavie
1st Falkirk	13th Motherwell
2nd Fort William Co	7th Perth
25th Glasgow	Scone Coy
45th Glasgow	11th Stirling
94 GLW (1S) Coy	1st View Park
14th Greenock	1st West Kilbride

IRELAND

1st Cork Co.
4th Dublin
32nd Dublin
Ireland

WALES

22nd Cardiff
1st Newport
8th Newport
1st Penarth
20th Cardiff Ex-Membs
25th Cardiff Ex-Membs

OTHERS

BB Badge Club
Collectors' Club
George Orr Assn.
Headquarters
Stedfast Assn
St. Neots

ENGLAND

1st Alford Company	10th Enfield	1st London Co	7th Plymouth	1st Water Orton
2nd Alton	10th Exeter	5th London Co	1st Ponteland	3rd West Bromwich
2nd Altrincham Co	1st Felixstowe	16th London	1st Port Sunlight	1st Westgate on Sea
4th Barking Co	Gateshead Batt	70th London	1st Preston Co	6th West Kent
52nd Birmingham	3rd Grays	1st Loughborough	2nd Scarborough	14th West Kent
73rd Birmingham	4th Halifax	1st Malvern	1st Sittingbourne Co	2nd Widnes Co
83rd Birmingham	Halton Battalion	1st Moreton	4th Southampton	5th Wigan
1st Bp's Stortford	1st Harpole Co	1st Morpeth Co	8th South Shields	20th WiganCo
1st Bournemouth	7th Hemel Hempstead	1st Newport (IOW)	18th South Shields	Wilts Battalion
Burntwood	4th Hillingdon	6th Northampton	1st St.Albans	10th Wolverhampton
1st Burton	1st Kempston	11th Northampton	5th St.Helens	1st Worcester
1st Cannock	1st Kidderminster	16th Northampton	1st St.Neots	
1st Colchester	1st Kings Sutton	North Staffs	1st Stonehouse	
1st Congleton	29th Leeds	8th North Staffs	2nd Sutton Coldfield	
2nd Croxley Green	5th Leicester	20th North Staffs	1st Tewkesbury	
5th Croydon	14th Leicester	27th North Staffs Co	6th Trafford	
1st Downham Market	1st Lichfield	30th Nottingham	3rd Wallasey	
1st Ealing	10th Liverpool Co	1st Oadby	1st Walsall Wood	
10th East Durham	35th Liverpool	Oldham & Dist Batt.	1st Waterlooville	

Scarf-Pins & Tie-Pins

The picture reproduced on page one showing Sgt. Jones depicts the typical dress of the smart BB boy in the 1890s. He wears around his neck a wide tie, cravat or scarf. Not considering himself fully dressed without one, he has adorned his scarf with a neat silver pin bearing the BB crest, no doubt the result of some competition won, in drill, efficiency or perhaps a tent competition from camp such as described here:

'The tents were critically examined every day; the lynx-eyed officers made a thorough search inside and around each tent for bits of straw, minute scraps of paper, and similar insignificant litter, the folding of blankets and the state of accoutrements were examined and marks were awarded accordingly. At the end of the week the two tents with the highest aggregate marks would be declared the winners, and the occupants of these tents would each receive a silver scarfpin bearing the design of the brigade anchor.' [1]

The Scarf-Pin is perhaps the oldest of the mufti badges of the BB and also one of the first to adorn uniform without creating problems with regulations. The earliest advertisement appears in the BB Manual of **1888** when Messrs. John Storer advertised: *'Scarf Pins 1/3'* [2] By **1891**, they are advertised as *'Silver Scarf Pins 1/3'* and as this section of the advert is in capitals, it idicates the pins were in demand.

In **1893**, there was more:

'Scarf Pins Representing Crest of the Boys' Brigade, (Suitable for Company Prizes) 1/3 & Satin - lined case 9d.'

Both pins and cases were obtainable from Messrs. Garlick of Bristol by **1893/4**. When, in **1895**, Messrs Farquharson of Houndsditch London started to stock the silver pins it also had another:

'White metal with enamelled BB Crest 8d.'

It was probably this kind of salesmanship, seeing a need for a cheaper pin, and meeting it, which made Farquharson a veritable giant amongst suppliers to all the brigades for many years. This enamelled pin is the one with a light blue shield and white metal silvered anchor crest, a small pin which could be worn on a scarf or coat, fully two years before the introduction of the Officers' Buttonhole Badge. A brooch version exists, with a squeeze joint, which may date from sometime post-**1900**. The scarf-pin type was still being marketed in the **1920s** [3] In **1904**, the blue enamelled anchor shield featured on a special key used to open the Headquarters of the 1st Warley (Essex) Coy. [4]

In **1902**, Farquharson again stole the lead by introducing enamelled Silver Scarf Pins for 1/3, as well as the cheaper white metal, and two sizes of non-enamelled anchor, 1/- and 1/3. [5]

As was the case on the various pendants, etc., small silver BB crests when made by a large jeweller could be fixed to a single stick-pin as easily as to a medal. It is not surprising, therefore, that at least one

of the pre-**1927** silver crests found on scarf-pins is indentical to those commonly found on small medals. The same applies to post-**1926** crests where one maker seems to have produced silver and sometimes bronze emblems for general use. These individual unmounted anchors can still sometimes be found. [6]

By **1914**, James A Ferrier [7] had taken over from John Storer in producing the Silver Scarf Pins and included 9ct Gold Pins for 7/6 and 5/-. Farquharson advertised large anchor pins of silver, 9ct, 15ct and even 18ct gold, in the mid **1920s**. In **1928**, Ferrier still advertised directly in the BB Manual. From **1927**, the new system of BB HQ looking after supplies meant that firms such as Ferrier could now service BB Supplies rather than sell direct. In the **1928**, BB Supplies Catalogue the Scarf Pins are detailed as 'tie-pins', but come in the same types and finishes as supplied by Ferrier. However, Ferrier continued to advertise in the BB Gazette. [8]

By **1931**, a new small post - union BB emblem was being used for tie pins in silver and gilt. In bronze form the same anchor appeared on the Old Boys' Union Badge of **1932** and gilt on the Jubilee Buttonhole Badge of the same year. Gilt and bronze anchors contined for many years. Originally the Old Boys' Badge was produced with a stud fastening for use with buttonholes, but in the late **1950s** and **1960s,** when fashions changed and buttonholes vanished from jackets, the badge became stickpin type.

In **1975,** there were three 'Stick-Pins' advertised in the BB Supplies Catalogue. Two of them were produced with different finishes; gold and 'silvery' and had a short explanatory description:

'A small BB Anchor on a long stickpin. Sometimes used as a brooch badge or lapel badge.'

Also in the same Catalogue there was advertised an Old Boys' stickpin Badge. It is not certain when the stickpin disappeared from the Old Boys' Badge to be replaced with a clutch-pin. Clutch-pin Buttonhole Badges came in during **1976.** By **1978,** the price of the Old Boys' Badge had increased from 10p to 26p, greater than inflation, suggesting a new consignment. In **1979** the Old Boys' Badge was advertised as 'Old Boys Badge Bronzed', no mention being made of stickpin or clutchpin. The cost of the badge by **1983** was 65p, more than the members Buttonhole Badge. By this time it was certainly a clutch-pin fastening.

The 'Tie Pins', which were stickpins in **1975,** were still available in **1979,** or at least one of them was:

'Tie Pin, Stickpin.... Silver finish with red cross...'

Presumably the gold option had gone. The supplies code for the silver finish was the same as the previous gold-finished item.[9] Also, in the **1979** Catalogue, options were available for fastening ties, as well as stickpins; namely 'tacks' and 'retainers'. The small anchors are, however, again being used for 'Scarfs' this time fastened to 'scarf rings' for fastening ladies scarves.

Some experimental tie pins of the stickpin type were produced in the **1970s,** the anchor emblem being replaced by the letters *'BB'* in a sloping style similar to the Automobile Association's *'AA'* logo. Some pins in this new style were produced for sale but were not popular.

The **1985/86** Catalogue gives no details of stickpin badges for ties or

'Old Boys'. All the tie products are called 'tacks' or 'clips'. No doubt obvious safety considerations were paramount here.

A Life Boy tie pin was produced (see photo. page 233), but unfortunately it can't be dated. The idea of using stickpin badges was common in the **1970s:** Warrant Officer Badges, Officers Collar Badges, and even one format of the **1976** Brigade Council Badge. By the **1980s** and **1990s** most badges were no longer being produced with stickpins.

REFERENCES

1. Gibbon, F.P, Comrades Under Canvas, A Story of Boys' Brigade Life, p 207. c.1908. RTS. R. Bolton Collection.
2. BB Manual 1888, advert John Storer & Son, 64, Buchanan St., Glasgow. BB Archive, BB HQ, Felden, Herts.
3. Farquharson catalogue, c.1920s pictured page   . No. 16.
4. T. Jon Ellis. 'An Extraordinary Gentleman'- F.C. Carey Longmore. Homeleigh Books,2000. p 25.
5. op.cit. BB Manual 1902. J.Farquharson Advert.
6. Unmounted silver anchor in R. Bolton collection, hallmarked 1919, Birmingham.
7. James A Ferrier, Manufacturing Jewellers and Silversmiths, 13, South Exchange Place Glasgow, later 62, Buchanan St., Glasgow.
8. BB Gazette, Oct. 1933, May 1935. etc.
9. Supplies Catalogue Code: 1975. 116811 [Gold], 116821 [Silvery]. 1979. 116811 Tie Pin, Silver finish.

Scarf Pins and Tie Pins 1886 -

BB 470

BADGES of the BRIGADE

VOLUME ONE
THE BOYS' BRIGADE

5. Medals

The Cross For Heroism The BB 'VC'

The BB Gazette of September 1902 had the first intimation of a Cross For Heroism:

'It is made of bronze, so it is not for its intrinsic value that it will be appreciated, but because it is to be awarded only to a Boy who has performed a really brave act, or a signal act of self-sacrifice.' [1]

The medal was designed by Mr G.G. Urquhart, Lieutenant, 115th Glasgow Company [2] The design of the medal has changed only once, in **1926,** when the cross was added behind the anchor upon union with the Boys' Life Brigade. The BLB had its own Bravery Award instituted in **1922** and discontinued after union with the BB. Some published 'Cross for Heroism' lists included the nine BLB Boys who held that BLB award.[3] (Details in Volume 2)

The ribbon was originally royal blue with white vertical stripes, but was changed to plain royal blue in **1941**, thus three different variations of the cross are possible, permutating medal design and ribbon colour.

In **1915**, the 'Diploma for Gallant Conduct' was instituted and there-

Photo: F & J Hare. Pinner.   BB Archive collection

Simon Herriott, aged 8, 2nd Ruislip Junior Section. The youngest winner of the BB Cross for Heroism, 1980.

This was awarded for his courage in saving the life of his young brother. Simon was attacked and stabbed by a mentally deranged man but had sufficient strength to rescue his little brother. Simon was in hospital under intensive care before recovering.

fore, two levels of award were possible from that date.

One hundred and ninety-seven Cross for Heroism awards have been gained to date of which six were awarded posthumously. Not for nothing has the award been dubbed 'The BB VC'.

It was **1904** before the first three medals were reported in the BB Gazette. The first recipient being Corporal James Morris of the 14th Capetown SA Company. He was 16 and saved the life of a woman at a railway level crossing. James died in August **1964**.

One of the first three awards was also the first posthumous award. Pte. James Conway of 1st Enfield Coy. was swimming with his younger brother in the River Lee when he noticed his brother was in difficulty. James swam to his rescue managed to get hold of his brother and get him near enough to the

edge for his father to sieze hold of the younger boy's hand and pull him to safety. James, however, was now exhausted and fell back into deep water and was drowned. When the Cross was received by James' parents, because of the boy's keenness and loyalty to the BB, they requested that the Company should keep the medal as a memorial to their son's bravery. The medal is still on display at Company HQ.[4]

Other boys who have gained the cross posthumously are ...

Pte Samuel Smart, May 1912
Sgt Ian Menzies, Jan. 1914
L/Cpl Cyril Chamberlain, 1921
Pte John Loan, 1953
Pte Glenroy Esmie, March 1974

In **1909,** L/Cpl Edmund Semper showed great courage in stopping a runaway horse, and Sgt Archibald Roberts from Cornwall saved a woman from being run down by a train.

In **1910,** Sgt. Walter Edwards of 11th Manchester attempted to rescue a man who had fallen down a mine shaft. In **1927,** Pte Patrick Kernan of 8th Dublin initiated a rescue from an attempted robbery.

During the Second World War many boys showed outstanding courage and performed deeds well beyond the limits of their own personal safety. In **1940,** Cpl Kenneth Clements of 76th London attempted to rescue his grandmother from her burning home, set alight by bombs during an air raid. Two months later L/Cpl George Hammond of 82nd London res-

Bournemouth BB, Auxiliary Fire Service Messengers 1940
Photo: The Boys' Brigade

cued two little children from the debris of a bombed building during a heavy air raid.

Again in **1940,** a local newspaper carried news of 16-year-old Pte Ronald Orme of the 9th Manchester Coy. The headline read:

'100 neighbours signed epic of 16-year old bugler He was a Hero 4 times over'.

Ronald was an ARP messenger on duty at the door of an underground shelter when ten incendiary bombs fell nearby. Ronald was putting the incediaries out when a bomb hit the shelter. He crawled under the debris, found two babies, brought them out one by one, shielding them from shell splinters with his tin helmet. Ronald helped to carry out six adults when help arrived. He then climbed a 45 ft. drain pipe to hold a hose. When the fire was under control he helped to rescue people from another house across the road. The Air-raid warden, Mr Thomas Heys, headed a list of 100 neighbours who signed an account of Ronald's gallantry and forwarded it to Boys' Brigade Headquarters. Small, black-haired, pale-faced Ronald, "Nobbie" to his friends, told the reporter:

'Its a lot of rot really. Least I can do

now, I suppose, is to try for my fireman's badge with the BB. I'm not even a squad leader.'

Two boys stand out with distinction in having gained both the Cross for Heroism and the Diploma for Gallant Conduct. Andrew Bruce of 1st Falkirk won the Cross in **1926** when he was 13 by saving someone from drowning. Then, in **1928,** he saved another, from drowning, being awarded the Diploma. Charles Barff, 14, of 4th Leeds achieved the distinction in reverse order but in the same year, **1931.** [5]

The Cross for Heroism is today the only BB award which is recognised on a worldwide basis. Its young recipients represent the epitome of true 'Christian Manliness' as laid down by William Smith in the object of the Brigade.

REFERENCES

1. BB Gazette, Vol X1 Sept. 1902, p13. BB Scottish Archive, Carronvale.
2. ibid.
3. Lists produced in BB Diaries, 1932, 1933 etc.
4. BB Gazette, Vol XIII Oct. 1904, p18.
5. Adapted from an article in Jan 1995 Gazette, p 37. R. Mandry.
6. Lowestoft Journal 31/8/1909
7. Cross & Rechabite Medal in the R. Bolton collection.
8. Records of the Commonwealth War Graves Commission. G.W. Mantripp L/Cpl 5376.
9. The Cross awarded to Leslie Thorn in 1928, the 100th issued, was a pre-union pattern. Cross and certificate held by BB Archive, BB HQ, Felden

BB HEROES

Date	Rank	Name	Age	Company
1904	Cpl	James Morris	16	14th Capetown
	Sgt	Charles Hayes	16	27th Liverpool
	Pte	James Comway	15	1st Enfield [P]
1905	Pte	James Hocking	15	2nd Plymouth
	Pte	Percival Hocking	13	2nd Plymouth
	Pte	James Bew	14	1st Middlesbrough
	Pte	Robert Donaldson	13	2nd Perth
	Cpl	William Baillie	16	4th Sunderland
	Cpl	Peter Jefferies	15	4th Leith
1906	Pte	Alexander McVicar	12	1st Jamestown [Aust]
	Pte	James Fisher	15	18th Bristol
	Cpl	Albert Kerr	16	1st Irvinestown
	Pte	James Rogers	13	13th Nottingham
	Pte	George Clarke	13	1st Portsmouth
	L/Cpl	Edward Cox	17	1st Worcester
	Pte	John Minhinett	14	2nd Plymouth
	Pte	Harry Washington	16	3rd Halifax
	Pte	George Hebenton	15	9th Dundee
1907	Sgt	William Haston	16	4th Leith
	Cadet	A. Stafford [Boys' Naval Brig.]		7th S. Melbourne [Aust]
	L/Cpl	G. Williams	--	2nd Derby
	Sgt	William Burgess	17	5th Birmingham
1908	Pte	Archibald Anderson	13	1st Bridge of Allen
	Cpl	John McIntyre	15	7th Perth
	Cpl	Harry Walker	15	8th Sheffield
	Cpl	Herbert Gardner	15	1st Kilkenny
	Pte	Moody Spratt	15	37th Belfast
	Sgt	William Cheshire	17	1st Hastings
1909	Sgt	John Peterson	14	1st Lerwick
	L/Cpl	Edmund Semper	14	6th Sheffield
	L/Cpl	Eugene McCormack	14	1st South Shields
	Sgt	Robert Butchard	17	49th Edinburgh
	Sgt	Archibald Roberts	17	1st Pool [Cornwall]
	Pte	Robert Dalrymple	14	47th Glasgow
1910	Pte	Campbell Clifford	14	9th Cardiff
	Pte	Harry Bosworth	13	14th Birmingham
	Pte	James Bishop	14	1st Cromer
	Pte	George Mantripp	14	2nd Lowestoft
	Sgt	Walter Edwards	17	11th Manchester
	Pte	George Danton	13	73rd London
	L/Cpl	Edward Howard	13	2nd Falmouth
	Sgt	William Hathaway	17	5th Cheltenham
	Pte	Albert Marrs	17	20th Belfast
1911	L/Cpl	John May	17	1st Southwold
	Pte	William Clarke	15	94th London
	Sgt	John Young	17	86th Glasgow
	L/Cpl	Arthur Harris	15	1st Newport
	Pte	George Tilke	13	9th Cardiff
	Pte	Samuel McGowan	15	1st Newton Stuart
	Pte	George White	14	5th Sheffield
	Cpl	Walter Bower	14	8th Nottingham
	Pte	A.F. Jones	14	17th Nottingham
	Cpl	Thomas Fraser	17	2nd West Kent
	Cpl	Illtyd Davies	13	13th Cardiff
1912	L/Cpl	John Inston	14	1st Hoddesdon
	L/Cpl	James Burrell	16	1st Burnley
	Pte	William Bednall	16	5th Birmingham
	Pte	Samuel Smart	15	5th Nottingham [P]
	Pte	Hubert Rankine	12	1st Calderbank
	Sgt	Gerald Haslam	17	25th Sheffield
	L/Cpl	Christopher Bailey	16	41st Manchester
	Pte	Arthur Jones	12	10th Birmingham
1913	Sgt	Marshall Cooper	16	47th Aberdeen
1914	Cpl	Archibald Lapin	16	39th Belfast
	Pte	William Winton	13	106th Glasgow
	Sgt	Ian Menzies	15	1st Oban [P]
	Sgt	James Massie	16	12th Aberdeen
	Pte	Arthur Langley	13	4th Cambridge
1915	Pte	Sidney Henshall	--	8th Nottingham
	Cpl	Thomas Ellison	14	1st Morpeth
	Pte	Frederick Tuck	14	1st Morpeth
	Pte	Charles Davenport	16	10th Oldham
1916	Cpl	Stanley Smith	16	5th Bristol
	Pte	John Mayoram	13	3rd Ipswich
	Pte	Richard Beney	12	1st Brighton
1917	Cpl	Alexander MacDonald		35th Aberdeen
1918	Pte	Fred Pettifer	14	1st Bournemouth
	Cpl	Arthur Cousins	15	8th Nottingham
1920	Pte	James Price	16	3rd Halifax
1921	Pte	Harry Case	--	8th Dublin
	Pte	Norman Coates	--	8th Dublin
	L/Cpl	Edward Gow	--	76th Glasgow
	Pte	Percy Warnes	15	3rd Northampton
	L/Cpl	Cyril Chamberlain	12	1st Exeter [P]
	Pte	Frank King	13	1st Exeter

George William Mantripp

In **1909**, 14-yr-old George, the only son of George and Anna Mantripp of 458 London Rd., South Lowestoft was a member of the 2nd Lowestoft Coy part of St. John's Church. Unusually, for the time, George had learnt to swim and save life at the Morton Rd Council School. On the morning of Monday 26th July he was walking just south of the Groyne between Lowestoft and Pakefield when he heard cries for help from one of the boys who was bathing there having suffered an attack of cramp and being thrown on to one of the pieces of submerged concrete. Quickly taking off the most cumbersome of his clothing he plunged into the sea. The boy, Alfred Reynolds, after much difficulty was finally saved by George at considerable cost to himself. George's body and legs had been severely lacerated by the hidden underwater concrete.[6] Pte. Mantripp was awarded a special certificate of The Royal Humane Society and the Silver Medal of the Independent Order of Rechabites for this act of bravery.[7]

Sadly, almost exactly seven years later, on 9th July **1916,** George, now L/Cpl Mantripp of the Oxford & Bucks Light Infantry was killed in action near Loos, France. He has no grave but is recorded on the Loos Memorial, panels 83 - 85.[8]

Private Terence Baker, aged 14, of the 1st Rayleigh Company, for saving the life of a boy from drowning in the Chelmer-Blackwater Canal, on the 8th of August **1934.**

'A party of Boys had been fishing from a barge when one of them, attempting to cross from one barge to another by a plank, fell into the water. The adjacent lock gates were partially open, and there was consequently a strong current which swept the Boy into deep water, where he quickly sank. Baker, although small for his age, dived in fully dressed and, swimming out to the drowning Boy who was much bigger than himself, succeeded in reaching him. He was in great danger of being swept under one of the barges or dashed against the lock gates, but after a struggle he reached safety and saved the Boy's life.'   Official citation, BB Gazette.

Year	Rank	Name	Age	Company
	Pte	Robert Hilliard	13	17th Nottingham
	Pte	Robert Addison	15	1st Middlesbrough
1922	Pte	Percy Love	16	14th Northampton
	Cpl	Robert McGeoch	16	164th Glasgow
	L/Cpl	John Bishop	16	164th Glasgow
1923	Pte	John Buyers	13	50th Aberdeen
1924	L/Cpl	Charles Randle	17	16th Nottingham
1925	Cpl	Frank Harwood	14	1st Walton-on-the-Naze
1926	Pte	Sinclair Henderson	16	44th Edinburgh
	Pte	Andrew Bruce	13	1st Falkirk
1927	Pte	Patrick Kernan	16	8th Dublin
	Pte	William Jones	13	23rd Liverpool
	Pte	Arthur Mallory	14	14th Leeds
1928	L/Cpl	David Wren	16	1st High Bonnybridge
	Pte	Leslie Thorn	12	9th Thames Valley
	L/Cpl	James Elrick	14	1st Fraserborough
	Pte	David Miller	14	38th Belfast
1930	Sgt	John Frew	17	1st Cowdenbeath
	Pte	George Bradshaw	15	2nd Nottingham
	Pte	William Cunningham	13	1st Kirkcaldy
1931	Pte	Charles Clark	15	7th London
	Pte	Charles Barff	14	4th Leeds
	Pte	Frederick Priest	15	2nd Cleethorpes
1932	Pte	Henry Whitby	15	88th Manchester
1933	Pte	Alec Hurley	15	62nd London
	Pte	Vincent Shelley	12	1st Cannock
	Pte	Samuel McCracken	15	3rd Portadown
	Pte	Raymond Goss	13	5th Wellingborough
	Pte	William Pearce	12	9th Nottingham
	C/Sgt	Thomas Hughes	17	17th Liverpool
	Pte	Maurice Mallard	17	17th Northampton
	Cpl	Walter Jones	17	1st Turk's Island
1934	Pte	Neil Dougall	15	1st Oban
	Pte	John Kursa	13	133rd London
	Pte	Leonard Holyoak	15	11th West Kent
	Pte	Albert Goode	15	1st Nottingham
	Pte	Terence Baker	14	1st Rayleigh
	Pte	Frederick Hicks	13	18th Bristol
	Pte	George Boyter	13	2nd Gourock
1935	L/Cpl	James Collins	14	41st Dundee
	Cpl	James Greig	14	21st Aberdeen
	Pte	Robert Rudge	12	3rd Wigan
	Pte	Edward Burford	13	1st Taunton
	L/Cpl	Harry Gornall	14	4th Windsor [Ontario]
	Pte	Thomas Fleming	15	1st Falkirk
1936	Cpl	P. Kneebone	16	4th Plymouth
	Pte	Roland George	12	1st Gorleston
1937	Pte	Gerald Wickett	13	2nd Plymouth
	Pte	William Riddoch	13	4th Inverness
	Pte	Frank Riley	13	1st Whitle-le-Woods
1938	L/Cpl	William Garnham	14	2nd Gorleston
1939	Cpl	James Alexander	15	1st Collace
	Pte	Harry Faulkner	13	13th Leeds
	Pte	Ewen Cameron	13	282nd Glasgow
1940	Pte	Thomas Gosling	13	1st New Lanark
	Pte	Donald Evans	12	5th London [Ontario]
	Pte	Donald Blaney	12	5th London [Ontario]
	Cpl	Kenneth Clements	18	76th London
	Pte	Ronald Orme	16	9th Manchester
1941	Pte	Henry Huggon	13	3rd Carlisle
1942	Pte	Thomas Bailey	13	1st Herne Bay
	Pte	Frederick Waters	13	1st Herne Bay
1943	Sgt	Daniel Berry	17	59th Edinburgh
	Pte	Alfred Shaw	14	3rd Grimsby
	Pte	John Hudson	13	1st North Seaton
1944	Cpl	Ronald Edwards	15	6th Romford
1945	Cpl	Norman Stevens	16	57th London
	Pte	Wilfred Ellis	14	2nd Bournemouth
	Cpl	Thomas Stevens	17	2nd Hastings & St Leo'ds
1946	Pte	Leonard Bradshaw	14	7th Johannesburg
	Sgt	Stanley Radeby	18	11th Ebenezer
	Cpl	Wilfred Fritz	17	11th Ebenezer
1947	Pte	James Lucock	15	11th Liverpool
	Pte	Johnston Sandlan	13	1st Clydebank
	Pte	Norman Trim	12	2nd Plymouth
	L/Cpl	Alexander Hogarth	16	243rd Glasgow
1949	Sgt	Robert Mitchell	18	3rd Lurgan
1951	Cpl	M. Jennings	17	11th Johannesburg
	Pte	C. Dennis	13	16th Birmingham
1953	Pte	Glen Lawson	14	1st Springs [S.Africa]
	Pte	Harvey McCreadle	12	1st Glenluce
	Pte	John Loan	12	1st Glenluce [P]
1955	Pte	Robert Maxwell	14	191st Glasgow
1957	Pte	Michael Peart	15	1st Oxford
	Pte	James Oliver	13	1st Morpeth
	Cpl	Thomas Campbell	17	173rd Glasgow
	Pte	Ian Halliday	16	127th Glasgow
1958	Pte	George Harris	15	1st Cookstown
	Sgt	Kenneth Mitchell	17	33rd Sydney [N.S.W.]
1959	L/Cpl	Lindsay Casey	15	4th Parramatta[N.S.W.]
1960	Pte	Roy Penn	14	1st British Virgin Is.
	Pte	Michael Marshall	13	32nd Edinburgh
1961	Pte	Gerald Lopes	14	1st St. Eustatius
	-	Thomas Connell	14	1st Bermuda
	-	Ian MacDonald	15	1st Bermuda

Year	Rank	Name	Age	Company
	L/Cpl	J. Barry Shannon	15	1st Portstewart
1963	Sgt	Alan Dore	17	5th Plymouth
1965	Pte	James Patrick	11	208th Glasgow
1966	Pte	John Hawley	15	118th New South Wales
1969	Pte	Derek Triplett	11	64th Edinburgh
	Pte	William Moore	15	1st Donaghadee
1973	J.S.	Richard Simpson	11	1st Shepshed J.S.
1974	Pte	Glenroy Esmie	12	32nd Jamaica [P]
1978	-	Leslie Vanderbeck	-	2nd N.Brunswick [Can.]
	L/Cpl	Alan Budd	16	18th Kingston & Merton
1979	J.S.	Lawrence Buckley	11	12th Wigan J.S.
1980	J.S.	Simon Herriott	8	2nd Ruislip J.S.
1983	L/Cpl	Christopher Clifton	15	2nd Sheffield
1984	Pte	David Thompson	13	1st Donaghadee
1987		John Bayliss		1st Aberbargoed
1996	Cpl	Alexander Sutherland	18	12th Dundee
1997	L/Cpl	Ben Wilson	16	73rd Birmingham

198 [Excluding BLB Awards]

List correct @ October 2000

1969

1995

Derek Triplett

Derek was only 11 years old and still at Royston Primary School, Edinburgh when the incident which was to win him the Cross for Heroism occurred. In 1968, he went fishing in Granton Harbour with his pal who took along his little brother. They climbed underneath the wooden beams of the pier until a rocky ledge was reached. The youngest boy, Ian Black, who was then aged nine, slipped and fell into the sea. Ian couldn't swim, obviously panicked and started to go under. Derek dived in, but had severe difficulty keeping the youngster afloat as Ian kept trying to drag him beneath the water. Eventually both reached the ledge and Ian's elder brother hoisted the youngster out. Derek, however, was too small to reach the ledge unaided, but too heavy to be hauled out, so he was obliged to swim a long distance to reach a suitable low wooden beam. The boys then just walked home.

Derek (above) is now married with two daughters and is employed as a forester with Lothian Region.

The Cross for Heroism

1902 - c.1928	c.1928 - 1941	1941 -

Ribbon as
per c.1928-1941

BB 511   **BB 512**   **BB 512**

BB 494 & BB 495 BACKGROUND NOTES

The medals are bronze with some colour variation. The ribbons are 1⅓" wide, either royal blue and white striped or plain royal blue, dependent upon the date of issue. (see above) There is a ring suspension and a bronze 'fold-over' brooch suspension bar on the pre-union medal and a plain bronze brooch suspension bar on the post-union. (see above) The shape is an ornamental, square-limbed Maltese Cross. The obverse has the BB anchor in the centre. After c.1928 (9) the anchor is backed by the Geneva Cross. The lettering is 'The Boys Brigade Cross For Heroism'. The reverse of the Cross is plain with details as laid down in Regulation Two. The medal is worn in uniform on the left breast. The medals were made by H.W. Miller, Ltd., of Branston St., Birmingham 18 and supplied in a presentation box. Medals are known in boxes inscribed D. Cunninghame, Medallists of Glasgow. The medals have no makers details on them.

Cross For Heroism - Detail

The Regulations for the Cross for Heroism, published in 1902:

1. The Cross may be awarded to any boy who, being a member of The Boys' Brigade, has performed a signal act of self-sacrifice for others, shown heroism in saving life or attempting to save life, or displayed marked courage in the face of danger.

2. The Cross shall be of bronze, and the ribbon of the clasp shall be royal blue and white. The name of the holder, together with the date of the act of heroism, shall be engraved on the Cross.

3. A duly attested narrative of the act of heroism which is deemed worthy of the award shall be lodged with the Brigade Secretary by the officer commanding the company to which the boy belongs.

4. The Brigade Executive shall be the sole judges as to the awarding of the Cross, and their decision shall be final.

The Squad Medal

From the oldest Company Medal

The oldest medal in the Boys' Brigade is a squad medal. To be precise, the Squad Medal of the 1st Glasgow Company. The 1st Glasgow 'Challenge Medal' was first awarded for the session **1885-1886** to Lance Corporal William Smith (no relation to the founder.)[1] Unfortunately, the original medal (See photo. page 215) was stolen during re-decoration of the Company premises and a replica has since been made. Like the original it bears the names of all recipients engraved on a special 'book' clasp.

The Company Prize

The awarding of medals was the cause of much soul-searching within the Brigade in the late 19th Century. Many companies awarded attendance squad medals, as one of the 'Company Prizes'. Details of a scheme appeared in the BB Gazette in October **1896** with suggestions as to the use of the 'Squad Medal':

'A Squad Challenge Medal, to be held for one year by the NCO whose squad

has the highest average attendance during the session, might come next on the list (after an attendance prize such as a Bible, Prayer Book etc.) The object of such an award is to encourage the Non-Commissioned Officer to exercise a supervision and control over the members of his squad, and at once to visit them when absent, as well as to stimulate each member to do his best for the honour of his squad. The usual plan is to have a clasp attached, which is held for one month by the NCO whose squad had the highest average during the previous month- this clasp to be ultimately retained by the winner of the medal. The clasp ought to be small, with suitable engraving and inscription. Cases have been known where such a clasp has found a resting place on the person of a mother, sister, or other friend, after the stalwart owner had retired from the Company! It is not advisable to offer individual prizes to the members of the winning squad, as it is better for the NCO to be in a position to appeal to the laggard to pull up for the credit of his squad, rather than for any personal reward to be gained. A good plan, however, is to parade the successful squad in front of the Company monthly, and at the annual Prize Giving, while the clasp or medal is pinned on the breast of the leader.'* [2]

A correspondent to the Gazette in **1896**, James Allen, (Capt. 1st Bannockburn Coy.), put forward a scheme in which the Squad Challenge Medal was to be awarded on a broader basis than attendance alone. Capt. Allen's idea included punctuality, cleanliness, obedience and behaviour in the ranks. It was mainly a way of being fair to those boys who sometimes had an unavoidable absence or lateness. In effect it was an attempt at an efficiency award. [3]

Alfred Kerr, (Capt. 14th Liverpool Coy.) read a paper on 'Prize Giving' to the officers of the Liverpool Battalion on 26th October **1898** and it was reproduced in the Gazette the next year. In a section headed 'Medals' Kerr states:

'I would not advocate their use, on the grounds that they are likely to bring ridicule in cases where they are worn to excess, on the simple uniform which our Boys wear, and to which they stand in rather striking contrast.' [4]

Eighteen months later Kerr addressed the Officers' Conference at the annual Brigade Meeting in Sheffield on 'Rewards and Decorations'. He had much to say on medals:

'As to medals these were highly thought of by the members of our Companies, but more so by the younger ones than the older. A number of medals on a Boy made him look ridiculous, and the multi-coloured ribbons indulged in by some Companies were not in harmony with the sober and simple uniform of the Brigade. While not in favour of medals, he suggested that a uniform ribbon should be adopted in the Brigade for all Attendance Medals, and another colour might be used for Drill, if such a reward were found to be advisable. From his critisism of medals, however, he excluded the Squad Challenge Medal, which he found to be an enormous help in interesting NCO's in their work' [5]

At the Sheffield Meeting Mr T.W. Cuthbertson, Brigade Treasurer, followed Mr Kerr, making reference to the BB Manual and the paragraph therein on 'Prizes'. He rated attendance as the most important requirement to qualify for a prize. The article in the Gazette goes on to say:

'The Squad Challenge Medal he placed next, although he pointed out that it had its dangers which must be guarded against. Boys who could not attend with perfect regularity might be forced out of a Company by a too zealous NCO or a squad intent upon winning the medal. The monthly clasp he considered an excellent feature, giving each squad a fresh start, as it were, at the beginning of each month. He recommended that the whole squad should be paraded in front of the Company when the clasp was presented to the NCO.... As to wearing of decorations, Mr Cuthbertson said, "Let there be only one Medal per Company. I believe this has been made a rule in one of the English Battalions, and I think it is a good one. It is positively ridiculous to see a lot of Boys in a Company with medals. Or if you think this is not fair, because the Squad medal is only open to NCO's, then let there be one other for the rank and file, say for the best at Drill. If medals are offered to you, have the courage to refuse; give your reasons, and they are sure to be respected; you will get the prizes in some other form.' [6]

No doubt, Mr Cuthbertson would have found many medal-bedecked CLB Companies of the time very interesting indeed.

'Toy Crimean Veterans'

The debate on 'Prizes' at Sheffield in **1900** continued with letters being read from Mr P.D.Adams and Mr A.E. Spender of London. Mr Spender's communication said:

'The question of Medals is open to a wide divergence of opinion, but the multiplicity of medals should be strongly discountenanced. Our aim should be as far as possible to check our Boys from being made the subject of ridicule as toy Crimean veterans. If medals are presented, let them be won by Boys not seeking to win them selfishly but in conjunction with others for the honour of a section, as in the case of the Squad Medal, where every member of the detachment contributes to the victory, and is proud to see his squad leader wear the reward. The medal should be a reward for Drill and general Efficiency, and should never be given as a mundane inducement to attendance at Bible-Class: ways other than this should be found.' [7]

In fact, it was the other 'inducements', regularised and standardised, which turned into the Badge System. So, between 1890 and 1910 BB medals were put firmly in their place; acceptable for Squad Challenge, but for very little else.

Various Designs

Before **1927,** and particularly in the early years of the Brigade, equipment and uniform were supplied direct by contractors upon receipt of an officially placed order on the appropriate regulation form. Medals, bearing the emblem of the Brigade, were no exception to this rule and were widely advertised in Brigade publications, particularly the Manual. Unfortunately, these advertisements were not usually illustrated, so we can but speculate as to the design and size. In the **1888** Manual (Edition 1), Messrs. John Storer & Son, Jewellers, of 64, Buchanan Street, Glasgow, advertised:

'A stock of Gold and silver medals and badges always on hand at wholesale prices.'

These were probably, as described, stock medals with BB anchors added in relief or engraved, or both. Then, as now, you got what you paid for and the limitations were only those of the wallet. In the **1890s,** however, some standard designs were issued which were 'struck' once a market had been established. Storer's advert of **1891/2** was offering *'Squad Challenge Medal & Clasp, in Case, Complete 17s.'* In **1893**, the same medal from Storer was being advertised as *'Squad Challenge Medal & Monthly Clasp'*. That year more suppliers were entering the market. James Farquharson, of Houndsditch, London, and Garlick & Sons of Castle St., Bristol, both advertised in the BB Manual. Advertisements appeared in **1895** from Storer and Farquharson, with the latter describing the medals as *'Bronze, Plated and Silver Star Medals'*. Bronze were 6d and came with pin hangers, plated were 2/- and silver 10/- both with clasp and ribbon. A case was available for the above from 1/6d. 'Star' can mean many things. Were these five-pointed stars, four- pointed stars (like the sergeants' star), or an eight- pointed star like the current Squad Medal ? The evidence suggests that they were either the four-pointed, or eight-pointed stars. Four-pointed star medals do exist from this time, in 'Bronze' and 'Silver' and with ribbons. These four-pointed stars are the same size and design as the later Sergeants' Star Badge. In other words, not very large. The sum of 10/- does seem a lot for one of these, even in silver. It is likely that they were the larger 'Squad Medals' and that this was the first year of their production. The advertising as 'star' medals was not used again, perhaps to avoid confusion with the smaller four-pointed stars. Examples of the star pattern, as per the current Squad Medal, do exist hallmarked **1896** and **1898**. The **1896** medal has a ribbon with equal vertical stripes of red, white and blue, typical of the period, with **1896 - 1898** clasps. An **1898** hall-marked medal with blue ribbon exists in its original Farquharson's box. [8] Farquharson's **1897** advert in the BB Officers' Manual described the medals as *'Silver Squad Challenge Medal in case 11/6.'* ...the same price as the **1895** 'star medal' advert. These medals are marked 'TBW' as the maker.

Perhaps the 'star' Squad Challenge medal was rather expensive for some companies. James Farquharson in **1902** brought out a *'Special design'* Medal in Bronze (1/-) and Silver (3/-). This was in addition to the silver Squad Challenge medal. The design was probably the *'Round struck medal'* with a BB emblem on the obverse surrounded by oak and laurel swatches; cheaper to produce than the star medal and an adaptation of a stock design. [9] At least one example exists of a silver, round-struck medal on a **1901-1902** engraved suspension brooch bar. Unfortunately, maker and hall-mark are indistinct but the maker could be 'W.J.D.', the brooch bar is certainly such. [10]

In **1902,** an announcement appeared in the BB Manual that: *'Medals will be worn on left breast'.* The Brigade had accepted the fact that medals would be worn. The plural *'Medals'* was used, but the rule was probably to coincide with the introduction of the BB 'Cross for Heroism' that year. In London a meeting held in **1903** [11] authorised the wearing of *Squad Challenge Medals* as follows:

'Silver for Commander, and bronze for Corporal. Medals to be worn for one month by N.C.O.'s of squads with best record, for the session. At the end of the session the bar to be presented to N.C.O. whose Squad has best record for the session.'

No more than two

The **1914** Manual made it clear where the Brigade stood as regards medals. Under the heading:

'Company Prizes': 'The leading Prize in many Companies is a "Squad Challenge Medal" to be held for one year by the NCO whose squad has the highest average attendance at Drill and Bible Class. A "Clasp" goes along with it, which is sometimes used throughout the Session as a "Monthly Clasp" held each month by the best Squad of the previous month and final-ly retained by the winner of the medal.'

'The Executive have laid down a Regulation that not more than two medals per Company are to be worn on parade (apart from the Brigade Cross for Heroism and Royal Humane Society Medal.)' [12]

This wording was to appear virtu-ally unchanged for the next fifty years.

The **1914** Manual had perhaps the largest number of potential suppli-ers of medals. Farquharson was selling its *'Silver Squad Challenge Medal with record bar & ribbon 10/-, with Case 1/6.'* Its *'Round Struck Medal'* was also still at the **1902** price of *'Bronze 1/- & Silver 3/-.'* J.S. & W.W. Lawson, James A Ferrier and Leckie-Graham were also advertising medals.

A uniform design?

In **1918,** there was a move to stan-dardise the *'Squad Challenge Medal'*.

Patterns for badges had been regu-larised, but here was one aspect of the Brigade 'uniform' that was still company based. The Northern Committee of the Brigade Executive stated that it could not endorse the view of the Southern Committee as regards:

'Adoption of a uniform Squad Medal' as this would *'destroy individuality'*, it would *'render obsolete a large num-ber of existing squad medals'* which have *'become historic'* in some com-panies and were often *'gifts of sup-porters.'* [13]

The Northern Committee got its way. The Squad medal would not become Regulation, a situation which persists.

During the **1920s** and **1930s,** the number of firms advertising medals reduced considerably. Farquharson continued to adver-tise its silver and bronze round medals and squad medals. James A. Ferrier and the Birmingham Medal Co. Ltd., both advertised medals. [14] After **1926,** the round medals and star squad medals were made with the new Cross & Anchor emblem, but retaining vir-tually the same designs. The 'round-struck' medal now had only laurel leaves around the emblem on the obverse.

It is probable that from about **1927**, the ribbon colour of the eight-pointed star squad medal, which had been blue since about **1900**, started to appear in BB Supplies in red as well as blue. BLB Service Medals had been on red ribbons. Three alternative uniforms existed in order to ease the transition, so it seems quite likely that former BLB companies may have requested a red ribbon on their squad medals, but this is only speculation, as most suppliers offered a choice of rib-bon.

The **1971** Manual had the first change in the wording of the advice regarding squad medals for more than fifty years:

'Annual or monthly competitions for the Squad Challenge Medal may be based on the highest average attendance at Company Parade Nights and Bible Class.' [15]

BB Supplies stocked only one type of medal described as *'Squad Challenge Medals'* and that was the 'eight-pointed, fluted star'. It is not known when BB Supplies started stocking these medals, but it was certainly pre-Second World War. [16] Bronze and silver medals were, and are, available with the bronze medals having a red ribbon and the silver, blue. Throughout the **1970s**, **1980s** & **1990s** both colours were available although the 'silver' option did disappear from the **1988/89** Catalogue only to be restored by popular demand. 'Silver' has in fact been described as 'Silver Plated', or even 'Silvery' (**1985** Cat.) and 'Bronze' described as 'Bronzed' for accuracy. Hallmarked silver medals supplied by the Brigade were made by Messrs. Smith & Wright and examples by that maker are known from **1939** and **1970**. [17]

The situation regarding squad medals in **2000** is still much as it was a hundred years ago. Medals are available of a standard design if required. If not, then companies continue to use their own. The 1st Glasgow medal, or rather its duplicate, is still in use today.

JAMES A. FERRIER,

Manufacturing Jeweller and Silversmith,

62, BUCHANAN ST., GLASGOW, C.1

SQUAD CHALLENGE MEDALS—
with Clasps, Sterling Silver, in Cases, 15/-, 17/6, 20/-, 22/6 each

SILVER BADGES and MEDALS—
with Brigade Crest, from 2/- to 10/- each

SCARF PINS OF BRIGADE CREST—
Silver, 1/-, in 9 ct. Gold. 7/6

SILVER CUFF LINKS—
with Brigade Crest, engraved, 5/6 per set
In 9 ct. Gold, 17/6 per set

ENGRAVING NEATLY DONE AT MODERATE PRICES

Medals & Badges made to Special Designs

Telephone : Central 7723

Advert from the BB Manual 1928

R. Bolton collection

REFERENCES

1. 'The Anchor', Magazine of 1st Glasgow BB. Special issue for the Company Centenary 1983. p 103. R. Bolton collection
2. BB Gazette, 1st October 1896. 'Prizes' p 27. BB HQ, Felden, Hemel Hempstead, Herts.
3. ibid. Letter from James Allen Capt. 1st Bannockburn Coy.
4. ibid. 1st April 1899, p 119.
5. ibid. 1st November 1900 pp 38 -39.
6. ibid. p 39.
7. ibid. pp 39 - 40.
8. Medals in private collection.
9. 1902 Officers Manual. Advert Section at end of book.
10. Round struck medals in private collection.
11. London Council Minutes 6/7/1903. BB Archive, Felden Lodge, Hemel Hempstead, Herts.
12. BB Officers Manual 1914 pp 38-39. R. Bolton collection.
13. Northern Committee Minute Book, No 1. [1915-1918], 11/7/1918. BB Scottish HQ, Carronvale, Larbert, Stirling.
14. BB Officers Manual 1931. pp 104-105, 111 and 119. R. Bolton collection.
15. Manual for the Use of Officers 1971. p 32. para 21. R. Bolton collection.
16. Hoey, A.E. Ex. Brigade Supplies Officer. To B. Mandry January 1998.
17. Hoey, A.E. .ibid. By 1974, Solid Silver Medals were not being advertised, but were supplied on request from special stock from the original batch.

The oldest medal in the Boys' Brigade

The 1st Glasgow Coy Squad Medal 1885

The first name engraved on the Brigade's original medal is that of L/Cpl W.H.Smith, for the session **1885-86.** *Mr William H. Smith,* pictured left at the 1933 Jubilee Celebrations, was one of the first boys to join the BB. He was then 14 years old and No. 16 on the register.

The medal photographs above (of the original medal) are reproduced from the special centenary edition of 'The Anchor' magazine of 1st Glasgow Coy. The winner for 1982-83, was Cpl. Douglas McLintock.

Company Silver Squad Medals

1906 -1910   1901-1902   1903   1896

| 1st Montrose Coy | 1st Weston-Super-Mare Coy | 1st Thetford Coy | 63rd Glasgow Coy |

SQUAD MEDALS BACKGROUND NOTES

The attractive 1st Montrose silver 'Squad Challenge Medal' and brooch suspension bar is typical of the ornate, high quality medals often used by BB Companies. It is engraved on the reverse with the names of the boys who wore it: Sgt. Spencer Cove with 97. 64% etc. Unfortunately, by 1910, the reverse was completely filled with engraving. The 63rd Glasgow medal is similarly ornate, decorated with filigree work. A standard BB emblem has been added to all of these medals with engraved B's. The medals above, unlike the struck medals, have been contructed from plates fastened together in sections by a Jeweller.

Star - Shaped Struck Medals

c.1891 - c.1927

c.1927 -

STAR-SHAPED STRUCK MEDALS BACKGROUND NOTES

The eight-pointed star medals have very little variation in the striking. The greatest variety is found in the metals, finishes and ribbons.

The earliest medals seem to be those of hallmarked silver and can often be found in presentation boxes stamped with the supplier eg. James Farquharson, London. The maker is 'TBW' with a Birmingham Assay mark. The boxed medals, which are the ones to have survived in the best condition, were most likely 'replicas' given to an NCO at the end of a session when his squad had been champion most times. In this case they are often engraved on the reverse. The suspension brooch - bar is depicted above and can be found engraved. Unfortunately, many medals in constant use for most of the 20th Century have much of their detail erased, a penalty for using silver! Examples are known in silver, white metal and bronze from the 1890s. Other finishes pre-1927 are bronzed gilding metal and frosted. Ribbons come in all widths, lengths and shades, but the most common width is $1\frac{1}{2}$". The most common colour was Royal Blue. Early medals are commonly found on vertical red, white and blue striped ribbons, sometimes with a number of clasps.

The eight - pointed fluted medal shown on the right above, is virtually identical to those currently available from BB Supplies. Over the years the quality of the striking has varied with more recent medals showing less well defined detail. Since 1927 the custom has been to make bronze medals and brooch suspension bars with red ribbons and silver medals with blue ribbons. Most 'silver' medals have been white metal, some having a 'chromed' shiny finish. Other variations include gilding metal 'brass'. The most recent medals (1990s) have smaller B's, as seen on the bronze medal above. The deeper brooch suspension bar is also typical of newer varieties. The medal pictured left, struck from a completely different die may be a one-off prototype but it has been in use. The orange-red enamel is usually found on medals from the 1930s.

Round Struck Medals

c.1902 - 1927

PRE- UNION ROUND STRUCK MEDALS BACKGROUND NOTES

There is a large variety of round-struck medals dating from around 1900 to 1927. The variations include the obverse design with variations in the oak and laurel leaf shapes and the bow.

The reverse has even greater variation in leaves and bow. The ribbon/suspension ring has either a straight 90° weld (above left), a double clutch (centre) or an embelished decorative top. Face edges of the medal are either milled or plain. The medals are either silver, white metal or bronze in original form. In the 1970s, the die of the obverse was used to re-strike a limited number (c.20) in gilt. The re-strike version with a blue ribbon and gilt suspension bar has a completely plain back, no wreath of any kind. On the originals, the methods of suspension vary, early versions use a direct brooch bar as shown above centre, others have plain bars and a ribbon. Common ribbon colours are royal blue and red, white, blue stripes. The medal was versatile and not always awarded as a 'Squad' medal. Examples are commonly found not ribboned with engraving on the reverse which indicates individual proficiency or competition success.

1927 -

POST-UNION ROUND STRUCK MEDALS BACKGROUND NOTES

Generally similar to the pre 1927 versions but with the post '26 anchor. Silver, white metal and bronze versions exist. All types seem to have the embellished decorated top under the suspension ring. The leaves are now all laurels, obverse and reverse, but there is much variety in the form of the reverse laurels and bow. Ribbons and suspension brooch bars vary when used, royal blue remaining common. Maker: JF&S.

Maltese Cross, Struck Medal   1910s - 19??

MALTESE CROSS STRUCK MEDAL BACKGROUND NOTES

The emblem is engraved in pre - '27 versions. This medal was sold by Messrs James Farquharson & Sons, Houndsditch, London, as an alternative to the round struck medal, frequently being the medal featured in its adverts in the BB Manual. Usually found with a blue ribbon. The cross behind the anchor is sometimes finished in red enamel.

The Daily Telegraph

Medals   The 'Blue Riband' of London

On Saturday 10th May 1906 the 3rd Enfield Coy. marched out for the final of the first ever Daily Telegraph Shield Competition at The Royal Albert Hall. Strictly speaking this was a London District BB Competition, but, held in a national arena and supported by a national newspaper, the Competition took on a status which could not be matched outside London. There was, understandably, much tension in the air, but this caused no unsteadiness in the ranks. The 3rd were hopeful to continue the success of the previous year when they had won the 'Meares Colours' for drill.

The Competition in the Royal Albert Hall was to be the pinnacle of a year's work in the Company under the captaincy of Thomas R. Plowman and was, in fact, only the final hurdle in a test of all - round efficiency including drill, bible-class, clubroom and band. The Drill Competition final pitted two first-rate companies against each other to decide who would win the giant circular Daily Telegraph Shield, set to be the most coveted trophy in the whole of the London District. The judge was Capt. Strackey, 3rd Battalion Grenadier Guards, Commandant School of Instructors, Chelsea. On this first occasion it was the 66th London who would provide the competition for the famous 3rd Enfield. The result was 66th London: 228 points, 3rd Enfield: 234 points. Capt. Plowman was on hand to receive the magnificent shield.[1]

More than a month after the memorable win in the arena of the Royal Albert Hall, on a Wednesday evening in mid-June, the 3rd held a typically Edwardian sing-song and tea in celebration of its victory. At that time the 'Daily Telegraph Medals' were presented to each of the boys. The Company had also been presented with a 'replica' D.T. 'plate' some 255mm in diameter made of wood with a picture of the D.T. shield at its centre.[2]

The 3rd Enfield went on to dominate the Competition for the Shield between **1906** and **1920** appearing in every final except one (**1908**) and winning it seven times. In the **1920s** it was the 1st Enfield which would take on the winners mantle on more than one occasion.

The Daily Telegraph Medals, being presented to every boy in the winning Company, gave the competition its title the 'blue riband' of London BB competition. The bronze medals, appropriately, had a blue ribbon and were suspended from either a silver or bronze brooch clasp with wording 'The Boys' Brigade'. Some medals can be found with different coloured ribbons due to the fact that the winning company sometimes substituted for the blue ribbon its own company 'colour' (eg. yellow).

Initially, the medals seem to have been produced each year, the first ones being made by Mappin and Webb and then in **1909** by Elkington and Co..[3] Later, a decision seems to have been made to get a batch of medals made to distribute each year and the firm of Birmingham Medal and Badge Company, is listed as the manufacturer.[4]

The medals continued to be awarded through the First World War and into the **1930s**. After **1926**, the BB emblem should have been changed, but this was not done. Perhaps there was still plenty of the old stock remaining. However, by **1932**, when the 94th London were winners, the medal supply seems to have dried up with the last of these special medals being awarded that year. The 94th won the Competition again in **1933**, but was not presented with medals. Subsequent winners would only be presented with plain medallions.[5]

The 'Daily Telegraph Cup' Medal is much more of a problem to trace. A request for information, put out in November **1995** to the London Stedfast Association, revealed not a scrap of information. However, such a medal does exist and was obviously competed for by the Bands from the Brigades and Scouts. The London District BB Band Competition for the 'Devonshire Cup' was introduced in **1923**, but this was for Bugle Bands. The Brigade boy on the obverse is clearly playing a fife. It remains a mystery.

REFERENCES

1. Wilson, Robert, supplied details from 1st Enfield. Dec. 1995.
2. ibid.
3. Medals in collections of 1st Enfield, John Russell, Dorset, and R. Bolton. Engraved on edge with dates 1907-1909.
4. Fiddaman D.R. Ast. Publicity & Promotions Manager, Daily Telegraph, in a letter to R Wilson [op.cit] 20/3/1984.
5. White L, Pinner [Ex. 94th London Coy.] and Garvey Chas. F. [Ex.58th London Coy.] in letters to R. Bolton 12/1995.

The Daily Telegraph Shield Medals   1906 - 1932

Reverse 1   **Reverse 2**   **Reverse 3**

Obverse 1

> Position of Maker's name
> Mappin & Webb 1906 - c.1908.
> Elkington. 1909 -

THE DAILY TELEGRAPH MEDALS BACKGROUND NOTES

The medals are bronze and have the BB (pre-'27) crest on the obverse which does not vary in style except for 'milling' at the edges: Mappin and Webb not milled, Elkington milled. The variation is on the reverse in the 'winged victory' figure. Mappin & Webb and Elkington use an identical figure, 'Reverse 1', but this is completely re-drawn in later types, most noticeable around the head and shoulders of the figure. The winged victory figure on 'Reverse 2', which includes examples from the early 1920s, has a thin faced figure with a definite 'scowl'. Later in the 1920s 'Reverse 3', the head of the figure is changed to a fuller face and with scowl removed, the rest of the figure remaining identical. In the later medals there are variations with and without milling, but milled edges are the most common. Examples from the late 1920s seem to be thinner gauge metal than earlier types. It was common practise to have the medals engraved, either around the edge, army style, easier on earlier types, or with the date only on the obverse each side of the anchor. Single and double suspension rings are found at the top of the medal. The ribbon is royal blue $1\frac{1}{4}$" wide although often found with different 'company' ribbons, eg yellow.

Brooch suspension bars are either white metal or bronze with the wording 'The Boys' Brigade'. They have axle pins and circular catches. There are two sizes of lettering.

Daily Telegraph Cup Medal   c.1910

THE D. T. CUP MEDAL BACKGROUND NOTES

The Medal is bronze. The obverse has two figures, a Scout Drummer and a Brigade Fife Player with the wording 'The Daily Telegraph Cup'. The reverse has a lyre and trumpet motif with laurel leaves and space for engraving. There is a double suspension ring. The ribbon is royal blue $1\frac{1}{4}$" wide. The Brooch suspension bar is bronze with decorated edges and has the wording 'Band Competition'. It has an axle pin and circular clasp.

Small Medals,
Watch-Chain Fobs & Pendants.

In the early days of the BB it was commonplace for boys to be awarded **medals.** These were usually small silver pendants, not ribboned and often without brooch suspension clasps, etc., The reasons for this are many, but perhaps the two most important were the fashion for wearing a watch-chain fob, or pendant, and the lack of an all-embracing award system.

These 'mini-medals' were awarded for competition, proficiency and efficiency in such activities as: drill, attendance, shooting, member of best squad, tug of war, signalling, band, best tent etc.. Often the medals were boxed and after being awarded, remained surrounded in cotton-wool in the drawer at home.

Most medals were silver or even 9ct. gold, frequently produced by local jewellers, they were often made to order. Some large jewellers such as John Storer in the **1890s** or James A Ferrier in the **1930s**, advertised in the BB Manual and the BB Gazette selling direct, or supplying bulk orders to other retailers such as Messrs. Farquharson of London and Garlick of Bristol. To assist in the production of these medals small silver crests were made which could be easily fastened to medal 'blanks' a much cheaper method than striking a complete medal. For instance the BB anchor was made without the 'B's' which would be engraved in the medal after the anchor was affixed. These were often advertised in the **1880s** & **1890s** as:

'Special Silver Shield badges with embossed Brigade crest.'[1]

JACK M. CUTLER,
Wholesale and Export,
Everything for Clubs, Associations, Leagues, Institutions, Friendly Societies.

72 GREAT CLYDE STREET, GLASGOW.

Hall Marked
SILVER MEDALS
with Blue Enamel Centre
as illustrated herewith.
4/6 each.
Prices in Gold on application.
Sketches and Quotations of Shields, Cups, Trophies, and Badges submitted.
Catalogues Post Free
on mentioning
"The Boys' Brigade Gazette."

Meda. No. 28.

The term 'badge' didn't mean the metal crest with a brooch pin- that was a 'brooch' for the use of ladies only. Some of the blanks used had the usual embellishments of laurel leaves, scrolls, crowns and acanthus leaves, but others were carefully hand engraved and appropriately cut out to form signalling flags, company colours, St. Andrew's crosses, shamrock leaves and even BB boys with rifles. The addition of part-enamelling, usually with blue, added to the attraction of these medals. After **1911**, the use of the circular Buttonhole Badge became common on silver fobs, a practice continued into the **1930s**. (See examples on page 223)

The reverse of these pendants was usually left blank for engraving with the name of the recipient, his company, the date and the activity. By the **1920s** and **1930s** they were often awarded with just the name of the activity, leaving space for the recipient to get any personalised engraving done. Needless to say, this was done infrequently.

During the **1910s** & **1920s** firms such as W.J.Dingley and Butler Bros. of Birmingham were striking medals which included the BB crest. The catalogue of James

Farquharson & Sons in the **1920s** illustrated examples of two small struck medals in the shapes of a shield and a pointed maltese cross; pre-**1927** and post-**1926** versions of the same medal shapes are found today.

When the BB took control of selling BB Supplies in **1927**, a range of 'Silver Watch Chain Pendants' was on sale. There were six types ranging in price from 2/- to 5/-, clearly separated from 'Challenge Medals' for Squad Competitions, etc..[2] The quality of silver BB pendants was high during the **1920s** & **1930s** with red and blue enamelled crests made by Toye, Fattorini and Miller being common. The **1931** BB Supplies Price List illustrated for the first time five watch-chain pendants, two enamelled and three silver. The silver pendants shown are the same as numbers 5, 6 and 7 on the **1960** advertisement pictured on page   . The enamelled medals make use of the circular buttonhole coloured crest. Some of the larger Battalions, especially Glasgow, Birmingham, Northampton, and Manchester, had their own medals struck. Medals were still produced by adding a separate, now-post **1926**, emblem to a standard blank.

Production of enamelled BB medals stopped during the Second World War and what had been the 'Golden Age' (or should it be 'silver' age) of the **1920s** & **1930s**, was over.

In **1947,** the BB Gazette carried an advert for BB Supplies part of which read:

'Pendants, silver plated with BB Crest - ready in April 1/6 each from Brigade Offices.'[3]

The medals as advertized in the BB Gazette April/May 1960

The small medals of **1947 - 1953** started with eight types, but initially No.1 had no BB emblem, No.2 had the emblem stuck- on and Numbers 3 and 4 were engraved. Only medal Numbers 5 - 8 were struck and represented as they would later appear in the **1960** advert reproduced above. The fashion after the war, for small pendant medals, was for a wide range of styles within a restricted price range. The BB Supplies Price List for **1953-54** featured the range of medals in the format which would last for the next thirty years. The numbers 1 - 8 were retained, with the ninth being a special Sports Medal with various added centres illustrating individual sports. No's 1 - 4 were frosted silver with No's 5 - 7 being silver-plated or bronze and No.8 was a bronze version of No. 2. These medals turn up frequently. The Sports Medal, in a distinctive tablet form, originally had centres for A. athletics, B. cricket, C. football, D. gymnastics and E. swimming. In all the BB Supplies Catalogues up to the **1980s** the medals retained their numbers, so their progress can be followed.

In **1960**, the BB Supplies medal advertisement included five additional newcomers in the form of silver and enamelled pendants numbered 10 - 14. (See picture above)[4] No's 10 - 14 seemed to have a very limited lifespan, however, because by **1975** the Supplies catalogue had no mention of them. All the other **1960** medals are present. No's 1 - 8 are now silver-plated and 5 - 8 bronze. There were now no real silver options. In **1971**, the No. 9 sports medal included additional centres for rugby and table-tennis.

By April **1980**, the Supplies Catalogue retained medals 1, 3, 4, 5, 6, 7, and 8, but medal 9 had lost its 'cricket' option. Medal 2, a silver version of No. 8, had in fact, been unavailable since **1975**. The three remaining 'Traditional' silver plated medals (1, 3 & 4) were featured on the front of the price list.[5] The 'Traditional BB Medals' (1, 2, 3 & 4) all featured on the front of the April **1981** Price List along with a new range of medals. The new medals were described as 'Rose' and 'Scroll' medals, they had plastic 'decal' centres and were available in three finishes: 'Bronze, Silvery

and Golden'. The April **1982** List had all medals available, but by August only the Rose and Scroll Medals were obtainable and just two of the No.9 Sports medals remained, gymnastics and table tennis. Continuing with the changes the April **1983** Catalogue

JAMES FARQUHARSON & SONS, 59-64, Houndsditch, London, E.1.

BADGES, MEDALS Etc.

		£	s	d
1.	Watch Chain Pendant :— silver, 1/6 ; 9-ct gold, 8/6 ; 15-ct. gold, 12/0 ; 18-ct. gold	13	6
1A.	Watch Chain Pendant ; anchor surmounted by scroll – silver	3	0
2.	Shield Medal ; anchor in relief—silver ...	2	11
3.	Pointed Maltese Medal ; anchor in relief—silver	2	11
4.	Shield Medal ; anchor mounted—silver	2	10
5.	Plain Maltese Medal ; anchor mounted—silver	2	10
6.	Round Medal ; anchor in relief, wreath on reverse— ... silver, 4/6 ; bronze	1	3
7.	Maltese Medal ; anchor mounted—silver	3	3
8.	Star Medal ; anchor mounted—silver ...	3	3
9.	Maltese Medal ; anchor engraved, wreath surround— ... silver, 6/6 ; bronze	4	3
10.	Maltese Wreath Medal ; anchor engraved—silver 6/6 ; bronze	4	3
11.	Maltese Medal ; anchor engraved—silver	6	6
12.	Squad Challenge Medal, Star with bar and ribbon; anchor and rays in bold relief—silver, 14/0; silver-plated, 2/6; bronzed	2	0
13.	Squad Challenge Medal, Round with heavy ring edge ; anchor in centre ; complete with hook bar—silver	16	6
14.	Brooch for lady helpers ; anchor mounted on three bars— ... silver	2	6
15.	Scarf Pin ; small anchor— silver, 1/3 ; silver gilt	1	6
16.	Scarf Pin ; anchor set in blue enamel ground— white metal	1	0
17.	Scarf Pin ; large anchor—silver, 1/6 ; 9-carat gold, 9/0 ; 15-carat gold, 12/6 ; 18-carat gold	14	0
18.	Medal Bar ; small — ... silver, 1/2 ; bronze	0	8
19.	Medal Bar ; small,— ... silver	1	6
20.	Medal Bar ; large,— ... silver	1	4
21.	Medal Bar ; large,— ...silver, 3/3 ; bronzed	0	9
22.	Medal Bar ; large hook fitting (no ribbon)— ... silver	3	6

Cuff Links, oval and torpedo, plain or with B.B. anchor engraved on each oval—9-ct. gold ; ... plain **14/0**; engraved **17/6** per pair. Silver ; ... ... plain **2/6** engraved **4/0** per pair.

Medal Ribbon, Dark Blue or Marone— For Bars Nos. 18 and 19—**2d.** ;   Nos. 20 and 21—**3d.** length.

Ribbon is **not** included with bars **except when supplied with medals**.

The medals shown are only those of distinctively B.B. pattern.

We have in addition a very large variety of fancy and sports patterns in gold, gold centre, silver and bronze. Special illustrated list will be sent on request.

Engraving on medals at short notice, from **6d.** dozen letters.

A page from the Farquharson BB & BR Catalogue c.1924
BB Archive collection

---

was full of Centenary medals with just the two sports medals still available. The popular sports' medal had gone to three different strikings! In **1985/86**, the Catalogue makes no mention of any of the old medals, concentrating instead upon the Rose and Scroll types and a new 'Laurel' medal of similar style.

In the **1988/89** Catalogue *'BB and Sports'* medals were available coloured gold, silver, and bronze each in a wallet. *'Sports'* medals were available with cross-country, football, swimming, athletics, table-tennis, badminton, gymnastics, victory, bible knowledge, drill and first aid centres. The **1994/95** Catalogue described the medals as: *'BB Medals-Bronze, Silver or Gold medals for general use, supplied in a small blue wallet.'* These have plastic 'decal' inserts and were made from very cheap, thin metal.

Over the years there have been many 'one-off' small pendants etc.. In **1969,** the Brigade stocked a range of ladies' jewellery which included a pendant of a small BB anchor, of the type used for tie-pins or 'Old Boys' Badges, but finished in 'hard gold' plate. There was only one order of stock made for these which was exhausted by the mid **1970s**.[6]

New pendants were introduced in the **1960s** for 'key fobs', mainly for car keys. Originally these were chrome with enamelled BB emblems. By **1972**, the new introduction was a plastic circular BB emblem encapsulated in 'periglass' fitted with a small chain and key ring. Thirteen years later a new chromed metal anchor about the size of the old Three Year Service Badge, complete with chain and key ring, was being sold alongside the 'periglass' ring.

The Centenary celebrations in **1983** produced more pendants, for instance the Rose and Scroll medals having a plastic Centenary logo decal in place of the normal BB emblem. Ladies pendants and brooches were also produced using the metal Centenary Badge with a suspension ring fitting.

In **2000**, a ladies' pendant was produced in as limited edition of 200. Its design was based on that of the 'AD2000' badge.

REFERENCES

1. BB Manual 1888. Advert. Messrs John Storer, 64, Buchanan St. Glasgow. BB Archive, Felden.
2. The Boys' Brigade, Price List of Supplies for The Boys' Brigade and The Life Boys. 1928-9.
3. BB Gazette, April 1947. R. Bolton collection.
4. ibid. April/May 1960. Advert inside front cover.
5. BB Supplies, Price List, April 1980/No.3.
6. Gibbs Muriel, Brigade Archivist, in a letter to Rev. Ken Holman, 10th February 1986. R. Bolton Collection.

Fobs, Pendants & Small Medals

BADGES of the BRIGADE

VOLUME ONE
THE BOYS' BRIGADE

6. The Junior Organisations

The Boy Reserves Instructors' Badge

The Boy Reserves came into being in September 1917 following a meeting of The Brigade Council in Manchester. Essential parts of the new Boy Reserves Manual were published in January **1918**.[1] The idea was to cater for the younger boy, aged 9 - 12 yrs, as a

would wear the Badge on a glengarry. Honorary Instructors, initially only men, but, by **1919,** inclusive of ladies, wore the Badge on either a staff-sergeants' cap (men) or a navy-blue, felt, wide-brimmed hat turned up to form three corners, W.R.N.S. style.[2] Women Honorary Instructors who did not wear uniform wore the Badge as a brooch. BB staff-sergeants' acting as Honorary Instructors became known as 'Petty Officers' and initially wore the Badge either on an armband or the lapel.[3]

the BR Badge. The staff-sergeant, or other BB NCO helping with the BR Section, would now be officially rated 'Petty Officer' with the Instructors' Badge being worn on the cuff of the right sleeve.[4]

When, in **1926**, the BB united with the BLB, the Boy Reserves and the BLB 'Lifeboys' were merged to form 'The Life Boys' rendering all badges bearing the initials 'BR' obsolete.

The Peckham Boy Reserves c 1924

Photo. R. Bolton collection

preparation for entry into The Boys' Brigade.

The first metal badge to be used was a large nickel badge for the caps of 'Captains of Reserves' and 'Honorary Instructors'. Captains of Reserves, not already BB officers,

In **1923,** the Boy Reserves Manual was re-issued and included changes and greater detail. The hat was now 'recommended' for Lady Instructors whilst all non-BB Honorary Instructors and officers were to wear the glengarry with

REFERENCES

1. BB Gazette Vol.XXVI No 5. January 1918 pp 54 - 57. BB HQ Felden Lodge, Hemel Hempstead, Herts.
2. Brigade Executive Minutes 16-18/May 1919 BB HQ Felden Lodge, Hemel Hempstead, Herts.
3. Boy Reserves Manual. 1918. pp 14 - 17, BB HQ Felden Lodge, Hemel Hempstead, Herts.
4. ibid. 1923. pp 18 - 19 & 26 - 27.

The Boy Reserves Jersey Badge

Badges have never been a big feature of the junior part of the BB. Not until **1966** did any proficiency badges appear. Even uniform badges were kept to a minimum. It is worth reiterating the policy of the BB in **1918**:

'...it is the policy of The Boys' Brigade to keep down the number of badges, and to keep up the standards necessary to gain them, and it is well for the younger Boys to look upon the gaining of a badge as a real achievement, attainable only by elder Boys, and after considerable effort. There are, therefore, no badges in The Boy Reserves, and the spirit of work for work's sake, play for play's sake, and hobbies for hobbies' sake should be cultivated to the greatest possible extent. The Boy possessed of this spirit has the healthier outlook and will make the better man.'[1]

It is hardly surprising, therefore, that when the Boy Reserves started there were no metal badges for the boys with the one exception of a small star for Leading Reserves (See page 46). Even this star was abandoned after two years.

A crest was required for the Boy Reserves Uniform from its start in **1917**. The Brigade Executive simply recorded in their minutes:

'Boy Reserves - Crest to be worn by Boys on left breast.'[2]

The crest adopted was in cloth, probably due to expense, but also

to make the uniform serviceable for wear to school as,

'ordinary week-day clothing of a large number of small Boys...'[3]

The cap was not recommended for school use.

Apart from the avowed BB policy against badges the expense of the BR full uniform was the cause of some concern in the early years. An example here from the Edinburgh Battalion:

'The Secretary informed the meeting that he had been asked by Capt. Tait (54th) to bring up the subject of expense in clothing the Reserves, as the expense was considerably over 14/6 without shorts. He proposed that a cap with B.R. badge in front would be quite sufficient.'[4]

Cost was evidently not a problem everywhere because, in **1921**, the Brigade Executive approved the suggestion of the Consultative Committee for England and Wales,

'..that the badge on the Boys' jerseys should be made of metal was also approved.'[5]

The new metal badge was issued and even though it was 7d compared with 2½d for the woven version, it caught - on. [6]

In **1922**, there was an unsuccessful move to completely get rid of the cloth badge when the stocks started to run out. The request came from a meeeting of Directors and Advisory Committee of the Boy Reserves where the B.R. Cloth Badge had been discussed at length. It wanted the Executive...

'...to cease issue of the Cloth Badge

when present stocks became exhausted.'

The Executive decided not to discontinue the cloth badge, but to inform Messrs. Farquharson and Son to quote for the addition of cloth backing. A representative of Farquharson was at the meeting and stated that the cost would not exceed 1d per badge.[7] It would seem likely that the cloth badge was not surviving a regular wash! Perhaps this accounts for this badge not turning up today, or maybe they were just thrown away with the jumpers.

The metal brooch badge is also quite rare, possibly because of the relatively small numbers produced in just five years. In **1926,** there were 18,928 Boys in 646 sections. [8] Photographic evidence suggests that perhaps no more than a third of these used metal badges, say 6,000. In many Sections, due to the expense of 7d, the Reserve Section bought and issued the badges, taking them back when a boy transferred to the Company.[9] How many boxes of these were 'dumped' in **1926** when the BR was no more?

REFERENCES

1. BB Gazette Vol XXVI, No 5, 1st January 1918. p. 57.
2. Minutes of BB Northern Committee. 18-20 July 1917. BB HQ, Felden Lodge, Hemel Hempstead, Herts.
3. ibid. Boy Reserves Manual, 1923. p 27.
4. Edinburgh Battalion Executive Meeting Minutes. Meeting for those interested in Boy reserves, 30/11/1920, minuted 13/12/1920. BB HQ Edinburgh.
5. op.cit. BB HQ. Brigade Executive Minutes 28-29/5/1921.
6. ibid. Messrs Farquharson & Messrs Garlick & Sons. Adverts from BB Gazette 1/9/1924.
7. op.cit. Brigade Executive Minutes. 4/9/1922.
8. Gibbs Muriel, Boy Reserves to Junior Section, BB Archive Press, 1986. p 19. R. Bolton collection.
9. Ritchie J., of Edinburgh who was a Boy Reserve in 46th Edinburgh in 1926 under Capt. Tom Curr testifies that this loan system was used in his Section. (Jack Ritchie, Photo. p far left, back row.)

The Boy Reserves Badges

Captains', Instructors', & Petty Officers' Badge   1918 - 1926

BB 023

BB 023 BACKGROUND NOTES

Due to its variety of uses, on glengarry, Staff-Sergeants' and Ladies' Tricorn hats as well as on armbands, lapels and coat sleeves, the fastening is a brooch type for versatility. This pierced, solid nickel badge has a reliefed surface, but unlike the BB Officers' Cap Badge which is made up in two parts, it is made from one pressing. Most types were originally frosted, but the Leaders' Cap Badges would have been cleaned, the armband badges for Petty Officers perhaps being more likely to remain 'frosted'.

Boys' Jersey Badge   1921 - 1926

BB 024

BB 024 BACKGROUND NOTES

This circular brooch is unique amongst all BB badges. It is made from nickel with the emblem incused with blue paint rather than enamelling. In contrast to the silvery, shiny slightly-domed surface, the blue paint has a matt finish. The badge is shell-stamped. Variations occur in the colour of the blue infil and in the brooch fastening.

The Life Boys Uniform Badges

Boys' Jersey
Boys' Cap
Leaders' Collar
Leaders' Hat

The lifebuoy was the emblem of the Junior League of The Boys' Life Brigade, formed in 1920, and called naturally 'The Lifeboys'. The emblem had been widely used in the BLB for many years prior to 1920. When the BB & BLB united in 1926, the new Junior organisation was called 'The Life Boys', with the words 'Life' and 'Boys' now separated. This new creation, effective from 1st October 1926, was deliberately given a nautical flavour. The BB Boy Reserves had used sailor hats and these remained as did the lifebuoy logo with, appropriately, the 'BB' anchor in the centre flanked now by 'LB' rather than 'BR'. Boys aged between 9 years and 12 years, (from 1955, 8 years - 12 years) were known affectionately as 'The Young Brothers'.

The Lifeboys emblem 1920 - 1926

Photo: Ronald A. Chapman. The Boys' Brigade Archive collection.

The BLB 'Lifeboys' had worn a school cap with a metal, enamelled badge and jumper with a woven breast badge. Just as the BB and BLB continued with a number of uniforms during the transition period, so did The Life Boys. New metal badges for wear on the left breast were introduced as were smaller badges for use on the school caps. The decision to retain the popular metal breast badge, even though the Lifeboys had previously used only woven breast badges, was taken early, at a meeting of the BB Executive in January 1927. It was stated:

'Specimens of proposed metal Badges for the Life Boys Jersey, to be used alternatively to the woven Badge were

before the Meeting...'[1]

Throughout the decades from the late 1920s and even into the 1950s there was to be a continuing debate about the use of a single badge for boys' jerseys, metal or cloth, or both. The result was that both types were kept as alternatives.

The metal badge was a solid 'brass' brooch replica of the new Life Boy Emblem, $1\frac{7}{8}$" across with blue enamelling in the central area. A smaller, but in every other way identical, brooch only 1" across was produced for the school cap. The school cap ceased production during the War, although it was still being worn into the late 1940s.

The Gazette, in October **1946**, carried an official announcement that only one pattern hat was now available,

'...of the nautical persuasion...'[2]

Production of the school cap was not re-started after the War and so there was no longer any need for the small, brooch cap badge.

The War had nearly caused the demise of the metal breast badge too. It had become unavailable by **1942**. In **1946,** the Gazette announced that:

'The Committee favours an improved cloth badge'[3]

Was the writing on the wall for the metal badge? No. By June **1947** the Gazette stated that the metal jersey badges were...

'...now in production again'

The cost would be 6d per badge and the metal badge would in future be the uniform badge for the boys' jerseys. The woven badge would still be legal, but would be supplied no more.[4] The badges were produced without the blue enamelling.

Remarkably, in **1949**, the Gazette carried a further announcement about the Boys' Jersey Badge, indicating that a woven badge was available as an alternative. It would be a gold LB crest on dark blue.[5] Two months later it was being advertised:

'Embroidered Jersey Badge, New Style, obtainable 1/4 each.'[6]

It was to be **1954** before colour returned to the Jersey Badge, but the 'all-brass' type was to stay:

'Breast Badges. The metal badge for wear on uniform jerseys has for some years been subject to the austerity of

wear-time production. The Equipment Department is pleased to announce a return to the metal badge with blue colouring in vitreous enamel that will wear well and withstand all the polishing that a Boy's badge should receive. The coloured badges cost 1s 6d each and supplies are now available from Brigade offices and depots.

To meet the needs of Teams that may find the coloured badge too costly, the metal badge without colouring will continue to be sold at 9d.'[7]

Some Life Boy Teams used the coloured badge to distinguish 'Leading Boys', combined with a lanyard. e.g. 26th Edinburgh.

The metal Life Boy Jersey Badge continued through to the end of the Life Boys in **1966**. The Jersey Badge for the new Junior Section being of the woven type.

Cleaning the Life Boy Jersey badge until as much of the lettering as possible disappeared was something of a tradition, but difficult to do in a few years with a new badge. There were many types produced varying in colour from virtually bronze gilding metal to the golden brassy colour.

The Leaders of the newly formed Life Boys, in **1926**, continued for the rest of the session with their old uniforms, even though the new boys' badges were starting to appear. It was May **1927** before the Brigade Executive Life Boys Committee got round to uniform. It was proposed by Mr Alexander and Miss Webb (The 'Lady Demonstrator' **1925 - 1929**). Lady Leaders would wear:

'Bronze collar badges and three-cornered hat with plated crest. '[8]

Male leaders would also wear Bronze Collar Badges and a hat as per BB officers, but with LB plated crest. Instructors would wear a Staff-Sergeants' Field-Service Cap with LB crest.

The bronze collar badges, chosen to match the style of the BB Officer, were the same 1" size LB emblems as used on the boys' school cap, but in bronze finish rather than 'polishable' gilding metal. Needless to say, perhaps, the colours varied as much as on the BB Officers' Collar Badges. Generally, the Leaders' collar badges were 'stick-pin' like the BB Officers' Badge, but since they were to be used by Lady Officers, a brooch version was available.

In a further attempt to mimic the style of the BB Officer, the Life Boy Leaders' Cap badge was made in white metal in a pierced form, 1⅝" diameter. The badge design was otherwise, the same as the Officers' Collar, and boys' badges. To give flexibility the fastening was of the brooch type since most Leaders were 'Lady Leaders'. From **1927** to **1947** the badge was worn on the side of the large tricorn hat. From **1947**, the hats were re-styled and the badge worn at the front.[9]

In **1966**, The Life Boys was integrated into the BB as the 'Junior Section' and all the Life Boy Leaders Badges became defunct.

REFERENCES

1. Brigade Executive Minutes, [Life Boys Committee] 17/1/1927. BB Archive, BB HQ, Felden.
2. BB Gazette, October 1946, p 15. Author's collection
3. ibid. December 1946.
4. ibid. June 1947, p 94.
5. ibid. December 1949. p 32.
6. ibid. February 1950.
7. ibid. February 1954, p 51. Vol LXII, No 3.
8. Brigade Executive Minutes op.cit. 15/5/1927.
9. op.cit. BB Gazette February 1947, p 49.

The Life Boys, Uniform Badges

The Boys' Jersey Badge

1927 - 1942 & 1954 - 1966

1947 - 1966

BB 029

BB 029

BB 029

BB 029 BACKGROUND NOTES

This is often called the 'brass' jersey badge but it was produced in a variety of materials which accounts for the great difference in colour from dark brown to gilt. It was produced as both an enamelled and non-enamelled badge. It was not produced at all between 1942 and 1947. Only the non-enamelled versions being produced during the utility restrictions 1947 to 1954. After 1954, there was a choice of versions with teams employing one or both. Having a long history this badge has many variations in lettering, emblem, ropes, enamelling and fastenings. One version has the maker's name 'Ludlow London' on the reverse.

Boys' Cap Badge   1927 - c.1946

BB 028

Leaders' Collar Badge   1927 - 1966

BB 027

BB 027

BB 028 & 027 BACKGROUND NOTES

BB 028 is a small replica of the Boys' Jersey Badge (BB 029), alike in all respects except size, it was used on the alternative 'school cap'. There are non-enamelled versions found. It is only found with a vertical pin. BB 027 is the same size as BB 028 but bronzed, non-enamelled and appearing in stick-pin and brooch form. The badge can be solid or shell-stamped and the brooch version can have either a vertical or, more commonly, horizontal pin. The bronze colour varies considerably, one version being brown-painted similar to the finish found on the Cadet Officers' Collar Badge.

The Leaders' Cap/Hat Badge   1927 - 1966

BB 026.01

BB 026.04

BB 026.08

BB 026 BACKGROUND NOTES

These pierced nickel brooches have much variety in the emblem, lettering, lifebuoy and fittings. Initially, they were frosted. They have many degrees of impressing including a shell-stamped version. The badge produced by Miller (026.08), is distinguished by its characteristic attention to fine detail and by its larger, finer lettering.

The Life Boys Buttonhole Badge

The newly formed Life Boys Committee, meeting in May 1927, postponed discussion of a buttonhole badge until September.[1] If it had known what a hullaballo would be caused over the little badge it would probably have put it off permanently.

At the meeting in September a Mr Rickard proposed that the Executive be asked to approve the issue of a Buttonhole Badge for the Life Boys and he was seconded by Mrs Alexander,

'...and it was agreed that it should be square, used in diamond form, the same colour as the Lady Life Boy Leader's tie, with L.B. in silver.'[2]

The Life Boy diamond buttonhole

Just a few months had elapsed before the matter of buttonhole badges was back on the agenda. At the meeting in January 1928 there was...

'...dissatisfaction with the appearance of the Badge.'

The little badge had only just been produced when it was proposed by Mr Goddard and seconded by Mr Hay that a new design be prepared and the present one discontinued.

This motion was not carried.[3]

Throughout **1928**, the complaints continued. In March they came to a head at the Life Boy Leaders' Conference meeting at Hope. The April Gazette reported,

'Dissatisfaction with the new Button-Hole Badge was expressed by a large majority of the leaders present.'[4]

Spin

In a last ditch attempt to generate sales the BB Gazette in November **1928** carried an announcement full of 'hype' and what today we would call 'spin':

'It is now nearly a year since the introduction of the Life Boy Buttonhole Badge. Although there has been a large demand for this Badge, it appears that, while many leaders are wearing it, large numbers of Life Boys are not. The Buttonhole Badge is intended for wear by both leaders and Boys, and an announcement should be made at Team meetings that the Badge should be worn by every Life Boy. The cost is 3d each, in the form of a button, or with a brooch pin.'[5]

What they meant to say was:

'There has been a pitiful demand for the badge, the leaders are always complaining and refusing to wear it and the only way we can keep face is by saying that the boys don't like it. This will help our credibility and get a different one sanctioned by the Committee. In the meantime we have got to flog as much of the stock as possible to recoup some of our wasted investment.'

There are very few of these badges in collections and that speaks for itself.

Despite the plea in the Gazette the badges don't seem to have sold well only the Committee would not let it go. At its meeting in September **1929** several members expressed 'dissatisfaction' with the Buttonhole Badge. It decided that the matter would be considered in January and that,

'...other designs should be submitted to the Secretary.'[6]

Three new designs were submitted at the January meeting but none were accepted. Ideas, however, had obviously been forthcoming because by the end of the meeting the committee knew what it wanted: a design which reproduced the Life Boy Crest, if possible smaller than the present BB buttonhole badge. Just what the designs were is not known, but a design does survive from the period which could be described as 'transitional' because it retained the rejected square shape, but included part of the Life Boy emblem.[7] (See next page.)

The BB Gazette reported on the meeting of the Committee in January and stated that:

'It was decided to produce for next Session a new design of the Buttonhole Badge.'[8]

**One of the rejected 1930 design proposals
for the LB Buttonhole.**
It has the square diamond shape but includes the LB Lifebuoy.
R. Mandry collection

A New Badge

Finally, the saga was over. Specimens of the new Buttonhole Badge were produced at the Life Boys Committee meeting in May **1930**.[9]

The new badge really was a success. It was smaller than the circular BB Buttonhole and it had the emblem of the Life Boys enamelled in blue and white in a silvery white metal surround. When, in **1956**, the call came for a uniform Life Boy Service Badge it was this little badge which was put into a one - year diamond to create the 'new' Badge.

In **1935**, it was considered necessary to promote the Badge in the pages of the Gazette:

'Show the Badge.
Boys to-day love to wear badges on the lapels of their jackets. Many Life Boy Leaders have appealed to this natural 'instinct' and have used it to foster Team Spirit and pride in the organisation by introducing to the members of their Team the very attractive silver, blue and white Life Boy Badge (now sold at 3d, with either stud or pin fitting.)

In such Teams a tradition has been built up, and every Boy is just as eager to wear the Badge and show his membership "in private life" as he is proud to wear his cap, jersey and jersey badge for the Team parade. These little things have a bigger significance in the mind of a Boy than is sometimes imagined, and therefore the slight trouble taken in getting a supply of these badges and selling (not giving!) them to the Boys is well worth while. And what's more every Badge that's shown will make The Life Boys more widely known amongst possible recruits and grown-ups too! [10]

Virtually the same article was reprinted under the title 'Wear the Badge' in August **1958**.[11]

Wartime Economy

The Second World War brought with it all types of economy restrictions and one of these was the use of enamelling on badges. The attractive white and blue enamel disappeared from the buttonholes in the early **1940s** when stocks became used up and the utility badges came into use. The all-nickel badge was still quite attractive, however, and the number of surviving wartime types indicate many different production batches. Just as it would not be true to say that the enamelled versions stopped in **1939**, it was also a fact that at the end of the war, the enamelled versions didn't suddenly re-appear. It was some years before restrictions were lifted and so-called normal production resumed.

Until **1966,** and the change of name from 'Life Boys' to 'Junior Section', the little silver, blue and white badge was a real favourite. The jilted 'LB' diamond disappeared into obscurity, so much so that it is now one of the rarest badges to find. No doubt its reason for demise in **1930**, its lack of identity, is why so few of them turn up today. Few know what it is.

Lessons Learnt?

It must be said that often people don't learn from history. Mistakes are frequently repeated. Seventy years after the BB produced a small angular, single-colour enamelled badge with two initials, unrecognisable as a BB badge, a committee designed the Anchor Achievement Badge. Perhaps someone should put a few by for **2067** and make a real killing on the second - hand market!

REFERENCES

1. Life Boys Committee, 15/5/1927. BB HQ, Felden Lodge, Hemel Hempstead, Herts.
2. ibid., 17/ 9/ 1927.
3. ibid., 15/1/ 1928.
4. BB Gazette, Vol XXXVI, No 8, 1/4/1928. p. 132. Mitchell Library , Glasgow.
5. ibid., Vol XXXVII, No 3, 1/11/1928, p.47.
6. Life Boys Committee op.cit. 6/9/1929.
7. ibid., 12/1/1930.
8. BB Gazette, op.cit. Vol XXXVIII, No 6, 1/2/1930. p. 91.
9. Life Boys' Committee 11/5/1930.
10 BB Gazette, February 1935, p 100.
11 ibid., August 1958, p 125.

The Life Boys' Buttonhole Badge

1927 - 1930

BB 171

BB 171 BACKGROUND NOTES

This small, square unpopular little badge was not particularly attractive or well made. The silver initials 'LB' are rather crudely formed and the blue enamel uneven and poorly linished. There were two versions, brooch and stud. It was blatantly modern in nature, but the lack of any name or recognisable emblem soon led to its premature demise.

1930 - 1966   c.1940 - c.1950s

BB 172.07   **BB 172.09**

BB 172.25   **BB 172.29**

BB 172.12

BB 172.24   **BB 172.32**

BB 172 BACKGROUND NOTES

The white and blue enamelled badge had silver lettering. Made from gilding metal, sometimes not nickel - plated, to give the effect of brown ropes on the lifebuoy. Made in brooch and crescent lapel stud form, the studs have variations as do the brooch fittings. The badge has a solid construction. A number of makers were involved in production over the years, but mainly Messrs. Miller. There is however considerable variation in the emblem and colours of enamelling, etc.. Perhaps the most noticeable variation being the larger size Smith & Wright type. The detail on these larger badges is not so fine. During and after the Second World War utility measures caused a number of non-enamelled badges to be produced in brooch, crescent stud and foot stud variants including a lightly silvered, non-enamelled version. The larger Smith & Wright type was also produced non-enamelled, under utility conditions.

 ## The Life Boys, Scarf Pin

BACKGROUND NOTES

Presumably produced for Lady Leaders, very little is known about these pins. It is known that they were on sale in the 1930s and worn at the 1933 Jubilee Celebrations. The feature of this pin is the delicate pierced nature of the emblem having the ropes separated from the lifebuoy. Non-enamelled.

The Junior Section Badges

The Achievement Awards

The Life Boys operated a successful award scheme known as the 'Seal System'. In keeping with the BB policy of having few badges, the different coloured seals were kept on a wallchart and not displayed on the uniform. The Seals covered all aspects of proficiency.

In **1966,** a new programme came into being, called The Achievement Scheme. This recognised the fact that the Boys' Brigade, of which The Life Boys was now shortly to become an integral part as the 'Junior Section', had a wide selection of proficiency badges. The Scheme, wide - ranging in its content, was based upon the award of round plastic badges in six stages, white, green, purple, blue, red and gold. The peak of the system was the award of the 'gold' level in the session prior to promotion to the Company Section.

A Company Section badge, the 'Junior Section Service Badge', introduced in **1968**, recognised the achievement of this gold award with a special gold version being available in addition to the normal silver type. Previously, the Life Boy

Photo: Lichfield Mercury

All smiles! A proud member of the 1st Lichfield Junior Section shows off his Gold Achievement in July 1978, one of the first four 'Golden Boys' in his Company. Note: His Leading Boy Badge and 1977 Queen's Silver Jubilee Badge.

Service Badge was only produced in 'silver' (nickel) form for not less than two years' service. A transfer badge, recognising achievement in the junior organisation, dates back to the use of such badges in The Boys' Life Brigade when a boy could attain a particular 'Order of Merit'in The Lifeboys, 3rd, 2nd or 1st Class, with a special transfer badge reflecting each level of attainment, if applicable.[1]

Over the years, there have been few changes in the Achievement Badges, a measure, perhaps, of their success. The fastening changed, as has the method of

showing the obverse detail. The Gold Award seems to have produced the most types as the designers tried various ways of showing a gold anchor on a gold badge.

The new Gold Achievement Badge issued in **1993**, underwent a complete renewal, becoming the first badge to transfer along with its recipient from Junior Section to Company Section. A boy who may have had previously, only a short time to wear the gold badge on his junior uniform could now wear the same badge on his uniform for the rest of his service in the Brigade. The shape of the new badge conformed, generally, to the existing style of the Achievement awards by being circular and of similar size and colour. The new badge was, however, made from metal and had a re-designed anchor emblem including the new spelling of 'Steadfast'.

An interesting point concerning the plastic Achievement badges should be noted here. In **1976**, the Brigade Executive in an attempt to re-launch the **1968** 'Barrel Badges' abandoned the tacky aluminium brooches for badges produced in a similar way to the Junior Section Achievements, even including a similar 'cone/collet' fastening. Imitation is the best form of flattery.

The Junior Section Service Awards

It was **1982** before boys in the Junior Section were allowed to wear a service award. The Junior Section Service Badge was produced in plastic and was circular and smaller than the Achievement Awards. Each badge depicted a number from 1 - 6. The Service Badges were originally worn in the centre of the armband, bu,t in **1997**, were moved over to the side in order to make space for the new Anchor Boy Achievement where applicable. [2] The colours of the six badges mirrored the stages 1:white, 2:green, 3:purple, 4:blue, 5:red, 6:gold.

The Anchor Boy Achievement Badge

The Anchor Boy Achievement Badge (gained whilst serving in the Anchor Boys) has been covered elsewhere in this volume.

The Leading Boy Badge

The 'Leading Boy' in the Junior Section is a 'rank' which goes back

Photo: Wigan Post & Chronicle

Lawrence Buckley, Junior Section member of the 12th Wigan Company and winner of the BB Cross for Heroism in 1979.
Lawrence was allowed to wear his Leading Boy Badge
on the right breast.

to the Boy Reserves. The designation started with a star worn on the right arm in **1918**, then until **1922**, a cord sewn round the upper seam of the right sleeve of the jersey. In **1922,** a white lanyard was introduced (see photo. page 225). The change in jersey style for Juniors in **1971** and 'Health & Safety' considerations meant a change to a plastic 'Leading Boy' badge in **1972**, worn above the jersey badge.[3] The Leading Boy Badge is made from plastic with a raised gold border to tie-in with the design of the Achievement Badges.

Other Badges & Awards

Since its inception The Junior Section has only worn a woven breast badge. The Junior Section Cap Badge is identical to those of the Company and Senior Sections, but has a yellow plastic surround instead of red or blue. Shoulder

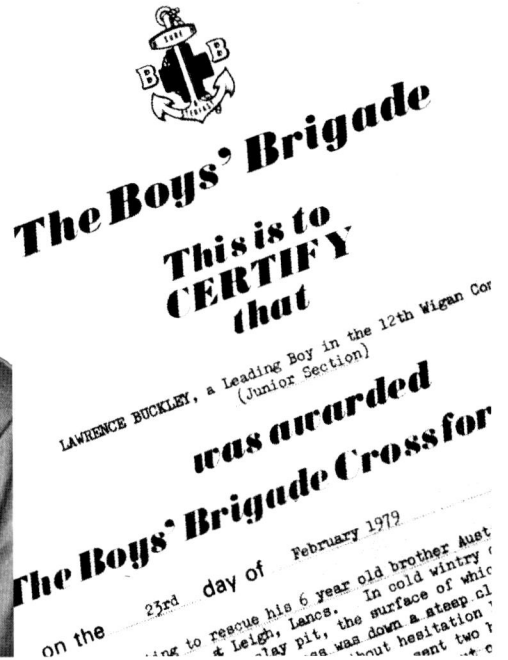

pennants have not been worn since the introduction of the new jumper in **1971**, company numbers being worn in the hats since **1970**. Additionally, shoulder titles, giving company designation have been part of the regulations since **1958** and can be worn at the top of the left sleeve of the jersey. Only a few other badges have been sanctioned for uniform wear over the years. In **1977**, permission was given for the Queen's Silver Jubilee Badge to be worn above the breast badge (see picture on page 234). In **1983,** the Brigade Centenary Badge was permitted to be worn in a similar manner as has the Junior Section 75th Anniversary Cloth Badge in **1992** for Juniors completing a 'Community Challenge'.[4] Junior boys awarded the Cross for Heroism wear the medal above their breast badge which can cause a problem if you are also a Leading Boy. (See photo. above)

REFERENCES

1. The Lifeboys Badges, c 1920, p 8. British Library. Ref: 4192.c26
2. BB Gazette, May 1997 Vol 105, No 4. p 76. R. Bolton collection
3. ibid., December 1972, January 1973 p 33.
4. ibid., September 1992, p 122.
5. ibid., August September 1981, p 137.

Wearing the Junior Section Badges

Right Arm

1966 - 1982

The maximun number of
Achievement badges.
Six stages, white, green, purple,
blue, red & gold.

1982 - 1997

The maximun number of
Achievement badges.
Six stages, white, green, purple,
blue, red & gold.
Junior Section Service Badge in
centre, 1-6.

1997-

The maximun number of
Achievement badges.
Six stages, white, green, purple,
blue, red & gold.
Junior Section Service Badge 1-6,
and Anchor Boy Achievement
Badge

The Leading Boy Badge   1972 -

BB 030.01

BB 030.03

BB 030 BACKGROUND NOTES

This is worn above the cloth Junior Section crest by 'Leading Boys' only. (Average three per Section.) It is a white
plastic injection moulded, reliefed, brooch. The relief is painted either gold or silver.

Doing Your Own Thing

Target Award

BB 600

BB 601

BB 602

BB 603

BB 604

These special Activity Awards of the 3rd Jersey Coy. were produced in **1992** and are still in use in **2000**. They mimic the standard colours used on the official BB badges. The decision to produce the unique badges arose from the involvement of five girls in the Company Section. As girls are, naturally, not allowed to wear BB badges the company decided that in order to have one common badge in the section everyone would wear these special awards. The size, shape and colours are similar to the official BB issue but the design is very much their own, incorporating the three fishes emblem of their Parish of St. Brelade.

Mystery Badges ? ?

This badge turned-up in the desk of BB Secretary Sydney Jones. It is gilt with blue enamel and has two lugs. Seemingly quite old and with 'Sure and Stedfast' it must be BB. But what was 'R.S.'? What does the number 47 at the top mean? Was it for uniform use or mufti? What is the significance of the rope surround. Is it pre-union or is it like the Life Boy badge which never included the cross? Is it from the UK? Does 'RS' stand for 'Reserve Section' ? Who knows?

The star cap badge pictured left is, perhaps, an experimental, non-pierced, sew-on type probably used when investigating alternative uniforms in the **1960s**.

The Welsh, Girls', Boys' Brigade 'Queen's Badge'?

As far as we know this badge is a special BB badge which has been sanctioned for use only by girls within the Principality of Wales - devolution indeed.

'Girls Sections' which run alongside BB companies have operated for years in the UK, they have badges which resemble those of the BB but have no initials 'BB' and certainly no motto 'Sure & Steadfast'. However, this badge is a BB badge complete with the official BB logo crowned with the Welsh Dragon and it has the wording 'The Boys' Brigade in Wales'. Having the same basic design as the new BB President's and Queen's Badges, it must have been produced post - **1994.**

We can find no official record that this badge exists, but here it is. It was photographed on an armband being worn by a girl wearing BB uniform to whom it had been awarded as her 'Queen's Badge'.

What were these badges used for?

Glossary

Terms used in the manufacture and description of badges & medals.

Frosted

Lugs

Fangs

Axle Joint

Safety Catch

Burnished

Collet

Due to the historical nature of brigade badges and medals, many of the processes, materials and machinery used in their manufacture have changed considerably over the years. Names for similar finishes and techniques vary considerably between badge manufacturers and users. Badge manufacturers often ascribe differing names to the same metal, finish or fastening.

FORCE MARKS

Throughout the book a standard terminology has been used in order to avoid confusion and misunderstanding. The purpose of this glossary is to provide the required detail inclusive of the miriad names which are used now, or may have been employed in the past. There has been much discussion as to which terms to use throughout the book and which to leave languishing in this glossary, and thus we can only apologise if your favourite descriptive term has been so relegated.

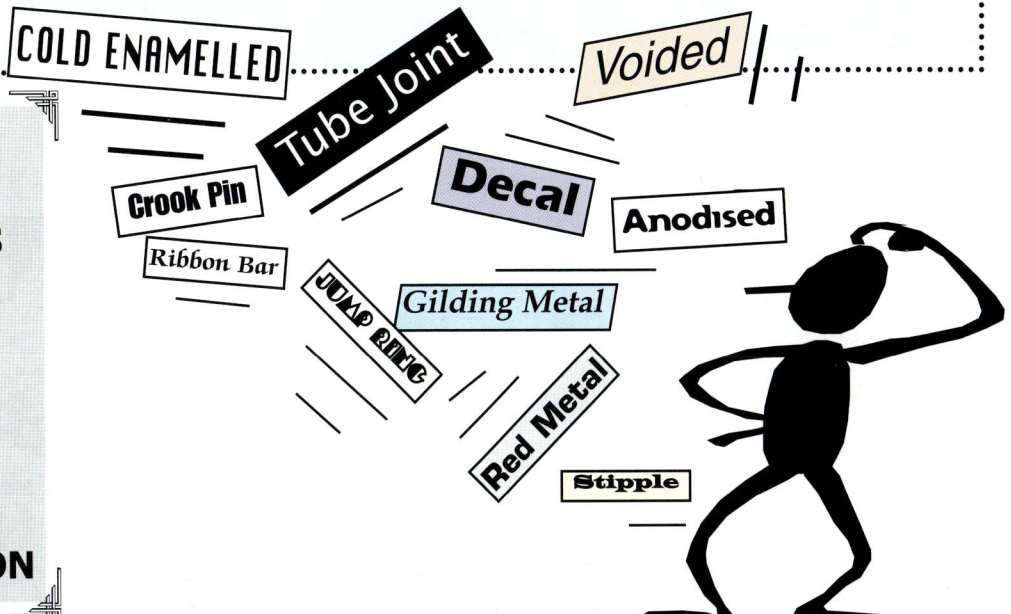

COLD ENAMELLED

Tube Joint

Voided

Crook Pin

Decal

Anodised

Ribbon Bar

JUMP RING

Gilding Metal

Red Metal

Stipple

Covering:

FASTENINGS

FINISHES

TEXTURES

CONSTRUCTION

Fastenings

Stick pin [Straight, no clasp]

Type a. [Fig.1]A long pin fastened to the back of the badge, normally at the top, bent parallel to the badge. Used in collar badges, tie /scarf pins, etc.. Designed for the pin to run between two layers of cloth. Sometimes supplied with a protective sheath.

Type b. [Fig.2] Similar to a] above, but the pin comes from a small tube fastened to the back of the badge.

Modern pins are fusion-welded onto the reverse. This is much stronger and more durable than the traditional soldered joint.

Brooch

Any version of a pin-and-clasp arrangement for attaching the badge to uniform, lapels, etc.. There are various types of pins and clasps. [See below].

Stud

Usually in a standard circular pattern [Fig.3], 'foot'[Fig.4], or crescent [Fig.5] . Designed to fit through a lapel buttonhole of a suit, blazer, etc.. A number of types exist.

Lugs

Loops, sometimes called 'shanks', soldered onto the reverse of a badge. [Fig.6] The badge is secured by using a spring/cotter pin. A backing plate can be used. Although usually in pairs, occasionally a badge has two sets. A similar method of fixing can be achieved by the use of a bar fitting with two holed plates protruding. This latter method is suitable for smaller badges and is less expensive to make. Used on the BB Cap Badges from the 1970s. [Fig 6A]

Tab/Slide

Flat flexible metal strip soldered to back of cap badge. Usually with curved end. Designed to fit into slot in cap. [Fig.7]

Fangs/Tags

Thin, flat, pointed metal strips of varying length and thickness soldered to the back of badges, numbers, etc.. They are designed to pierce the fabric and may then be folded to secure the badge in place. Many makers soldered two tags as one piece cutting it as a finishing process. Tags are pointed on the ends whilst Fangs taper throughout their whole length. [Fig. 8- Tags] [Fig. 9- Fangs]

Thread Holes

Used on badges to be sewn on to fabric. Single holes are common but often found in pairs.

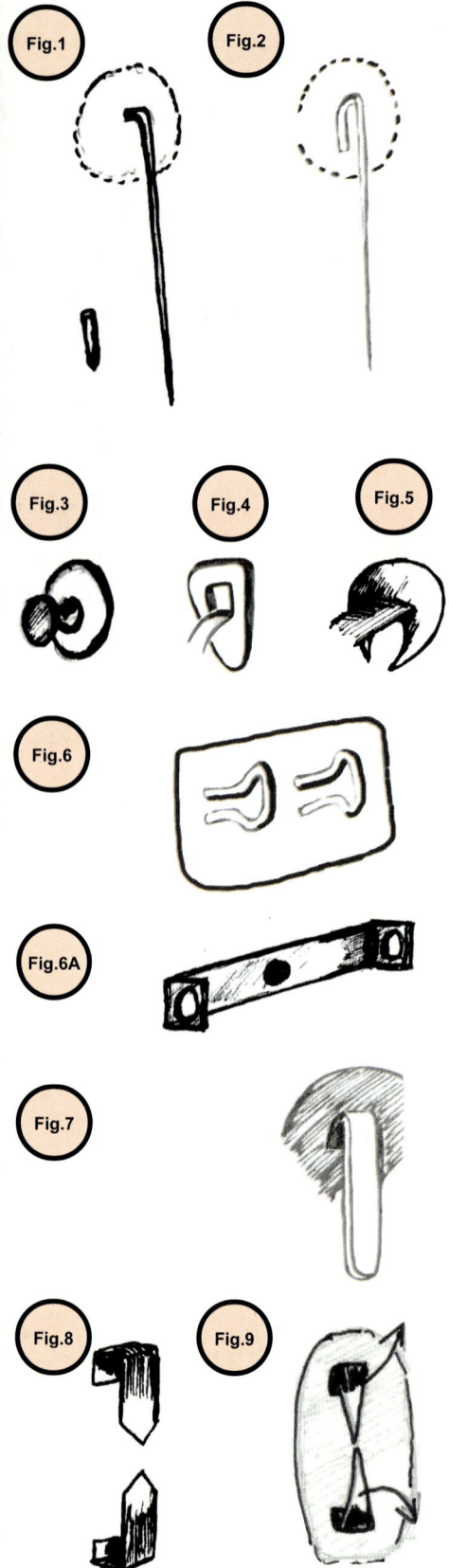
Fig.1 Fig.2 Fig.3 Fig.4 Fig.5 Fig.6 Fig.6A Fig.7 Fig.8 Fig.9

Plastic Clip

Various types are known. The system usually involves a peg and washer or collet. A circular plastic collar receives a peg from the back of the badge. Usually used only once, but some types are designed for repeated use. [Fig.10]

Fig.10

Bolt

Threaded bolt protrudes from the back of the badge and locks with a nut. The nut usually has a knurled edge. [Fig.11]

Fig.11

Brooch Pins/Mounting

There are three main directions of mounting brooch pins/clasps or bar brooches: vertical, horizontal or diagonal. Mounting is done by fusion welding, soldering or sometimes, less sucessfully, by glueing.

Fastenings for Tin/Button Badges

Button badges made from tin plate usually have a single wire pin, including a 'locking-tongue', inserted under a rim around the reverse of the badge. This is sometimes called a 'wire-brooch fitting'. Tin studs, stick pin and 'best brooch' [solid] fittings are also occasionally used. [Fig.12]

Fig.12

Joint

This is the name given to the method in which the pin is secured to the badge. Various types and styles are used for this moving part of the brooch fitting. There are many varieties of joint, only the types most commonly used on brigade badges are detailed here. [Fig.13]

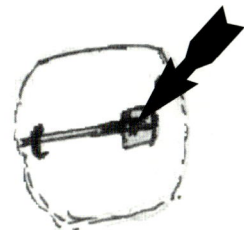
Fig.13

Axle Joint

A name we give to an early style joint, not used much after **1925**. The pin has part of the tubular hinge attached to it and fits between the other two parts of the hinge located on the badge. The whole assembly is secured by a small rod [axle] through all three elements. [Fig.14] This type of joint was not very strong for fitting through tough armlets and frequently lost the little rod. Various subsistitutes are often found in place of the rod. A coiled version also exists which often includes a small bridge. [Fig.15] The BB Brigade Executive commented on the weakness of the pin and, in **1925**, requested the use of a different arrangement.

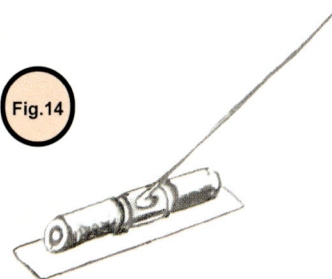
Fig.14

Fig.15

Squeeze/Clamped Joint

A brooch arrangement where a single stranded coiled pin is held in place between two metal plates each having a protrusion pointing inwards to retain the pin. The pin is tensioned over a 'bridge' in front of the clamp.[Fig.16]

Fig.16

Box Joint

As 'Squeeze' joint above, but with backing. A double- coiled pin is tensioned over the front of the box as a 'bridge'. [Fig.17] There are numerous arrangements and shapes. A reverse type requires end of pin to provide spring tension. [Fig.18]

Tube Joint (Standard Joint)

A simple design. The pin is bent through a small tube fastened to the reverse of the badge and folded under itself for tension. Generally used as the next generation after the 'axle' pin and before the onset of squeeze/clamped joints. As such it is the 'standard' brooch fastening adopted by many of the major manufacturers. Although requiring a separate fusion catch to be soldered to the badge, this joint is still used today because of its simplicity and strength. [Fig.19]

Crook Pin

After being coiled/clamped in a joint, the end of the pin is formed into a crook shape to provide greater tension. [Fig.20]

Coiled Pin

The pin is wrapped, usually more than once, around an axle or clamp. Some pins are 'rivet pins' which are not unlike the early 'axle', but are riveted in place as a hinge.

Bar Brooch

A complete unit of rivited hinge/squeeze joint, pin and domed safety catch. This is stuck, soldered or fusion-welded to the back of the badge. The safety clasp used on this assembly is usually the swivel type, but other catches are used. Common types are described as 'wide' or 'slim'. This is a modern brooch fitting and comes in hundreds of different types. [Fig.21]

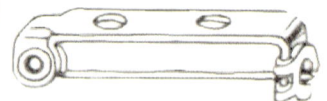

Clutch Pin

A modern pin attatchment. A short pin is welded to the back of the badge at a right angle with a shorter spacing pin by its side.[Fig.22] A separate circular butterfly-winged and sprung retaining-clip fits over the pin. [Fig.23]

Plastic Cone. Clutch/Collet

A short metal pin is welded to the badge, without a spacer. [Fig.24] A plastic cone with a central hole in its base is pushed on top of the pin. [Fig.25] Sometimes there is a plastic 'pin' and a washer clips into place on top of it.

Spring Pin

A metal wire pin bent to the form of a 'cotter pin'. [Fig.26] It is used to secure by passing it through lugs fastened to the reverse of the badge. Often described incorrectly as a 'split pin'.

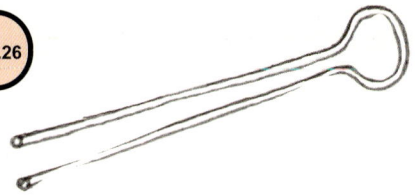
Fig.26

Clasps or Fusion Catches

These are the names given to the devices which secure the pointed end of the brooch pin. They are often produced in the same metal as the badge but can be made in any metal which is able to be soldered on to the reverse of a badge. There are a number of common types.

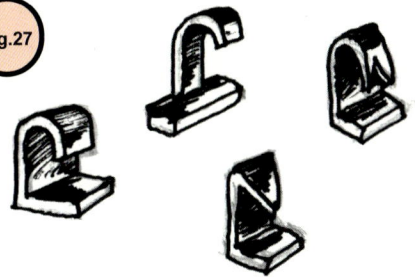
Fig.27

Flat-Rolled Catch

The catch consists of a flat piece of metal with about 25% soldered on to the badge and the rest bent at a right angle with the tip curved round to make the catch. The free end is either flat, curved, single-pointed, notched/forked, etc.. [Fig.27] Shortened to 'FRC' in book text.

Rounded Catch

A metal ring has been cut open to form a circular clasp. [Fig.28]

Fig.28

Hooked Catch

A small thin catch having the appearance of a reversed figure '2'. [Fig.29]

Fig.29

Safety Catch

Usually a domed safety catch but sometimes a more simple design. The domed catch is a hinged assembly in three hooked parts, the centre swivels round to completely enclose the pin. This rotational movement is made by moving a small 'handle' on outside of swivel. This catch is used mainly on bar-brooches.[Fig.30]

Fig.30

Medal & Pendant Rings

Fig.31

Medals often have a 'built-in' ring or slot from which the carrying ribbon is suspended. This will be part of the 'casting'. Sometimes medals are holed after striking in oder to use a loose 'jump ring'. [Fig.31]

Jump Ring

Fig.32

A small circular metal wire ring which is usually cut in one place. [Fig.32] This can be used to go through a hole or ring cast in the medal. The medal ribbon is carefully folded through the jump ring. Jump rings can be used when extra bars are being suspended between the medal and the ribbon.

Fixed Rings

Fig.33

Mounted on medal either flush or at right angles. They can be single or double rings.

Famous BB Artist Tom Curr, Capt. 46th Edinburgh Coy. with his Life Boy team c.1927. The boys are wearing new Life Boy Cap tallies, but retain their Boy Reserves metal Jersey Badges.
L. Howie collection

Finishes

Silvering

The badge is coated with a thin layer of silver and then laquered. Badges with this finish have not worn well. General rubbing during use causes so much wear that often the silvering is lost completely from the obverse of the badge.

Frosted Silver

The badge is sandblasted to give a rough matt surface all over. High places are then 'lapped' [burnished] to make them smooth. It is then silver-plated, the sandblasted areas retaining a snowy white 'frosted' matt effect and the smooth areas a glossy shine. The whole badge is then laquered to prevent tarnishing. This two-tone effect originally called 'frosted' by William Smith has been peculiarly termed 'french silvering' by many Boys' Brigade members over the years. The finish, whilst more durable than direct 'silvering', is liable to wear in patches when handled giving a most unsatisfactory grubby appearance. On BB badges the frosting was frequently deliberately rubbed off by BB boys and officers to reveal polishable nickel beneath. The finish ceased to be included on any badges ordered by the BB after **1942**. When badges started to be made from gilding metal or copper instead of solid nickel, the cleaning would often reveal the gold/brass- coloured gilding metal under-neath. Some early BB badges, even pre **1926**, were made from plated copper as well as nickel or solid silver, for example the Officers' Field Service Cap Badge.

Gilding/Gilt

This is not strictly a finish. A gold-coloured nickel coating solution is applied to the badge. Called 'electro-gild-ing' it is the first process in coating the metal badge. This coating enables a final 'finish' such as gold or chrome to be applied to gilding metal badges. 'Gilt' finish, in this context, means 'gold' finish.

Chrome

A shiny plated 'bright' finish, commonly used on modern enamelled gilding metal badges. Found on some BB nickel proficiency badges and probably sometime supplied by BB HQ since samples from HQ stock from the early 1940s have been found. It is possible that when gilding metal started to be used instead of solid nickel for BB badges, damaged and rubbed badges were chrome plated to hide the brass coloured marks which appeared under the remains of the frosted silvering. During the **1950s** the 'chrome' finish was very popular, epitomised by American cars and juke boxes of the period! The first official chrome BB badge was a lapel badge introduced for the **1953** Coronation. Varying qualities and colours are known, so batches may have been done by battalions, companies or individuals.

Bronzed

A coating on gilding metal applied using Ammonium Hydrosulphide. Often the detail is picked out by a process of exposing the badge to a solution containing carborundum and ceramic chips, thus producing high-lights.There is room for variation at each stage of the process, the state of the badge before bronzing may be altered, the strength of the solution, the amount of time exposed, degree of highlighting, etc.. Sometimes called 'pickling'.

Blackened

Sometimes badges are required to be 'black' and can be finished as per 'Bronzing' above. Occasionally badges were simply painted black. Not a very durable finish.

Laquered

A preservative coating of clear laquer is applied over the finish of badges when ex-factory. This could, for instance, be on top of a frosted silver or bronze finish. Tarnishing will not take place so long as the laquer remains intact.

Burnished

Lapping, or polishing metal. A matter of degree. On some brigade badges the gilding metal has simply been polished instead of a coating being applied.

Enamelled

Vitreous, glass enamel is the traditional enamel used on the earliest badges. Used prior to the introduction of epoxy resins and still favoured by some manufacturers. Generally this finish is transparent and the pattern on the surface of the badge shows through the colour. This is an expensive process today compared with the alternative 'cold' epoxy enamelling.

Cold Enamelled/Epoxy/New Enamelled

Also known as 'soft-enamelling'. A non-vitreous process using resin. Sometimes, particularly with early types, the coloured areas of the badge do not seem to be filled 'flush' as with vitreous enamelling. The resin is applied to the badge by hand using a syringe. The resin can be used in a number of ways: As on opaque colour, as a transparent colour mimicking vitreous enamel or as a clear coating giving either a flat or 'bubble' domed surface. Clear epoxy can be applied over paper, decals, coloured resins, gilt or chrome finishes. Clear coatings are sometimes termed 'acrylics'. New types can copy vitreous enamel so well that they can even be linished, enabling a flush surface to be applied to the finished badge.

Part-Enamelled

A description of an enamelled badge which has exposed non-enamelled areas, suitable for enamelling, which have been deliberately left uncoated for effect.

Anodised

Aluminium finish which imparts metal colours, usually bronze or silver.

Decal

A film of printed plastic which is inserted into the obverse of the badge. Sometimes printed paper stuck to metal or plastic badge. The process of using a printed plastic decal covered with plastic or resin is sometimes known as 'second-surface printed.'

Paint

Enamel or acrylic paint applied to the obverse of a badge. Most effective when surface is indented to take the paint, but usually wears away with age. Cheaper than vitreous enamelling, used before epoxy resins became widespread. Screen printing can be used on some badges fixing paint with modern curing methods.

'Staybrite'

Shiny gilt or chrome bright vacuum coating/plating on either metal or plastic badges. Often laquered. The biggest advantage is that polystyrene injection mouldings can be made to resemble polished metal. It is light-weight and untarnishable.

Celluloid

Term used for early plastic covered, printed tinplate badges. The 'plastic' is camphor and cellulose nitrate, a highly flammable material subject to discolouration with age.

Textures and Surfaces

Stipple

Used on obverse and reverse areas. Sometimes a mottled, beaten effect. Often composed of small raised dots. Usually clearly defined as: 1. Bold/Heavy/Large/'Seeded', 2. Medium, 3. Fine/Light/Small. When this pattern is used on reverse, the maker's name usually has to be boxed within a stipple-free area.

Reliefed

Chanelled-out, recessed, raised or chased to lift detail from background. Sometimes the chanelling is produced specifically to accept enamelling. When lettering is channelled-out and filled with enamel it is said to be 'incused'. When the area around the lettering is filled leaving the lettering un-enamelled it is called 'incised'. This technique is used mainly on the obverse.

Flat

Not reliefed or chanelled in any way either on obverse or reverse.

Domed

The whole badge forms a dome. A common feature of cap badges.

Bubble

A domed, clear, resin coating over obverse badge detail or decal.

Force Marks and Stamping

A range of marks on the reverse of a badge due to the varying force required to stamp detail on the obverse. The extremes are clear, but there are grades in between which may be described in order to identify batches etc. Generally each batch/production run will involve a similar force. The most common gradations are described below:

1 Shell-Stamped or 'Full Shell'

Every detail visible on the obverse is reproduced on the reverse, like a Jelly mould. This results in a thin metal 'shell'

2 Semi-Shell

Most details visible on the obverse are reproduced on the reverse. Usually heavier gauge metal than 'Full Shell'.

3 Impressed

Some detail of obverse shows through to reverse. Varying degrees of detail have been noted.

4 Depressed

A hollow behind some obverse feature, but not making a clear reverse impression of it.

5 Flat [Non-Reliefed] 'Solid'

Plain, no detail from obverse shows through on reverse. Some detail may be included as a deliberate force-mark. eg location points for brooch joints & catches, maker's name, stipple etc. There may also be a mark or marks bearing no relationship with the obverse.

Construction, Shape and Form

Stamped/Struck

This is the way most badges and medals are made using a force and die in a stamping machine. The term 'Struck' is used for medals.

Injection Moulded

This is the way badges made from High Impact Polystyrene [Plastic] are produced.

Pierced

A hole or holes are stamped out of the badge after the initial pattern has been stamped. Usually only one or two holes are pierced at once. This is an additional process which makes the badge more expensive. A badge with six holes could go through the machine two or three times. Variables include thickness of metal and size of holes. Badges could be described as 'Two pierced' or 'Three pierced' etc. During wartime, utility restrictions governed the amount of piercing allowed which meant that some badges, pierced in peacetime, were produced as 'solid'.

Voided/Open

The whole badge obverse design has the background pierced away. The ultimate in pierced badge technology. This process was popular for cap badges which employed cloth backing as the colour of the cloth would show through the holes. This is often the most expensive technique and can produce the most rejects at the factory.

Fretted

Often used as an alternative name to 'pierced', but strictly speaking should only be applied to those badges or medals cut by hand. Some CLB medals were cut this way in bronze, silver and gold. An expensive process, but in the days of cheap labour it was obviously cheaper than having lots of holes pierced by machine.

Pendant/Watch-Chain Fob/Key Fob

Pendants can be found either with rings for suspension or with no suspension ring. Often the non-suspension type would be in a presentation box. Generally for mufti wear and without ribbons. Sometimes ribbons were added for unofficial wear. Suspension from a brooch bar was sometimes normal for silver pendants awarded for intra-company activities, when they would be worn in uniform. Common reasons for award would be for camp tent competitions, drill, tug-of-war, etc.. Some pendants could be bought as membership badges, or to present to friends and supporters. For many years the description 'pendant' was used in the CLB to describe a medal. The CLB long service medal started life as a mufti watch chain fob but was ribboned and given its own brooch bar. Most brigades produced official pendants direct from HQ with approved emblems, etc.. These would be awarded for competitive activities such as sports. Sometimes the same badge would be produced as a watch-chain fob or buttonhole stud for men and as a brooch for women.

Medal

A pendant hanging from a ribbon used in the brigades for uniform wear. The ribbon will have specific colours, length and width. The order for wearing medals was established quite early by all brigades although sometimes this was changed. There are no miniatures of Brigade medals.

Button-Badge

Generally known today as a 'tin badge' or 'tin-button', although strictly speaking this term is applicable to badges which are made from tin and printed directly on to the tin as per drinks cans. Button badges were first produced using button-making technology in **1896** in the USA and were seen in Britain for Queen Victoria's Diamond Jubilee a year later. The earliest BB badge made using the 'button' technique was the Officers' uniform Buttonhole Badge first produced in **1897** when, just like a button, a thin shell-stamped obverse layer was given a backing. Tin badges were not taken up by the brigades until production of metal badges became difficult during the Great War. Early badges were covered in celluloid. Probably the greatest advantage to the brigades was the cheapness of production, whilst some have been used in uniform. Generally today, they are confined to mufti or 'fun' status.

Brooch Bar/Suspension Bar

A simple bar, often in hallmarked silver, used to suspend a pendant or medal either directly or by a ribbon. The bar has a brooch fitting as per a normal badge although the pin is often longer. Sometimes brooch bars are made for specific medals whilst others are universal. Bars directly supporting a medal usually have a hook of some type in the centre where the medal jump-ring goes through. Bars specifically for ribbons can be reliefed or decorated with patterns or words, left clear for engraving, or be hidden under the medal ribbon. N.B. not to be confused with 'Bar-Brooch'!

Bar/Clasp

This is a bar fastened on to the ribbon of a medal to denote a year, or level, etc.. There are two main types:
1. Fold-over style. Soft metal is used and ends are folded behind ribbon to grip the fabric.
2. Slide style. The bar, often silver or nickel, has a slot through which the ribbon passes.
Sometimes a bar is suspended between the medal and the ribbon by two jump rings.
For certain aspects of service a small metal emblem can be fixed into the ribbon of a medal, usually using fangs. Typical brigade patterns include, mitre, crown, star and rose.

Ribbon Bar

A short length of medal ribbon is made into a brooch, by covering a brooch bar. The brooch bar is often worn in place of the medal itself. Sometimes just 'Ribbon Bars' are awarded.

N.B. The word **'ribbon'** when applied to the obverse of a badge is the name given for a border containing lettering, etc..

Tie/Scarf/Cravat Pin

A badge is positioned on the end of a long single 'stick-pin' in the earliest type. More modern types have various kinds of clutch, bolt or safety catch.

How to Clean Badges and Buckles.

Here is a simple method for cleaning badges and buckles. Procure a pennyworth of whiting from a painter's shop (which will last over six months), a tin of metal polish ("Matchless" being a very good brand), and a small soft brush, the cost being about a penny.

You then proceed to clean your badge or buckle in the ordinary way with the polish; next take some whiting and rub over the badge with your fingers; next brush it off and finally rub with a dry cloth, and you will find that the badge is far superior to one cleaned only with polish.

For five weeks after this you need only rub with whiting each week, which easily brushes off; that is you use polish once in six weeks only.

When a badge or buckle is cleaned with nothing but polish, it is very hard to get all the dirt out of the crevices and between the letters, and it takes up a considerable amount of time to do it regularly; it also causes the leather near the buckle to go black, and this is very unseemly. But when you use whiting they are much brighter and the crevices devoid of any dirt whatever. In the case of the belt, it tends to keep the leather its proper colour.

Chevrons may also be cleaned with whiting.

Private W. T. SALTONSTALL.

**Extract from The C.L.B. 'Brigade' Magazine
July 1903**

Body Material

Nickel/White Metal

Very malleable/ductile. Either used solid or applied as a coating. Expensive today and not used in solid form for BB badges since the 1930s.

Gilding Metal [90% Copper & 10% Zinc]

Until recently, the most commonly used badge and medal material. It is a 'brassy' golden colour and has to be nickel-coated before being finished in chrome, gilt, bronze, etc.. It is a hard metal and needs more stamping than copper alone.

Brass [70% Copper & 30% Zinc]

A type of Gilding Metal! Not usually used for badges and medals due to the low resistance to heat, making it difficult to weld catches, etc.. Most badges traditionally described as 'Brass' are in fact a gilding metal with a lower percentage of zinc.

Bronze [90% Copper & 10% Tin]

Not commonly used, except for medals. Often today the term 'bronze' means 'bronzed' ie. bronze-coated.

Silver

A white metal, very malleable/ductile, used to make badges and medals, but more expensive than nickel, so not used much after the **1920s** for brigade badges and medals. Usually hallmarked with maker, assay office, date and quality. Sometimes simply labelled 'silver' or 'sterling silver'.

Gold

This most expensive metal is used to make some brigade medals and pendants. Hallmarked when solid with appropriate details. Some brigade badges are 'gold-plated' in order to prevent tarnishing, the word 'gold' then appears on them.

Copper/Red Metal

A most malleable/ductile metal. Commonly used until prices began to increase. Not as hard as gilding metal so the die is not damaged to the same extent. Now available more cheaply, it is being used much more for the making of badges and medals. It has a pinkish 'red' colour, hence the alternative name. Problems that were experienced with vitreous enamels darkening when applied over copper are now overcome by the use of epoxy resin 'cold-enamelling' techniques.

High Density Polystyrene/Plastic

Now much more frequently used as prices of metals rise. Brigade badges of all types have been produced using this material. With the number of coating techniques available today it is often difficult to distinguish a plastic badge from a metal one, although the plastic badge is invariably lighter in weight. Often used in conjunction with resins and decals.

Anodised Aluminium

Anodising adds a coloured finish to the metal. Aluminium has been used for brigade badges since the start of the twentieth century, originally having a novelty value and later being adopted because of their lightweight qualities.

Tin Plate

Thin steel construction plated with a layer of tin. The most common type of button badge is produced this way.

Pewter

A tin and lead alloy. Infrequently used except as a novelty. For example, it was used for a souvenir brooch for ladies by Glasgow BB for the **1983** BB Centenary Celebrations.

Woven Wire

A badge constructed from 'wire' thread, usually silver or gold, on to a cloth fabric base. Sometimes given a brooch fastening otherwise stuck or sewn in place. In the past, sometimes produced by hand, machine made today. Mainly used by the CLB/CL&CGB.

---

6   STEDFAST MAGAZINE   *August, 1957*

S T A N D
E A S Y

by
SANDY
MacCHEVRON

Illustrated by
TOM CURR

Extract from 'Stedfast Mag' No.47 August 1957.

'Sandy MacChevron' was Mr W.R.Smith, Capt. 55th Edinburgh Coy. BB

Tom Curr was Capt. 46th Edinburgh Coy. BB

DOC. FOULBREW switched off the batteries connected to the electrodes submerged in the glass tank. We crowded round attentively as he fished out Coote's foreign coin.

● "As you will perceive," began Foulbrew in his smuggest voice, seeing that for once the experiment had worked, "silver ions from the solution have been withdrawn and have been deposited on the cathode, or negative electrode. As rapidly as the silver has been withdrawn from the electrolyte, silver has been dissolved from the anode, or positive electrode. That, Boys, concludes the demonstration on electrolysis. Any questions?"

● His voice rambled on and on, but my thoughts had departed from the deposition of silver on foreign coins.

● Coote produced his foreign coin admiringly as we made our way home from school. Mouldy Greene, Wheelwright, Nobby Clarke, and one or two others had joined us. This, I felt, was the time to put my ideas across.

● "How many of you chaps clean your badges every week?" I commenced, laying the foundation for the next statement.

● Wally Brown didn't sound too enthusiastic as he stated, "Four blooming one year service badges, three year's service badge, first aid, PT, education, arts and crafts, piper's and swimming badges . . . takes me an age."

● Coote, even though his armoury wasn't anything like Wally Brown's, agreed it was a fag. "Especially," he concluded, "some of those second-rate efforts with a white deposit all over the surface."

● "If only they'd keep bright," put in Mouldy Greene, whose cheerful remarks were enough to brighten anyone's life.

● "That's just it, chaps," I enthused seeing that opinion was going the way I wanted it to. "What we want is a surface that keeps clean, with just an occasional rub."

● Bodger had joined us, and his ears flapped approvingly at my last remark. "What's brewing, MacChev?" he queried. "You've got something up your sleeve, I reckon. Let's have it."

● I drew a deep breath and crossed my fingers.

● "Some of you saw Doc. Foulbrew's experiment on electrolysis last period today. Put a lovely layer of silver on Coote's German pfennig." Coote handed round the specimen once more. "Needs a bit of a rub up, of course, but once that's done it's good for months," I concluded.

● "You mean, MacChev, that if we could do the same to our badges we could cut out a lot of the donkey work." Bodger was quick in the uptake.

● "Now, let's see," I said, checking over the mass of wires, jars, chemical liquids, and other contraptions. "DC supply from accumulators, chromic acid bath, and rod of chromium. Seems OK."

● "It'd better be." Wally Brown's voice was anything but encouraging. "That's my one year service badge you've got in there. So no backfires, MacChev, or else . . ."

● Bodger threw the switch. A few bubbles of gas indicated that something was going on. Nothing startling occurred, however, so we sat down to wait. I took the opportunity of suggesting that our haversack slides and belt buckles might be the next step.

● "After all," Nobby Clarke agreed, "the cap numerals are chrome, so why not the rest of the metalwork?"

● Wheelwright, who had joined us by this time wasn't so sure. His opinion, a good cross-section of the "old Brigade," he summed up, "seems if we streamline everything there'll be no uniform left to clean, chaps. I can see the point of MacChev here wanting his belt buckle chromed—anything would be better than the muck he sports on it at parade night."

● Bodger's interjection cut short my reply. "Time's up. Let's have a dekko at the badge, MacChev."

● We switched off and I triumphantly fished out the wire to which the badge was attached. Wally Brown seized it anxiously whereupon it bent and crumpled like a piece of silver paper.

● "Ass," he howled. "Look what you've done."

● Coote, however, saved my bacon. "It's OK chaps. Shows it's working. Only thing we forgot was that instead of dissolving chromium off the anode and hence on to the badge, we got the terminals mixed up and dissolve the badge into the chromium. Let's try another." So saying he swapped the accumulator connections.

● Wally could see it was no use trying to back out now, and produced another service badge grudgingly.

● Half an hour later he was glancing admiringly at a bright chrome badge.

● "A polish up on my old man's Lion Cup drill outfit and Bob's your uncle," I chortled. Even Mouldy Greene had cheered up.

● The whole Company had seen Wally's gleaming service badge on parade. After dismissal we cornered our squads and sold them on our idea. Handfuls of badges were handed over readily as we explained the set-up.

● "At a shilling a head, fellows, you've got a real bargain," I assured them. "For a token fee to cover our costs, no more drudgery for the rest of your BB lives."

● "See you have them back next Friday or there's one BB life that will terminate very abruptly," warned Wheelwright.

    *   *   *

● I didn't like the look in Skip's eye as he addressed the assembled parade. I liked less what he had to say.

● "The Brigade Executive have permitted Battalions the choice of returning to the pre-war practice of chrome plating all metal work on uniform, or of keeping them as they are. Our Battalion is going over to chrome."

● He paused. Why did he have to keep looking at me, I wondered. I was soon to know . . .

● "Furthermore, through the generosity of an ex-member who owns an electro-plating plant, all your equipment will be done free of charge within the next two weeks."

    *   *   *

● Looks like I'll be paying back shillings for weeks yet. These ungrateful bounders just couldn't understand that we didn't make a penny from their badges. Oh, well, guess that's what comes of sticking in too much at school.

● Just the same though, I'd like to hear what you chaps think about chrome metalwork on our uniforms. After all, you're the chaps who know more about them than anyone else.

Acknowledgements

Special thanks to Mr. David Aubrey Q.C. Llanfaches, S. Wales, without whose invaluable help and encouragement this book would not have been produced.

Aberdeen and District Battalion, BB (James F Reaper)
Kevin Aitchison, Edinburgh
Paul Arkinstall, 2nd Sutton Coldfield Coy. The Boys' Brigade.

Mr J. A. Bates. Stedfast Association, London.
1st Bearsden Coy. The Boys' Brigade
The Bodleian Library, Oxford (Mrs Christine Mason, Principal Library Assistant)
1st Bournemouth Coy. The Boys' Brigade
Philip Boyd, Kilmacolm, Renfrewshire
BB Scottish Headquarters, Carronvale House, Larbert (Margaret Bannantyne, Rev. W.H. Moore and staff who helped us to get 'doon the dunnie')
BB Brighton & Hove Battalion, 88, London Road, Brighton (Chris Hinton, Batt. Secretary)
BB Birmingham Battalion, Hatchett St, Birmingham (Roger Green, Batt. Secretary)
Ronnie Breingan, Rozelle, Ayr. 1st Alloway Coy. The Boys' Brigade.
The British Library, Colindale Avenue, London
British Red Cross Museum and Archives, Barnett Hill, Guildford (Mrs Helen Pugh) and the Edinburgh Branch.

William Cameron, Oxgangs, Edinburgh
Mary Care, The Boys' Brigade Headquarters, Felden, Herts.
John Cooper, Capt. 101st Glasgow Coy. The Boys' Brigade.
Duncan Curr, Baberton, Edinburgh

Gillian Daley, Dublin Battalion The Boys' Brigade.
Peter Dawson, Manchester Battalion The Boys' Brigade.
Alastair Dinsmor, Blantyre, Strathclyde
Duke of Edinburgh's Award Office, Windsor.
BB Dundee Battalion Archive, Dundee

T. Jon Ellis, Ingatestone, Essex
Mrs Muriel Ellis, Former BB Archivist.
Edinburgh Battalion BB Archive, Edinburgh (Mr. S. Rose)
The Central Public Library, Edinburgh
1st Enfield Coy. The Boys' Brigade.

Messrs. Firmin & Sons, Birmingham. (Peter Williams and Janet Horton)
Ian Fleming, 5th Croydon Coy. The Boys' Brigade.
Maurice Forsyth, Belfast Battalion, The Boys' Brigade.
Foundry Boys Religious Society, Glasgow
Ian Frame, Millport, Isle of Cumbrae

Chas F. Garvey, Ex-member 58th London Coy. The Boys' Brigade.
Jack Gilchrist, Archivist and Historian, 40th Edinburgh Coy. BB
The Girls' Brigade, England & Wales, Headquarters, Didcot, Oxfordshire,
University of Glasgow, Business Record Centre
Neville Gray, Metheringham, Lincoln
The Art Gallery and Museum, Kelvingrove, Glasgow

Allen D. Hambly, Cardiff Battalion BB
Malcolm Hayden, Director, Finance & Administration, The Boys' Brigade.
Terry Hissey, Christ Church Roxeth & Harrow Co. CL&CGB.
A. E. Hoey, Former Boys' Brigade Supplies, Officer.
David Howie, ex-President East District, Edinburgh BB.

Imperial War Museum, Southwark.
John Inglis, 2nd Prestwick (Kingcase) Coy. The Boys' Brigade.

Mike Jackson-Baker

Mrs J. Jacombs, Badges Plus, Birmingham
Sydney Jones OBE, Brigade Secretary, The Boys' Brigade

Ken King, Codicote, Hitchin, Herts.

Mr. R. Landine, Star Promotions Ltd.
Stephen G Lane, 1st Barnet Coy. Archivist, The Boys' Brigade.
5th London Coy. The Boys' Brigade.
D. G. Lynn, Newtownabbey N. Ireland.

Hugh McCallum, Bearsden, Glasgow (Honorary Officer, 1st Glasgow)
Mr W. McGorman, BB Old Boys' Union, Northern Ireland.
David MacNab, Edinburgh Boys' Brigade.
Eddie Menday, London District BB Publicity Officer.
Mitchell Library, Glasgow

National Library of Scotland, Edinburgh
National Railway Museum, York
John Neil, OBE, Former Battalion Secretary, Glasgow
New College Library, Edinburgh (Pam and Pat)
The New Library (Music), Oxford

George Oakton BEM, Birmingham (Dec'd)

F. C.Parry Ltd.
John Peak/Stephen Peak, Badges Plus. Birmingham
R. Allan Percival, Resource Centre Manager, The Boys' Brigade
Plymouth Battalion, The Boys' Brigade, (Roger Scobie)
Enoch Pratt Free Library, Baltimore, Maryland, USA
The Public Record Office, Kew

Jack Ritchie, Edinburgh. Ex-member 46th Edinburgh Coy. BB
Douglas Rolland, Capt. 1st Glasgow Coy. The Boys' Brigade.
John Russell, Lytchett Matravers, Dorset. BB Stedfast Assn. London.

Saint Andrew Ambulance Association, Glasgow
Chris Sanders, Edmonton, London
Scottish United Services Museum, Edinburgh Castle (Allan Carswell, Curator of Uniform and Mrs Philip, Librarian)
W. R. Smith, Edinburgh
John Springhall, The New University of Ulster, Coleraine, N. Ireland.
E. R. Staniford, O.B.E. (Dec'd) Bletchley.
Strathclyde Regional Archive (Mitchell Lib.) Glasgow

Derek Triplett, Edinburgh

United BB & GB of America, Baltimore, USA.

The Victorian and Military Society, Guildford (Ralph Moore-Morris)

Alan G. Watts, Capt. 5th London Coy. The Boys' Brigade.
Mr L. White, Pinner, Ex-member 94th London Coy. BB.
Alex Wilson, Bournemouth Scouts (Dec'd)
John Wilson, 11th Birmingham Coy. BB.
Doug. Wilson, Warehouse Manager, BB Supplies, St. Neots.
Robert Wilson, 1st Enfield BB.

BB BADGES
NUMERICAL LIST: TYPES & STAR - RATING

No.	Title of Badge	Variations/Types	★ Rating
	A Colour Key and explanation of the Star - Rating appears on page 279		1 2 3 4 5 6
001	**Officers Cap**, 1885 - 1926	10	★★★
002	**Officers Cap**, 1927 - 2006	28	★
003	**Officers Buttonhole**, 1897 - 1903	4	★★★★★
004	**Officers Field-Service Cap**, 1899 - 1926	4	★★★★
005	**Officers Field-Service Cap** & Epaulette 1927 - 2006.	11	★★
006	**Officers Collar**, 1916 - 1926	7	★★★
007	**Officers Collar**, 1927 - 2006	28	★
008	**Cadet Officer Cap**, 1918 - 1924	1	★★★★
009	**Cadet Officer Collar**, 1918 - 1924	2	★★★★★
010	**Cadets Cap**, 1918 - 1924	6	★★★★
011	**Boys Alternative Cap**, 1918 - c.1927	2	★★★★★
012	Boys Alternative Grey Uniform **Shoulder Title**, 1919 - 1932	1	★★★★★★
013	**Warrant Officer, Cap**, Collar & Epaulette, Badge 1927 - 2006	36	★
014	**Pipe Majors Cap**, 1935 - 1976	2	★★★★
015	**Boys Field-Service Cap**, 1927 - 1970	18	★
016	**Crossbelt Boss**, Sgt's & S.Sgt's Pre'27	6	★★★
017	**Crossbelt Boss**, Sgt's & S. Sgt's Post '26	11	★★
018	**Lady Officers Pocket**, 1970 -	2	★★
019	**Small anchor**. Boys F/S Hat 1970, Sen. Collar etc 1970 - 2006	11	★
020	**Chevrons**; L/Cpl, Cpl, Sgt. S/Sgt. 1999 -	4	★
021	**Numerals Half-Inch**, 1,2,3,4,5,6,7,8,0. 1918 - 1971	1	★
022	**Numerals One-Inch**, 1,2,3,4,5,6,7,8,0.1885 - 1970	2	★
023	**Boy Reserves Instructors**, 1918 - 1926	3	★★★★
024	**Boy Reserves, Boys Jersey**, 1921 - 1926	2	★★★★★
025			
026	**Life Boy Leaders Cap**, 1927 - 1966	12	★★★
027	**Life Boy Leaders Collar**, 1927 -1966	17	★★
028	**Life Boy, Boys Cap**, 1927 - c.1946	3	★★★★
029	**Life Boy Jersey**, 1927-1966	29	★★
030	**Leading Boy**, 1972 - 2006	3	★
031	**Cabin Boys**, 1950s?	3	★★★★
032	**Pilot Jacks**, 1950s - 1960s	1	★★★★★
033	**Imps**.	1	★★★★★
034	**Anchor Boys**	1	★★★★★
035	**Five-Pointed White Star**, c.1890 - 1904	1	★★★★★
036	**3-Year Anchor**, S/Sgts Cap, Large Anchor, Pre '27.	14	★★★☆
037	**3-Year Service**, S/Sgts Cap, Seniors Collar, L. Anchor Post '26	51	★
038	**Boys Long Service**, 1927 - 1968	35	★
039	**1 Year Efficiency Diamond**. 1904 - 1926	13	★★
040	**1 Year Service Diamond** 1927 - 1968.	104	★
041	**Life Boy Service Diamond**, 1956 - 1968	10	★★
042	**Junior Section Service Diamond**, 1968 - 1971	13	★★
043	**Service**, 1968 - 2006	11	★
044	**Junior Section Service**, Coy. Badge, 1971 - 1994	13	★
045	**Junior Section Gold Achievement**, J/S & C/S 1993 -	3	★
046	**Seniors' Award** 1991-	1	★
047	**Anchor Boy Achievement**, 1997 -	2	★
048	**Junior Section Service**, Figure 1, 1982 -	1	★
049	**Junior Section Service**, Figure 2, 1982 -	1	★
050	**Junior Section Service**, Figure 3, 1982 -	1	★
051	**Junior Section Service**, Figure 4, 1982 -	1	★
052	**Junior Section Service**, Figure 5, 1982 -	1	★
053	**Junior Section Service**, Figure 6, 1982 -	1	★
054	**World War 1, National Service**, 1915 - 1921	2	★★★★
055	**World War 2, National Service**, 1940 -	5	★★★★

056	King's, 1914 - 1926	2	★★★★★
057	King's, 1927 - 1953	15	★★★
058	Queen's, 1953 - 1968	20	★★★★
059	Queen's, 1968 - 1994	18	★★★
060	Queen's, 1994,	3	★★★★
061	President's, 1968 - 1994	21	★★★
062	President's, 1994,	3	★★★★
063	Founder's, 1962,	7	★★★★
064	Duke of Edinburgh's Award, 1958 -	4	★★★★★
065	Duke of Edinburgh's Award, 1958 -	8	★★★★
066	Duke of Edinburgh's Award, 1983 -	4	★★★
067	Ambulance, 1891 - 1893	1	★★★★★★
068	Ambulance, 1893-c.1923	7	★★★
069	Ambulance/First Aid, c.1923 - 1968	39	★
070	Arts & Crafts, 1927 - 1968	30	★
071	Athletics, 1946 - 1968	6	★★★★
072	Band, 1914 - 1968	10	★★★
073	Bugler's, 1909 - 1968	26	★★★
074	Camper's, 1927 - 1968.	30	★
075	Drummer's, 1921 - 1968	25	★★★
076	Education/Citizenship, 1927 - 1968	18	★★
077	Expedition, 1964 - 1968	4	★★★★
078	Fireman's, 1927 - 1968	26	★
079	Gymnastics/PT, 1917 - 1968	39	★
080	Life Saving, 1915 - 1926	1	★★★★★
081	Life Saving, 1927 - 1968	11	★★★
082	Piper's, 1921 - 1968	10	★★★★
083	Seamanship, 1946 - 1968	2	★★★★★
084	Sergeant's Star, 1902 - 1926	3	★★★
085	NCO's Star, 1927 - 1968	18	★★
086	Gold & Silver Scout's, 1911 - 1927	3	★★★★★
087	Scripture Knowledge. 1958 - 1968	8	★★★
088	Signaller's, 1911 - 1968	22	★★
089	Swimmer's, 1927 - 1968	19	★★
090	Wayfarer's, 1927 - 1968	26	★
091	Arts, 1968 - 1976	3	★★
092	Athletics, 1968 - 1976	3	★★
093	Bandsman, 1968 - 1976	3	★★★
094	Bugler, 1968 - 1976	3	★★
095	Camping, 1968 - 1976	4	★★
096	Christian Education, 1968 - 1976	3	★★
097	Crafts, 1968 - 1976	3	★★
098	Canoeing, 1968 - 1976	3	★★★
099	Communications, 1968 - 1976	3	★★★★
100	Drill, 1968 - 1976	3	★
101	Drummer, 1968 - 1976 & 1974 Prototypes	7	★★★☆☆
102	Expedition, 1968 - 1976	3	★★
103	First Aid, 1968 - 1976	3	★
104	Hobbies, 1968 - 1976 & 1974 Prototypes	7	★
105	International, 1968 - 1976	3	★★
106	Life Saving, 1968 - 1976	3	★★★
107	Naturalist, 1968 - 1976	3	★★★
108	Physical Recreation, 1968 - 1976	3	★
109	Piper, 1968 - 1976	3	★★★
110	Safety, 1968 - 1976	3	★★
111	Sailing, 1968 - 1976	3	★★
112	Seamanship, 1968 - 1976	3	★★★★
113	Sportsman, 1968 - 1976	3	★★
114	Swimming, 1968 - 1976	3	★★
115	Arts, 1976 - 1983	2	★★
116	Athletics, 1976 - 1983	2	★★
117	Bandsman, 1976 - 1983	2	★★★
118	Bugler, 1976 - 1983	2	★★★
119	Camping, 1976 - 1983	2	★★

120	**Christian Education**, 1976 - 1983	2	★★
121	**Crafts**, 1976 - 1983	2	★★
122	**Canoeing**, 1976 - 1983	2	★★★
123	**Communications**, 1976 - 1983	2	★★★★
124	**Drill**, 1976 - 1983	2	★
125	**Drummer**, 1976 - 1983	2	★★★
126	**Expedition**, 1976 - 1983	2	★★
127	**First Aid**, 1976 - 1983	2	★
128	**Hobbies**, 1976 - 1983	2	★
129	**International**, 1976 - 1983	2	★★
130	**Life Saving**, 1976 - 1983	2	★★★
131	**Naturalist**, 1976 - 1983	2	★★★
132	**Physical Recreation**, 1976 - 1983	2	★
133	**Piper**, 1976 - 1983	2	★★★
134	**Safety**, 1976 - 1983	2	★★
135	**Sailing**, 1976 - 1983	2	★★
136	**Seamanship**, 1976 - 1983	2	★★★★
137	**Sportsman**, 1976 - 1983	2	★★
138	**Swimming**, 1976 - 1983	2	★★
139	**Target 1**, 1968 - 1976	19	★
140	**Target 2**, 1968 - 1976	16	★
141	**Target 1/Target**, 1976 - 1983/1983 -	20	★
142	**Target 2** 1983 -	8	★
143	**Activity** Leadership,[Inc. proto's] 1983 -	17	★
144	**Activity** Adventure, 1983 -	8	★
145	**Activity** Community, 1983 -	9	★
146	**Activity** Interests, 1983 -	8	★
147	**Activity** Physical, 1983 -	8	★
148	**Junior Section White Achievement**, 1966 -	10	★
149	**Junior Section Green Achievement**, 1966 -	10	★
150	**Junior Section Purple Achievement**, 1966 -	8	★
151	**Junior Section Blue Achievement**, 1966 -	12	★
152	**Junior Section Red Achievement**, 1966 -	8	★
153	**Junior Section Gold Achievement**, 1966 - 1993	8	★
154	**President's Badge, Miniature**, 1980 - 1984	5	★★★
155	**President's Badge, Miniature**, 1994 -	9	★★★
156	**Queen's Badge, Miniature**, 1968 - 1994	1	★★★
157	**Queen's Badge Miniature**, 1994 -	1	★★★
158	**Founder's Badge Miniature**, 1962	1	
161	**Dechmont Camp** 1933 -	1	★★★★
162	**Eton Camp**, 1954 -	3	★★★★★
163	**Caribbean Camp**, 1958. [A]	2	★★★★
164	**Caribbean Camp**, 1958. [B]	2	★★★★
165	**Scone International Camp**, 1983.	2	★★★★
166	**Ayr Centenary of Camping**, 1986.	2	★★★★
167	**Aberdeen International Camp**, 1991.	1	★★
168	**Manchester Battalion Camp.** 1936 - c.1968	3	★★★
169	**Bromley Battalion Camp Badge.** Date?		
170	**1st Chelmsford Coy. Camp Badge.** Date?		
171	**The Life Boys, Buttonhole.** 1927 - 1930.	2	★★★★★★
172	**The Life Boys, Buttonhole.** 1930 - 1966.	32	★★☆
173	**BB Buttonhole**, 1911 - 1926.	9	★★★★
174	**BB Buttonhole**, 1927 - 1934.	9	★★★
175	**BB Buttonhole**, 1934 -	65	★
176	**Jubilee, 1933 Buttonhole**, 1932 - 1933	5	★★★
177	**Glasgow Battalion Ex-Members** Jubilee Buttonhole 1933.	2	★★★★
178	**Coronation Buttonhole** 1937. English.	2	★★★
179	**Coronation Buttonhole** 1937. Scottish.	3	★★★
180	**Coronation Buttonhole** 1953. English.	4	★★★
181	**Coronation Buttonhole** 1953. Scottish.	3	★★★
182	**Prince of Wales Investiture**, 1969.	3	★★★★★

183	**Queen's Silver Jubilee**, 1977. English.	2	★★
184	**Queen's Silver Jubilee**, 1977. Scottish.	1	★★
185	**Windsor Royal Review**, 1994.	3	★★★☆☆
191	**Brigade Centenary Buttonhole**, 1983.	10	★
192	**Miniature Brigade Centenary Buttonhole**, 1983.	2	★★
193	**Glasgow Centenary**, 1983		
194	**7th Wishaw** Coy.BB Centenary.	1	★★★★
195	**Cumbernauld** Battalion, BB Centenary.	1	★★★★
196	**14th Belfast** Coy. BB Centenary.	1	★★★★
197	**13th Edinburgh** Coy. BB Centenary.	1	★★★★
198	**Chelmsford** Sharing Day, BB Centenary.	1	★★★
199	**1st Banff** BB Centenary Year 1983	1	
200	**1st Newport** BB 83. 1983.		
201	**Motherwell** Battalion, BB Centenary. 1983	1	★★★
202	**Brigade Centenary** Fun Badge	1	★★
203	**Weston Camp** 1982, BB 83	1	★★
211	**Brigade Council, 1905**, Aberdeen.	1	★★★★★
212	**Brigade Council, 1909**, Dublin.	1	★★★★★
213	**Brigade Council, 1925**, Dublin.	1	★★★★★
214	**Brigade Council, 1926**, Brighton.	1	★★★★★
215	**Brigade Council, 1933**, Glasgow [Red Scroll & White Scroll].	2	★★★★☆
216	**Brigade Council, 1938**, Dunoon.	1	★★★★
217	**Brigade Council, 1948**, Belfast.	1	★★★★
218	**Brigade Council, 1949**, Birmingham.	1	★★★★
219	**Brigade Council, 1950**, Brighton.	3	★★★★
220	**Brigade Council, 1951**, St. Andrews.	2	★★★★
221	**Brigade Council, 1954**, Glasgow.	1	★★★★★
222	**Brigade Council, 1958**, Aberdeen.	1	★★★★
223	**Brigade Council, 1968**, Belfast.	1	★★★★★
224	**Brigade Council, 1974**, Sheffield.	1	★★★
225	**Brigade Council, 1975**, Brighton.	1	★★★
226	**Brigade Council, 1976**, Aberdeen.	2	★★★★★
227	**Brigade Council, 1977**, Manchester.	2	★★★★
228	**Brigade Council, 1983**, Glasgow.	1	★★★
229	**Brigade Council Choir, 1985**, Birmingham.	1	★★★★★
230	**Brigade Council, 1993**, Southampton.	2	★★★
231	**Brigade Council, 1995**, Inverness.	1	★★
232	**Brigade Council, 1997**, Newcastle [N.I.],	1	★★
233	**Brigade Council, 1998**, N.W.Kent, [Inc Prototype]	2	★★☆☆☆
234	**Brigade Council, 1999**, Dundee,	1	★★★
235	**Brigade Council, 2000**, Brighton & Hove.	1	★★
241	**Cleveland Hike** [A].	5	★★★★
242	**Cleveland Hike** [B]	1	★★★★
243	**West Lowland Hike**, [A]	2	★★★★
244	**West Lowland Hike**, [B]	2	★★★★
245	**West Lowland Hike** Jubilee	1	★★★
251	**National Band Contest** 1980.	1	★★★★
252	**National Band Contest** 1981.	1	★★★★
253	**National Band Contest** 1982.	1	★★★★
254	**Scottish Band Contest**	2	★★★★
255	**Dundee Band Contest** 1986	1	★★★★
256	**Glasgow Battalion**, Central Band.	1	★★★★
257	**Stedfast Silver Band.**	1	★★★★
258	**World's Largest Band**, 1983.	1	★★★
259	**London Band, ID** 1983.	3	★★★
260	**Troon 2000** 21st Scottish Band Comp, 2000.		
265	**Junior Section 75 Yrs**	2	★★★
266	**Clydebank** Battalion, Junior section 75 yrs.	1	★★★★
267	**Felden Brickie** Fund-Raising.	2	★★★
268	**BB Badge Collectors' Club.**	10	★★★
269	**BB Collectors' Club** 2000	1	★

281	**Scottish Cross-Country** Run	2	★★★
282	**Scottish Cross-Country** Run 1989	1	★★★
283	**Scottish Cross-Country** Run 1990	1	★★★
291	**Bowling Club.** 1st O.B.	1	★★★★
292	**Bowling Club.** 9th O.B.	2	★★★★
293	**Bowling Club.** 13th O.B.	1	★★★★
294	**Bowling Club.** 21st O.B.	2	★★★★
295	**Bowling Club.** 34th O.B.	2	★★★★
296	**Bowling Club.** 58th O.B.	4	★★★★
297	**Bowling/Rugby.** Northants O.B.	1	★★★★
301	**Welsh Centenary,** Newport 1987	3	★★★
302	**N. Irish Centenary,** 1988	2	★★★
303	**Eire Centenary,** 1991	1	★★★★★
311	**Edinburgh** Battalion Rest Hut. 1919	1	★★★★★
312	**1st St. Andrews** Coy. 50 Yrs 1944	1	★★★★★
313	**Bradford** Battalion 50 Yrs 1954	1	★★★★★
314	**Airdrie, Coatbridge** & District Battalion, 50 yrs. 1972	1	★★★★
315	**1st Cambusnethan** Coy, 50 Yrs. 1973	1	★★★★
316	**1st Bletchley** Coy, 50 Yrs 1976		
317	**85th Birmingham** Coy, 21 Yrs 1979		
318	**40th Edinburgh** Coy, 90 Yrs. 1980	1	★★★★
319	**Hartlepool** Battalion 50 Yrs 1980	1	★★★★
320	**10th Leith** Coy. 75 Yrs 1981	1	★★★★
321	**1st Fraserburgh** Coy. 60 Yrs 1981	1	★★★★
322	**1st Newport,** 94 Yrs. 1981		
323	**1st Cupar** Coy. 50 Yrs 1981	1	★★★★
324	**89th Birmingham** Coy 21 Yrs 1981 (A)	1	★★★★
325	**89th Birmingham** Coy 21 yrs 1981 (B)		
326	**1st Old Kilpatrick** Coy 50 Yrs 1982	1	★★★★
327	**8th Airdrie** Coy 50 Yrs 1983	1	★★★★
328	**Clydebank** Battalion 50 Yrs 1984	1	★★★★
329	**5th Wishaw** Coy. 40 Yrs 1984	1	★★★★
330	**Glasgow** Battalion Centenary 1985	2	★★★★
331	**4th Carluke** Coy 10 Yrs 1985	1	★★★★
332	**Edinburgh** Battalion Centenary 1986	2	★★
333	**Ayr** Battalion Centenary 1986	1	★★
334	**49th Glasgow** Coy. Centenary 1986	1	★★★
335	**14th West Bromwich** Coy. 25 Yrs. 1986	1	★★★★★
336	**1st Wellingborough** Coy. Centenary 1986/7	1	★★
337	**1st Aberdeen** Coy. Centenary 1987	1	★★★
338	**2nd Dumbarton** Coy. Centenary 1987	1	★★★
339	**76th Glasgow** Coy. Centenary 1987	1	★★★
340	**Sheffield** Battalion Centenary 1988	1	★★★
341	**2nd Paisley** Coy. Centenary 1988	1	★★★
342	**25th Edinburgh** Coy, 25 Yrs 1988	1	★★★
343	**Enfield Battalion.** 100 Yrs.1988	1	
344	**73rd Birmingham** Coy. 50 Yrs 1989	1	★★★
345	**41st Edinburgh** Coy. 25 yrs 1989	2	★★★
346	**1st Alloway** Coy. 10 Yrs 1989	1	★★★
347	**N. Scottish District** Conference 75 Yrs 1989	1	★★★★
348	**40th Edinburgh** Coy. Centenary 1990	1	★★★
349	**Aberdeen** Battalion, Centenary 1991	2	★★★
350	**Dundee** Battalion, Centenary 1991	1	★★★
351	**Liverpool** Battalion Centenary 1991	1	★★★★
352	**1st Barnet** Coy. Centenary 1991	5	★★★
353	**1st Helensburgh** Coy. 75 Yrs 1991	1	★★★
354	**1st Auchinleck** Coy. 50 Yrs 1991	1	★★★
355	**2nd Cambusnethan** Coy.1991	1	★★★
356	**2nd Prestwick** Coy. 10 Yrs 1991	2	★★★
357	**6th/8th Dundee** Centenary 1991	1	★★★
358	**Nottingham** Battalion 1992	1	★★★★
359	**5th Aberdeen** Coy. 1992	1	★★★
360	**1st Harpole** Coy 50 Yrs 1992	1	★★★

361	**4th Fraserburgh** Coy. 40 Yrs 1992	1	★★★
362	**Glasgow** Battalion 'Cen Plus Ten' 110 Yrs, 1993	1	★★★
363	**Perth & District** Battalion Centenary 1993	1	★★★
364	**Hawick** Centenary 1993	1	★★★★
365	**Somerset** Battalion 25 Yrs 1993	3	★★★
366	**3rd Edinburgh** Coy. Centenary 1993	1	★★★
367	**6th Perth** Coy 1993	1	★★★
368	**7th Perth** Coy Centenary 1993	1	★★★
369	**Paisley** Battalion Centenary 1994	1	★★★
370	**1st St Andrews** Coy. Centenary 1994	1	★★★
371	**182nd Glasgow** Coy. 75 Yrs 1994	1	★★★
372	**1st Troon** Coy. 75 Yrs 1994	1	★★★
373	**Northampton BB/GB** HQ 25 Yrs. 1994	1	★★★★
374	**Cardiff & Vale of Glamorgan** Battalion Centenary 1995	4	★★★
375	**3rd Aberdeen** Coy. Centenary 1995	1	★★★
376	**1st Girvan** Coy. Centenary 1995	1	★★★
377	**268th Glasgow** Coy. 60 Yrs. 1995	1	★★★
378	**1st Colne** Coy. 40 Yrs 1995	1	★★★
379	**60th Glasgow** Coy 50 Yrs 1995	1	★★★
380	**Oldham** Battalion Centenary 1996	1	★★★
381	**3rd Cardiff** Coy. Centenary 1996	1	★★★
382	**10th Leith** Coy. 90 Yrs 1996	1	★★★
383	**1st Fraserburgh** Coy. 75 Yrs 1996	1	★★★
384	**2nd Bearsden** Coy. 50 Yrs 1996	1	★★★
385	**1st Morningside** Coy. 60 Yrs. 1996	1	★★★
386	**3rd Greenock** Coy. Centenary 1997	1	★★★
387	**2nd Witham** Coy. 25 Yrs 1997	1	★★★
388	**1st Castle Bromwich** Coy 25 Yrs 1997	1	★★★
389	**14th Croydon** Coy 40 Yrs 1997	1	★★★
390	**7th Coatbridge** Coy. 50 Yrs 1997	1	★★★
391	**Greenock** Battalion Centenary 1998	5	★★★
392	**2nd Sutton Coldfield** Coy. 50 Yrs 1998	2	★★
393	**1st Annaghmore** Coy. 40 Yrs. 1998	1	★★★★
394	**Edinburgh, Leith & District** Battalion 1 Yr. 1998 - 1999	1	★★
395	**1st Loughborough** Coy. 60 Yrs. 1998	1	★★★
396	**1st Ellon** Coy. Centenary 1998	1	★★
397	**2nd Gourock** Coy. Centenary 1998	1	★★★
398	**25th Glasgow** Coy. Centenary 1998	1	★★
399	**10th Brighton** Coy. Centenary 1999	1	★★
400	**85th Birmingham** Coy. 40 Yrs [A] 1999	3	★★
401	**85th Birmingham** Coy. 40 yrs [B] 1999	3	★★
402	**3rd Wallasey** Coy. 40 Yrs 1999	1	★★
403	**1st Southend On Sea** Coy. 90 Yrs 1999	1	★★
404	**1st Troon** Coy. 80 Yrs.1999	1	★★
405	**1st Margate** Coy 80Yrs 1999	3	★★
406	**6th Mansfield Coy. 60 Yrs.** 2000		
407	**18th West Kent** Coy 2000	1	★
408	**4th Kirkaldy** Coy. Centenary 1993	1	★★
451	**1st Thames Valley**, Richmond, Coy. Pre 27.	1	★★★★★
452	**16th Nottingham** Coy. Pre 27.	1	★★★★★
453	**1st Aberdeen** Coy.	1	★★★★
454	**1st Whitehaven** Coy.	1	★★★
455	**Redbridge** '79.	1	★★★
456	**85th Birmingham** Coy.	1	★★★
457	**12th** Coy BB Week, 1986	1	★★★
458	**16th London** Coy. 'Billy Bear'.	1	★★★
459	**London** District ID.	2	★★★
460	**Chelmsford** Uniformed Organisations Day, 1979	1?	★★★★
461	**Chester Rd** Brigades. 3rd Sutton Coldfield BB	1	★★★
462	**Northfield** Church Club.	1	★★★★
463	**Hartlepool & West Hartlepool BB & CLB.** c.1901.	1	★★★★★
464	**BB-GB Flag** Badge	1?	★★★★
465	**8th Grimsby** Coy, Fun Badge	1	★
466	**13th** Company. Pre '27	1	★★★★★★
467	**12th Glasgow** Coy.	1	★★★★

No.	Description	Qty	Rating
468	Hamilton & District Battalion 'Big Event', 1999	2	
469	Hamilton & District Battalion 'Big Event', 2000	1	
470	BB Initial Buttonhole	2	★★★
471	Old Boys Union, Watch fob, 1907 - 1932	1	★★★★★
472	Ex-Members, 1932 -	10	★★
473	Stedfast Association, Buttonhole.	5	★★
474	Stedfast Association Northern Ireland	1	★★★
475	Old Boys Union N. I.	4	★★★★
476	Regnal League 1934 -	4	★★★★
477	Port Glasgow Old Boys Union	2	★★★★★
478	Renfrew Old Boys Union	1	★★★★★
479	Old Boys Union, Northern Ireland, Pre '27 & Post '26	2	★★★★☆☆
480	BB Friend, 1980 -	6	★
481	O.B.A. Hat [A] 1931 - c.1934	1	★★★★★
482	O.B.A. Collar [A] 1931 - c.1934	1	★★★★★
483	O.B.A. Hat [B] c.1934 - 1936	1	★★★★★
484	O.B.A. Collar [B] c.1934 - 1936	1	★★★★★
485	C.O.B.A. Hat [C] 1936 - 1945	1	★★★★★
486	C.O.B.A. Collar [C] 1936 - 1945	1	★★★★★
487	C.O.B.A. Buttonhole, 1936 - 1945	1	★★★★★
488	BB Associate Member, 2000 -	1	★★
491	Officers' Long Service, Bronze 1996 -	2	★★★
492	Officers' Long Service, Chrome 1996 -	2	★★★
493	Officers' Long Service, Gilt 1996 -	2	★★★
500	Brigade, Millennium Buttonhole, 1999 - 2000	2	★
501	Brigade, Limited Edition, Millennium Buttonhole, 1999 - 2000	?	★★★☆☆
502	101st Glasgow Coy. Millennium Buttonhole, 1912 - 2000	1	★★
503	1st St. Combs Coy. Millennium Buttonhole, 1933 - 2000.	1	★★
504	London Stedfast Association, Millennium Buttonhole, 2000.	1	★★
505	Bath 2000, Buttonhole.	1	★★
506	1st Campsie Coy. Millennium Buttonhole, 2000	1	★★
511	Cross For Heroism, Bronze, Blue Ribbon. 1902 - c.1928	1	★★★★★★
512	Cross For Heroism, Bronze, Blue, and Blue & White Ribbon c.1928 -	2	★★★★★★
601	Anchor Boys Fun Badge		★
602	Junior Section Fun Badge		★
603	BB Juniors Fun Badge		★
604	Brigade Fun Badge		★
611	London District, 100 Group	1	★★★

Star - Rating Guide:

NB This is a rarity index and not a price quide.

★	Very Common
★★	Common
★★★	Hard to Find
★★★★	Scarce
★★★★★	Rare
★★★★★★	Very Rare

☆ Extra star[s] indicates additional distinctive types which are rarer.

Colour Key

Relating to Sections in Book

1. Uniform Badges
2. Efficiency/Service Badges
3. Proficiency Badges
4. Buttonhole & Mufti Badges
5. Medals
6. The Junior Organisations
7. Ex-Members & Friends

BADGES of the BRIGADE

Checklist

Checklist